THE INFOGRAPHIC HISTORY OF THE WORLD

SECOND EDITION

Published by Firefly Books Ltd. 2016

First printing

Publisher Cataloging-in-Publication Data (U.S.)

A CIP record for this title is available from the Library of Congress

Library and Archives Canada Cataloguing in Publication

A CIP record for this title is available from Library and Archives Canada

Published in the United States by
Firefly Books (U.S.) Inc.
P.O. Box 1338, Ellicott Station
Buffalo, New York 14205

Published in Canada by
Firefly Books Ltd.
50 Staples Avenue, Unit 1
Richmond Hill, Ontario L4B 0A7

Color reproduction by FMG
Printed in Hong Kong

Conceived, designed, and produced by Collins
An imprint of HarperCollinsPublishers
1 London Brigde Street
London, SE1 9GF

For Collins:
Commissioning Editor: Craig Adams
Head of Production: Anna Mitchelmore
Proofreader: Mark Bolland

MIX
Paper from
responsible sources
FSC C007454

FSC™ is a non-profit international organisation established to promote the responsible management of the world's forests. Products carrying the FSC label are independently certified to assure consumers that they come from forests that are managed to meet the social, economic and ecological needs of present and future generations, and other controlled sources.

Find out more about HarperCollins and the environment at
www.harpercollins.co.uk/green

2-2

THE INFOGRAPHIC HISTORY OF THE WORLD

SECOND EDITION

Valentina D'Efilippo & James Ball

FIREFLY BOOKS

You can, if you like, judge a lot about this book by its cover: we've made it an infographic of the content. We've labeled this version a bit more thoroughly – you can see that the front cover shows roughly how many years each of the book's four sections cover, while the back shows how many pages of the book are devoted to each. Handy, huh?

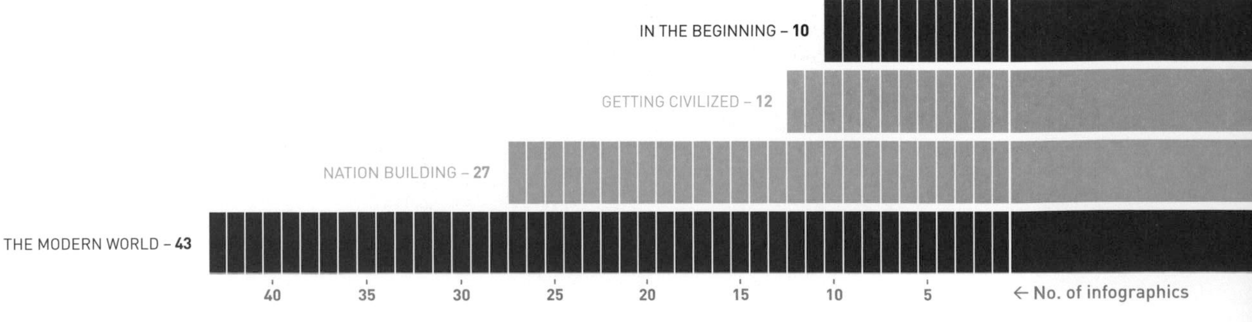

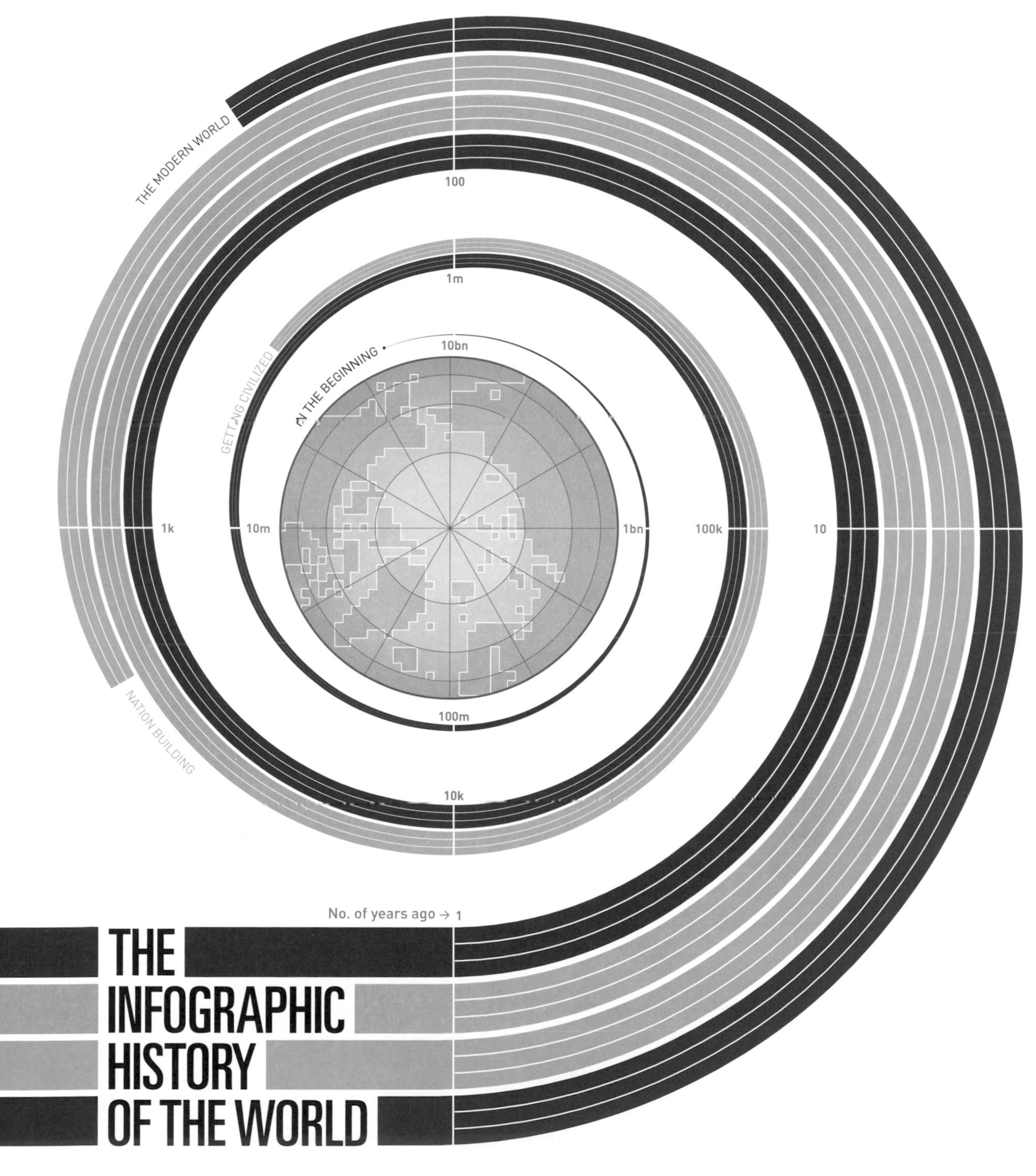

THE INFOGRAPHIC HISTORY OF THE WORLD

Pixel pusher. Paper lover. Data geek. **Valentina D'Efilippo** is a multi-disciplinary designer with an appetite for creativity and innovation – across all formats and media. After studying industrial design in Italy, she moved to London and gained a post-graduate degree in graphic design. Since then, her passion for visual communication and digital media has taken form in data visualization, art direction, and interaction design. She has worked with a number of leading agencies contributing to award-winning campaigns for global brands looking to sell more cars, oil and beer. Valentina founded London-based Italika Design in 2011.

James Ball is a multi-award-winning data journalist working on the Guardian's investigations team. He was a core journalist on several of the newspaper's data-driven investigations, including the Reading the Riots project, its reporting on WikiLeaks' Guantánamo Bay files, and the Offshore Secrets series. Before joining the Guardian, he worked with Channel 4 Dispatches, Panorama and ITN with the Bureau of Investigative Journalism, and was a freelancer working for WikiLeaks during its publication of 250,000 U.S. embassy cables. James is a lecturer on City University's Interactive and Investigative Journalism courses, and lives and works in central London.

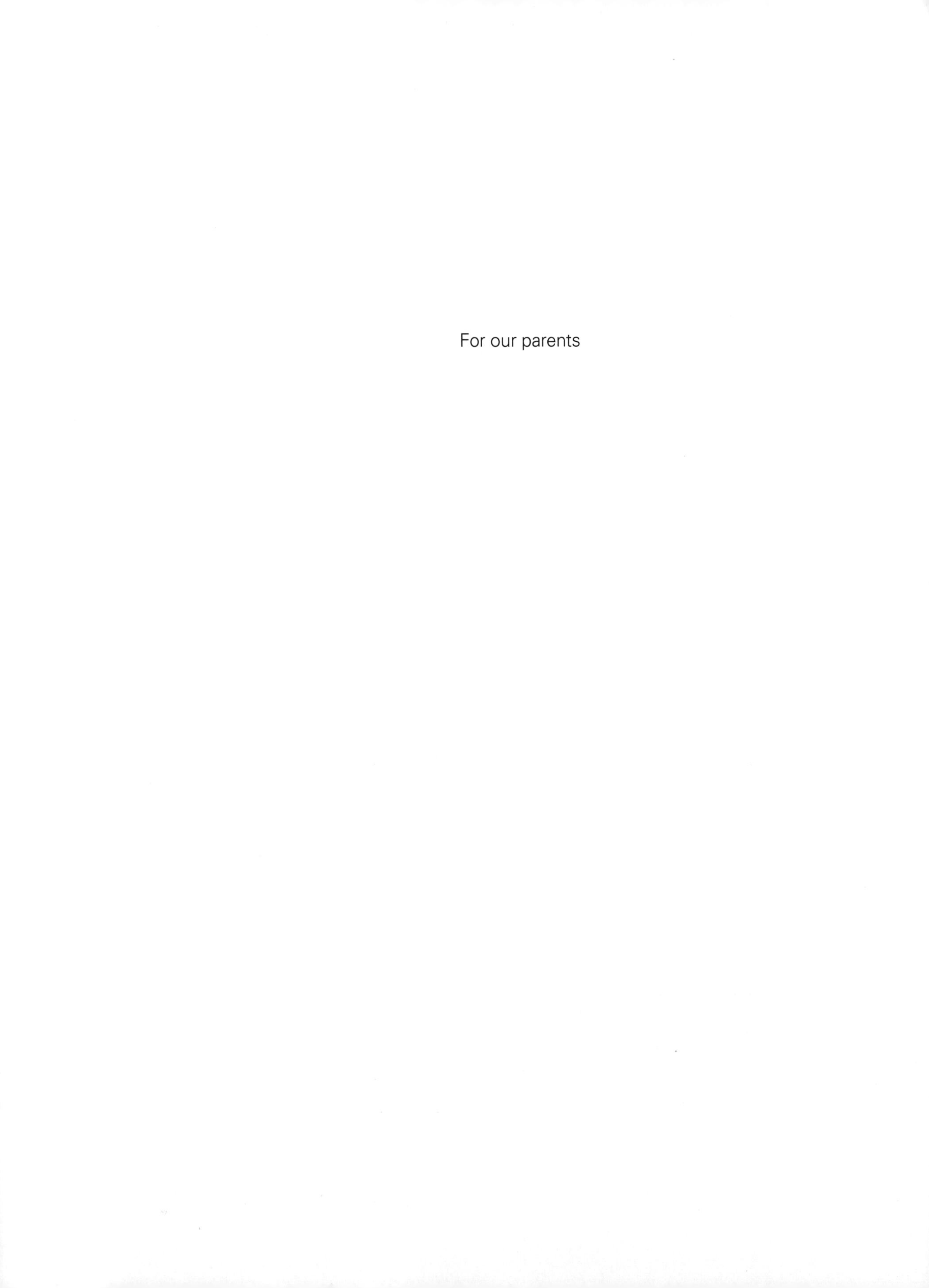

For our parents

This book can be read cover-to-cover, so feel free to start at the dawn of time and go forth from there, or dip in and out if that's more your style. Whichever method works for you, we've chosen to highlight a couple of things here to help you get your bearings.

We've broken down the history of the world into four sections, which correspond (very) roughly to certain phases of history: before humanity, before civilization, before 1900 or thereabouts, and the modern era. The design style progresses throughout: the more colors you see, and the more modern the fonts and style, the nearer the present day you're likely to be.

Also, keep an eye on the silhouettes in the bottom left-hand corner of the book: they evolve throughout, often dressing themselves appropriately.

Most spreads in the book tell the story of a single topic – but a few go across two or three: if you don't see a title, flick back a page or two, and you'll see one.

Not all infographics were created equal. They all have different levels of complexity, so it's worth keeping these three tips in mind:

1 – There's a question for every spread, which pithily summarizes exactly what you're looking at. Use it to instantly get acquainted with a topic.

2 – Read the text! What the infographics show is, of course, neatly (and entertainingly) summarized by the text, so find out what's generally going on before jumping into the detail.

3 – Use the key. Spreads with more complex infographics have a key that shows you how they've been constructed. A quick glance at the key tells you all you need to know about what the infographic reveals.

For those who want to know more about the sourcing or technical details of each of the graphics, there's an appendix with more details and commentary towards the back.

Finally, remember that there's been a lot of history since the beginning of time, and choosing what to include or leave out has often left us scratching our heads. We often allude to interesting topics and events that we didn't have space to elaborate on, so please have as much fun as we did researching them – by using the internet and a huge pile of books to find out more about the fascinating nuggets of history that are waiting to be discovered.

EDITOR'S NOTE

The inspirational E. H. Gombrich wrote that "anyone who can handle a needle convincingly can make us see a thread which is not there."

A story whose elements are woven together into a seamless and coherent whole can be not only satisfying and memorable, but also often perceived as persuasive. Unwittingly, we are prone to ignoring the quality and quantity of data on which a story is based in favor of a good yarn.

James' uncanny ability to surgically extract and pithily summarize a fundamental point has been as much a source of joy as Valentina's wondrous and seemingly limitless creativity. In the process of bringing the idea behind the book to life, the authors have strived to create a history with enough artifice and artistry to entertain, yet also one that is honest about the fact that data doesn't always present you with an unquestionable truth.

I hope that this book inspires you to do your own research – to explore the full complexity of the phenomena that there simply wasn't space on these pages to include, and that you enjoy the process as much as we did.

Craig Adams

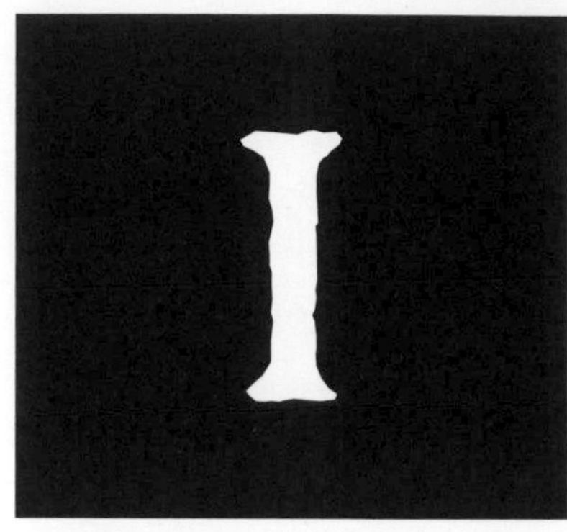

In the Beginning

Getting Civilized

Nation Building

The Modern World

VISUAL INDEX

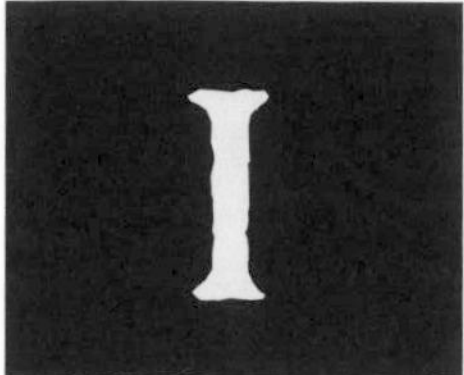

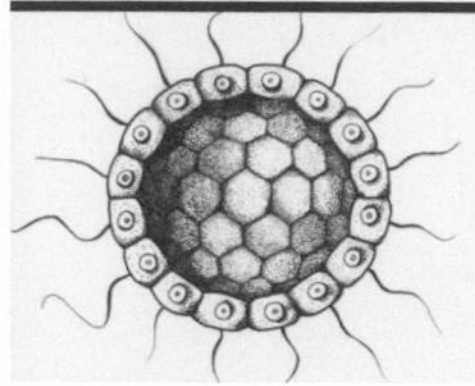

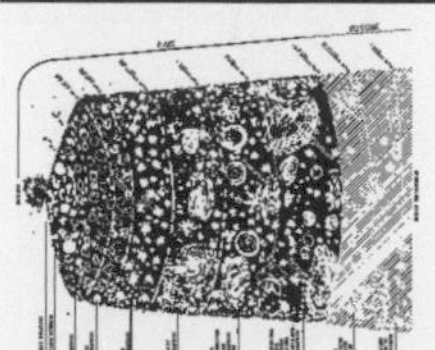

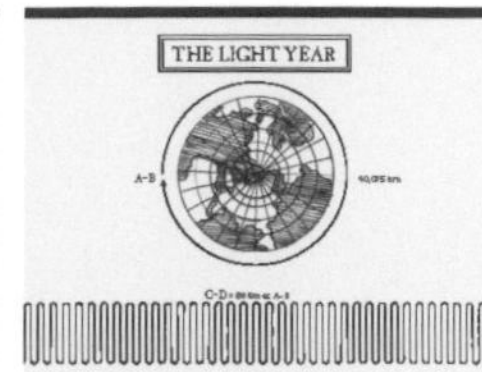

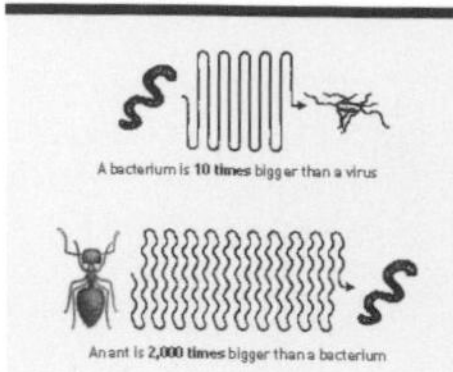

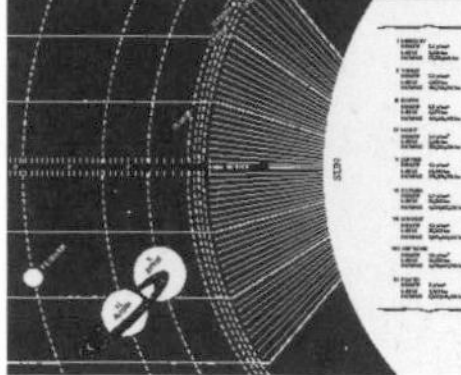

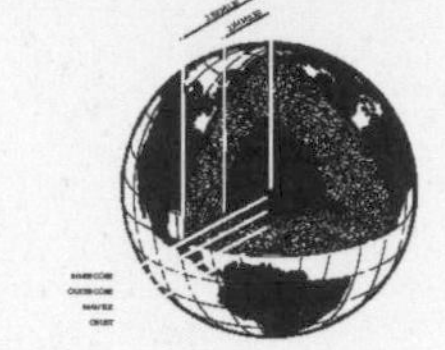

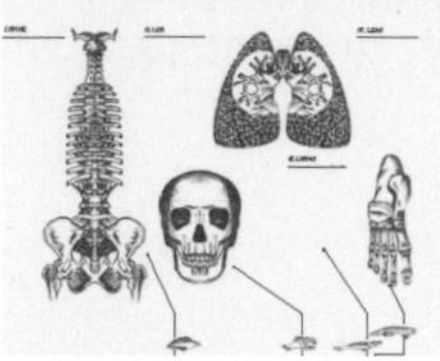

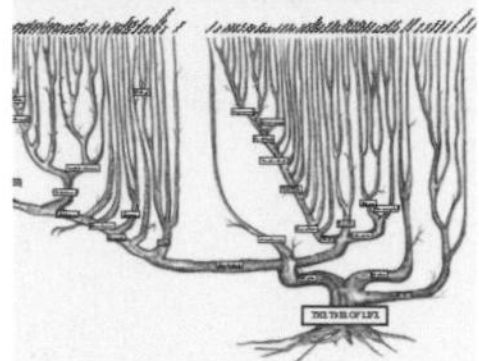

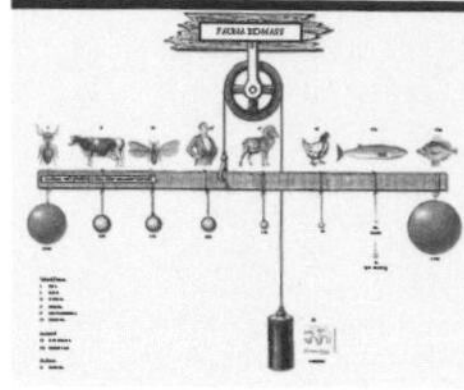

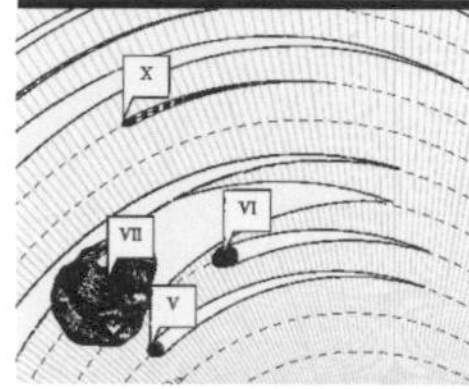

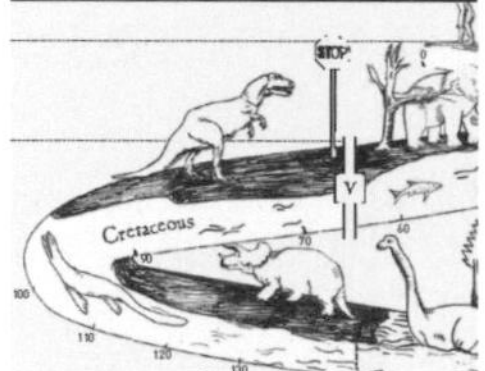

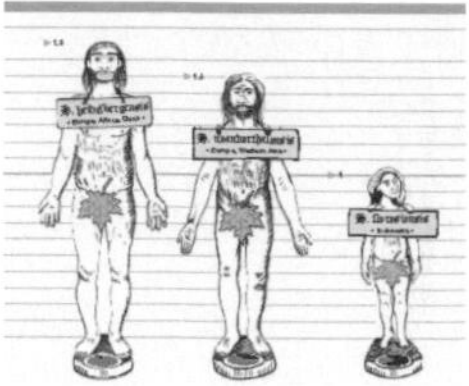

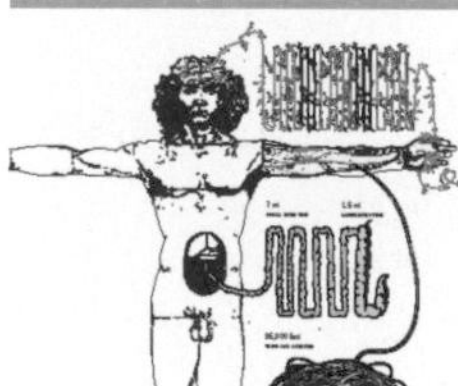

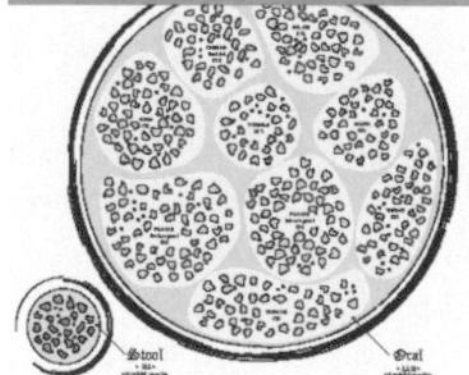

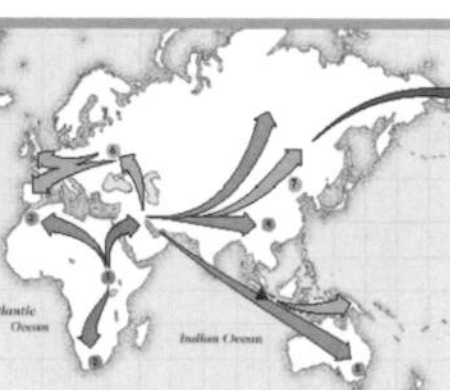

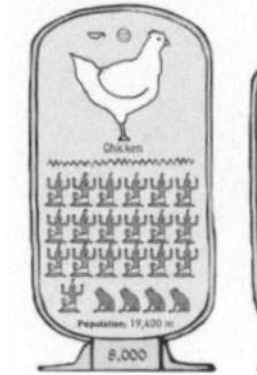

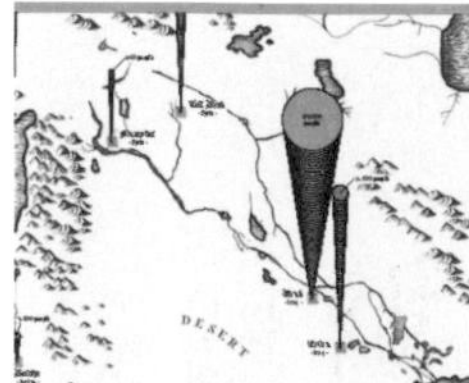

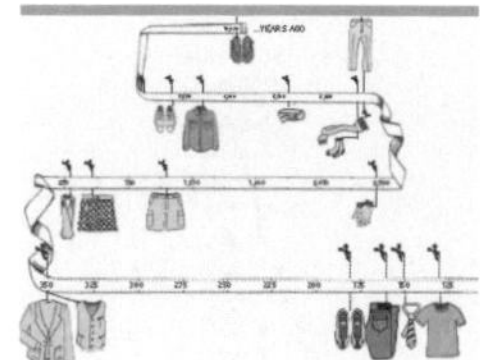

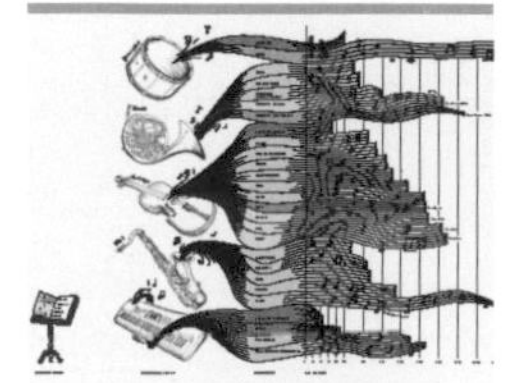

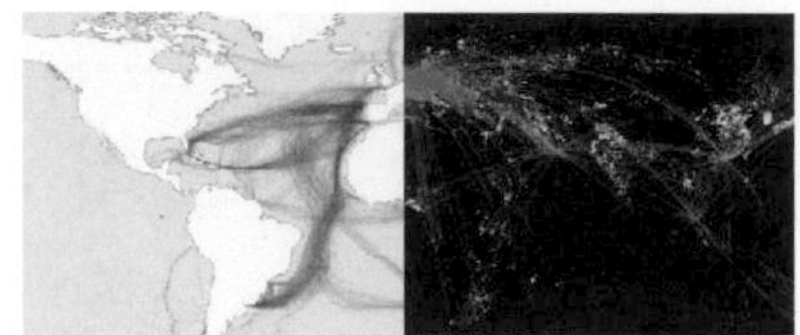

092–093 211

Dr. James Cheshire is a lecturer at the UCL Centre for Advanced Spatial Analysis. James' research focuses on the analysis and visualisation of large population datasets, but he will map any data he can get his hands on. His work has been featured in the likes of *National Geographic* magazine, *The Times Atlas Of London* and the *Guardian*. You can follow his latest projects at spatialanalysis.co.uk.

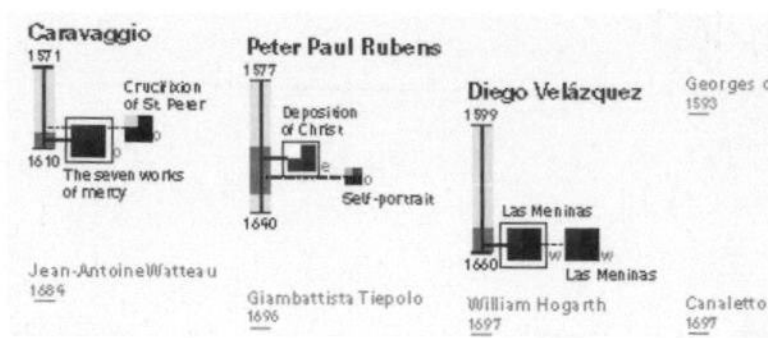

104–105

Accurat is an information design agency: we analyze data and contexts and we design analytical tools and visual narratives that provide awareness, comprehension and engagement. Accurat was founded in 2011 by Giorgia Lupi, Simone Quadri and Gabriele Rossi.

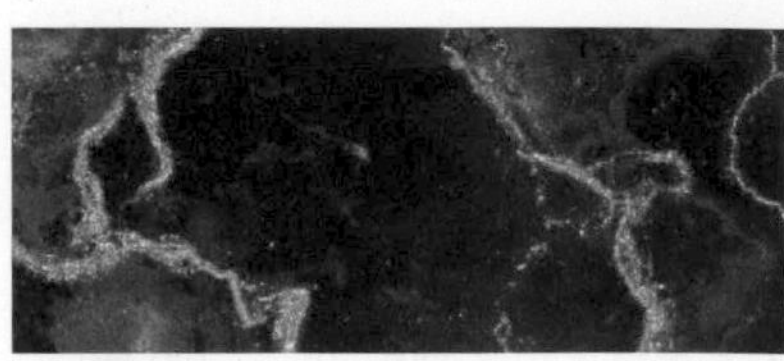

184–185

John Nelson is a cartographer and designer in Lansing, Michigan. As the User Experience & Mapping Manager at IDV Solutions, John helps Fortune 500 and governmental clients integrate and visualize data. He is a regular speaker at GeoScience and technology conferences and writes about usability, design, and visualization at uxblog.idvsolutions.com. John was the winner of the 2004 National Geographic Society Award for Cartography and his work has been featured in several science and visualization publications.
When he's not doing these things, John revels amidst a lively whirlwind of family, chickens and gardens.

200–203

Ruslan Enikeev. Russian engineer living in Singapore, explorer of the information space; waits for a time when data will be equal to knowledge and a robot will be able to ride a stream of abstraction.

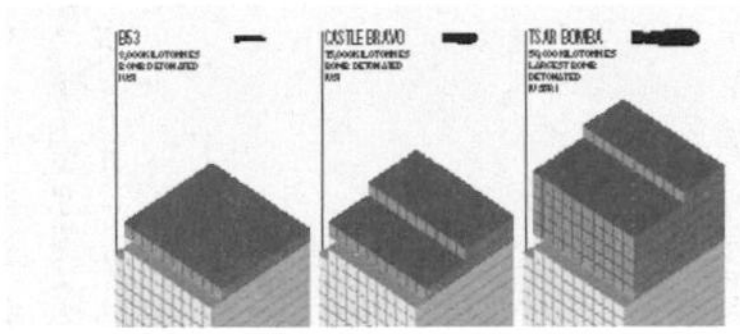

206–207

Maximilian Bode is a designer and artist based out of Brooklyn, NY. He is the former art director for *The New Yorker* magazine and his work can be found in print, in pixel and on gallery walls.

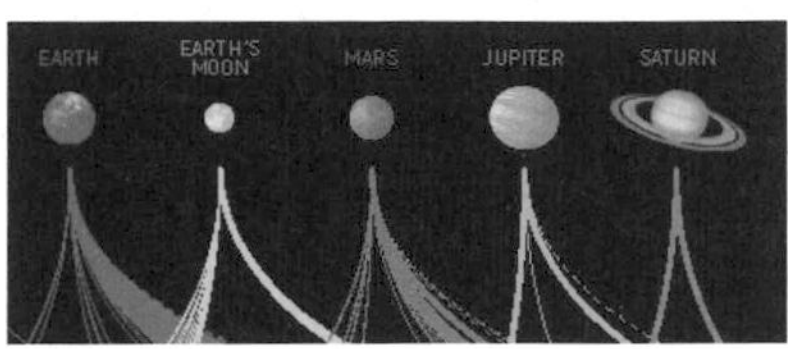

212–213

NASA's Jet Propulsion Laboratory is the lead U.S. center for robotic exploration of the solar system, and conducts major programs in space-based Earth sciences and astronomy. JPL spacecraft have visited all of the planets from Mercury to Neptune. In total, JPL has 22 spacecraft and 10 instruments conducting active missions. All of these are important parts of NASA's program of exploration of Earth, the solar system and the universe beyond. JPL has developed a special relationship with Moore/Boeck and its team of designers who have created various infographics for our audience to better understand the complexities of our space missions.

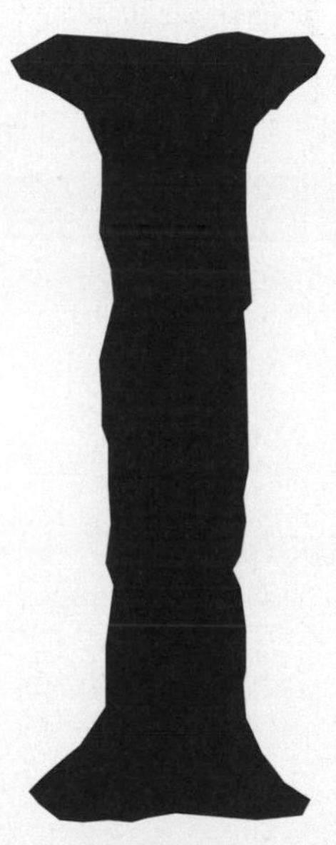

In the Beginning

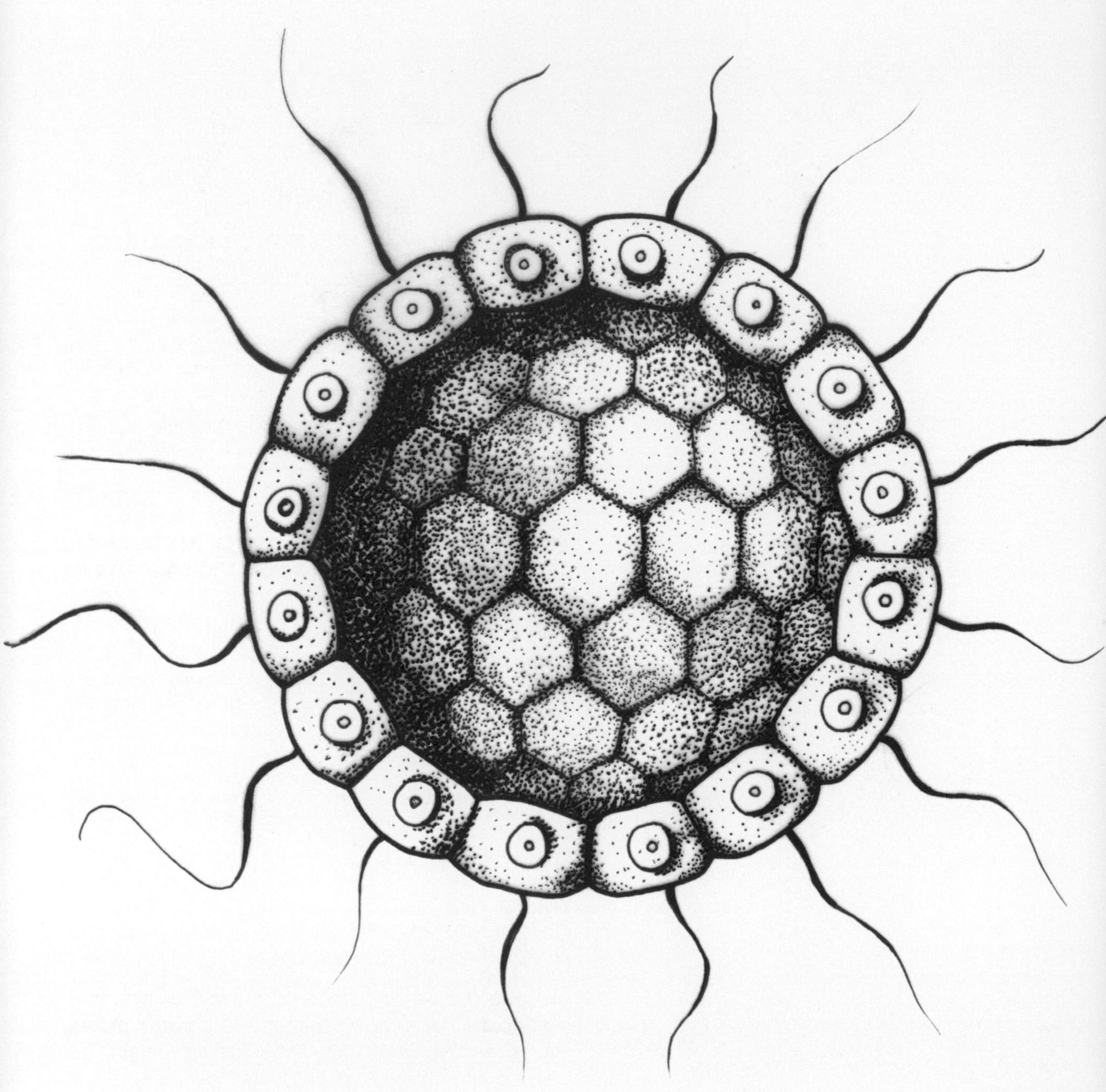

"In the beginning, there was nothing, which exploded," wrote Terry Pratchett.

Science's answer to creationism – the Big Bang – might not answer all, or frankly even any of our philosophical questions about the world we live in, but there's no shortage of detail on what happened.

In fact, 13.8 billion years of history have passed since the Big Bang, but historians (and humans, for that matter) have been around for hardly any of it. As a result, we could be forgiven for having missed some of the details of what's been going on.

Until now.

Consider this first section of our book a whistle-stop tour of history before humanity. And for good measure, we'll throw in a little geology and astronomy too.

What's in the solar system? Which animals lived and died before we showed up? How did we evolve? We'll cover all of that and more, as well as looking at what's around on Earth – rare metals for example (and – news you can use – why they're hard to find for your iPads).

To end the section on a high, we'll explore the asteroids that have crashed into our home planet in recent years – and which ones might be paying us what could be a terminal visit in the not-too-distant future.

A sneak preview before we worry anyone too much: the most dangerous asteroid we know of at the moment has a 1-in-625 chance of hitting us – and even that tiny risk doesn't come up until 2040.

So, plenty of time for reading, then.

In the beginning

Our story starts 13.8 billion years ago* in quite literally the middle of nowhere, shortly before what has to go down as a pretty notable event: the explosion that began our universe. But how to recount what's happened since then in one short book?

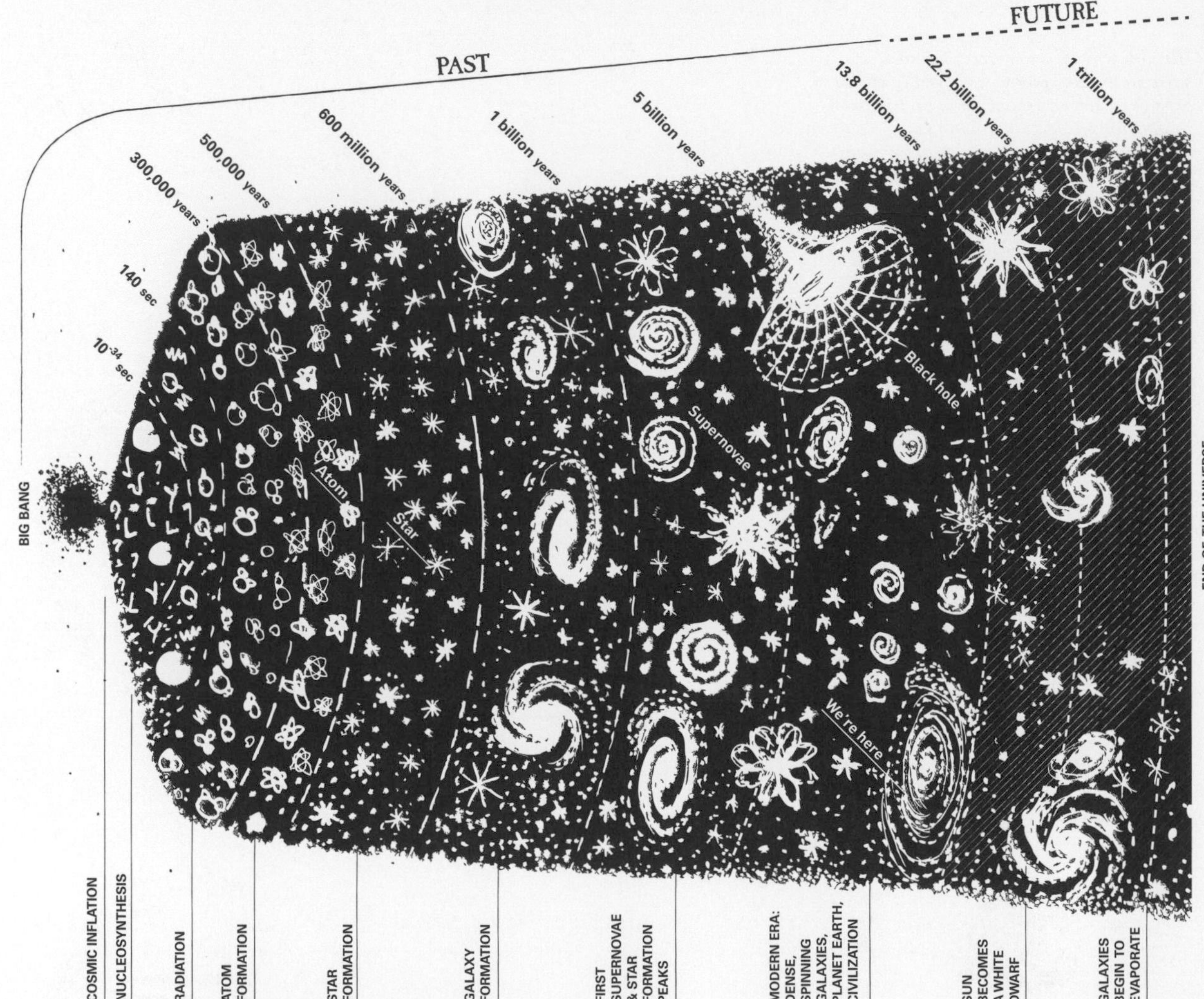

Our first thought was to give a page to every century, but as it turns out, that's a book 138 million pages long, about 900 meters thick, and – frankly – quite a few of those centuries are pretty boring. But these figures give you a sense of just how incomprehensible galactic history is. So we've tried to put some human scale on things.

At 13.8 billion years ago, the universe was a single, tiny point; far smaller than the period at the end of this sentence. In the first trillionth of a second of the universe's lifespan, gravity was born. Within a second, most basic forces (and most of the basic physical rules on which our universe runs) were in place. From this point, the universe was expanding constantly at the speed of light.

If your first thought on reading this was "No! Surely you mean 6,000 years ago" then in all honesty, this book probably isn't for you. But keep reading! The rest will really wind you up...

THE AGE OF...

... THE UNIVERSE

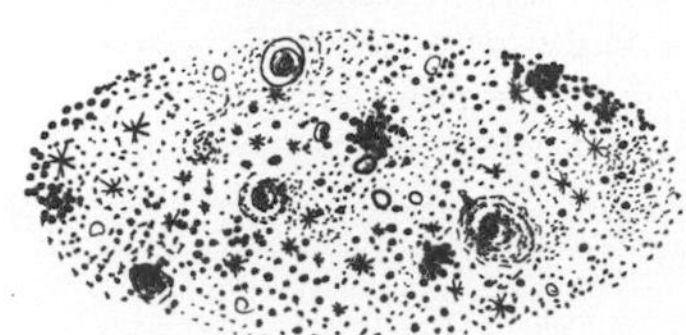

The universe as we know it, full of stars surrounded by planets, expanding all the time, will carry on (according to the current model) for around 100 trillion years – after which there won't be enough gas for new stars to form. This makes the universe young. If we imagine its current form in terms of a human lifespan, the universe is just four days old. It's still finding its feet.

TIMELINE (BILLIONS OF YEARS)

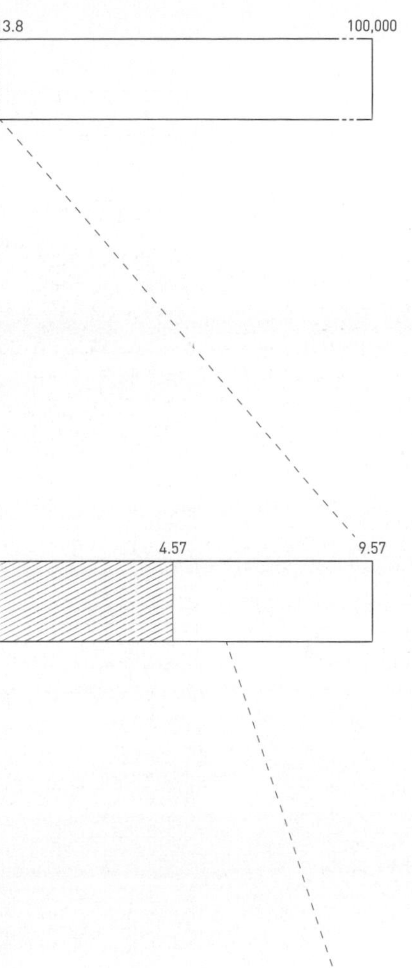

IN HUMAN TERMS

... THE SUN

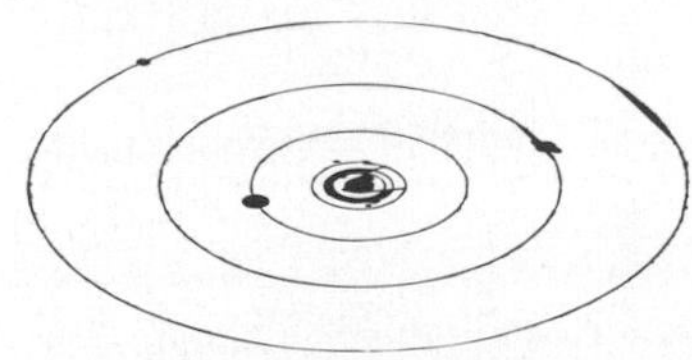

Sticking with time – we'll move on to space in a minute – our Sun is around 4.57 billion years old and it's only got around 5 billion more years to go before it becomes a red giant (and expands to consume all the planets). Relatively speaking, in human terms, that makes it around 38 years old.

... THE EARTH

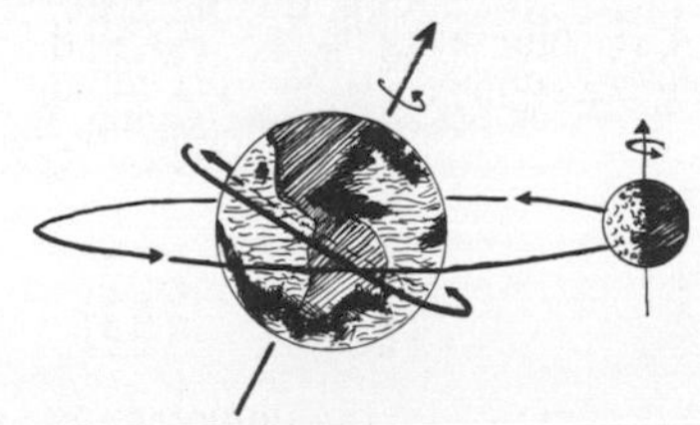

But what about Earth? Obviously, whatever is left of Earth won't survive the Sun's expansion. But don't worry – the planet will be uninhabitable long before then. Earth is almost as old as the Sun – it's been around for over 4.5 billion years – but it's only got around 1.4 billion years until the Sun's heat boils off the water (among many other nasty effects). In human terms, the Earth as we know it is about 61 years old. But hey, it doesn't look bad for it, does it?

If the time spans in the universe's age and history seem incomprehensible, that's nothing compared with trying to determine distance. The sizes here are utterly, mindbogglingly big. Unfathomable. Whatever we try to imagine, we fall far short.

But let's try anyway! A decent start is to try to get our heads around the "light year." If we were paying attention in physics at school we'd recall that this is how far light travels in one year – and given that light is the fastest thing going, that's a long way.

THE LIGHT YEAR

It really is – imagine flying all the way around the world, approximately 40,000 km. Now imagine repeating this 80 times over. That's a pretty long way, right? Now imagine repeating this feat every single day for 8,079 years. At the end of that time you'll have traveled one light year.

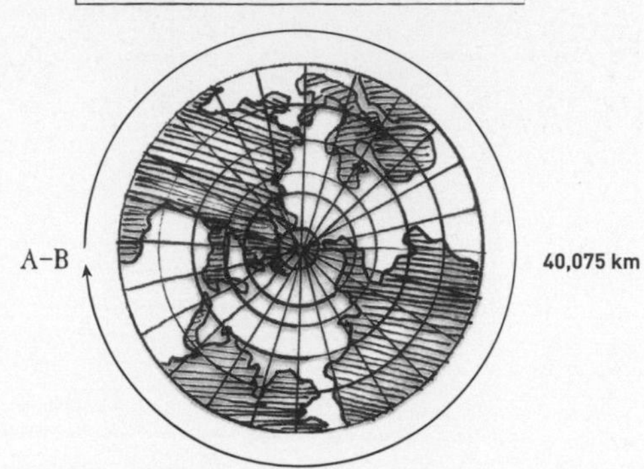

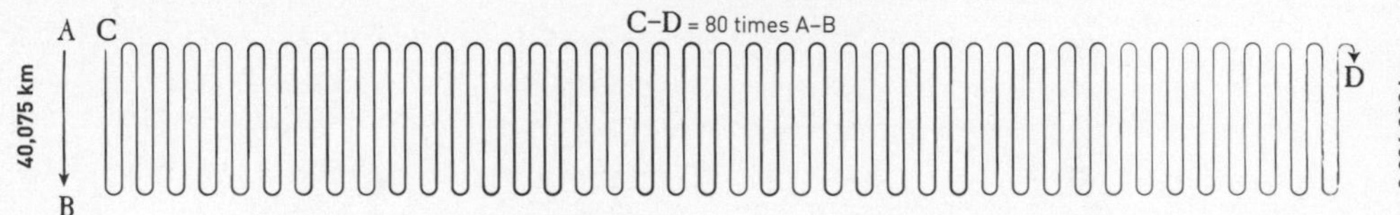

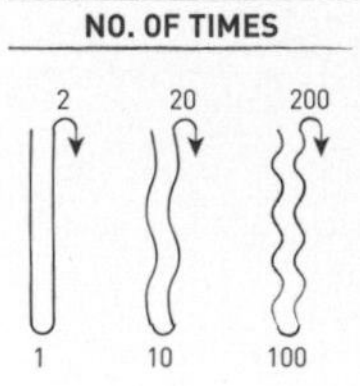

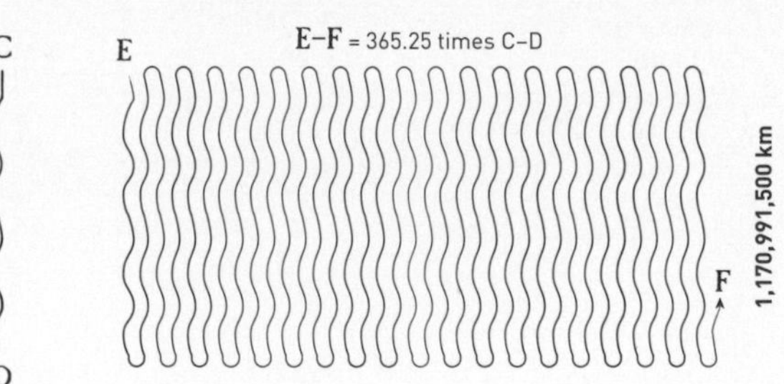

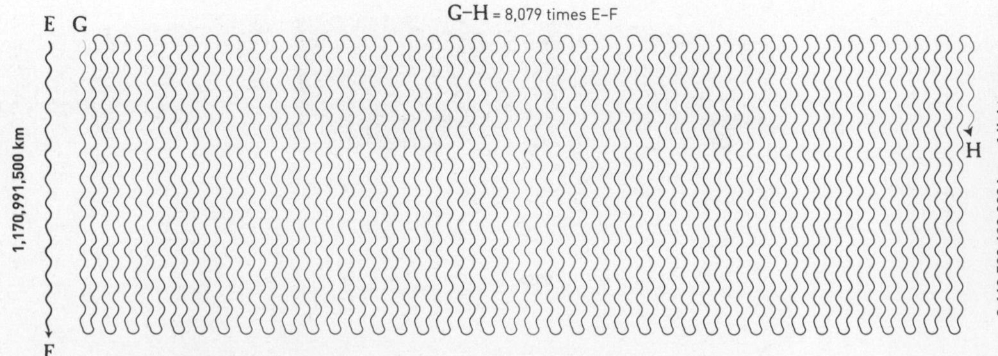

THE SCALE OF...

... THE SOLAR SYSTEM

1,050 times smaller than a light year

Our solar system is much smaller than a light year: its distance across is equivalent to almost eight years of our theoretical (and totally impossible) round-the-world journey.

The solar system is **115,500,000** times smaller than the Milky Way

... THE MILKY WAY

110,000 light years

But the solar system is just a tiny, tiny part of our Milky Way galaxy, which is a huge 110,000 light years across. That's 116 million times bigger than the solar system. The numbers are already incomprehensible, and we're just getting started.

The Milky Way is **249,000** times smaller than the universe

... THE OBSERVABLE UNIVERSE

27,400,000,000 light years

The universe is 249,000 times bigger than the Milky Way – it's 27.4 billion light years across. But your brain gave up a while ago, right?

One final try. Let's shrink the scale of both you and the universe, to make it more comprehensible. Imagine being the size of a virus.

An ant is 20,000 times longer than you are. A human is 20 million times bigger than you are.

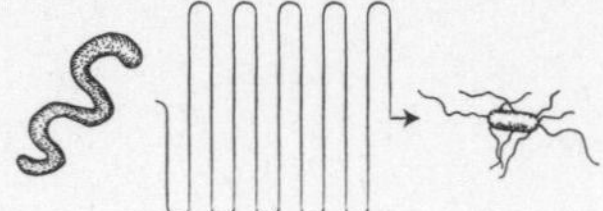

A bacterium is **10 times** bigger than a virus

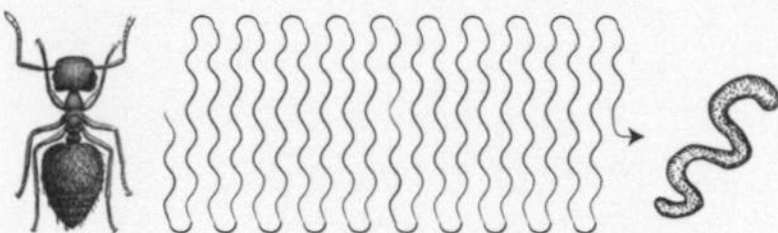

An ant is **2,000 times** bigger than a bacterium

A human is **1,000 times** bigger than an ant

As a virus, your size relative to a human is now about the same as a human versus the circumference of the Earth. In short, you're really, really small.

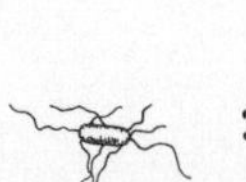
:

=

:

NO. OF TIMES

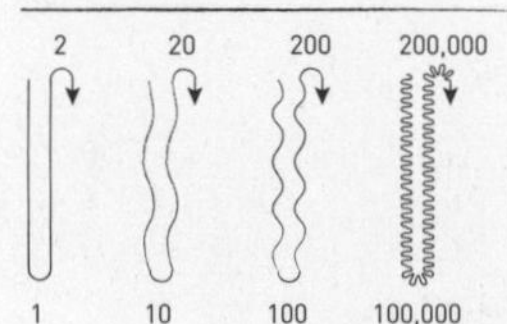

PICTOGRAMS AND ACTUAL SIZE

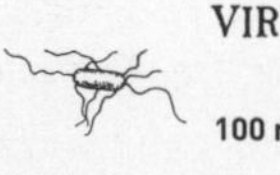

VIRUS

100 nm

BACTERIUM

1,000 nm

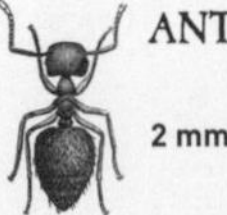

ANT

2 mm

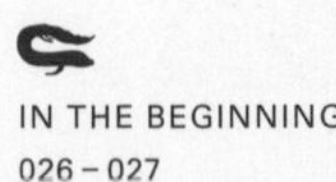

But even with everything shrunk by a factor of 20 million, the scale of the universe is still colossal. To travel from one end of the universe to the other as a human would be the equivalent of a virus having to travel to the Sun and back. Not once. Not twice. But more than 40 million times (about 86 million single trips).

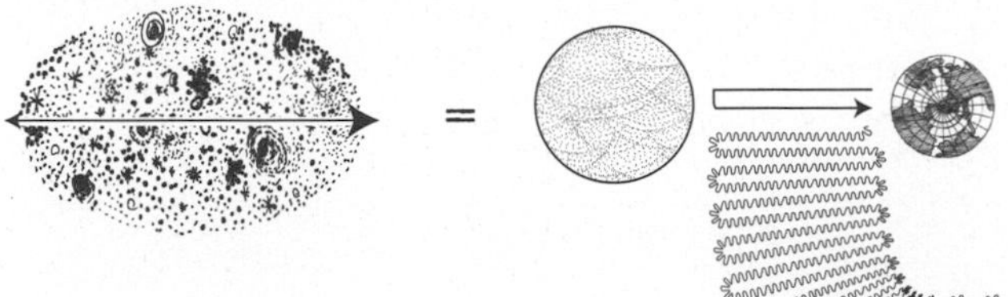

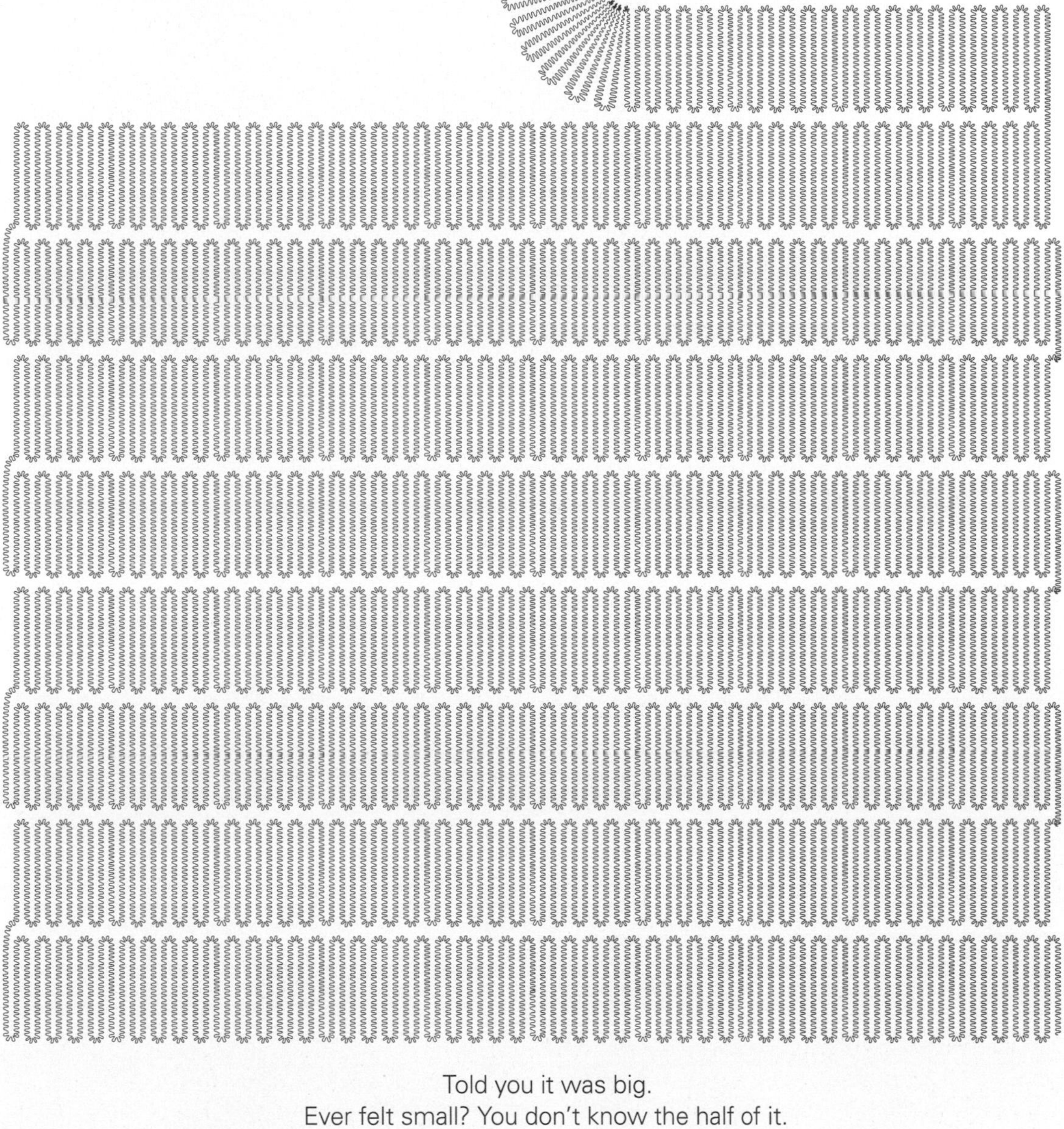

Told you it was big.
Ever felt small? You don't know the half of it.

HUMAN

2 m

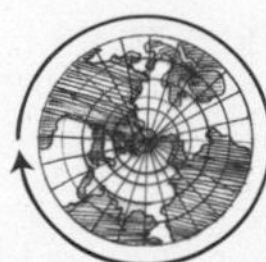

EARTH'S CIRCUMFERENCE

40,075 km

SUN–EARTH DISTANCE

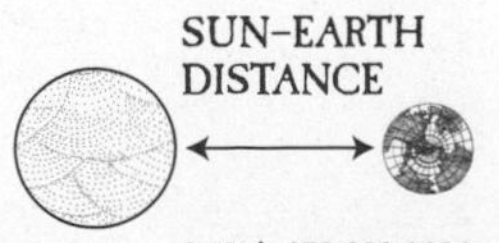

1 AU (≈150,000,000 km)

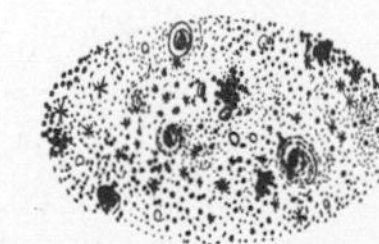

UNIVERSE

27.4 billion light years (≈ 1,732,806 bn AU)

WHERE ARE THE PLANETS IN OUR SOLAR SYSTEM?

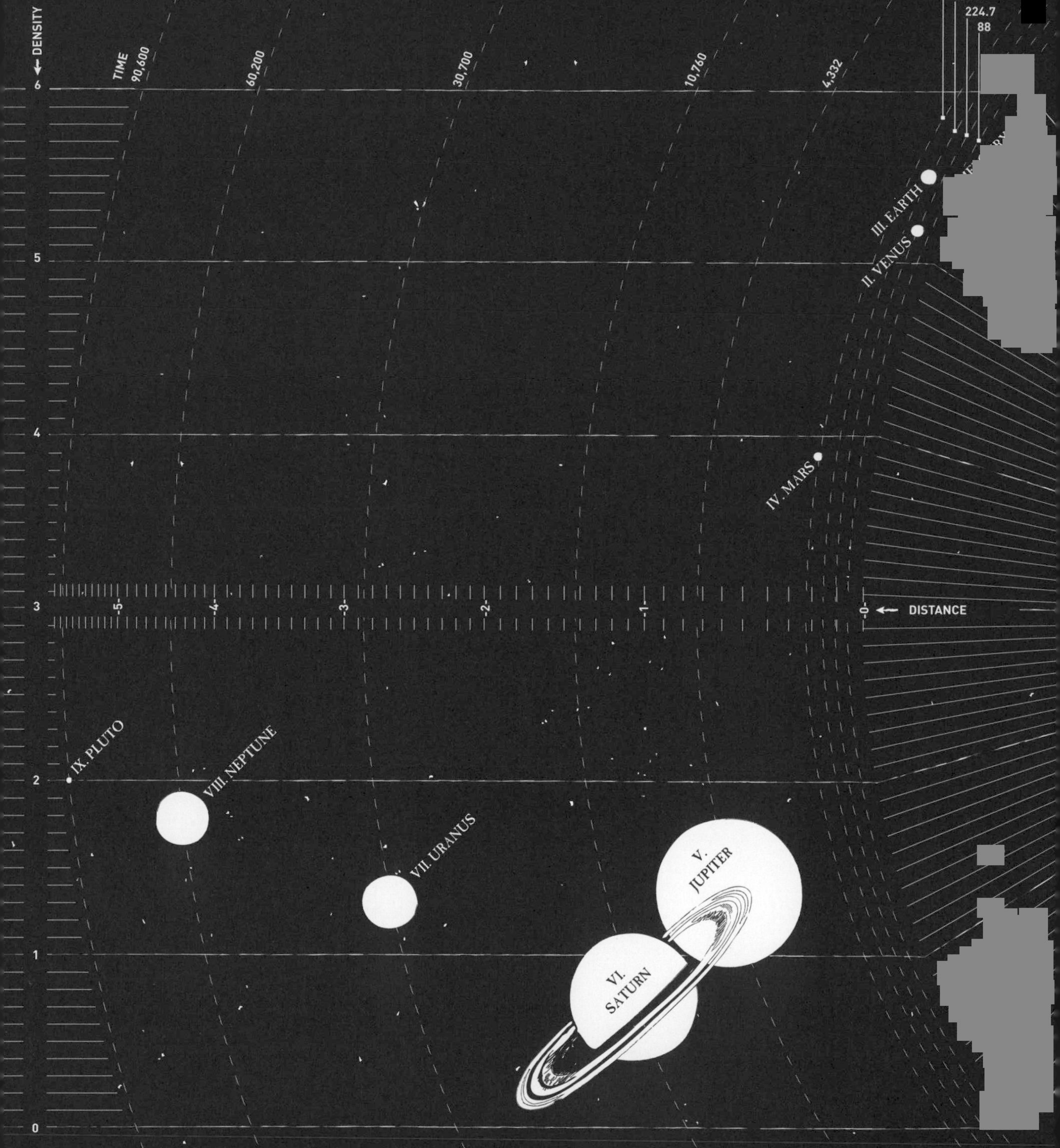

IX. PLUTO
VIII. NEPTUNE
VII. URANUS
VI. SATURN
V. JUPITER
IV. MARS
III. EARTH
II. VENUS

DENSITY: 6, 5, 4, 3, 2, 1, 0

TIME: 90,600; 60,200; 30,700; 10,760; 4,332; 687; 365.2; 224.7; 88

DISTANCE: -5, -4, -3, -2, -1, 0

TIME	DENSITY	DISTANCE
No. of days to complete orbit	g/cm³	km (in billions)

Bang goes the neighborhood

The big has banged, the universe exists, and a small corner of a galaxy known as the Milky Way has been colonized by a book-buying species known as humanity. It's probably a good idea to get to know the neighborhood.

Earth {III} is, despite what almost all of us were taught in school, the third of eight, not nine planets. **Pluto** {IX}, described for decades as the ninth, is smaller than many moons and asteroids, has an erratic orbit, and just doesn't meet the technical criteria. Alas.

The solar system isn't all that friendly a place. In fact, it's downright remote – partly because we're all so spread out. If you were looking down on the area of the planets' orbit and picked a spot at random, there's only a 1 in 22,900 chance you'd pick a planet. Compared with the size of space, or even the size of the Sun, the planets are tiny.

Really tiny. If you squeezed all the planets together into one giant ball, it would kill us all. It'd also still be 600 times smaller than the volume of the Sun.

Our planetary system has one neat party trick. To try it, you'll need a swimming pool about 120,000 km squared, filled with water (Earth would fit in this pool more than 100 times over). If you put **Saturn** {VI} in a plastic bag and dropped it in, it would float – it's the only planet that'd do so.

Earth is the densest planet in the solar system, and only **Jupiter** {V} has noticeably more gravity (you'd weigh 2.5 times more there than here). Earth also has the highest book sales of any planet, making us glad we targeted this volume here rather than **Uranus** {VII}.

And – sorry, we can't continue this calumny any longer. Pluto is the ruler of the underworld in Greek mythology, and Mickey Mouse's dog in Disney's. An 11-year-old girl named it shortly after its discovery. We can't take that away from her. Pluto, you're a planet.

SUN

I. MERCURY
DENSITY: **5.4 g/cm^3**
RADIUS: **2,440 km**
DISTANCE: **59,223,860 km**

II. VENUS
DENSITY: **5.2 g/cm^3**
RADIUS: **6,052 km**
DISTANCE: **104,768,294 km**

III. EARTH
DENSITY: **5.5 g/cm^3**
RADIUS: **6,371 km**
DISTANCE: **149,668,992 km**

IV. MARS
DENSITY: **3.9 g/cm^3**
RADIUS: **3,390 km**
DISTANCE: **224,503,488 km**

V. JUPITER
DENSITY: **1.3 g/cm^3**
RADIUS: **69,911 km**
DISTANCE: **778,278,758 km**

VI. SATURN
DENSITY: **0.7 g/cm^3**
RADIUS: **58,232 km**
DISTANCE: **1,421,855,424 km**

VII. URANUS
DENSITY: **1.3 g/cm^3**
RADIUS: **25,362 km**
DISTANCE: **2,873,644,646 km**

VIII. NEPTUNE
DENSITY: **1.8 g/cm^3**
RADIUS: **24,622 km**
DISTANCE: **4,490,069,760 km**

IX. PLUTO
DENSITY: **2 g/cm^3**
RADIUS: **1,161 km**
DISTANCE: **5,837,090,688 km**

The distance from the Sun is an average because the orbits of the planets do not make perfect circles, but rather very slightly flattened ones, or ellipses.

Producing a planet

The planet Earth, measuring about 4,000 miles from surface to core, resembles nothing so much as an intergalactic gobstopper.

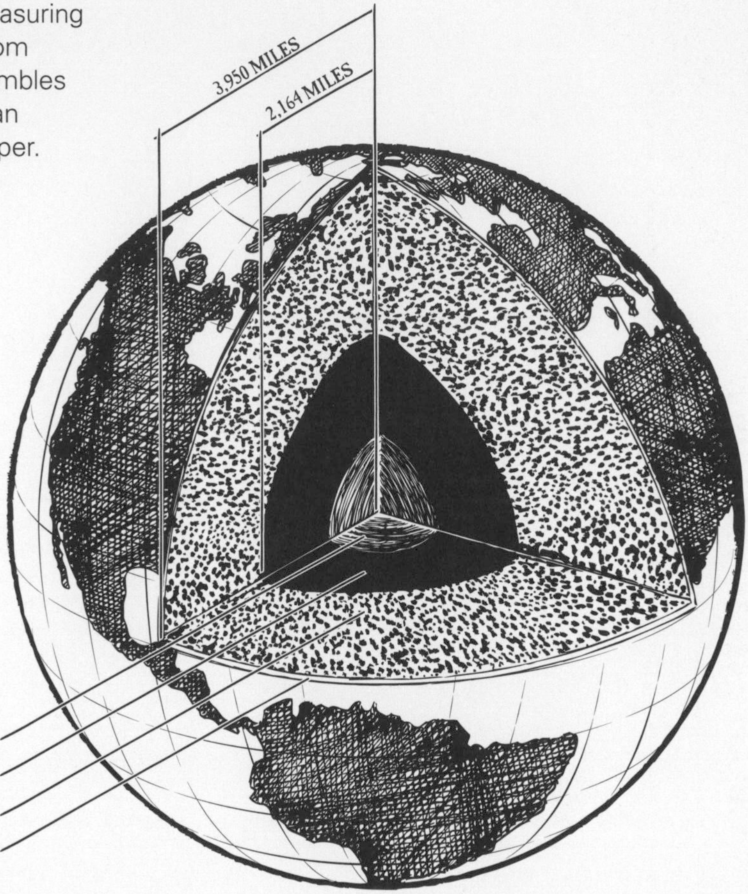

3,950 MILES
2,164 MILES
INNER CORE
OUTER CORE
MANTLE
CRUST

The central 2,000 miles or so are made up of compressed iron and nickel, with the mantle surrounding it (most of the remaining 2,000 miles) being composed of silicon, oxygen and (even more) iron.

So far so good – but let's be honest, we don't live in the center of the Earth, we live on the surface of it. And so, it's the material that makes up the 37 miles of the crust, the 37 miles that we call home, that really matters.

If you took a million 1 g samples (one metric ton, in other words) of the Earth's crust, and broke them down into their constituent elements, here's what you'd get. Almost half would be **oxygen** {O}, usually mixed with silicon or metals to make ores. The second-most abundant element would be **silicon** {Si} – almost none of it of a grade good enough for computing, but found on beaches everywhere, and perfectly good for glass. **Aluminum** {Al}, **iron** {Fe}, **calcium** {Ca} and **sodium** {Na} would make up a huge part of the rest: those six elements alone would make up more than 90% of our one-ton sample.

It's the rare metals that really count, though, especially for the high-tech gadgets we enjoy. iPads, smartphones and the like rely on so-called "rare earths," 95% of which are mined in China, including **neodymium** {Nd} and **lanthanum** {La}, which at 38 g and 32 g per ton each, aren't quite as rare as you'd think. Even **uranium** {U} is more common than you might suspect: one gram out of every 500,000 is made up of the stuff.

If you want to look for something really rare, try gold: only one gram out of every 500 million of the crust is made of **gold** {Au}. No wonder even Olympic gold medals only use a thin 6 g coating of the stuff. There's gold in them thar' hills – but, unfortunately, not much of it.

CRUST ELEMENTS TABLE

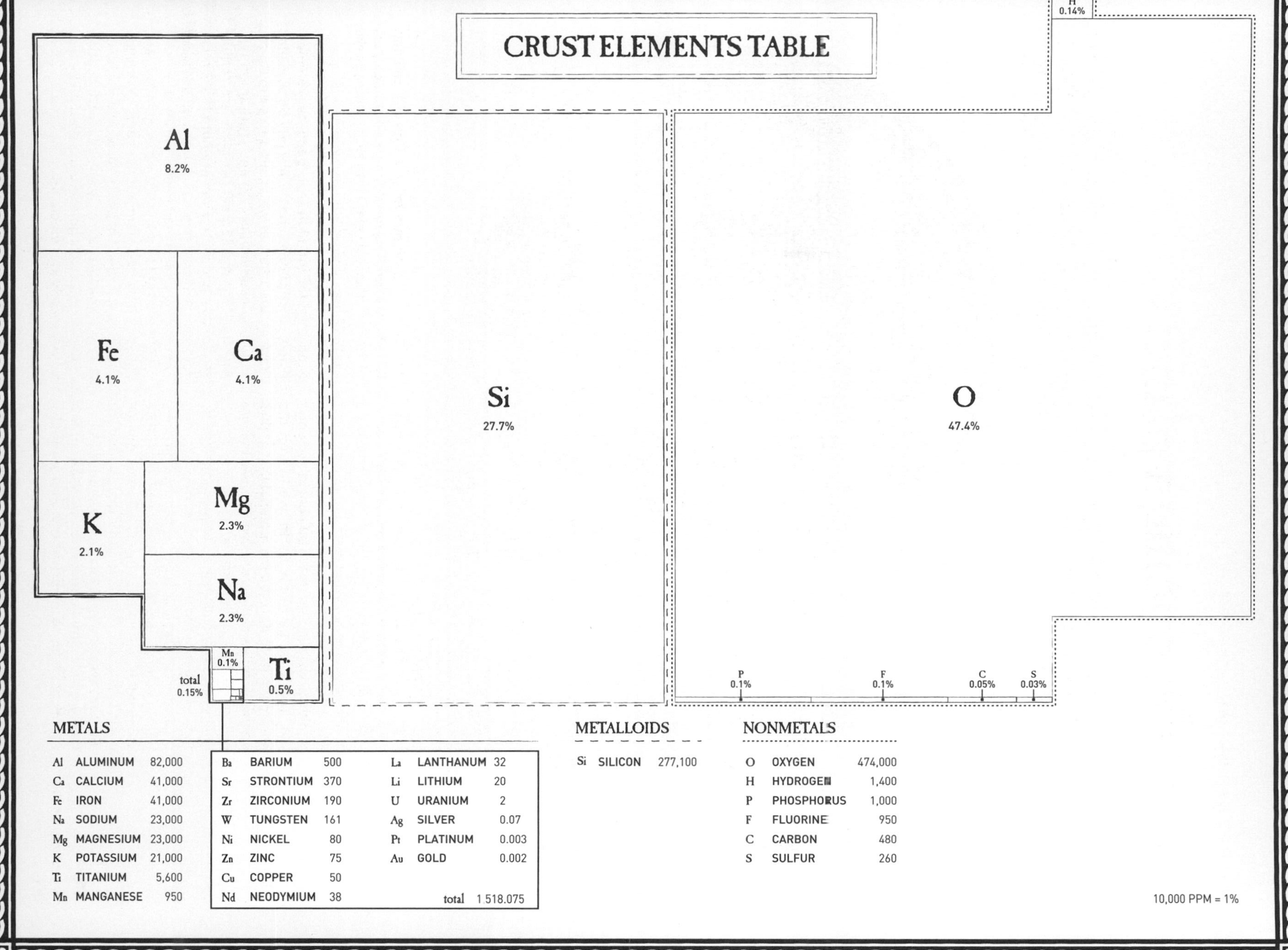

METALS

Al	ALUMINUM	82,000
Ca	CALCIUM	41,000
Fe	IRON	41,000
Na	SODIUM	23,000
Mg	MAGNESIUM	23,000
K	POTASSIUM	21,000
Ti	TITANIUM	5,600
Mn	MANGANESE	950

Ba	BARIUM	500	La	LANTHANUM	32
Sr	STRONTIUM	370	Li	LITHIUM	20
Zr	ZIRCONIUM	190	U	URANIUM	2
W	TUNGSTEN	161	Ag	SILVER	0.07
Ni	NICKEL	80	Pt	PLATINUM	0.003
Zn	ZINC	75	Au	GOLD	0.002
Cu	COPPER	50			
Nd	NEODYMIUM	38		total	1,518.075

METALLOIDS

Si	SILICON	277,100

NONMETALS

O	OXYGEN	474,000
H	HYDROGEN	1,400
P	PHOSPHORUS	1,000
F	FLUORINE	950
C	CARBON	480
S	SULFUR	260

10,000 PPM = 1%

Evolution revolution

How long does it take to design a human being? The short answer is that, provided you can find a man and a woman who love each other very much, it can be done in about 40 weeks. The longer answer, though, is more interesting. Thankfully. Some of our most significant and interesting features as a species have been more than 500 million years in the making – and it's only in the last century that we've been able to begin piecing the evolutionary jigsaw together.

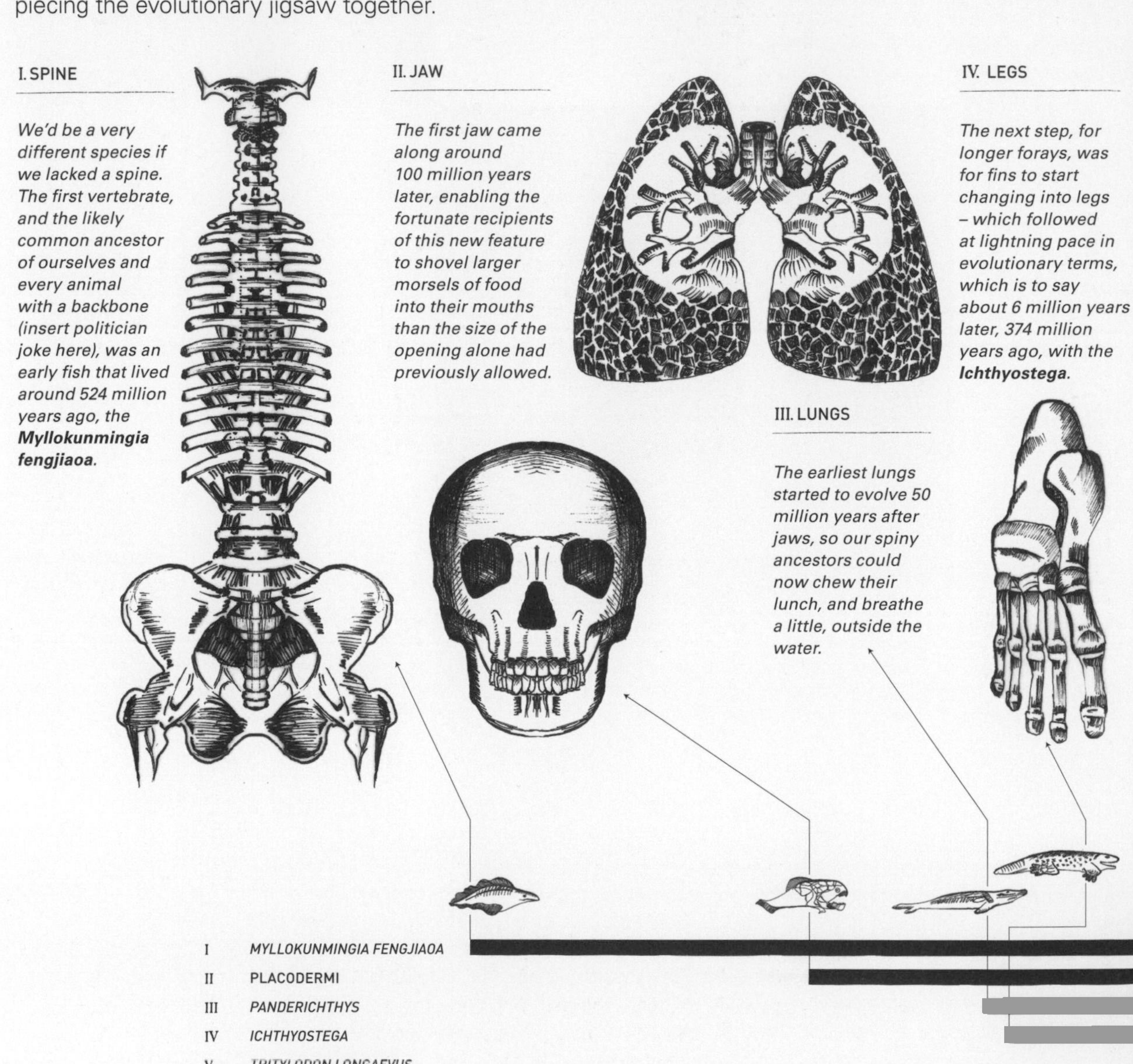

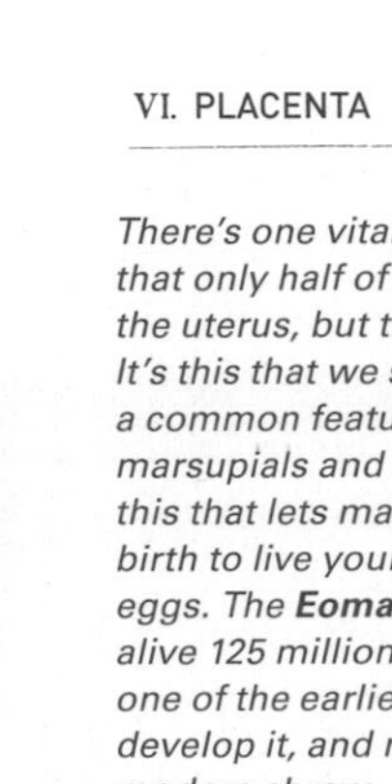

V. DIAPHRAGM

These early amphibians and reptiles kept evolving and changing, eventually producing the cynodonts – one of the earliest groups of animals that began to resemble modern mammals. One of their key features? The humble diaphragm, essential for our modern lung structure and generally lighter torsos.

VI. PLACENTA

There's one vital addition that only half of us have – not the uterus, but the placenta. It's this that we share as a common feature with marsupials and others, and it's this that lets mammals give birth to live young rather than eggs. The ***Eomaia scansoria****, alive 125 million years ago, was one of the earliest animals to develop it, and resembled a modern shrew.*

VII. THUMBS

From here, essentially, size matters. Mammals all have a neocortex, so for us, brains are primarily (in some respects) a question of scale. Our two big developments: opposable thumbs and a bipedal frame, which ran synchronologically. Opposable thumbs were first observed in animals from around 60 million years ago – but they could only really fully develop when they were free to be used, around the time when our ancestral knuckles stopped scraping the savannah floor. As thumbs improved, we spent less time on our forelegs. Consequently, our bone structure changed, allowing thumbs to develop yet further.

VIII. BIPEDAL LEGS/STRUCTURE

Eventually – about 3 million years ago – our bipedal ancestors emerged. From there, the rest is (quite literally) history.

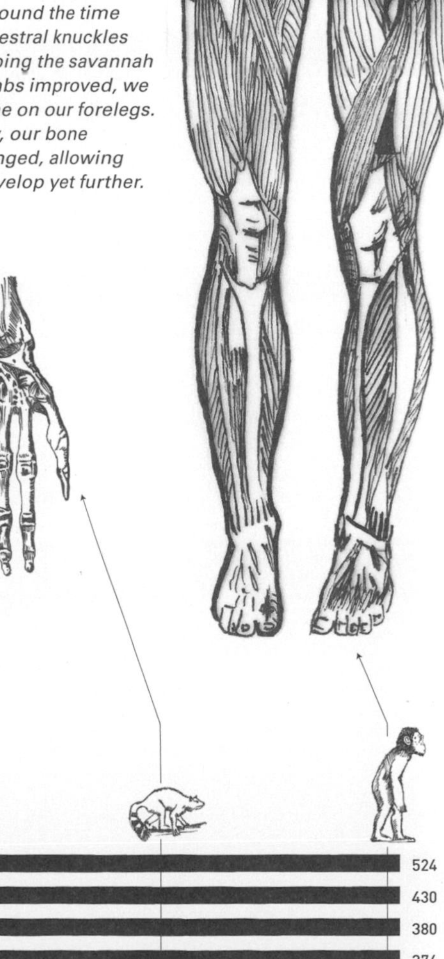

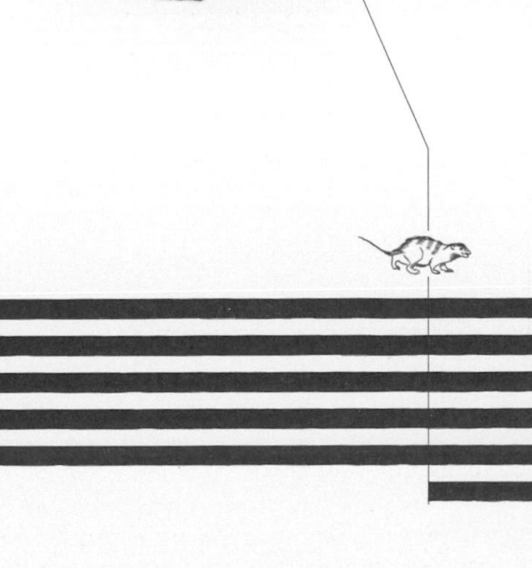

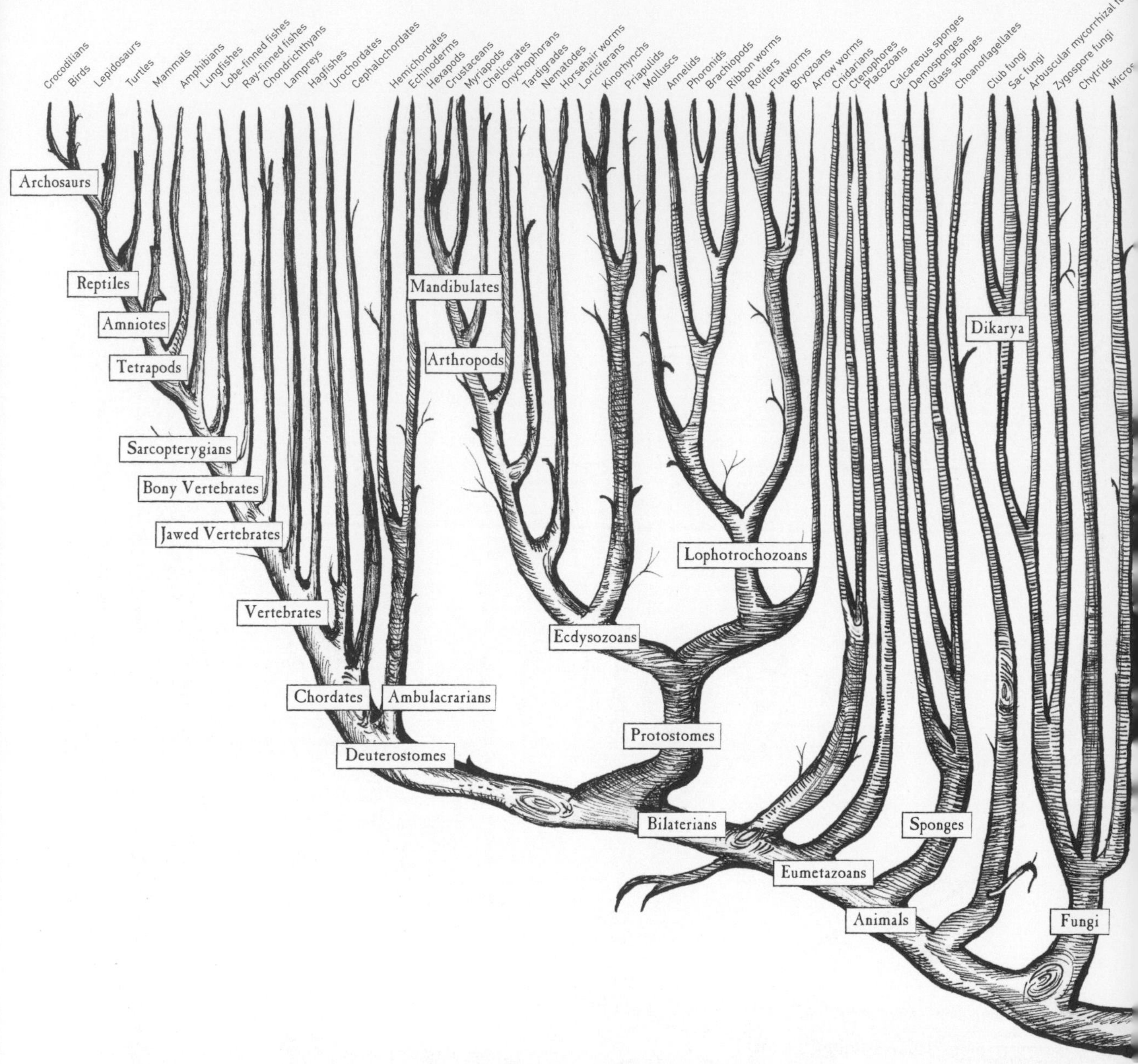

From tiny sapling to towering tree, the growth of life on Earth is pretty complex. What's fun to look at though, is just how each of the groups of organisms that call this planet home branched off and went their separate ways. As this (stylized and simplified) tree of life shows, our branch of the family tree diverged from bacteria a long time ago.

Fungi go their own way much later – just before we get towards what we call animals – while the far left of the graphic shows our fellow vertebrates (the animals who managed to develop some backbone). If we're being literal, none of us are a monkey's uncle – but we're certainly its cousin. Maybe once-removed.

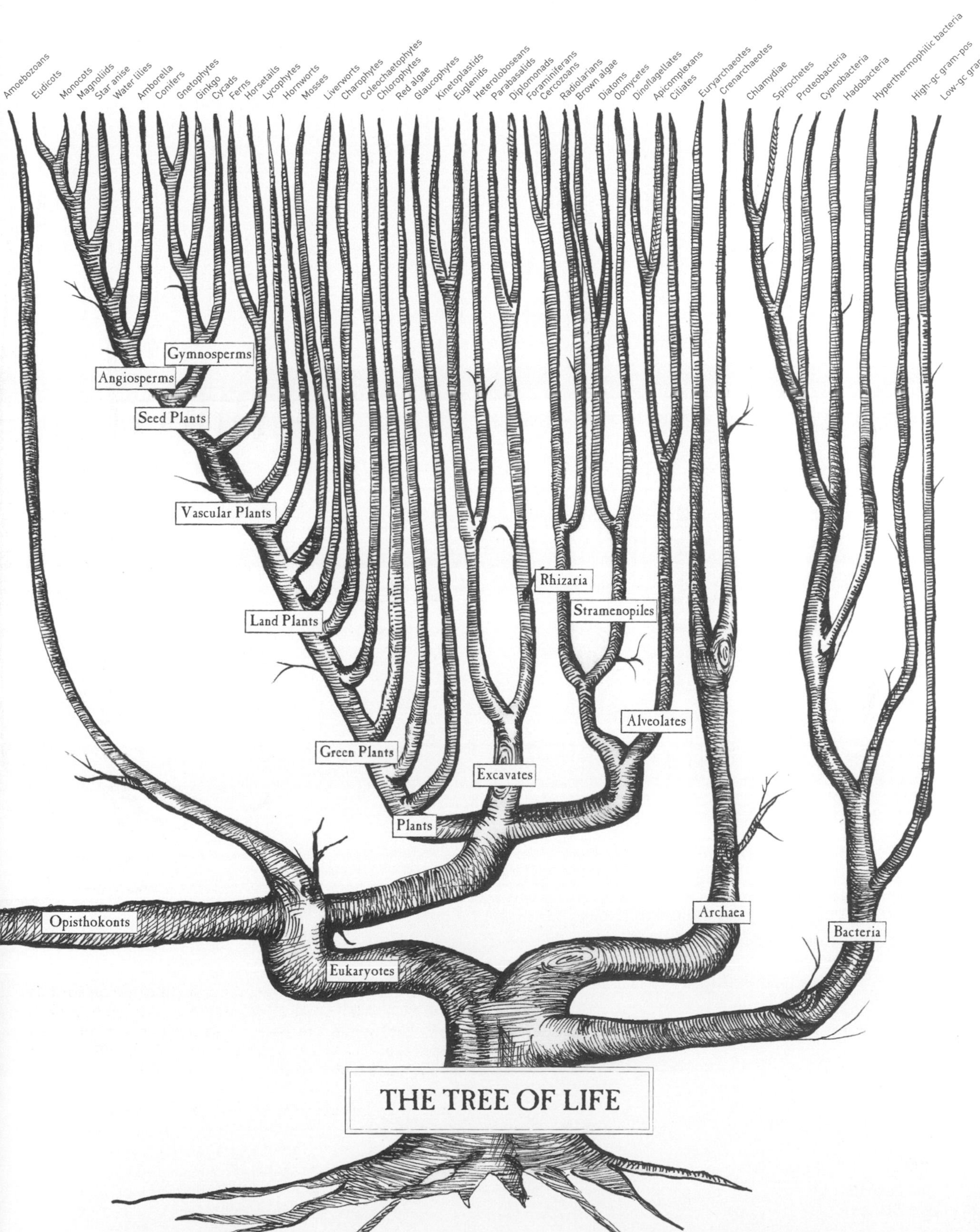
Amoebozoans
Eudicots
Monocots
Magnoliids
Star anise
Water lilies
Amborella
Conifers
Gnetophytes
Ginkgo
Cycads
Ferns
Horsetails
Lycophytes
Hornworts
Mosses
Liverworts
Charophytes
Coleochaetophytes
Chlorophytes
Red algae
Glaucophytes
Kinetoplastids
Euglenids
Heteroloboseans
Parabasalids
Diplomonads
Foraminiferans
Cercozoans
Radiolarians
Brown algae
Diatoms
Oomycetes
Dinoflagellates
Apicomplexans
Ciliates
Euryarchaeotes
Crenarchaeotes
Chlamydiae
Spirochetes
Proteobacteria
Cyanobacteria
Hadobacteria
Hyperthermophilic bacteria
High-gc gram-pos
Low-gc gram-pos
Gymnosperms
Angiosperms
Seed Plants
Vascular Plants
Land Plants
Rhizaria
Stramenopiles
Alveolates
Green Plants
Excavates
Plants
Opisthokonts
Eukaryotes
Archaea
Bacteria
THE TREE OF LIFE

Critical mass

Humans are quite fond of referring to ourselves as Earth's dominant species, and from our perspective that certainly seems to be true. Just look around, and evidence of our presence is everywhere. But by most measures, our presence is much less noticeable.

This is most starkly obvious if you look at biomass – the total mass (weight) of living things on the planet. For obvious reasons, this is hard to estimate, but roughly speaking there are 1.7 trillion tonnes of living biomass on the planet, if you exclude bacteria. The overwhelming majority of this – more than 99% – is plant life. We are among the 1%.

And indeed much less even than that: the total sum of **human mass {IV}** is about 350 million tonnes. Before you start thinking we should go on a diet, that compares with about 520 million tonnes of **cows {II}**, about 4,200 million tonnes of **fish {VIII}** and 2,700 million tonnes of **ants {I}** (and that's a conservative estimate).

Bacteria, left out of the previous estimate, are likely to weigh close to the same as all other living things put together. One current estimate puts the total mass of **bacteria {IX}** at around 1.3 trillion tonnes – around 4,000 kg of bacteria for each kilogram of human on the planet.

One area, though, where humanity's impact is sadly evident is the **blue whale {VII}** – once there were around 36 million tonnes of blue whale roaming the Earth. Today, there are less than half a million.

But compared with the Earth itself, we're just a tiny fraction of a tiny fraction. The total mass of fresh water on the planet is more than 2,000 times larger than the mass of all living things – and living creatures make up less than a ten-trillionth of the mass of the planet. We're smaller than we think.

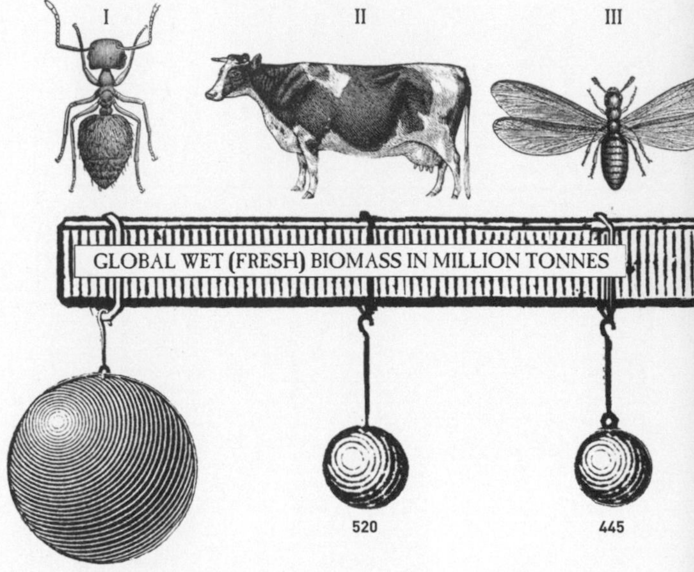

TERRESTRIAL

I ANTS

II CATTLE

III TERMITES

IV HUMANS

V SHEEP AND GOATS

VI CHICKENS

MARINE

VII BLUE WHALES

VIII MARINE FISH

GLOBAL

IX BACTERIA

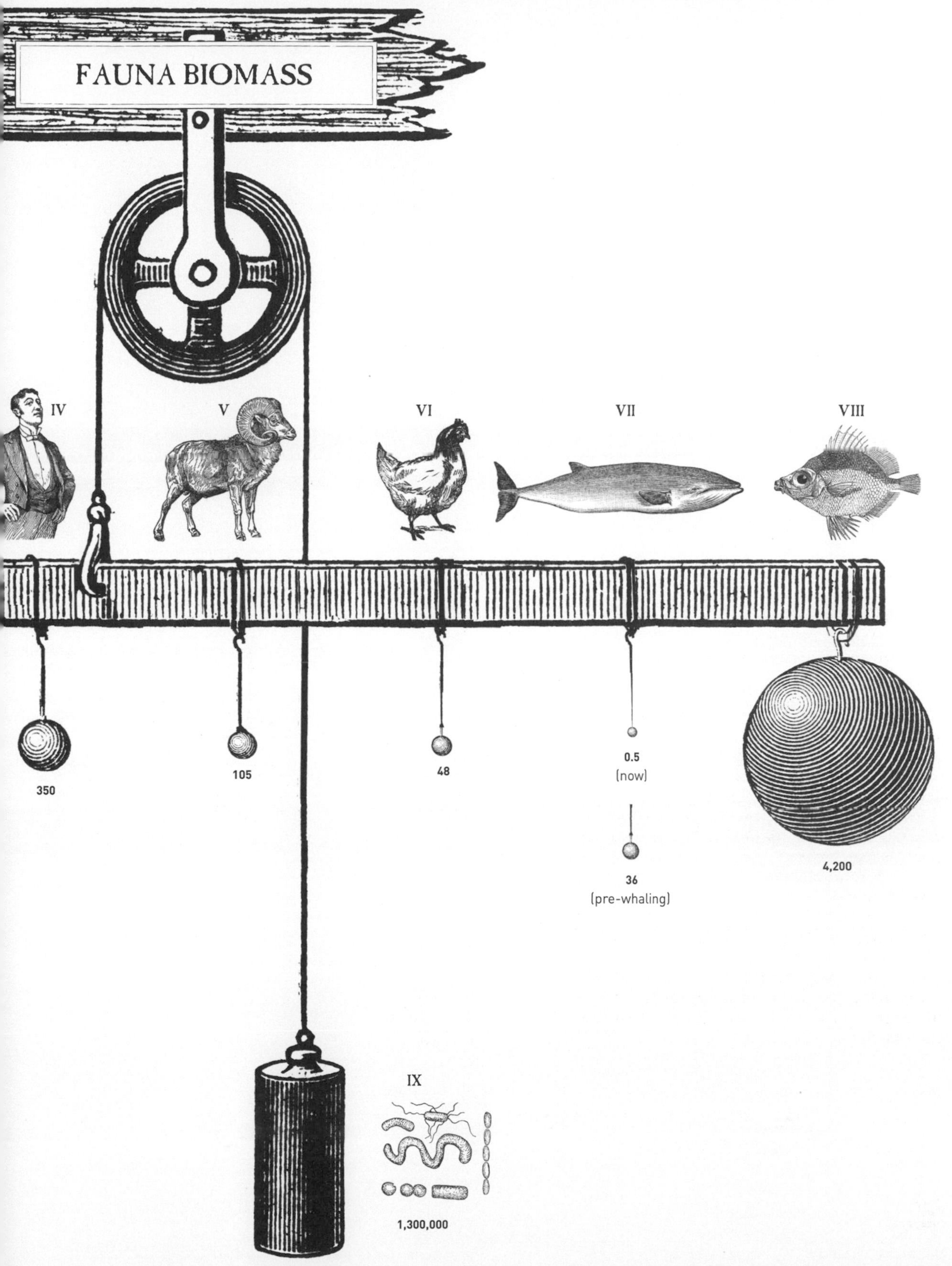
FAUNA BIOMASS
IV
V
VI
VII
VIII
350
105
48
0.5
(now)
36
(pre-whaling)
4,200
IX
1,300,000

The impact zone

Getting smacked around by an asteroid is no fun whatsoever, or so we assume. We have to guess, because much like the mafia, asteroids are pretty good at eliminating witnesses: just try looking for a dinosaur to ask about the experience.

Statistically speaking, Earth can expect to be struck by an asteroid about 50 meters across, which leaves a crater a kilometer in diameter, once every 1,000 years. Ominously, we're well overdue: we haven't been hit for around 55,000 years. Hopefully, the asteroids haven't noticed that.

Thankfully, NASA is keeping an eye on the skies and for the moment it's not too worried. It has a threat matrix that ranges from 0 to 10. So far, out of more than 1,000 asteroids it's monitoring that will come close to Earth, only two have a score higher than 0 – and both are a "1."

That doesn't mean we're totally out of the woods, though. One of the two scored asteroids, the pithily named **"2011 AG5"** {I} has a 1-in-500 chance of hitting Earth on one of four occasions between 2040 and 2047. It's a pretty huge 140 m across – not enough to wipe out life on Earth, but big enough to make sure we'd feel it.

The biggest asteroid, **"2010 AU118"** {XXI}, near the top of the watchlist, is 894 m across, which is getting toward global-extinction territory. NASA is watching for 37 separate potential collisions with Earth this particular rock could make before 2106, but it's not as bad as it might sound: its odds of actually hitting us on any of those occasions are less than 1-in-10,000.

Out of those on the watchlist, **"2010 RF12"** {XV} has the best chance of striking – 6.5%. The initial rush of worry that might cause, however, should be tempered: it looks to be a mere 7 m across. Asteroids this size hit roughly once a year and usually we never even notice.

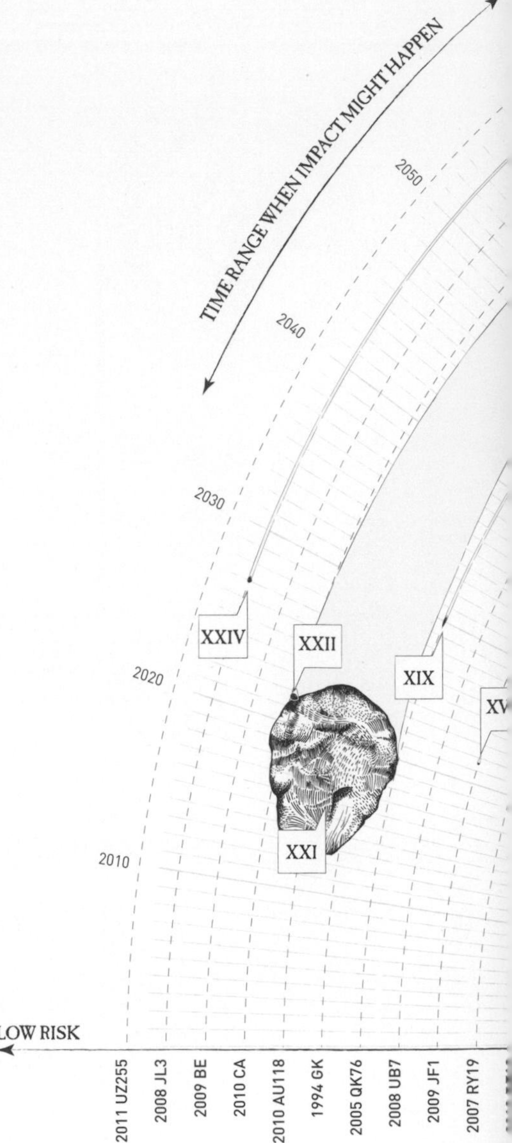

IMPACT PROBABILITY

(CUMULATIVE)

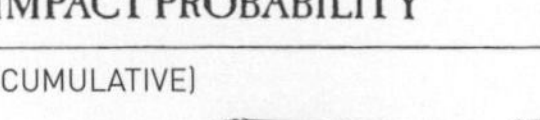

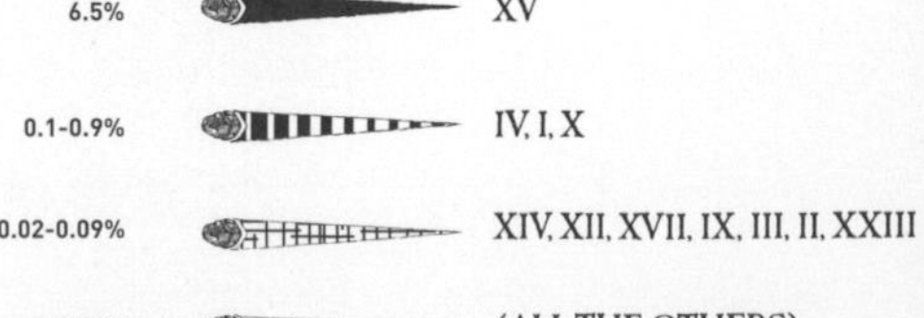

6.5%	XV
0.1-0.9%	IV, I, X
0.02-0.09%	XIV, XII, XVII, IX, III, II, XXIII
0-0.01%	(ALL THE OTHERS)

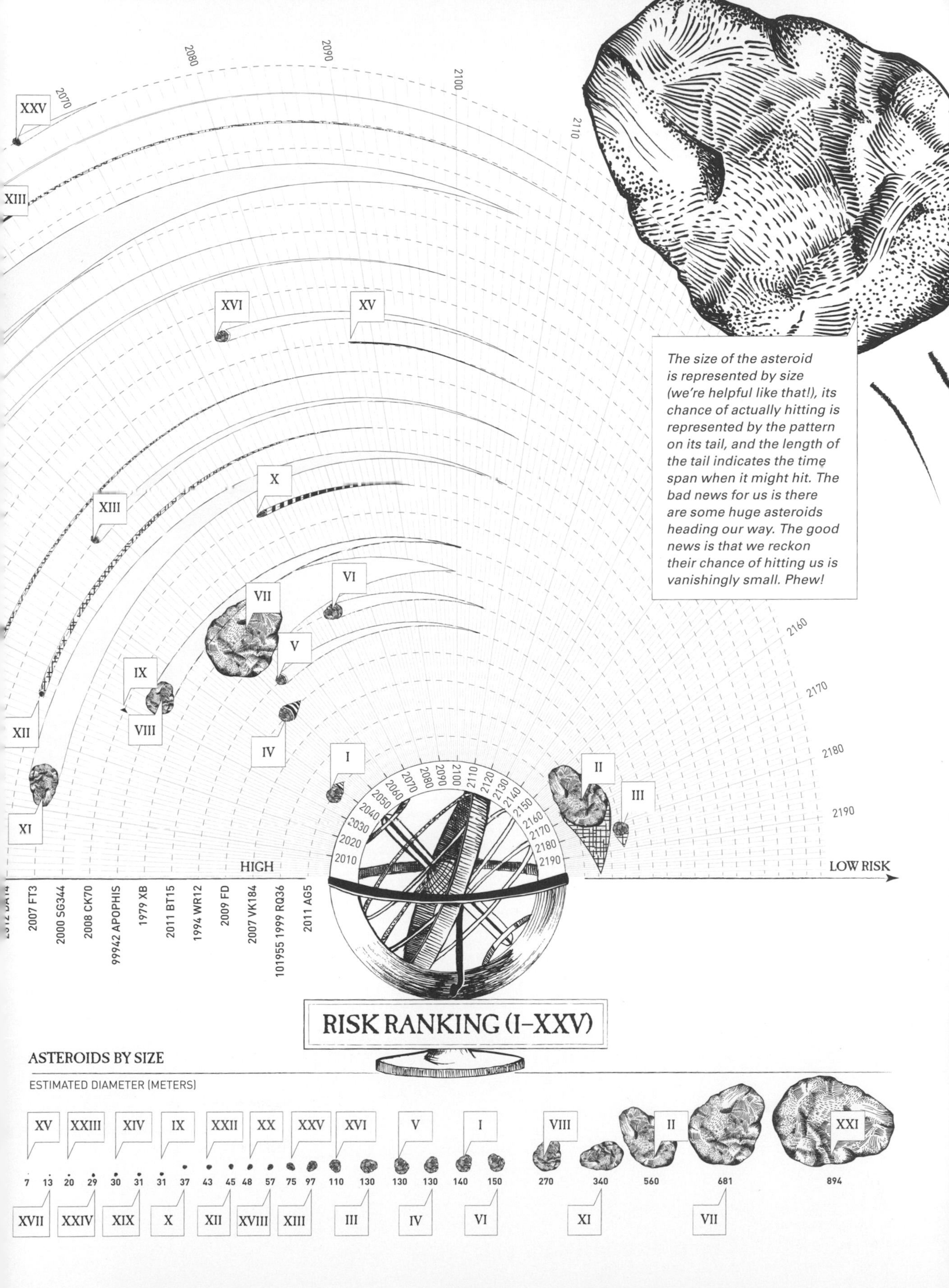
The size of the asteroid is represented by size (we're helpful like that!), its chance of actually hitting is represented by the pattern on its tail, and the length of the tail indicates the time span when it might hit. The bad news for us is there are some huge asteroids heading our way. The good news is that we reckon their chance of hitting us is vanishingly small. Phew!
HIGH
LOW RISK
2007 FT3
2000 SG344
2008 CK70
99942 APOPHIS
1979 XB
2011 BT15
1994 WR12
2009 FD
2007 VK184
101955 1999 RQ36
2011 AG5
RISK RANKING (I–XXV)
ASTEROIDS BY SIZE
ESTIMATED DIAMETER (METERS)
7 13 20 29 30 31 31 37 43 45 48 57 75 97 110 130 130 130 140 150 270 340 560 681 894
XV XXIII XIV IX XXII XX XXV XVI V I VIII II XXI
XVII XXIV XIX X XII XVIII XIII III IV VI XI VII

Distinctly extinct

"It's not that I'm afraid to die. I just don't want to be there when it happens," said Woody Allen.

Woody might not manage to miss his own death, but he's certainly not been around for the death of pretty much everything else that has ever existed. This is because pretty much every type of life form had disappeared without a trace long before humans turned up: 98% of the species that have walked, swum or flown on the planet are no longer with us.

When we think of extinctions, we tend to think of the dinosaurs and the meteorite we believe blasted them off the face of the planet some 66 million years ago {V}, making way for the era of the mammal (and the so-far short era of *Homo sapiens*).

But in reality, this was just one of several mass-extinctions over the last 500 million years, and almost certainly not the largest. The problem with extinct species is, of course, that they're no longer around for us to count. The best proxy we have is to look for fossils, but even these are tricky – if humanity went extinct tomorrow, hardly any of the seven billion of us would leave one behind.

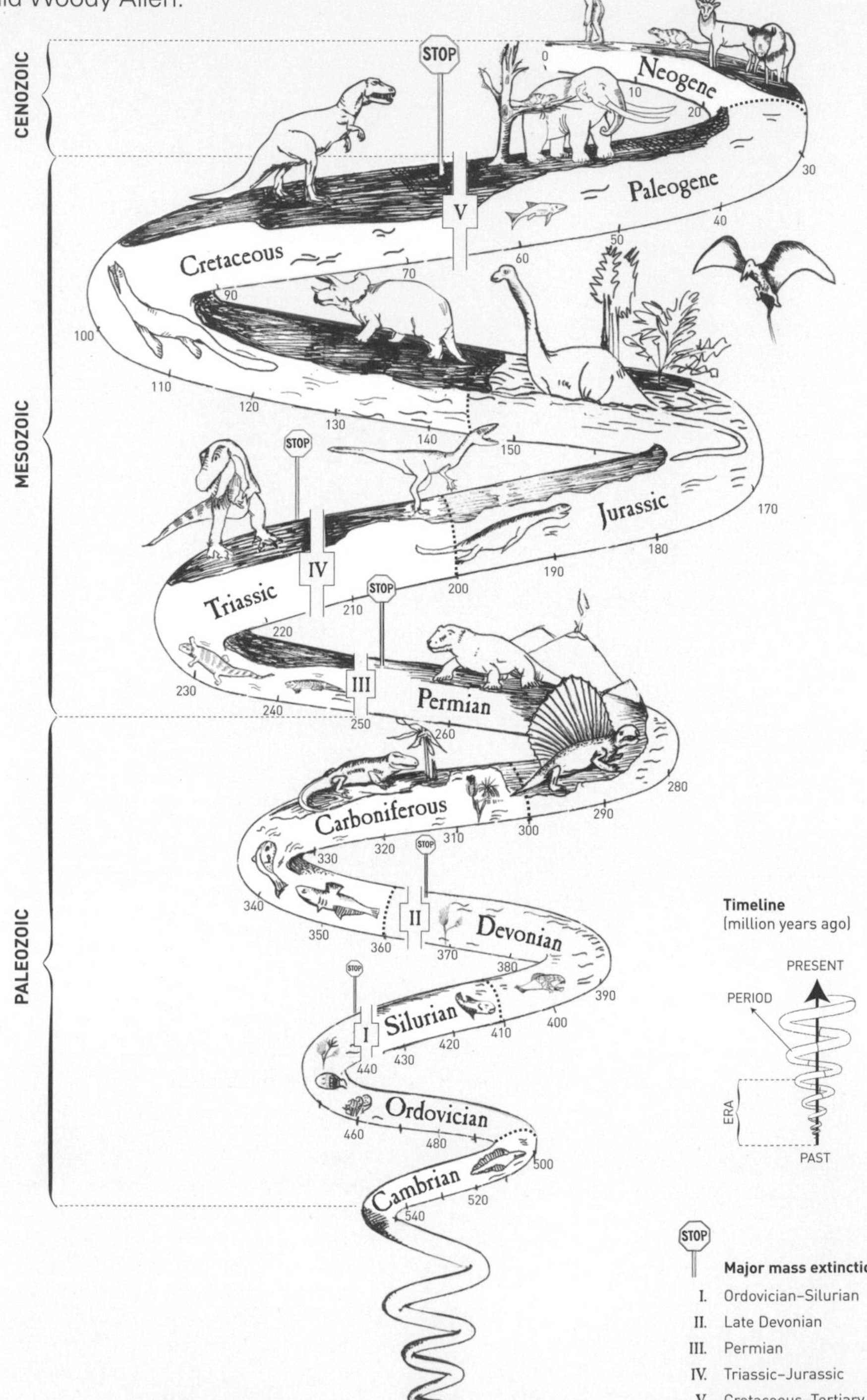

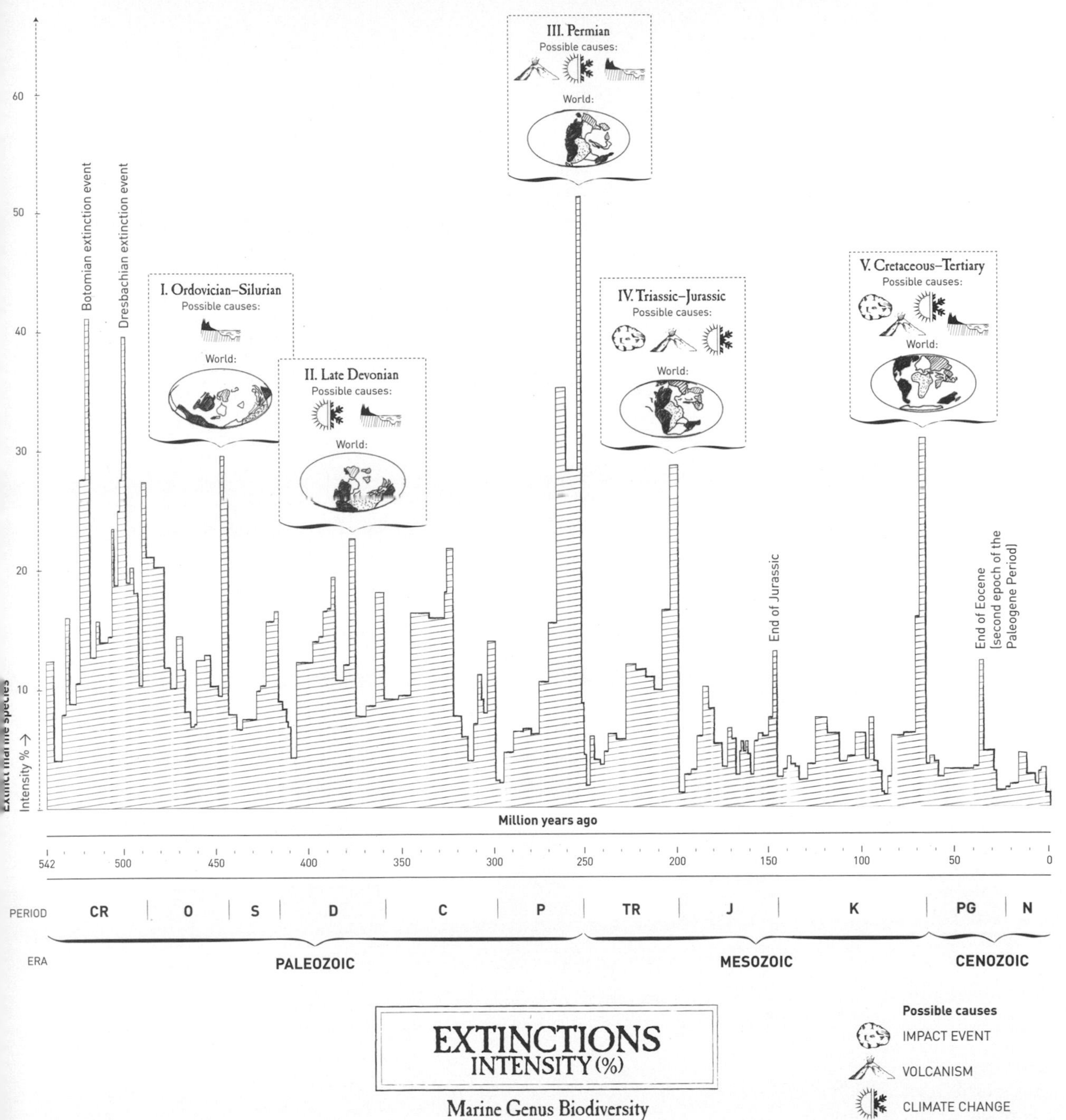

EXTINCTIONS
INTENSITY (%)

Marine Genus Biodiversity

Marine species are the easiest to find as they're the most likely to fossilize – and looking through a 540-million-year record, there is a constant level of "background" extinction, but also a few noticeable spikes, or "mass die-outs."

The biggest by far occurred around 250 million years ago **{III}**, and saw the death of at least 50% – and potentially up to 95% – of marine species. The majority of land animals and even insects of the time sadly bit the dust, too. Eerily, we don't really know why it happened – even Columbo might find it tricky to find just "one more thing" to ask about in solving a murder mystery that's millions of years old. Another meteorite could be a suspect, as could volcanic activities, continental drift, or even a sudden change in the Earth's atmosphere.

Still, as we're more highly evolved, we'd never let anything as silly as a mere change in the planet's atmosphere prove any kind of risk to us, would we?

Getting Civilized

About two million years ago, the first of our ancestors we'd (maybe grudgingly) recognize as humans started walking the earth. Though, like many distant relatives, we probably wouldn't want to invite them to many social occasions.

By modern standards, their personal hygiene wasn't up to much, and their table manners were terrible.

This section of the book chronicles our early history: our journey from nomadic tribes struggling to eke out an existence among other species to the clothed, always-online, latte-sipping sophisticates we are today. It's not always been the most sanitary of journeys. Along the way, we look at what makes up a man (short answer: miles and miles of biological tubes), the bugs and parasites we carry around, and the road not quite traveled – the Neanderthals and other close relatives who died out not all that long ago.

Thankfully, there's also the story of civilization: domesticating animals, developing language, making tools, and most crucially (it's the origin of the word "civilization," after all) – founding cities.

A good start, but still a long way to go: it took more than 9,000 years from the founding of the world's first city before there was anywhere decent to buy a cupcake. Those ancients had their priorities all wrong.

All in the family

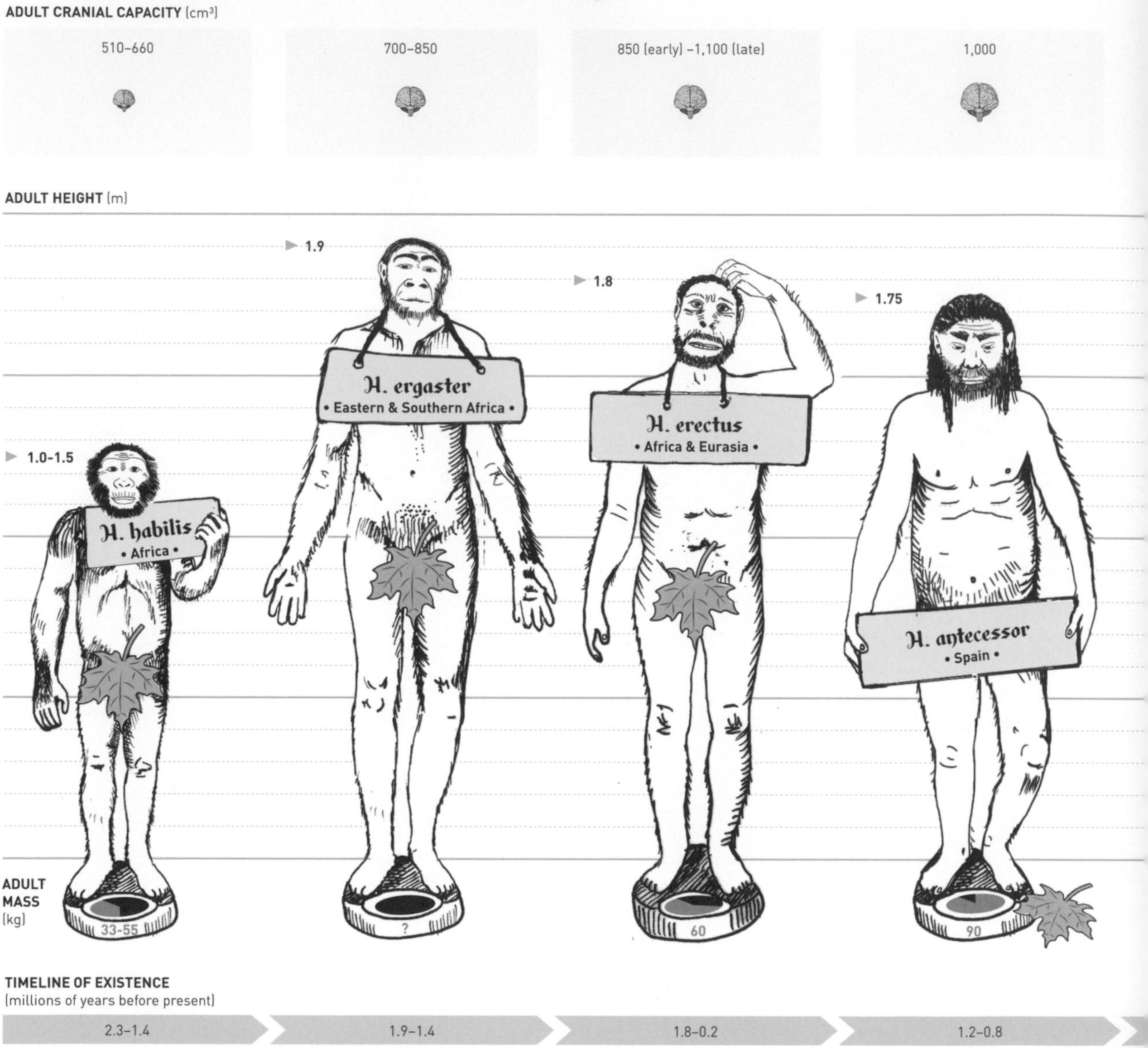

ADULT CRANIAL CAPACITY (cm³)

	H. habilis	H. ergaster	H. erectus	H. antecessor
Region	Africa	Eastern & Southern Africa	Africa & Eurasia	Spain
ADULT CRANIAL CAPACITY (cm³)	510–660	700–850	850 (early) –1,100 (late)	1,000
ADULT HEIGHT (m)	1.0-1.5	1.9	1.8	1.75
ADULT MASS (kg)	33-55	?	60	90
TIMELINE OF EXISTENCE (millions of years before present)	2.3–1.4	1.9–1.4	1.8–0.2	1.2–0.8

As a species, humans make pretty awful relatives. When it comes to our nearest genetic kin, it's not so much that we never call or write (though we don't), it's more that we let our nearest family members die – or might even have killed them ourselves.

When we think about other near-human species – like the Neanderthals – we tend to imagine comically stupid cavemen, outpaced and outgeared by our intellectually superior forefathers (and foremothers). And why not? It's fun!

But the fossil record isn't quite on our side. Both ***Homo neanderthalensis*** and the species believed to be our shared ancestor, ***Homo heidelbergensis***, had cranial capacities that could, on occasion, rival our own (although *heidelbergensis*'s were generally smaller).

Both species lived for longer than humans (we've managed about 200,000 years so far). None of the near-human species came close to ***Homo habilis***, though, who it seems might have been around for more than a million years. But

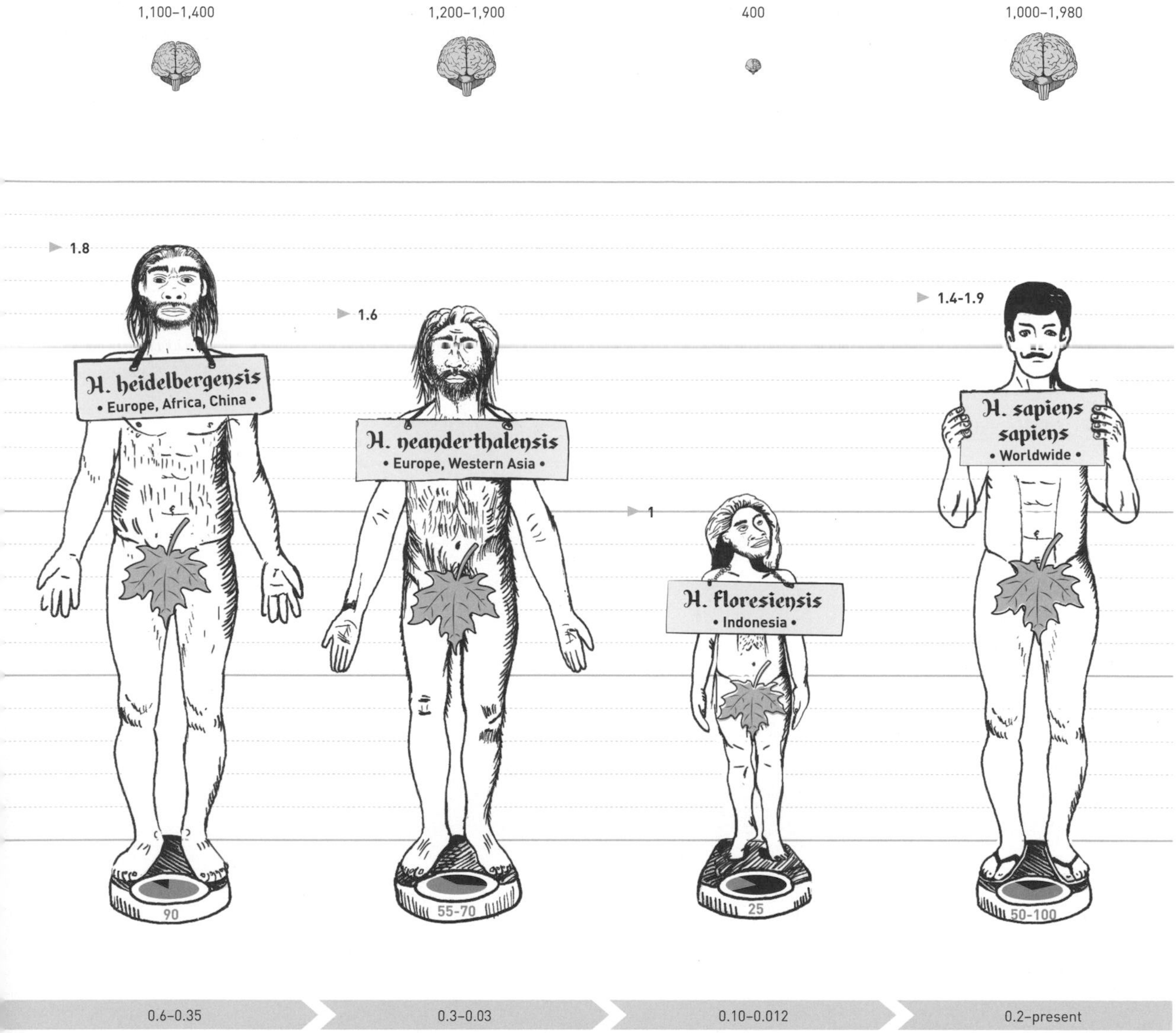

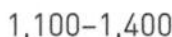

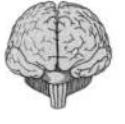
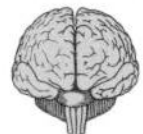

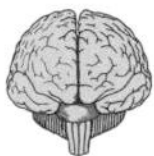

400

1,000–1,980

1.8

H. heidelbergensis
• Europe, Africa, China •

90

0.6–0.35

1.6

H. neanderthalensis
• Europe, Western Asia •

55-70

0.3–0.03

1

H. floresiensis
• Indonesia •

25

0.10–0.012

1.4-1.9

H. sapiens sapiens
• Worldwide •

50-100

0.2–present

given they were short, with brains less than half the size of ours, and without the intellectual faculties to invent even a primitive Xbox – we're probably ahead overall.

Maybe the saddest absence from this hypothetical family gathering, especially for *Lord of the Rings* fans, is ***Homo floresiensis***: the best candidate for a species resembling a hobbit. The one-meter-tall remains, unearthed on one of Indonesia's islands, would be around two-thirds of a typical person's height, and half their weight. And what happened to our nearest and dearest: the Neanderthals? When ***Homo neanderthalensis*** and ***Homo sapiens*** finally came into contact, the former died out – and fast. The nice theory is that they were outmatched and outcompeted for food. The nasty one is that we killed 'em.

I'd bet even the in-laws aren't that bad. Thankfully.

Species classification

H. = Homo
• ORIGIN •

What makes a man?

For generations, philosophers have wondered what makes a man. Thankfully, modern science makes the answer pretty straightforward: we're more or less just a load of hot air. Or, to be more precise, warmish oxygen.

%	ELEMENTS
65	OXYGEN
18	CARBON
10	HYDROGEN
3	NITROGEN
1.4	CALCIUM
1.1	PHOSPHORUS
0.25	POTASSIUM
0.25	SULFUR
1	OTHER

Were you to break a man up into his constituent elements (sounds painful, so pick someone you don't like much), around two-thirds of what's left, by mass, would be **oxygen** { } (most of it from water). The next biggest component would be **carbon** { }, then **hydrogen** { }.

If you were to hang around and look through the trace elements left over, you'd find tiny amounts of **zinc, magnesium, titanium, nickel** and even **arsenic** { } (though fewer than 5 grams of each). The typical human even contains around a tenth of a gram of **gold**. Who knew?

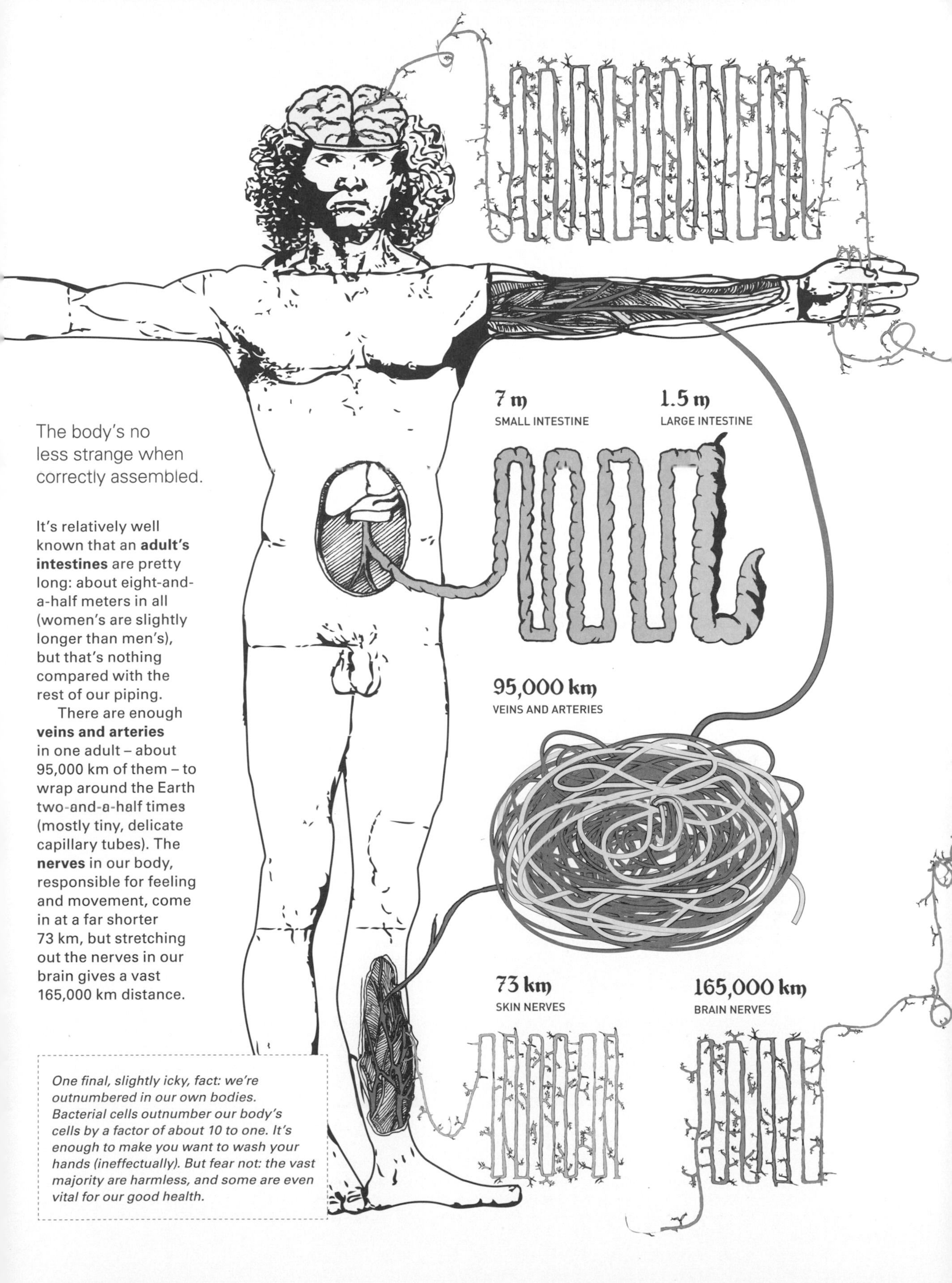

The body's no less strange when correctly assembled.

It's relatively well known that an **adult's intestines** are pretty long: about eight-and-a-half meters in all (women's are slightly longer than men's), but that's nothing compared with the rest of our piping.

There are enough **veins and arteries** in one adult – about 95,000 km of them – to wrap around the Earth two-and-a-half times (mostly tiny, delicate capillary tubes). The **nerves** in our body, responsible for feeling and movement, come in at a far shorter 73 km, but stretching out the nerves in our brain gives a vast 165,000 km distance.

One final, slightly icky, fact: we're outnumbered in our own bodies. Bacterial cells outnumber our body's cells by a factor of about 10 to one. It's enough to make you want to wash your hands (ineffectually). But fear not: the vast majority are harmless, and some are even vital for our good health.

Our little friends

Do you detest insects, bugs and all manner of creepy-crawlies? Do you check under the sheets for them before bed? Ever had a rush of panic that there's something tiny and alive crawling on you, somewhere? If so, turn the page. Right now. Don't even think about what we might say next. We can guarantee you won't like it.

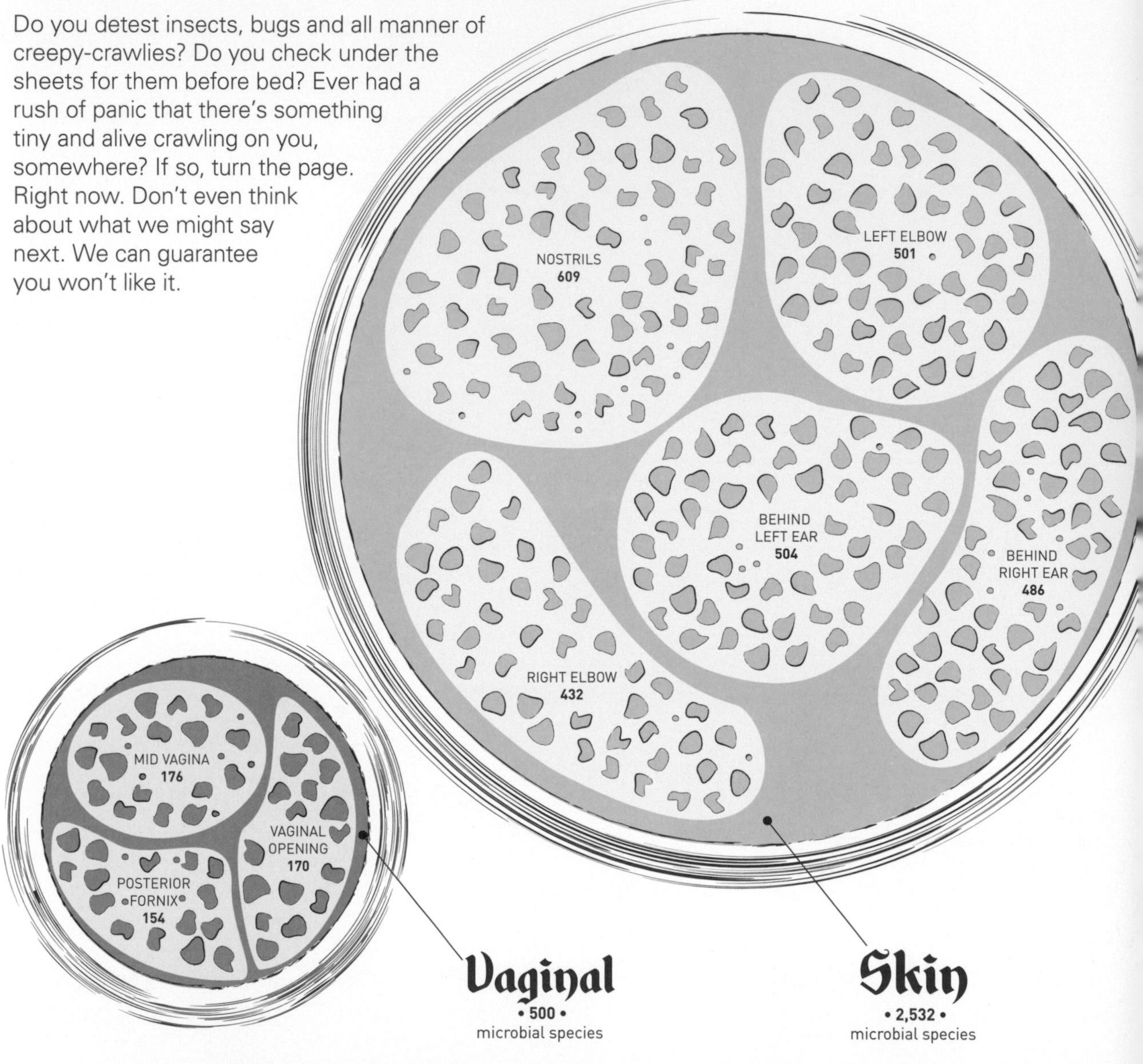

NOSTRILS 609
LEFT ELBOW 501
BEHIND LEFT EAR 504
BEHIND RIGHT EAR 486
RIGHT ELBOW 432

MID VAGINA 176
VAGINAL OPENING 170
POSTERIOR FORNIX 154

Vaginal
• 500 •
microbial species

Skin
• 2,532 •
microbial species

As humans, we like to think of ourselves as industrious, bright workers; loyal and entertaining friends, and more. We don't tend to think of ourselves as a fantastic place to live, or a great little habitat. Alas, to thousands of minuscule species, that's exactly what we are.

And we're not just talking teeny little parasites here; some of these things are bigger than you might think. Maybe the eeriest is the demodex – these tiny, half-millimeter-long mites live on humans, inside our hair follicles. They're particularly fond of eyelashes. And you've almost certainly got them on your face right now. Just to make it worse, they move. They prefer the dark, and can travel about 10 cm a night. Not bad for little fellows, huh?

But these guys are nothing, frankly, compared with the bacteria and other microbes that call us home. Probably the best habitat we offer is the gut – microbiologists' answer to the rainforest –

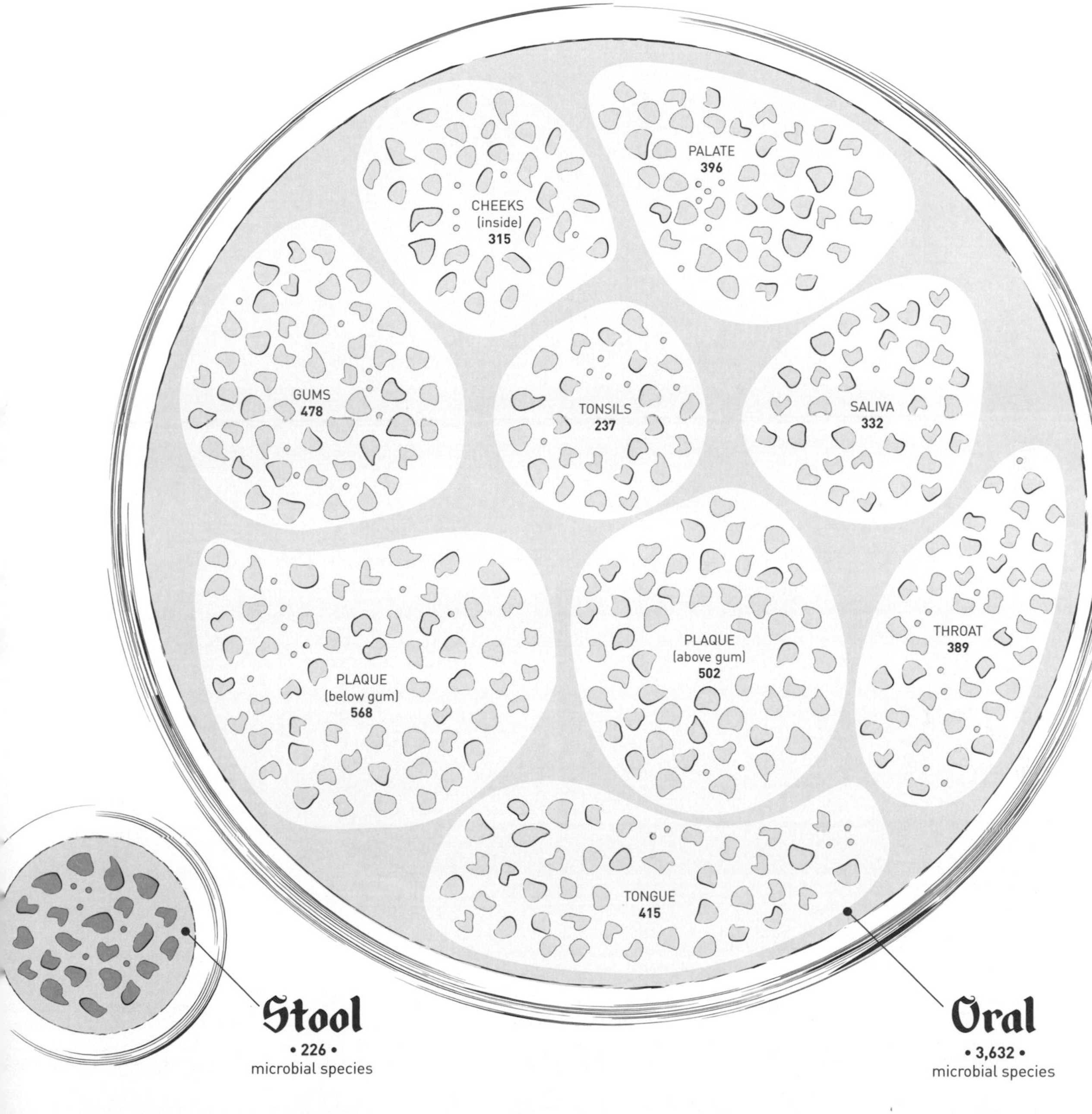

CHEEKS (inside) 315

PALATE 396

GUMS 478

TONSILS 237

SALIVA 332

PLAQUE (below gum) 568

PLAQUE (above gum) 502

THROAT 389

TONGUE 415

Stool

• 226 •
microbial species

Oral

• 3,632 •
microbial species

and the Human Microbiome Project has looked at the attractive residential opportunities on the surface of our skin.

We have a whole range of climates: stuff that likes to live on our **tongue { }** (average person: 415 species) differs from the stuff that likes our **palate { }** (average person: 396). Your **nostrils { }** are home to another 600 or so microbial species – almost 400 more than would typically be found in your **poo { }**. The different microclimates we offer are amazing in their variety: not only is the inside of your **elbow { }** a good spot, the elbow of the arm you write with will typically have a greater diversity of microbes than the other.

In all, we play host to so many species that for every one human gene there are about 360 microbial genes also present.

Lucky that the human body isn't a democracy, isn't it?

PETRI DISH:
total number of species per body part

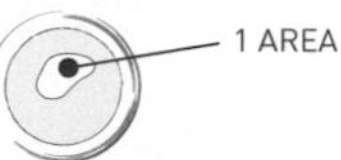

IN EACH AREA:

= 1 SPECIES

= 10 SPECIES

How we spread

The year 70000 BCE (or thereabouts) was a bad time to be a human being. The supervolcano Toba had erupted (we think) and darkened the sky for years, destroying crops, ruining habitats and generally making life miserable for our early ancestors.

"Out of Africa"

DIRECTION OF MIGRATION
(thousands of years ago)

- 200-100
- 50-99
- 20-49
- 0-19

FOSSIL SITES

1. **Omo Kibish** 98,000–192,000 years ago
2. **Klasies River Mouth** 64,000–104,000 years ago
3. **Dar-es-Soltane** ca. 80,000 years ago
4. **Liujiang** ca. 68,000 years ago
5. **Lake Mungo** ca. 50,000 years ago
6. **Kostienki** ca. 45,000 years ago
7. **Tianyuan** ca. 42,000 years ago
8. **Oregon Cropolite** ca. 14,000 years ago
9. **Monte Verde** ca.15,000 years ago

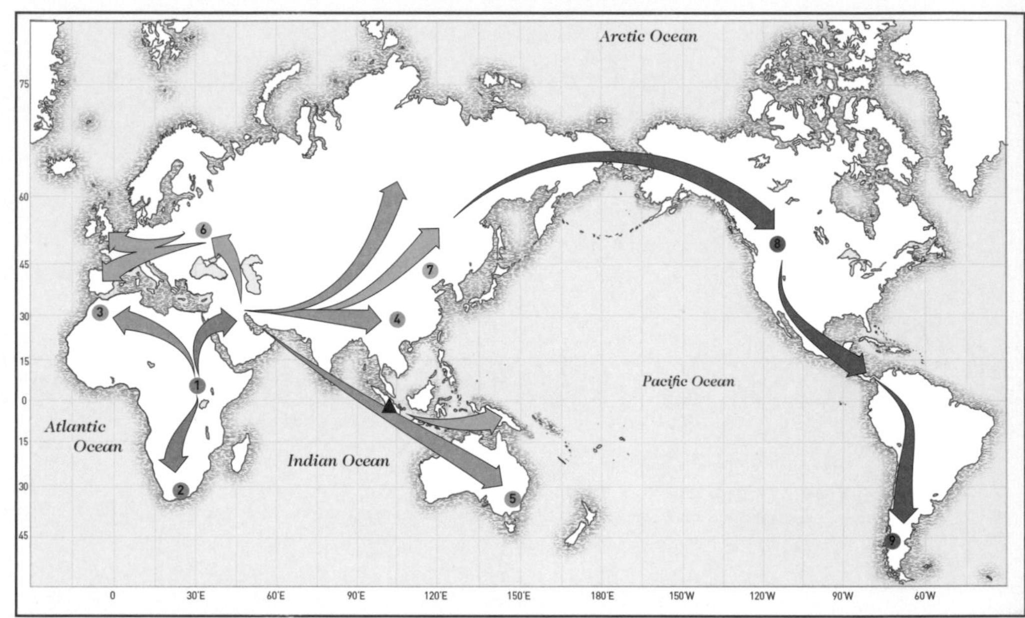

▲ **Toba eruption**, 74,000 years ago

In fact, the situation was so bad we came to the brink of extinction: it's estimated that only between 1,000 and 10,000 breeding couples survived in Africa. To give that some modern-day context, there are about 1,600 pandas alive in the wild today, and between 3,000 and 9,800 tigers. Even worse for our ancestors, there were almost certainly no welfare charities keeping an eye on us, either.

Fortunately for us – spoiler alert – our ancestors pulled through, and got on with spreading right across the world. The various mini ice ages that followed the catastrophe aided this process hugely. As different tribes migrated in search of better hunting and foraging, they could walk virtually everywhere: from Africa to Asia, across to Europe, and even down to Australia, across a land bridge created by lower sea levels.

Africa and South Asia came first, with treks across to Northern Europe (and round to Southern Australia) not really taking place until around 40,000 years ago. By 15,000 years ago, small numbers of our ancestors populated every continent, having made it across modern-day Russia into North America, and then down into South America.

Those 55,000 years or so also provided ample time for recovery. Estimating the earliest human populations, of course, involves a bit of approximation, but one set of figures estimates that by 10000 BCE there were around 4 million humans on the earth. By 0 CE, this had hit 170 million. We were off and running.

So maybe – just maybe – it's worth keeping an eye on those pandas. They might not look like much now, but in 70,000 years or so they could be a force to be reckoned with...

World population growth

It took Homo sapiens *many thousands of years to establish a population size of 1.6 billion, which we achieved around the year 1900. The next 1.6 billion took just 60 years, however, and by the end of the century there were more than 6 billion of us. So how long until we hit a nice round 10 billion? According to UN estimates, that will happen just after 2200, and might just stabilize. Volcano-permitting, of course.*

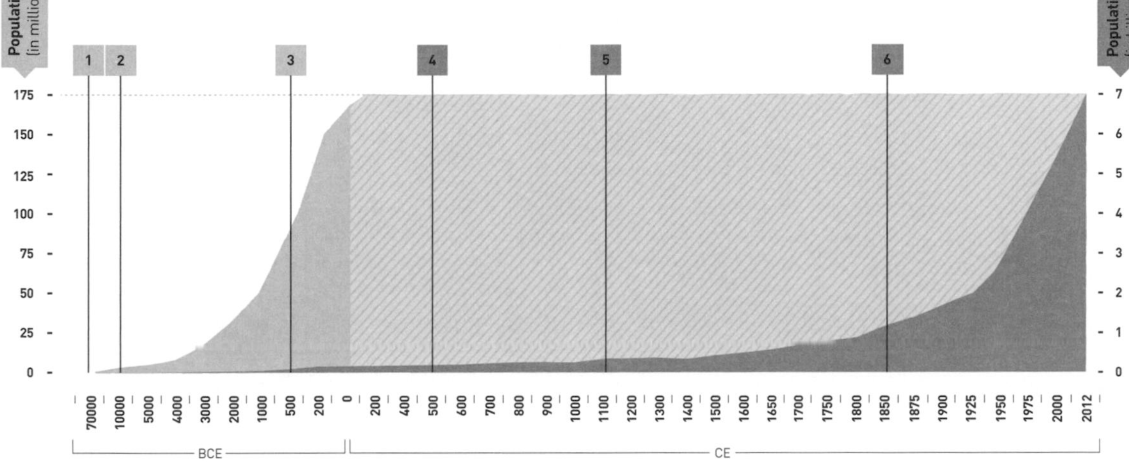

70000 BCE

WORLD POPULATION: **5,500**

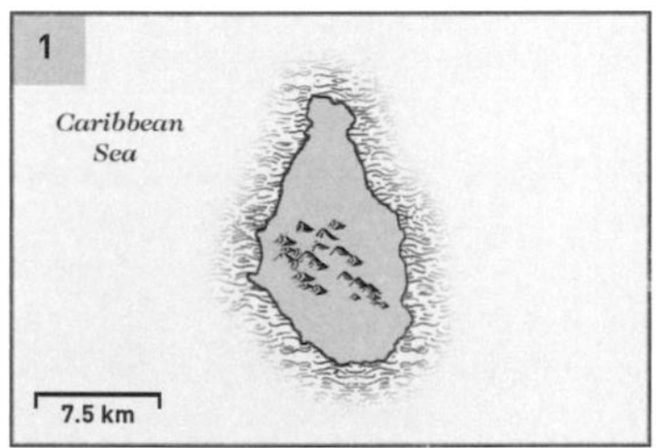

MODERN POPULATION COMPARISON:
MONTSERRAT (5,164 inhabitants)

10000 BCE

WORLD POPULATION: **4 MILLION**

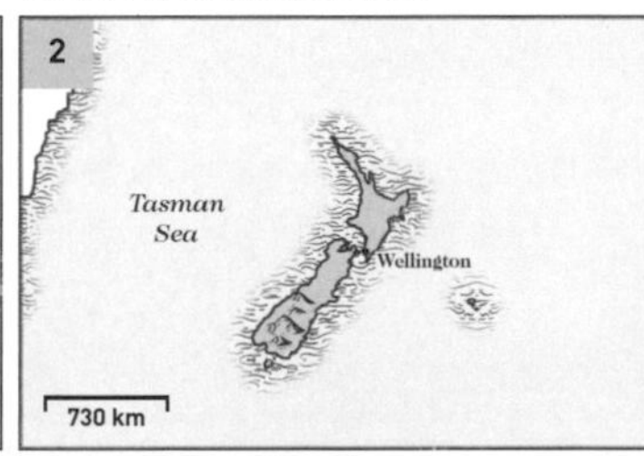

MODERN POPULATION COMPARISON:
NEW ZEALAND (4,327,944 inhabitants)

500 BCE

WORLD POPULATION: **100 MILLION**

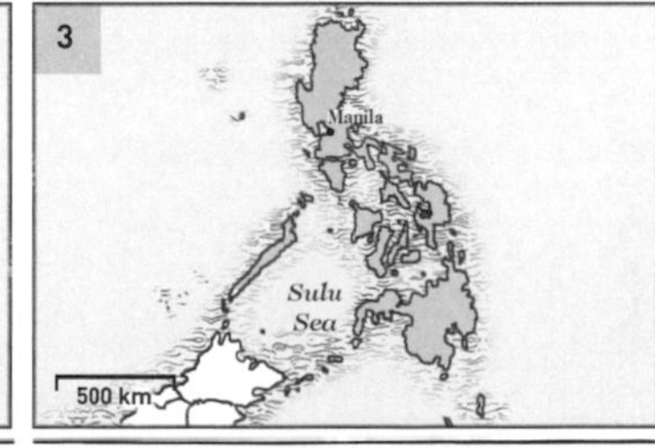

MODERN POPULATION COMPARISON:
PHILIPPINES (103,775,002 inhabitants)

500 CE

WORLD POPULATION: **190 MILLION**

MODERN POPULATION COMPARISON:
BRAZIL (199,321,413 inhabitants)

1100 CE

WORLD POPULATION: **320 MILLION**

MODERN POPULATION COMPARISON:
UNITED STATES (313,847,465 inhabitants)

1850 CE

WORLD POPULATION: **1.2 BILLION**

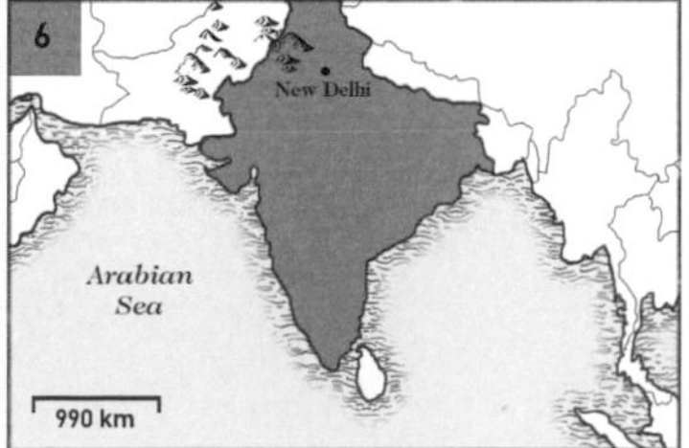

MODERN POPULATION COMPARISON:
INDIA (1,205,073,612 inhabitants)

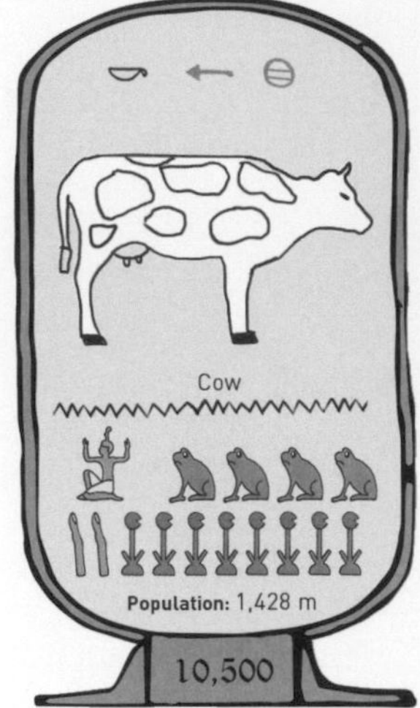

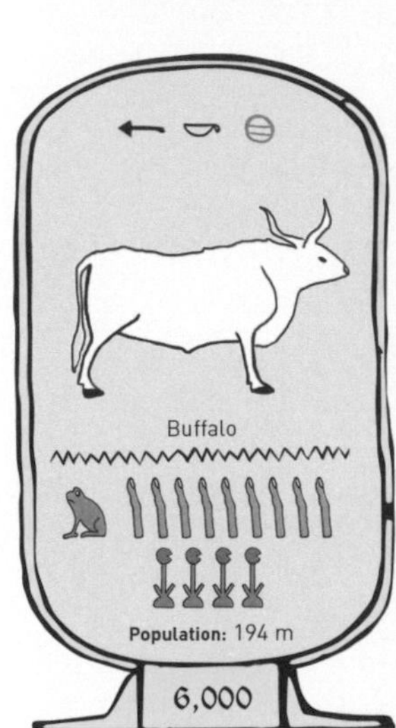

REGION OF ORIGIN

- AMERICA
- ASIA
- EURASIA
- EUROPE
- MIDDLE EAST
- UNKOWN (or multiple origins)

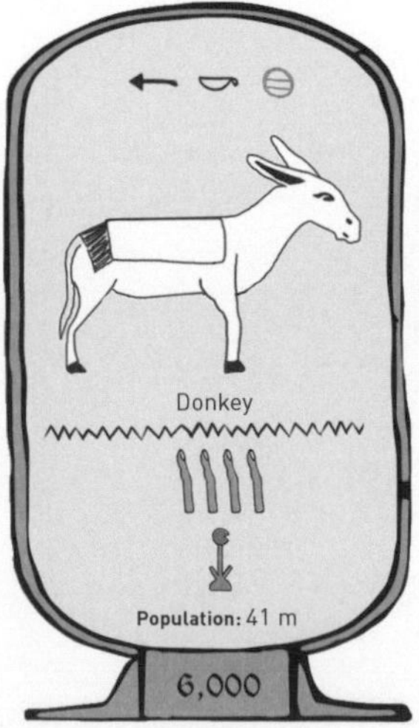

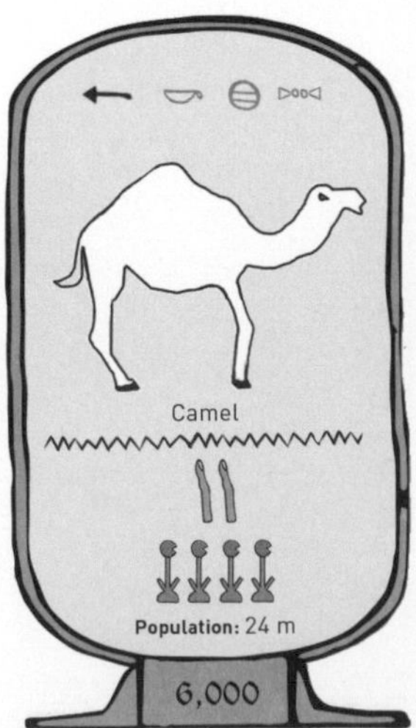

The taming of...

While William Shakespeare's 16th-century play was largely preoccupied with taming shrews (or rather, conveying a misogynistic take on courtship and marriage), our early ancestors had quite different priorities.

Many animals have reciprocal relationships with other species – ostriches and zebras, for example, occasionally hang out together to help warn each other of predators – but humanity has made recruiting and domesticating animals a speciality.

Pride of place in this relationship surely goes to the species we've christened our "best friend": the **dog**. Estimating exactly how early dogs were tamed is difficult, but some archeological evidence seems to suggest humans and wolves coexisted from around 34,000 years ago. The mutual benefits are clear: wolves benefitted from the warmth of fires and extra hunting opportunities, while humans were far more successful on hunts when accompanied by wolves (or dogs). It was the start of a beautiful friendship.

Other animals were perhaps less fortunate. Between 11,000 and 10,000 years ago, we started domesticating animals for food: **goats**, **sheep** and **cows**. We benefitted as they lived (milk and cheese, for example), and then, of course, we ate them. **Horses** took a little longer, and despite being exceptionally useful, they've only been domesticated for around 6,000 years.

What's perhaps most amazing is just how many animals we now keep. While there are only around 58 million horses in the world – they're expensive and not many people (or so we thought) eat them – there are around a billion each of **pigs**, sheep and goats, around 1.4 billion cows, and a staggering 19 billion **chickens** wandering the Earth: almost all of them domesticated.

And what of those first wolves drawn to the fire more than 30,000 years ago? Well, they certainly proved to be more popular pets than shrews, and more than 500 million of their descendants now live across the world as humanity's faithful companions.

DIAGRAM KEY

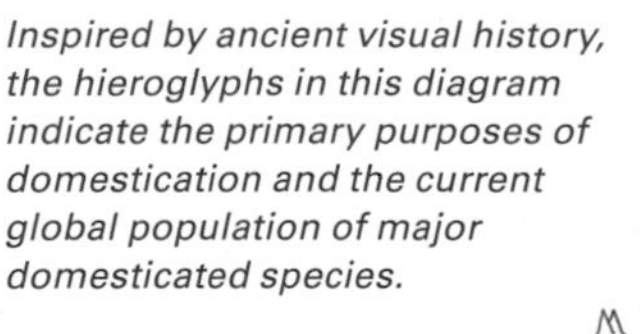

Inspired by ancient visual history, the hieroglyphs in this diagram indicate the primary purposes of domestication and the current global population of major domesticated species.

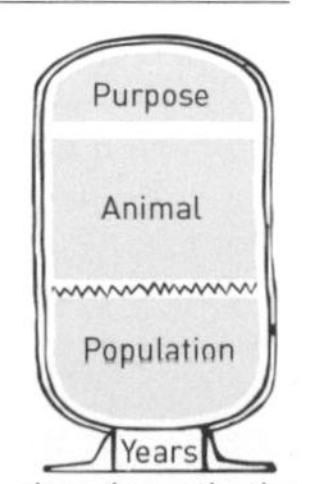

PURPOSE

Work
i.e., transportation, protection, hunting

Commodities
i.e., pelt, leather, fiber, wool

Food
i.e., meat, milk, eggs

Scientific research

Companionship
i.e., pets, ornament and show

POPULATION

The Egyptians had a base 10 system of hieroglyphs for numerals. Here we use:

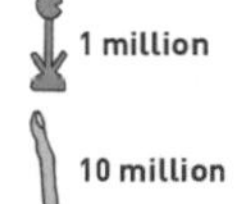

City livin'

To live around 12,000 years ago it really helped to be a fan of camping. It would also have helped to be a fan of many other things: lice, foraging, violence, poor dental hygiene and short life expectancy – but when it came to living options, there wasn't a whole lot of choice: humanity was a nomadic race. Until, over time, we weren't.

Pinning down anything from this early in our species' history is tough, but archeologists have dug up evidence of various early settlements, almost all of which are in the Middle East.

It's not even clear why some of our ancestors stopped moving around, especially given that the first decent coffee shop was thousands of years away, but there are two interesting theories.

The optimistic one stems from evidence that trade between tribes was already alive and well. So when a group hit on a luxury good, it was worth their while staying put – even if it made foraging harder – to collect and trade the spoils.

The pessimistic one is that when a given area had a large number of groups competing with one another, permanent, sheltered settlements – like the town of **Basta { }** in modern-day Jordan – were easier to defend, and therefore a wise move.

All these years later, few of the earliest cities still remain. Basta, which seems to have been home to between 600 and 1,000 settlers, was abandoned around 6900 BCE. Of the eight early cities we've gathered data for, only one remains today: the city of **Jericho { }** – a relatively small town by modern standards, with 20,000 residents.

The reason for abandonment? Most often, something as simple as the shifting of a river, and with it the town's prosperity. Sounds like an ancient phenomenon, but it's one that's had an impact right up until the last century.

Maybe those of us who still like to lug around a tent are onto something after all. Provided it's sunny out, of course.

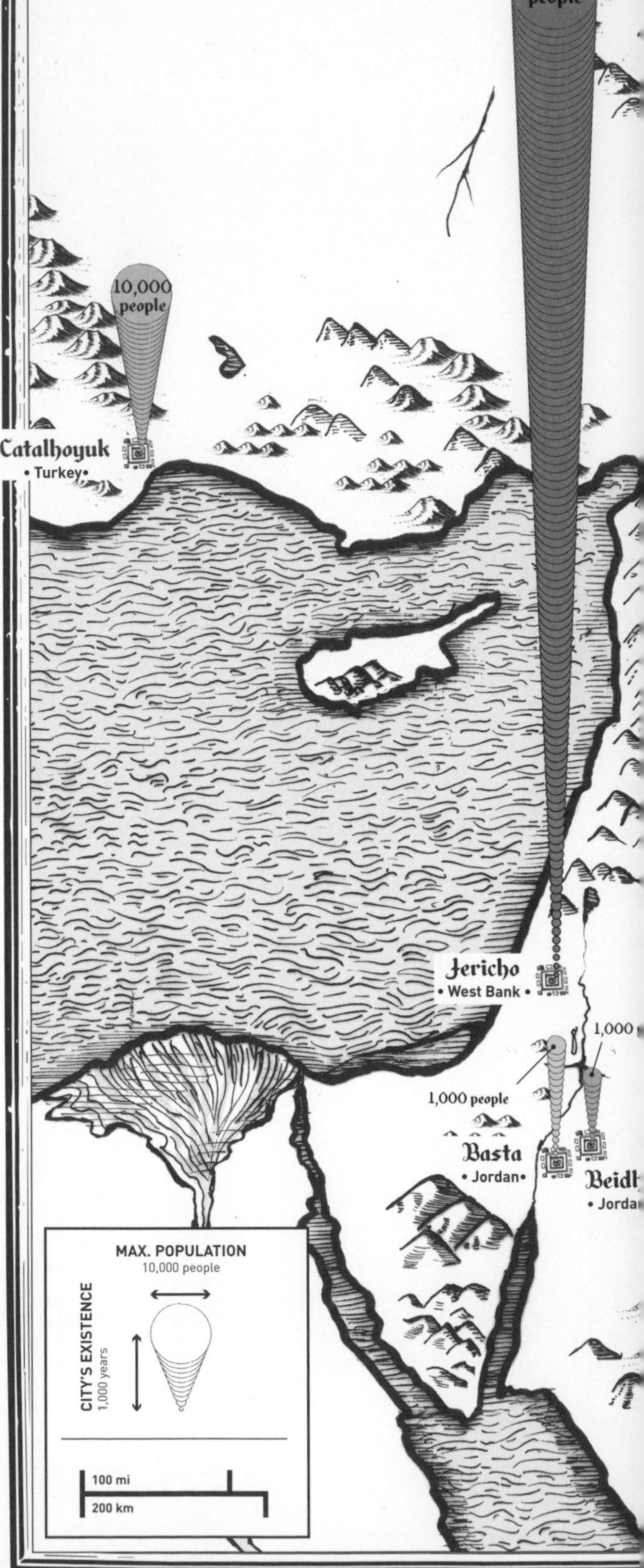

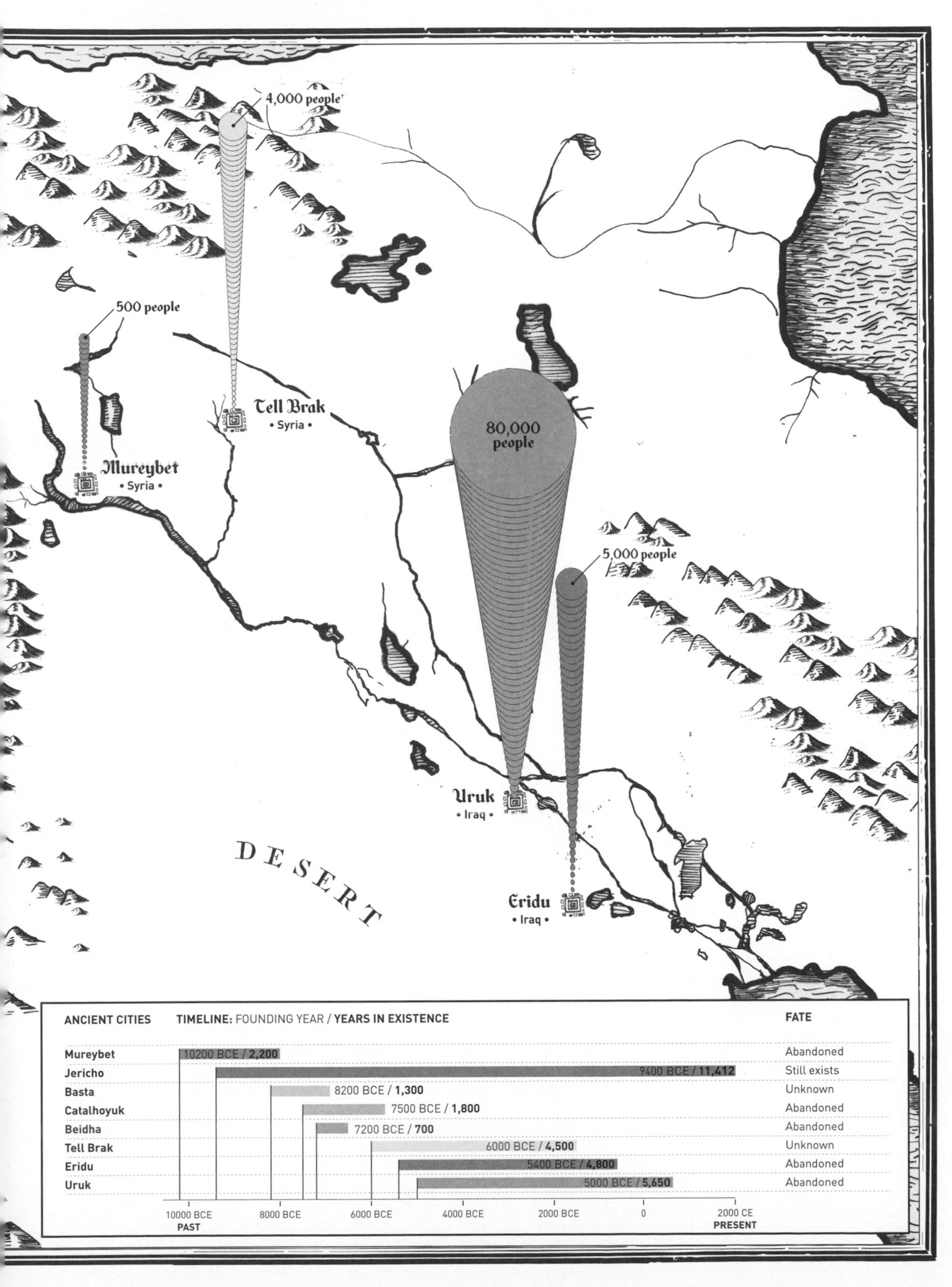
4,000 people
500 people
Tell Brak
• Syria •
Mureybet
• Syria •
80,000 people
5,000 people
Uruk
• Iraq •
DESERT
Eridu
• Iraq •
ANCIENT CITIES
TIMELINE: FOUNDING YEAR / YEARS IN EXISTENCE
FATE
Mureybet 10200 BCE / 2,200 Abandoned
Jericho 9400 BCE / 11,412 Still exists
Basta 8200 BCE / 1,300 Unknown
Catalhoyuk 7500 BCE / 1,800 Abandoned
Beidha 7200 BCE / 700 Abandoned
Tell Brak 6000 BCE / 4,500 Unknown
Eridu 5400 BCE / 4,800 Abandoned
Uruk 5000 BCE / 5,650 Abandoned
10000 BCE PAST
8000 BCE
6000 BCE
4000 BCE
2000 BCE
0
2000 CE PRESENT

HOW HAS CLOTHING CHANGED THROUGHOUT HISTORY?

Dressing it up

Time travel is much harder than it looks on TV. Although there are a couple of minor difficulties, like the fact that it's probably impossible, and the Earth's tearing round the Sun means you'd probably find yourself dying horribly in a vacuum if you did somehow manage it, there are other, more everyday issues to worry about.

female

10,000 ...YEARS AGO

5,300 4,600 3,900 3,200

350 780 1,210 1,640 2,070 2,500

350 325 300 275 250 225 200 175 150 125

30 40 50 60 70 80 90

NOW

TIMELINE

Garment invention

The tape measure represents how long ago the garments were introduced. At each turn the scale changes.

REGION OF ORIGIN

- AFRICA
- NORTH AMERICA
- ASIA
- EUROPE
- UNKNOWN

How, exactly, would you get your clothing right? We're not just talking about fashion (everyone gets that wrong now and then), but how do you make sure you're not wearing a garment that's not yet been invented?

The constituent parts of our daily dress have vastly different histories: some date back millennia, others mere decades. One neat example is the **dress {■}**. At its core, a modern dress – though the fashion police might disagree – is functionally almost identical to the tunic, a garment nearly three millennia old that was regularly worn in Ancient Greece.

Sandals {■}, the first ever form of footwear, date back around 10,000 years, and if you're the sort of person who'd insist on wearing socks with them, that's a fashion faux pas that's been possible for 2,800 years. Other items have a

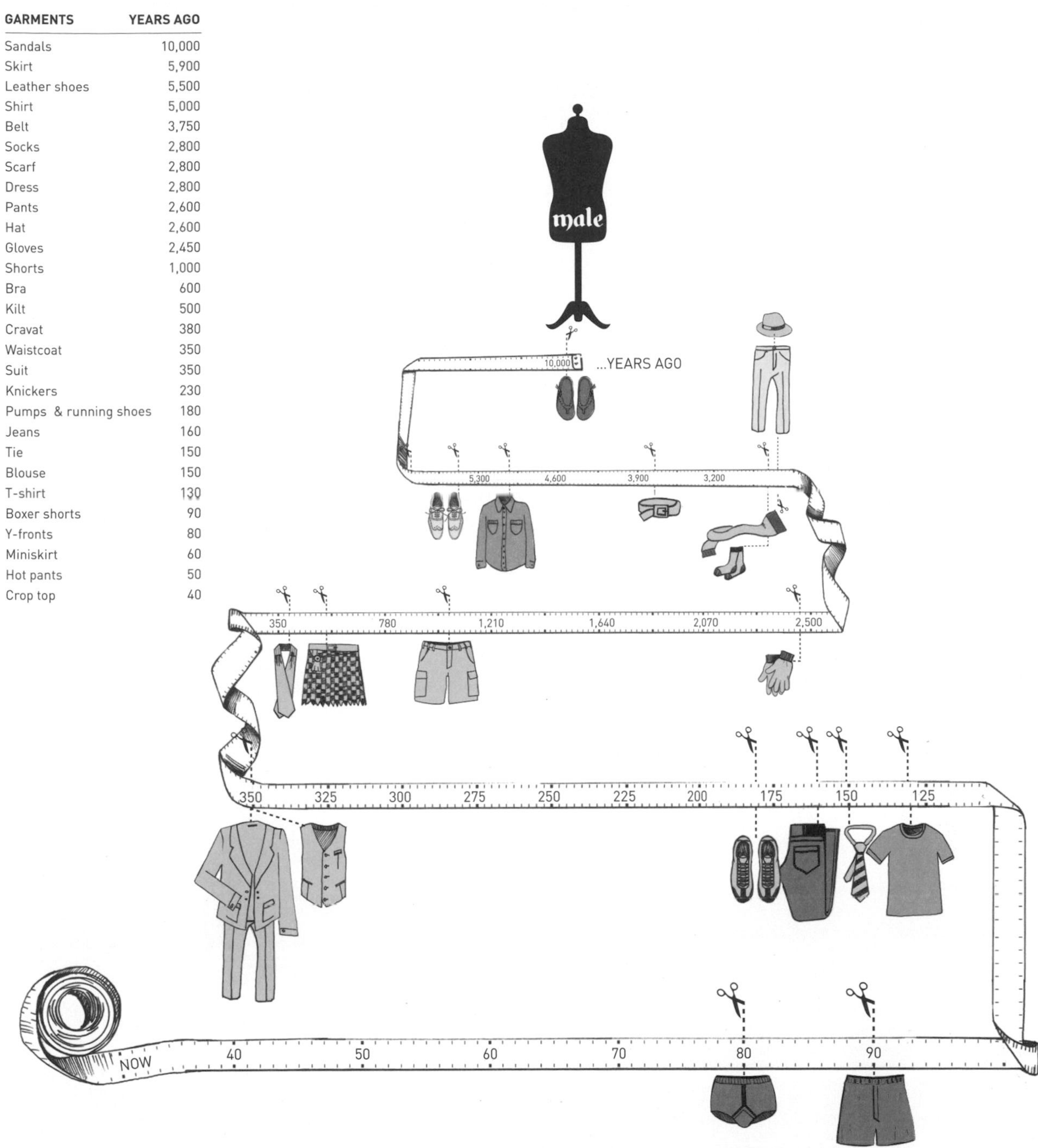

GARMENTS	YEARS AGO
Sandals	10,000
Skirt	5,900
Leather shoes	5,500
Shirt	5,000
Belt	3,750
Socks	2,800
Scarf	2,800
Dress	2,800
Pants	2,600
Hat	2,600
Gloves	2,450
Shorts	1,000
Bra	600
Kilt	500
Cravat	380
Waistcoat	350
Suit	350
Knickers	230
Pumps & running shoes	180
Jeans	160
Tie	150
Blouse	150
T-shirt	130
Boxer shorts	90
Y-fronts	80
Miniskirt	60
Hot pants	50
Crop top	40

quirkier history. Take the **bra {■}** – originally thought to have been an invention of the early 20th century, historians recently unearthed a remarkably similar garment from some time between the mid 14th and 15th centuries in Austria. Comfort seems to be a function of place just as much as time.

Other garments evolve: about 400 years ago the ruff evolved into the **cravat {■}**, and for almost all of us outside certain niche band followings, the cravat shifted to the **tie {■}** in the last century or so.

As for the ubiquitous modern uniform of **jeans {■}** and **T-shirt {■}**; that would work more or less any time in the last 130 years – unless you're trying to get a table in a decent restaurant, in which case you're probably out of luck.

Makin' sweet music

There's a half-decent argument for saying music is older than humanity – assuming you're willing to count drummers as musicians, which involves you in an age-old debate well beyond the scope of data to settle.

Several species of animal – and not just that gorilla from the Cadbury ad – have been observed using forms of percussion. Hard to know whether it's merely fun, just warning signals, or if there could – just maybe – be some artistic intent behind it.

While the **drum {■}** may have the unique distinction of being the world's oldest instrument, the **drum kit {■}** itself is far more recent, having only been around for 130 years, making it a relative newcomer in the musical world.

The first primitive **flutes {■}** that have been uncovered by archeologists appear to be around 43,000 years old – though probably would've sounded worse than a five-year-old's recorder class – while primitive **trumpets {■}** date back around 10,000 years. Even the **harp {■}**, one of the most complex stringed instruments around, dates back more than five millennia.

Still, to get anything sounding like modern music, you can't go back all that far. The **piano {■}** is only about 300 years old, and the **guitar {■}** only slightly older at 400. For obvious reasons, the **electric guitar {■}** has only just turned 80.

That's even less, believe it or not, than an item with inauspicious beginnings but at least as much influence on most modern recorded music as any of the above: the **synth {■}**. The first "additive" synth (one that changes the timbre of an instrument) was demonstrated 115 years ago in the U.S.. Frankly, it's amazing it took until the 1980s to show us what it could do.

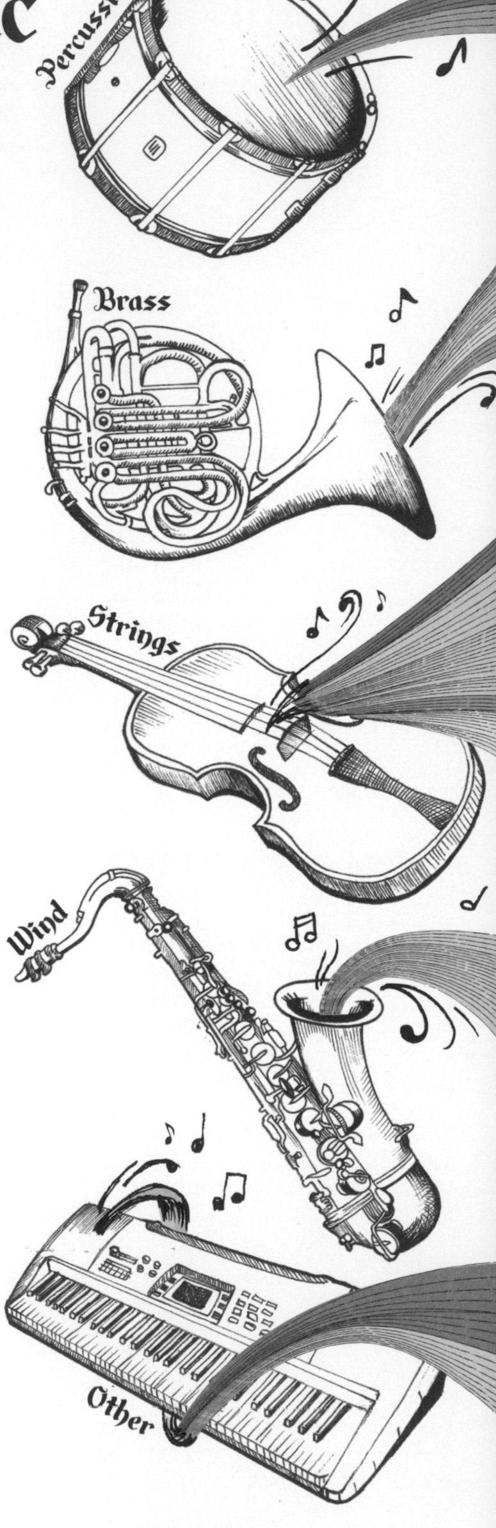

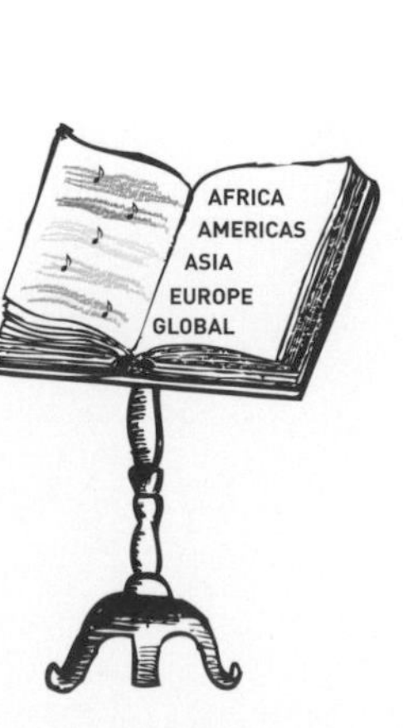

REGION OF ORIGIN

INSTRUMENT FAMILY

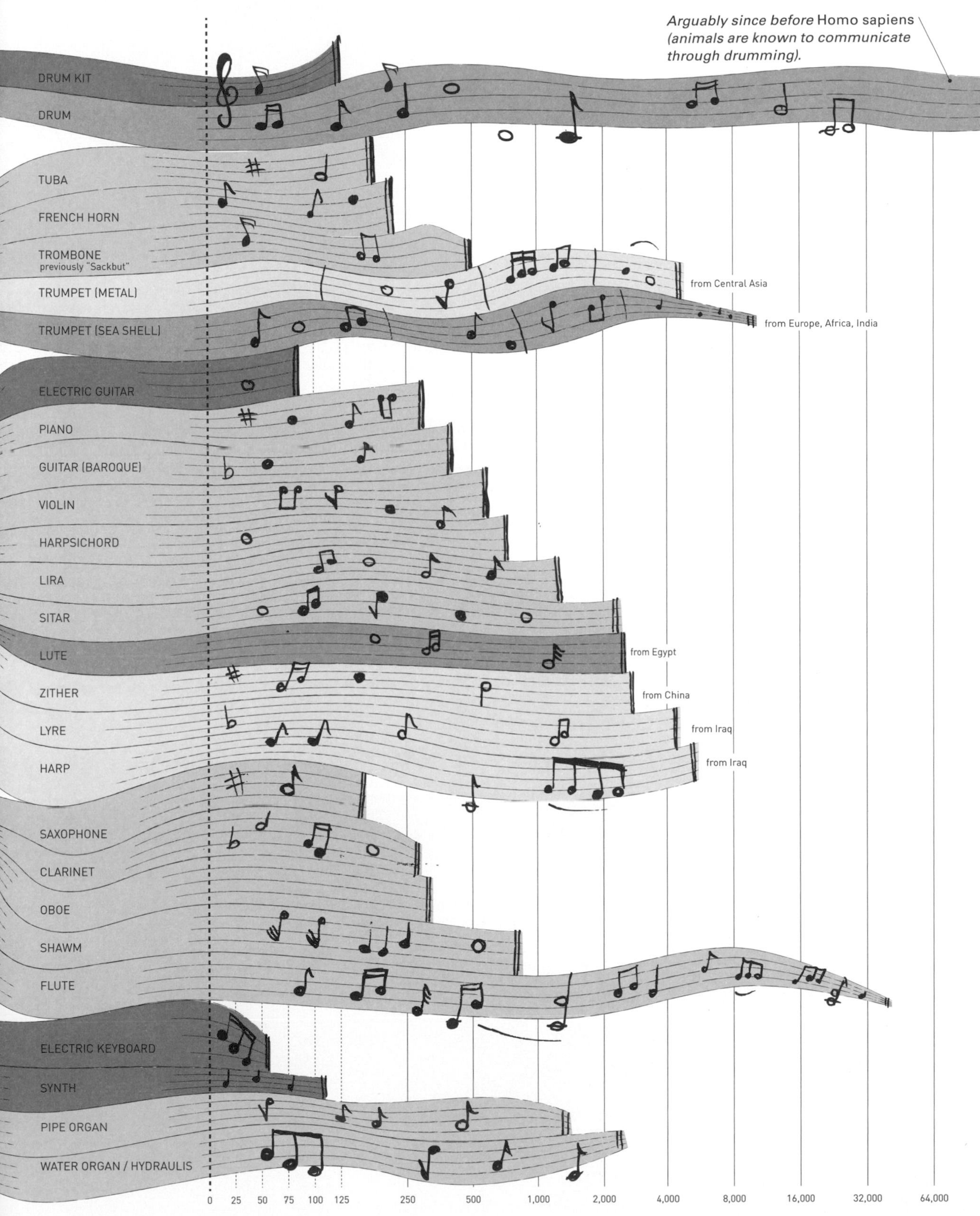

Arguably since before Homo sapiens (animals are known to communicate through drumming).
DRUM KIT
DRUM
TUBA
FRENCH HORN
TROMBONE
previously "Sackbut"
TRUMPET (METAL)
from Central Asia
TRUMPET (SEA SHELL)
from Europe, Africa, India
ELECTRIC GUITAR
PIANO
GUITAR (BAROQUE)
VIOLIN
HARPSICHORD
LIRA
SITAR
LUTE
from Egypt
ZITHER
from China
LYRE
from Iraq
HARP
from Iraq
SAXOPHONE
CLARINET
OBOE
SHAWM
FLUTE
ELECTRIC KEYBOARD
SYNTH
PIPE ORGAN
WATER ORGAN / HYDRAULIS
0 25 50 75 100 125 250 500 1,000 2,000 4,000 8,000 16,000 32,000 64,000
INSTRUMENT
AGE (YEARS)

Painting by numbers

This might irk the pragmatically minded, but the evidence all points one way: art predates civilization. While an efficient, organized species might have focused its energies on plumbing, agriculture or urban development first, our early ancestors seem to have been more interested in engaging with their muse.

The oldest known **cave paintings {■}** were discovered in Spain and date back around 41,000 years. That wasn't all we were up to at that time, either: the oldest **sculpture {■}** ever found dates back around 40,000 years, too. Not long after that, our creative efforts brought forth early jewelry and ornamentation. That's not to say early art was necessarily what we might describe as "good."

The first examples we have of recognizable humans are about 8,000 years after the first cave paintings, and despite earlier attempts, formal perspective in art – now thought of as a rather essential technique – is only about 600 years old. In earlier art, size wasn't used to suggest scale, but rather importance. The tools of the trade have also come a long way. Basic **watercolors {■}** were used as far back as cave painting, while basic printing has been used to decorate cloth in China for almost 2,000 years. Perhaps, then, it's surprising that the **pencil {■}** (which has always been made from graphite, never lead) is only about 450 years old.

As for what to draw on, the earliest options were papyrus (a variant of paper) or parchment (typically animal skin), which was used when trade disputes shut down the availability of the former. China discovered paper at around the same time, but it didn't widely reach the West for over a millennium.

Once paper caught on, we got pretty attached to it. Which is handy, as this book would have been quite pricey if we'd had to print it on vellum.

TIMELINE

Present

CE

1900 → 1990
1600 → 1890
1000 → 1500
0 → 900
0
0 → 900
1,000 → 9,000
10,000 → 29,000
30,000 → 39,000

BCE

Past

REGION OF ORIGIN

- NORTH AMERICA
- ASIA
- EUROPE
- MIDDLE EAST
- UNKNOWN (or multiple origins)

PAINTING & DRAWING

Acrylic paint 1946 U.S.
Blacklight paint 1934 U.S.
Pencil drawing 1660 Germany
Watercolor ca. 10000 BCE Egypt
Painting ca. 32000 BCE Spain
Murals (cave painting) ca. 39000 BCE Spain

PRINT-MAKING

Linocut 1905 Germany
Offset printing 1875 U.K.
Lithography 1796 Bohemia
Embossing 1796 U.K.
Etching 1500 Germany
Movable type 1040 China
Silk printing 960 China
Engraving ca. 3000 BCE Mesopotamia
Woodblock ca. 3000 BCE Mesopotamia

SCULPTURE

Casting & modeling ca. 4000 BCE Unknown
Carving ca. 38000 BCE Germany

PHOTOGRAPHY & FILM-MAKING

Digital photography 1988 Japan
Color photography 1861 U.K.
Photographic camera 1822 France
Pinhole camera ca. 500 BCE Greece

OTHER

Computer art 1960 U.K.
Geometric perspective ca. 1400 Unknown
Collage ca. 200 BCE China
Mosaic ca. 1500 BCE Mesopotamia
Stylized humans in art ca. 6000 BCE Unknown

The Mona Lisa "paint by numbers" diagram represents global chronological advances in visual art. The painting is broken into segments to reveal when (bottom to top, left to right) and where (by color) each discipline (by pattern) originated.

Mona Lisa: A timeline of visual art

Learnin' the lexicon

The very basics of language aren't just restricted to humanity. Anyone who's watched a wildlife documentary or two has seen monkeys warn one another of incoming predators – and anyone who owns a dog can probably manage to communicate with it well enough to get it to sit and fetch. But if you've ever tried to have a conversation with our canine or simian cousins you'll have noticed that communication is not the same thing as language.

There's a lot of disagreement, but it seems as if the *Homo* genus (of which our species, *Homo sapiens*, is a part) had the capacity for sophisticated speech 200,000 years ago – but it was only with our species that the capacity actually started to get used.

Whether modern languages diverged from an original "mother tongue" or grew up separately, there's no shortage of human languages across the world today. Of these, English is overwhelmingly the most widely spoken: not because it has the most native speakers, but because it's everyone's fallback language of choice.

The data on the evolution of English is pretty amazing, and there's no doubt that the lexicon has grown substantially over the last few centuries. One way to measure this trend is to have a look at dictionaries. The first known alphabetical dictionary { ■ }, issued in 1604, had just 2,543 entries, though it was pretty incomplete, even for the time. Lexicographers quickly got their act together, though. By 1696, the reference volume of choice { ■ } had more than 17,000 entries, while Samuel Johnson's seminal 1755 dictionary { ■ } – the authoritative work for more than 150 years – had 42,773. Today, revising the ***Oxford English Dictionary*** { ■ } is the work of decades, not years, and the latest edition (with supplements) has entries for more than 300,000 words.

Even that might drastically understate the real reach of our language. So many words are slang, or technical vocabulary, or never reach a dictionary – a "black market" of language, as it were. A seminal study for the journal *Science* last year used the millions of books scanned into Google to establish the real size of English: since 1950, the number of words in use in English has soared from around 500,000 to more than one million.

That's 700,000 under-the-radar English words – the undocumented immigrants of language. The good news for us? "Infographic" isn't one of them. Believe it or not, the word's been around since the 1960s.

Who knew?

Evolution of alphabetical dictionaries

	TITLE	YEAR	NO. OF ENTRIES
■	*A Table Alphabetical*, 1st edition	1604	2,543
■	*A Table Alphabetical*, 4th edition	1617	3,264
■	*The New World of English Words*, 1st edition	1658	11,000
■	*The New World of English Words*, 5th edition	1696	17,000
■	*The New World of English Words*, revised	1706	38,000
■	*A General Dictionary of the English Language*	1755	42,773
■	*Oxford English Dictionary*, 1st edition	1928	252,200
■	*Oxford English Dictionary*, 2nd edition	1989	291,500
■	*Oxford English Dictionary*, 2nd edition, 3rd additions series	1997	301,306

Diagram

Using a page from Dr. Johnson's 1755 A General Dictionary of the English Language *we show the number of entries in each dictionary by taking each character (except spaces) to represent 196 dictionary entries.*

A GENERAL
DICTIONARY
OF THE
ENGLISH LANGUAGE.

10 characters
2,543 entries

17 characters
3,264 entries

56 characters
11,000 entries

87 characters
17,000 entries

194 characters
38,000 entries

218 characters
42,773 entries

1,288 characters
252,200 entries

1,488 characters
291,500 entries

1,538 characters
301,306 entries

A

A, The firſt letter of the European alphabets, has, in the Engliſh language, three different ſounds, which may be termed the broad, open, and ſlender.

The broad ſound reſembling that of the German *a* is found, in many of our monoſyllables, as *all, wall, malt, ſalt*; in which *a* is pronounced as *au* in *cauſe*, or *aw* in *law*. Many of theſe words were anciently written with *au*, as *fault, waulk*; which happens to be ſtill retained in *fault*. This was probably the ancient ſound of the Saxons, ſince it is almoſt uniformly preſerved in the ruſtic pronunciation, and the Northern dialects, as *maun* for *man*, *haund* for *hand*.

A open, not unlike the *a* of the Italians, is found in *father, rather*, and more obſcurely in *fancy, faſt*, &c.

A ſlender or cloſe, is the peculiar *a* of the Engliſh language, reſembling the ſound of the French *e* maſculine, or diphthong *ai* in *païs*, or perhaps a middle ſound between them, or between the *a* and *e*; to this the Arabic *a* is ſaid nearly to approach. Of this ſound we have examples in the words, *place, face, waſte*, and all thoſe that terminate in *ation*; as, *relation, nation, generation*.

A is ſhort, as, *glaſs, graſs*; or long, as, *glaze, graze*: it is marked long, generally, by an *e* final, *plane*, or by an *i* added, as, *plain*.

A, an article ſet before nouns of the ſingular number; *a* man, *a* tree; denoting the number *one*, as, *a* man is coming, that is, *no more than one*; or an indefinite indication, as, *a* man may come this way; that is, *any* man. This article has no plural ſignification. Before a word beginning with a vowel, it is written *an*, as, *an* ox, *an* egg, of which *a* is the contraction.

A is ſometimes a noun; as, a great *A*, a little *a*.

A is placed before a participle, or participial noun; and is conſidered by Wallis as a contraction of *at*, when it is put before a word denoting ſome action not yet finiſhed; as, I am *a* walking. It alſo ſeems to be anciently contracted from *at*, when placed before local ſurnames; as, Thomas *a* Becket. In other caſes, it ſeems to ſignify *to*, like the French *à*.

A hunting Chloë went. *Prior*.

They go *a* begging to a bankrupt's door. *Dryd.*

May pure contents for ever pitch their tents
Upon theſe downs, theſe meads, theſe rocks, theſe mountains,
And peace ſtill ſlumber by theſe purling fountains!
Which we may every year
Find when we come *a* fiſhing here. *Wotton*.

Now the men fell *a* rubbing of armour, which a great while had lain oiled; the magazines of munition are viewed; the officers of remains called to account. *Wotton*.

Another falls *a* ringing a Peſcennius Niger, and judiciouſly diſtinguiſhes the ſound of it to be modern. *Addiſon on medals*.

A has a peculiar ſignification, denoting the proportion of one thing to another. Thus we ſay, The landlord hath a hundred *a* year; The ſhip's crew gained a thouſand pounds *a* man.

The river Inn, that had been hitherto ſhut up among mountains, paſſes generally through a wide open country, during all its courſe through Bavaria; which is a voyage of two days, after the rate of twenty leagues *a* day. *Addiſon on Italy*.

A is uſed in burleſque poetry, to lengthen out a ſyllable, without adding to the ſenſe.

ABA

For cloves and nutmegs to the line-a,
And even for oranges to China. *Dryden*.

A is ſometimes, in familiar writings, put by a barbarous corruption for *he*.

A, in compoſition, ſeems to have ſometimes the power of the French *a* in theſe phraſes, *a droit, a gauche*, &c. and ſometimes to be contracted from *at*; as, *aſide, aſlope, afoot, aſleep, athirſt, aware*.

If this, which he avouches, does appear,
There is no flying hence, nor tarrying here.
I gin to be *a weary* of the ſun;
And wiſh the ſtate of the world were now undone.
Shakeſpeare's Macbeth.

And now a breeze from ſhore began to blow,
The ſailors ſhip their oars, and ceaſe to row;
Then hoiſt their yards *a-trip*, and all their ſails
Let fall, to court the wind, and catch the gales.
Dryden's Ceyx and Alcyone.

A is ſometimes redundant; as, *ariſe, arouſe, awake*; the ſame with riſe, rouſe, wake.

A, in abbreviations, ſtands for *artium*, or arts; as, A.B. bachelor of arts, *artium baccalaureus*; A.M. maſter of arts, *artium magiſter*; or, *anno*; as, A.D. *anno domini*.

AB, at the beginning of the names of places, generally ſhews that they have ſome relation to an abbey.

ABA'CKE. *adv.* obſolete. Backwards.

But when they came where thou thy ſkill didſt ſhow,
They drew *abacke*, as half with ſhame confound,
Shepherds to ſee them in their art outgo. *Spenſ. Paſt.*

ABA'CTOR. n. ſ. [Lat. *abactor*, a driver away.] Thoſe who drive away or ſteal cattle in herds, or great numbers at once, in diſtinction from thoſe that ſteal only a ſheep or two. *Blount*.

A'BACUS. n. ſ. [Lat. *abacus*.]

1. A counting-table, anciently uſed in calculations.

2. In architecture, it is the uppermoſt member of a column, which ſerves as a ſort of crowning both to the capital and column. *Dict.*

ABA'FT. *adv.* [of abaftan, Sax. Behind.] From the fore-part of the ſhip, towards the ſtern. *Dict.*

ABAI'SANCE. *n. ſ.* [from the French *abaiſer*, to depreſs, to bring down.] An act of reverence, a bow. *Obeyſance* is conſidered by Skinner as a corruption of *abaiſance*, but is now univerſally uſed.

To ABA'LIENATE. *v. a.* [from *abalieno*, Lat.] To make that another's which was our own before. *Calv. Lex. Jur.* A term of the civil law, not much uſed in common ſpeech.

ABALIENA'TION. *n. ſ.* [Lat *abalienatio*.] A giving up one's right to another perſon; or a making over an eſtate, goods, or chattels by ſale, or due courſe of law. *Dict.*

To ABA'ND. *v. a.* [A word contracted from abandon, but not now in uſe. See ABANDON.] To forſake.

Thoſe foreigners which came from far
Grew great, and got large portions of land,
That in the realm, ere long, they ſtronger are
Than they which ſought at firſt their helping hand,
And Vortiger enforced the kingdom to *aband*.
Spenſer's Fairy Queen, b. ii. *cant.* 10.

To ABA'NDON. *v. a.* [Fr. *abandonner*. Derived, according to *Menage*, from the Italian *abandonare*, which ſignifies to forſake his colours; *bandum* [*vexillum*] *deſerere*. *Paſquier* thinks

The language tree

The Bible tells a simple tale of the origin of the world's many tongues. Humanity, it claims, once lived all together and spoke just one language. The people worked together on a great tower in the center of a great city until God came and scattered them, altering their languages until hundreds existed, and the tower – the Tower of Babel – was abandoned.

Proto-Indo-European languages

Like all the best stories, this one contains an element of truth: many of our languages share the same root, and changed as we spread out and wandered into new lands. While it's probably not true that we all spoke one language, many of the world's most prolific languages have the same origin: **Proto-Indo-European**, spoken around 6,000 years ago.

It lies at the root of the language tree for many present-day tongues: English, Spanish, Hindi, German, French, Urdu, Russian and more. Almost half of all humans on the planet are native speakers of an Indo-European language, and we can count hundreds of such languages even if you ignore the thorny issue of where to draw the line between what some would think of as a dialect and others might consider a language in its own right.

If language is a tree, it's a gnarly and complex one: it's not as if languages subdivide and never re-merge. Take English: at various points in its history (usually thanks to invading or being invaded) it's come into contact with Latin (the Romans), Germanic languages (Vikings), French (the Normans) and others. It has constantly evolved and assimilated words and structures, and every few hundred years changes so much that a speaker of a few hundred years before would struggle to understand.

Perhaps language is less of a tree than a river: while the banks stay roughly where they are, the water is always moving, separating, recombining ... but never the same.

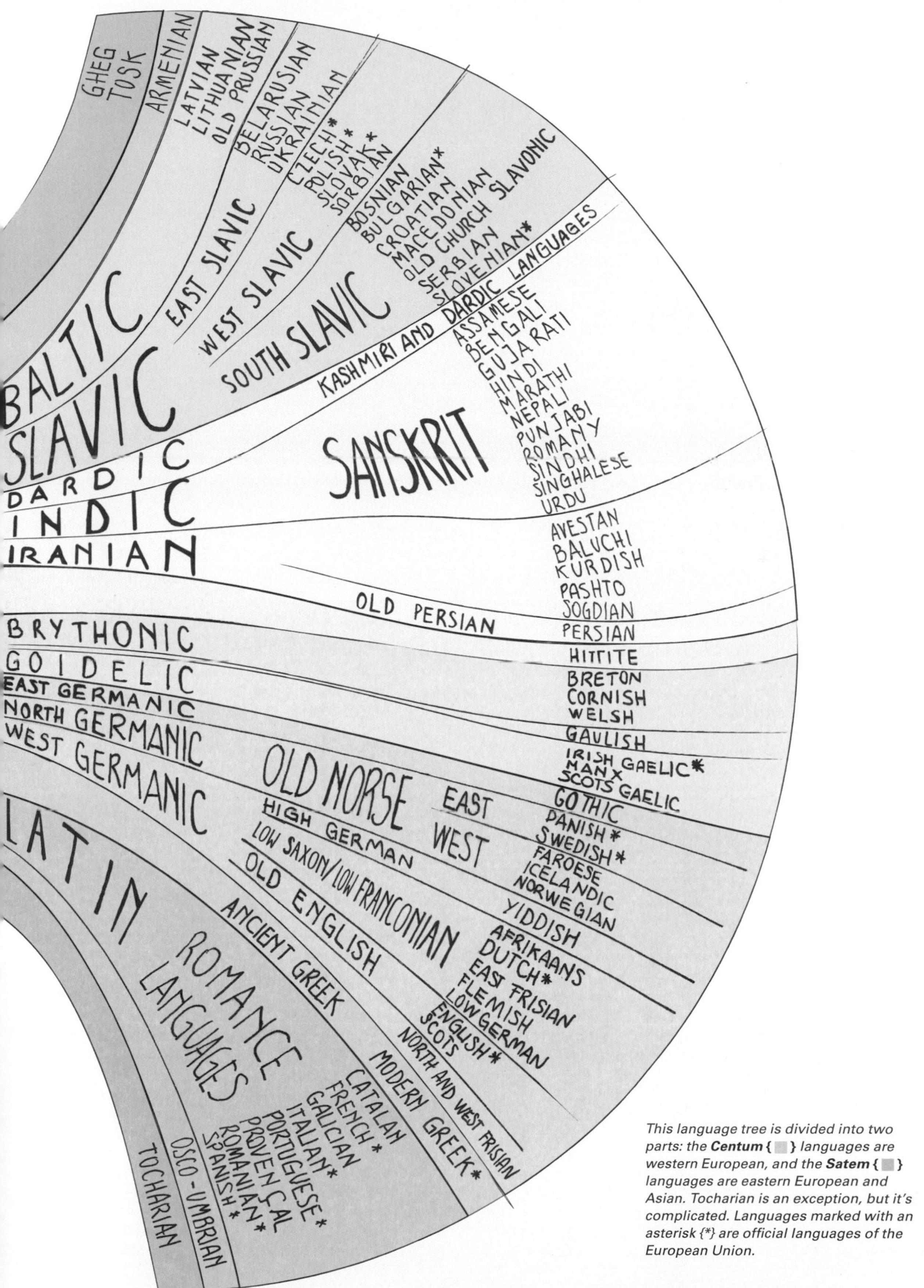

*This language tree is divided into two parts: the **Centum** { } languages are western European, and the **Satem** { } languages are eastern European and Asian. Tocharian is an exception, but it's complicated. Languages marked with an asterisk {*} are official languages of the European Union.*

Getting to the Iron Age

Most of us are dimly aware of the "three ages" theory of early history – how our early ancestors started with primitive stone tools, discovered the smelting of metal, and then progressed to the iron and steel we still use today. But that's a general picture, and it hides all the interesting detail.

First off, the Stone Age is far, far older than our species is. *Homo sapiens* (that's us) has existed for around 200,000 years – but we reckon the first stone tools crafted by our near ancestors date back around 2.6 million years. Those guys were cleverer than we tend to give them credit for.

What came next was a pretty interesting interplay of technology. Other than gold, metals take a fair bit of work to transform them into a usable state. Because they're impure when you've just dug them out of the ground, they need smelting (at quite high heat) to be able to extract the good stuff. Even copper required more heat than a typical campfire could offer.

It was – we think – the discovery of pottery that made smelting viable: pottery kilns were considerably hotter than a campfire. Progress then came at a comparatively whirlwind pace: while the **Stone Age {■}** lasted for millions of years, the **Bronze Age {■}** lasted for a couple of thousand, and the **Iron Age {■}** even fewer.

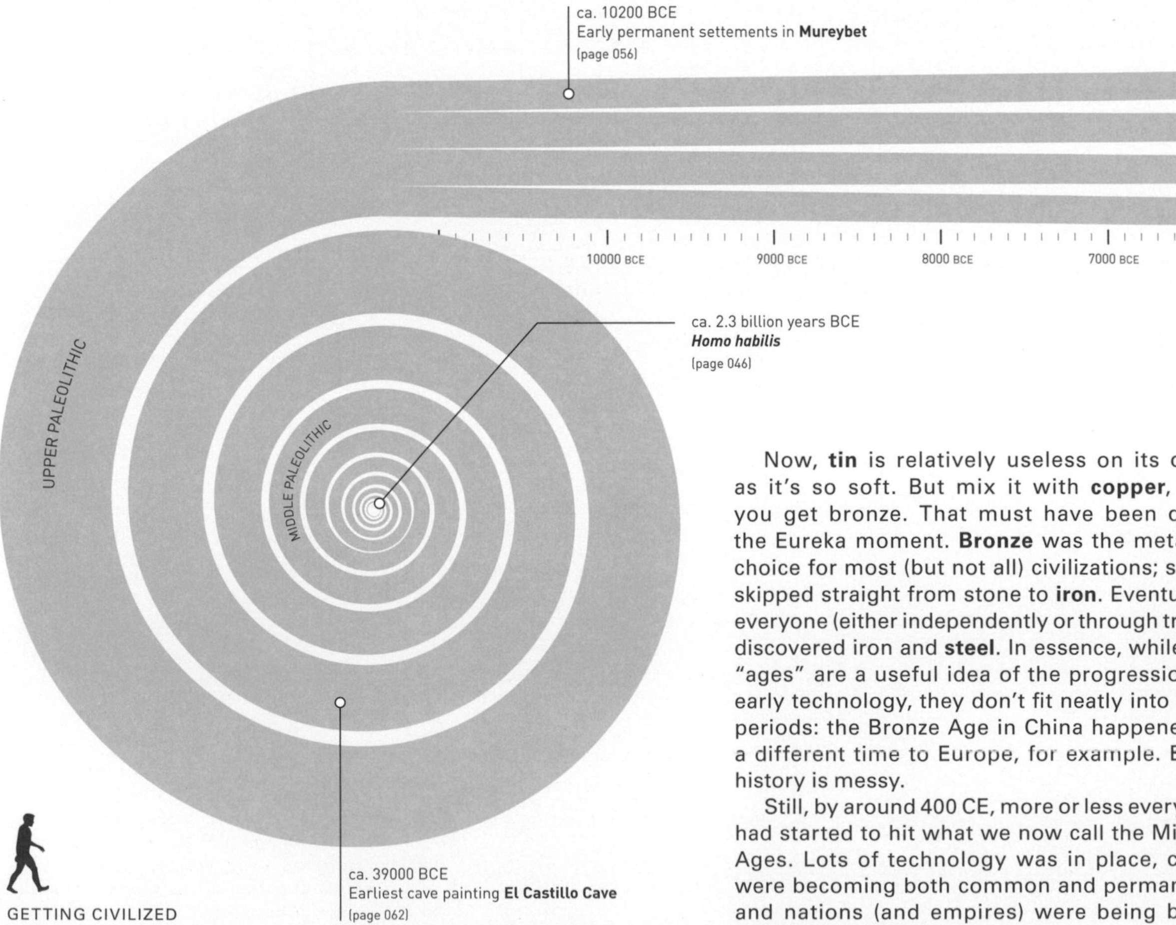

Now, **tin** is relatively useless on its own, as it's so soft. But mix it with **copper**, and you get bronze. That must have been quite the Eureka moment. **Bronze** was the metal of choice for most (but not all) civilizations; some skipped straight from stone to **iron**. Eventually, everyone (either independently or through trade) discovered iron and **steel**. In essence, while the "ages" are a useful idea of the progression of early technology, they don't fit neatly into time periods: the Bronze Age in China happened at a different time to Europe, for example. Early history is messy.

Still, by around 400 CE, more or less everyone had started to hit what we now call the Middle Ages. Lots of technology was in place, cities were becoming both common and permanent, and nations (and empires) were being born. Civilization was dawning.

Stone Age

The Stone Age saw the tool use of humanity, and our recent ancestors, become more sophisticated than those of other species: basic tools for rudimentary agriculture, weapons and the earliest roots of pottery – not to mention the first domestication of animals.

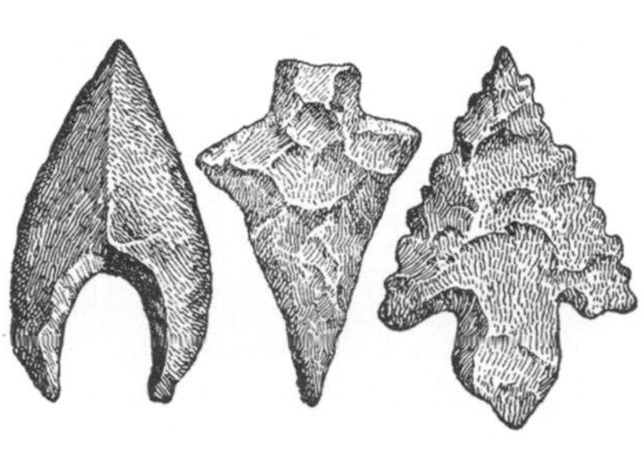

Bronze Age

The Bronze Age marked an unignorable change in the sophistication of tool use: the kilns used for more advanced pottery allowed for the melting and smelting of metals. Alloys (mixtures of metals) soon followed, leading to better weapons and tools alike.

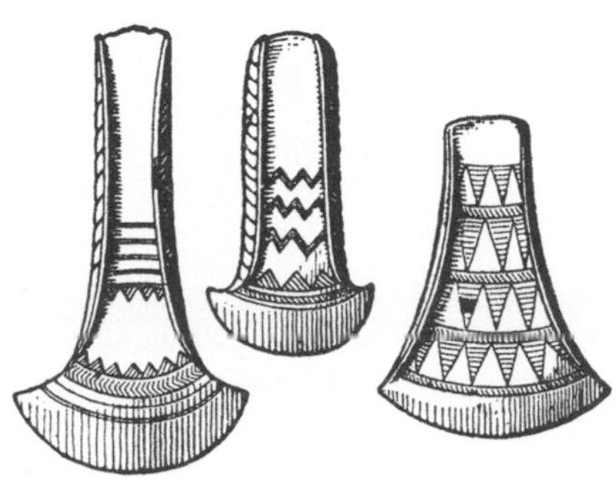

Iron Age

This age marked the evolution of the techniques first used in the Bronze Age (for most civilizations) for more robust metals and far more sophisticated tools – materials still used in industrial production and households alike to this day.

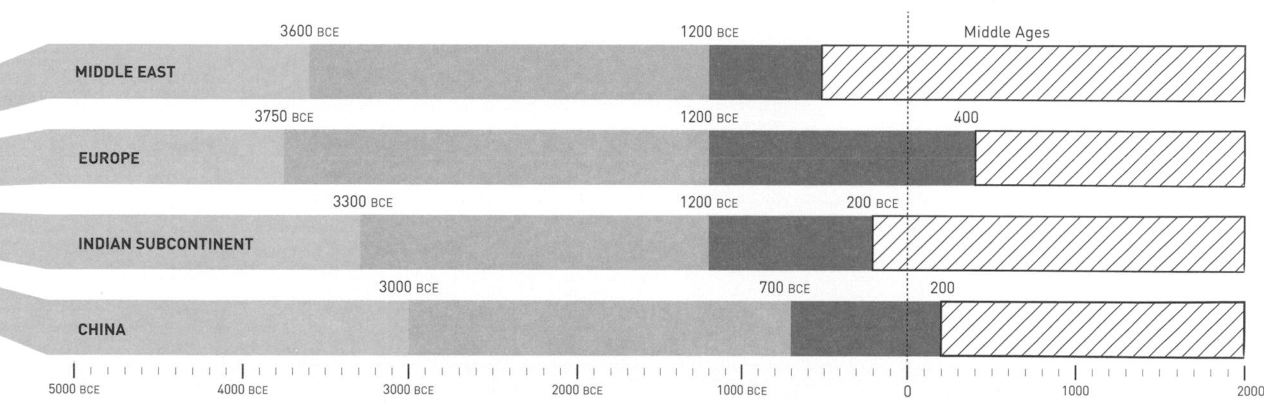

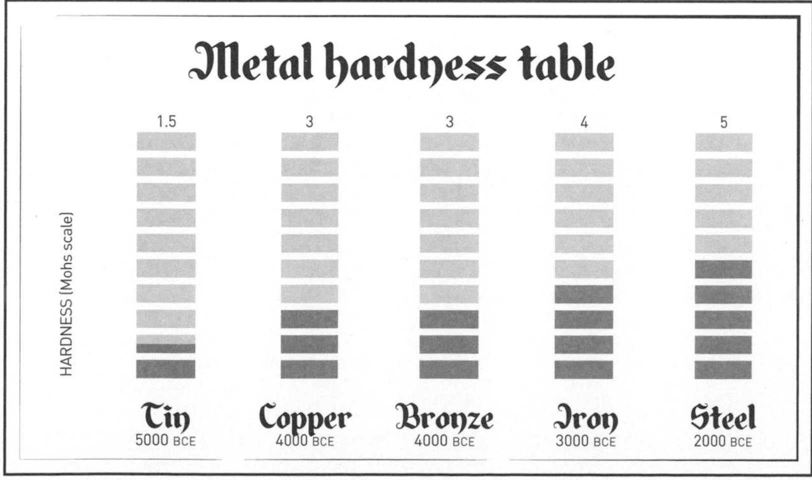

Nation Building

The story of the last 4,000 years is one of nations being founded, breaking apart, going to war and coming together. Along the way we see siege warfare, the abolition of slavery and the invention of pants.

Thankfully, what was once (or regularly) razed has always been built back, and humans have become more abundant and sophisticated.

Much more importantly for the writers and designers of a book of data-driven graphics, it's also the part of our story where historians and mathematicians began keeping records. We get our hands on the good stuff.

We use this to chronicle the rise and fall of empires, the tolls of wars throughout the ages, history's longest-lasting rulers and the age of discovery.

We also look at a few bits of history less often traversed: the falling cost of an hour's extra light and what that meant for society. An idea of how a peasant might have spent his day. When our clothes were invented. And what different ancient civilizations gave us.

So next time you're at a dinner party and conversation turns, inevitably, to the Byzantine Empire (again), this time you'll be well prepared...

I used to rule the world

And so we come to what we like to call the Classical era, when humanity was getting its act together, had the basics of technology down, and was preparing to found some major world civilizations. Humanity's tribes, which were scattered across numerous continents, now began to put down roots.

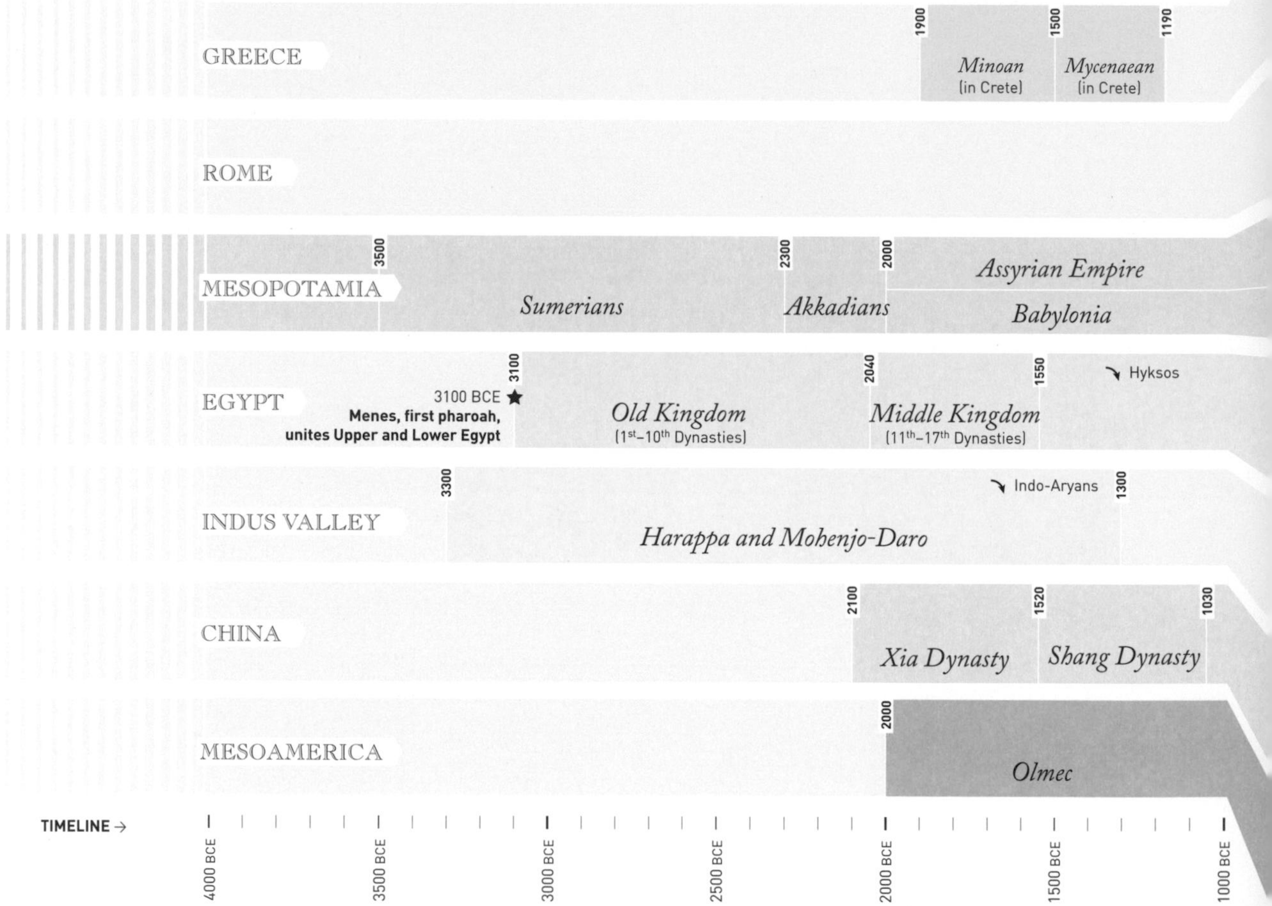

GREECE — 1900 *Minoan* (in Crete) 1500 *Mycenaean* (in Crete) 1190

ROME

MESOPOTAMIA — 3500 *Sumerians* 2300 *Akkadians* 2000 *Assyrian Empire* / *Babylonia*

EGYPT — 3100 BCE ★ Menes, first pharoah, unites Upper and Lower Egypt — 3100 *Old Kingdom* (1st–10th Dynasties) 2040 *Middle Kingdom* (11th–17th Dynasties) 1550 — Hyksos

INDUS VALLEY — 3300 *Harappa and Mohenjo-Daro* — Indo-Aryans 1300

CHINA — 2100 *Xia Dynasty* 1520 *Shang Dynasty* 1030

MESOAMERICA — 2000 *Olmec*

TIMELINE → 4000 BCE | 3500 BCE | 3000 BCE | 2500 BCE | 2000 BCE | 1500 BCE | 1000 BCE

INVASION
MAJOR WAR
★ MAJOR EVENT

What followed was a chaotic, overlapping sequence of rulers, empires, wars and more. It can make it quite hard to keep track – so we've made this at-a-glance guide to the ancient world. Interestingly, it also shows the impressive effect a few individuals can have on the course of history.

Take **Mesopotamia { }**. Its earliest settlements date back to 5000 BCE. After thousands of years in existence, Cyrus the Great succeeded in conquering his neighbors, and founded the first **Persian Empire { }**. But what goes around, comes around: a mere two centuries later Alexander the Great came and not only conquered the first Persian Empire, but did it just a year after doing the same to Egypt.

A few centuries later, and the **Roman Republic { }** was top dog – conquering Greece and Carthage in turn. Around the time of Julius Caesar, in the first century BCE, there began a struggle for power, and the Republic became an **Empire { }** (yes, that's where George Lucas got the idea from). A mere 500 years later, in 476 CE, the Western Roman Empire collapsed.

Despite the Holy Roman Empire in the east continuing through to 1453 CE, it's 476 CE which is generally considered to mark the end of the Classical Era. But hey, it was fun while it lasted.

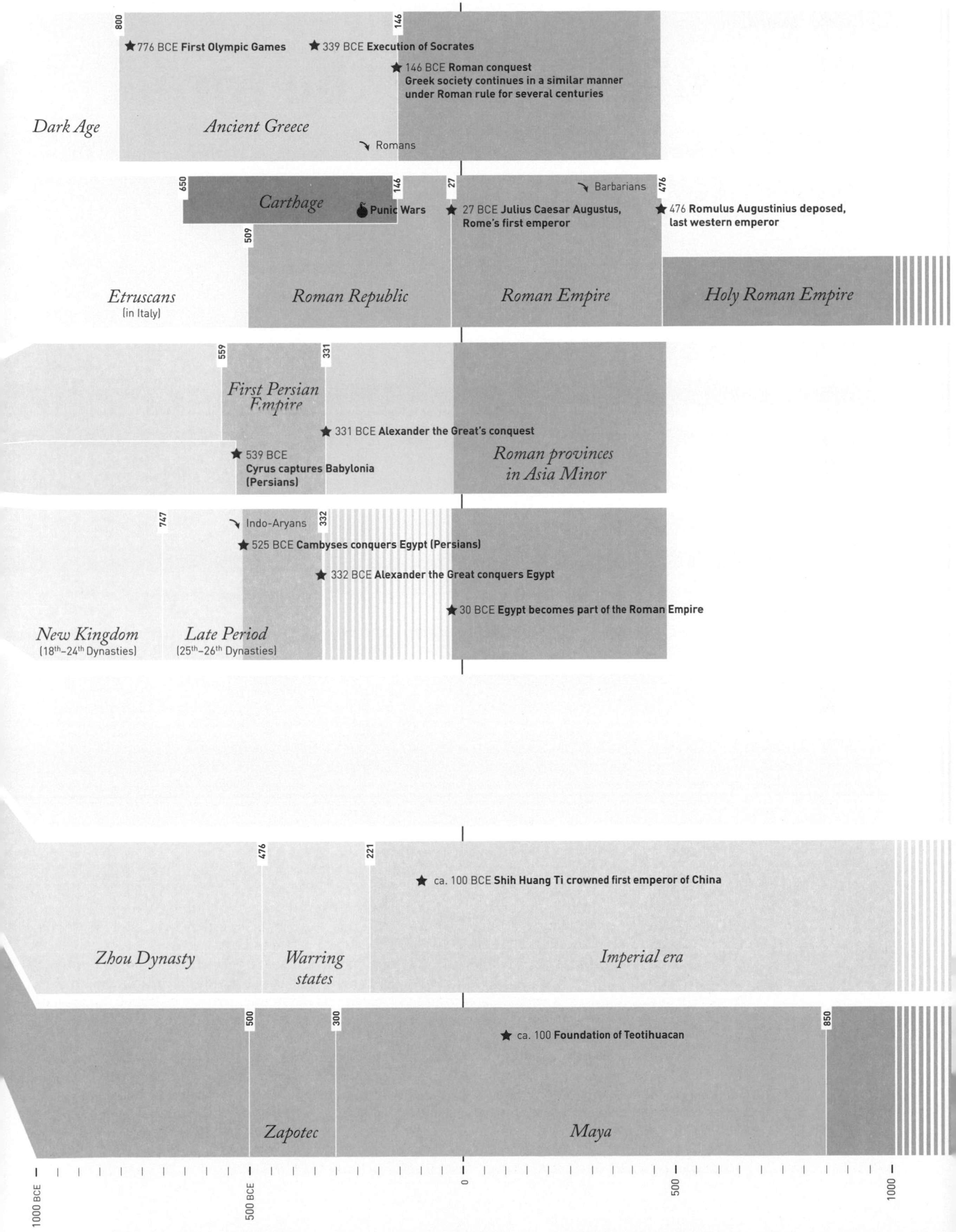

Dark Age
Ancient Greece
800
776 BCE First Olympic Games
339 BCE Execution of Socrates
146
146 BCE Roman conquest
Greek society continues in a similar manner under Roman rule for several centuries
Romans
650
Carthage
146
Punic Wars
27
27 BCE Julius Caesar Augustus, Rome's first emperor
Barbarians
476
476 Romulus Augustinius deposed, last western emperor
509
Etruscans
(in Italy)
Roman Republic
Roman Empire
Holy Roman Empire
559
First Persian Empire
331
331 BCE Alexander the Great's conquest
539 BCE
Cyrus captures Babylonia (Persians)
Roman provinces in Asia Minor
747
Indo-Aryans
332
525 BCE Cambyses conquers Egypt (Persians)
332 BCE Alexander the Great conquers Egypt
30 BCE Egypt becomes part of the Roman Empire
New Kingdom
(18th–24th Dynasties)
Late Period
(25th–26th Dynasties)
476
221
ca. 100 BCE Shih Huang Ti crowned first emperor of China
Zhou Dynasty
Warring states
Imperial era
500
300
850
ca. 100 Foundation of Teotihuacan
Zapotec
Maya
1000 BCE
500 BCE
0
500
1000

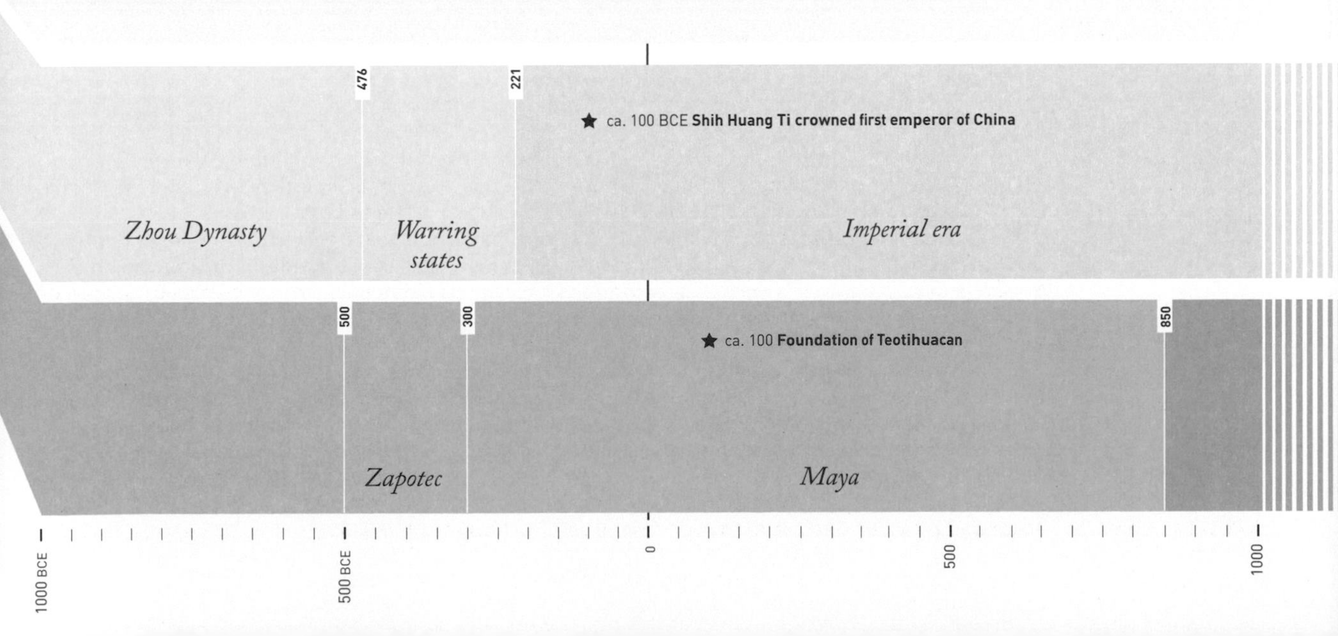

What did they ever do for us?

Ancient civilizations could have tried harder to be more helpful to historians. They were terrible at storing their stuff in ways that would make it easy to find and work out centuries later, and were often pretty shoddy in their approach to record keeping (particularly pre-writing).

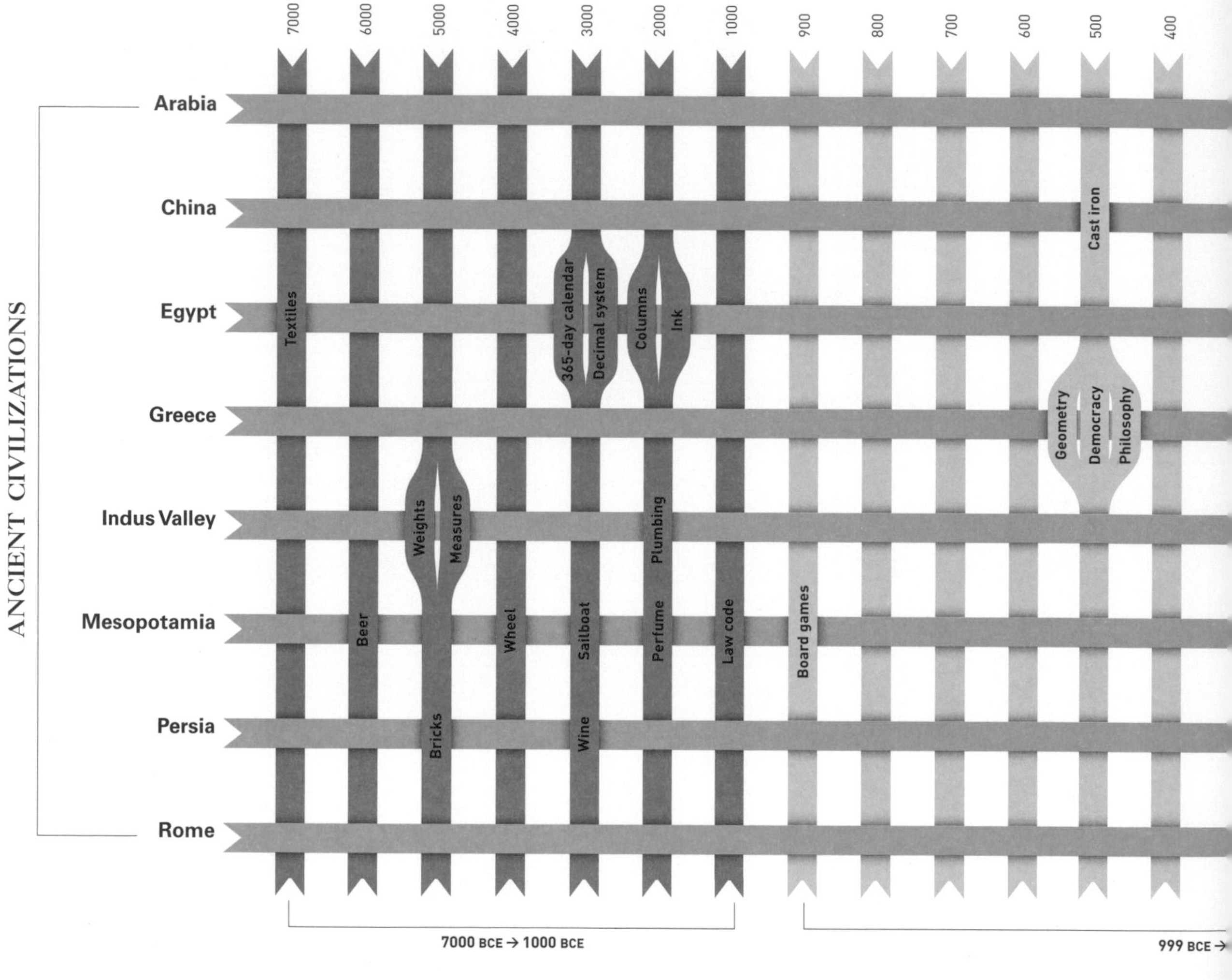

7000 6000 5000 4000 3000 2000 1000 900 800 700 600 500 400

ANCIENT CIVILIZATIONS

Arabia

China
Cast iron

Egypt
Textiles
365-day calendar
Decimal system
Columns
Ink

Greece
Geometry
Democracy
Philosophy

Indus Valley
Weights
Measures
Plumbing

Mesopotamia
Beer
Wheel
Sailboat
Perfume
Law code
Board games

Persia
Bricks
Wine

Rome

7000 BCE → 1000 BCE

999 BCE →

That makes trying to work out exactly each civilization's contribution to humanity quite tricky: we might find a civilization has a certain technology, but how do we know it was the first? If two have a similar one, did they invent it independently, or did one give it to the other? Is the oldest example of, say, **bricks** we've found really the oldest that existed?

So it's clear that establishing exactly what anyone did is a delicate business – but from what clever people have (literally) dug up, there's a lot that's intriguing. While we tend to credit Greece with some ingenious theoretical innovations – **democracy**, many of the foundations of modern **philosophy**, and some key **geometric** and **engineering principles**, other civilizations were more concrete in their approach.

The Romans were quite a practical bunch compared to the Greeks, and **concrete**, as it happens, is one of their inventions, along

We've woven together the inventions of some of the great early civilizations here – but textiles is a perfect example of an invention whose source is debatable. We highly recommend investigating further on the web – the debates are pretty interesting.

MILLENNIUM
CENTURY
year 0
CENTURY
Civilization
invention

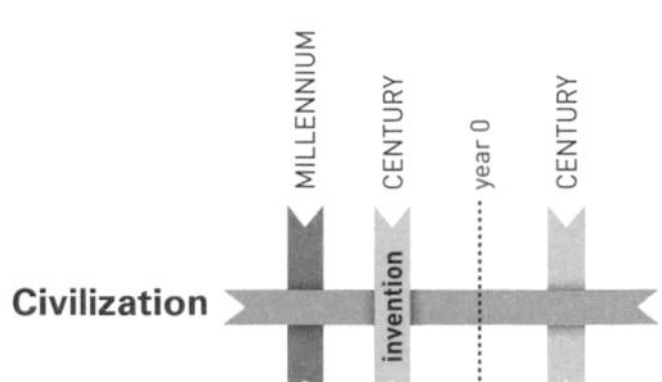

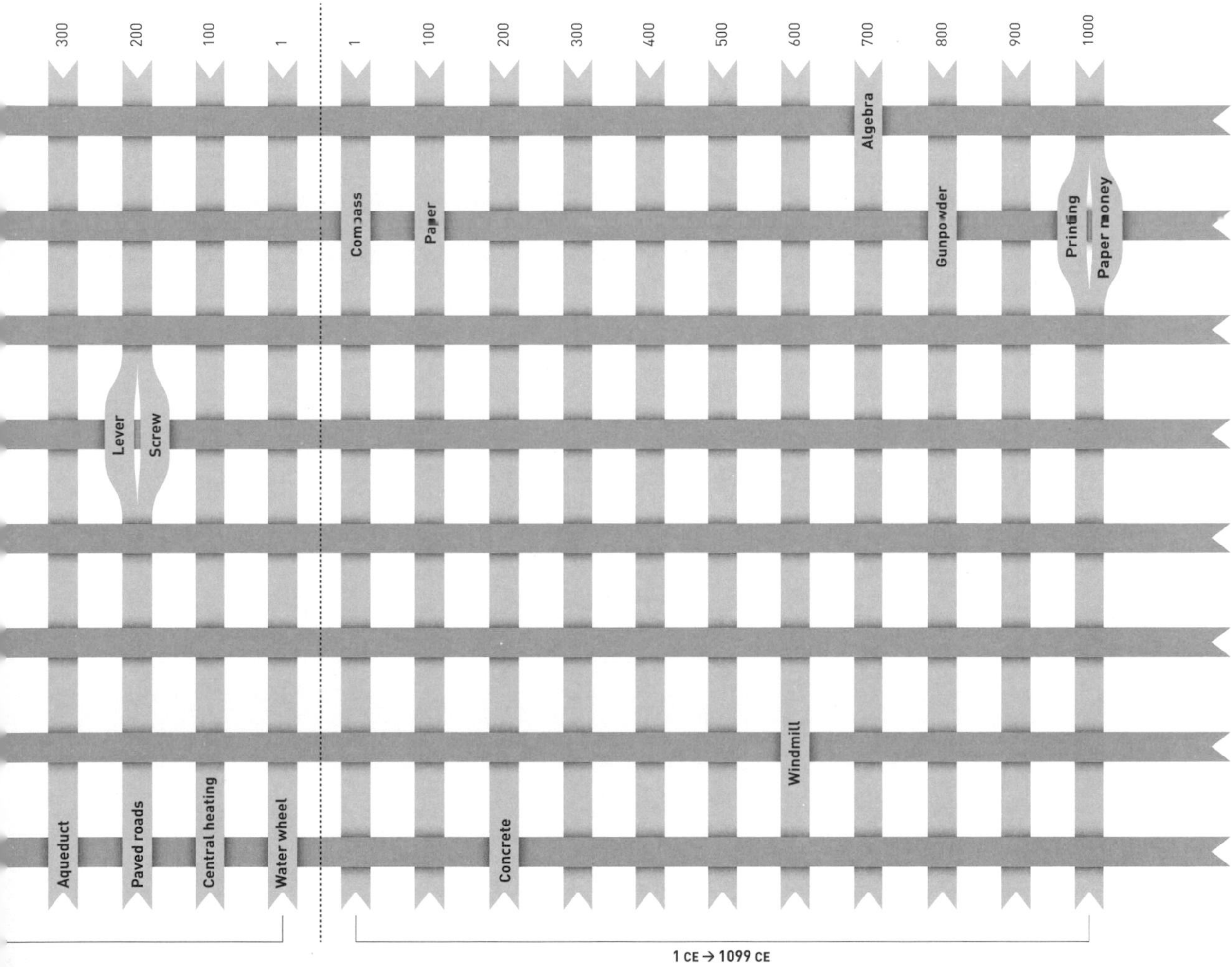

300
200
100
1
1
100
200
300
400
500
600
700
800
900
1000
Algebra
Compass
Paper
Gunpowder
Printing
Paper money
Lever
Screw
Windmill
Aqueduct
Paved roads
Central heating
Water wheel
Concrete
1 CE → 1099 CE

with another creation that's pretty useful – **central heating**. They don't win all the building innovation awards though: the oldest bricks ever found date from around 5000 BCE in Persia.

Some inventions happened earlier than you might think. The Indus Valley civilization, which seems to have collapsed hundreds of years before Jesus' time, had basic **plumbing** (as did the Romans, Greeks and others).

We've grouped a few great inventions from some of the brainiest ancient civilizations together – but if you feel inclined to pick a winner, remember that the value of any of these depends on your circumstance. In peacetime you might be tempted to choose **wine** or democracy, but if war suddenly broke out you'd probably wish you had the recipe for **gunpowder**.

Age of empires

"Empire" is a word that brings up a pretty mixed bag of feelings across the West these days. For a number of geeky men, it relates to a few pretty decent computer games.

But for those of us who paid at least some attention in school, it might hark back to a time of national pride and dominance, but for many it also heralds oppression, war, insurrection and, of course, slavery.

But there were plenty more empires than just the few we think about – typically the **British Empire { ■ }** and **Roman Empire { ■ }**. The vast majority of empires, caliphates and dynasties herald from **Asia { ■ }**. We've compiled reams of information on 30 of the biggest here.

It's pretty hard to contest the dominance of the British Empire: it ruled a fifth of the world's landmass, its commonwealth exists to this day, and it dominated a huge proportion of the world's modern economic powerhouses.

But beyond that, comparison gets difficult: do we look at the size of an empire at its peak? The proportion of the world's populace under its auspices? How peaceful or violent it was? Or its longevity?

Most of these are totally subjective, and there's really no accounting for taste. Even what might qualify as an empire is up for debate, so please take it as a given that no great political statements are meant by our selections. We've stuck to size (at an empire's peak), and an idea of how long each lasted, to build a timeline.

We think the results look pretty interesting.

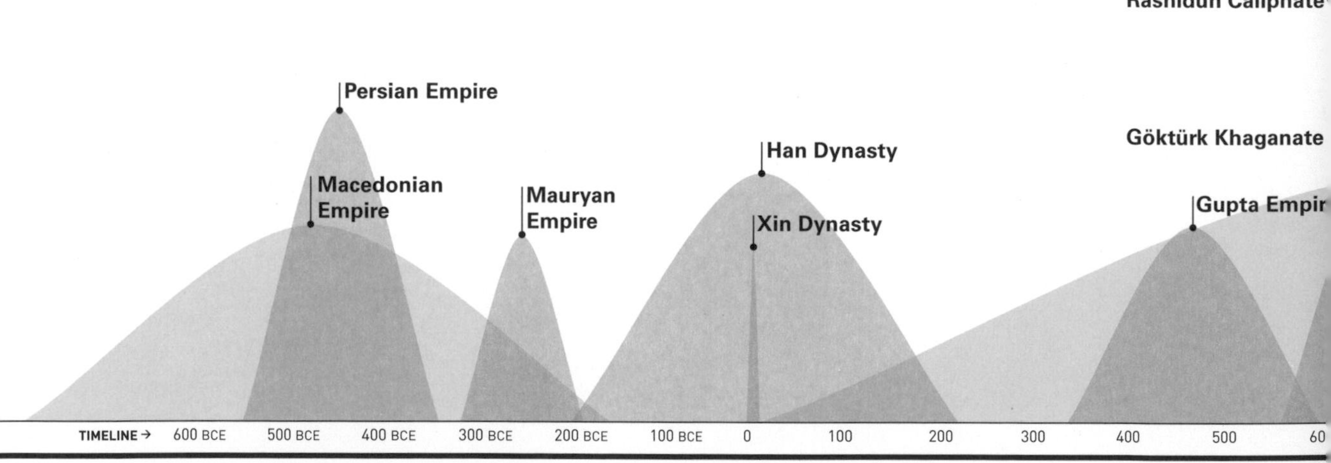

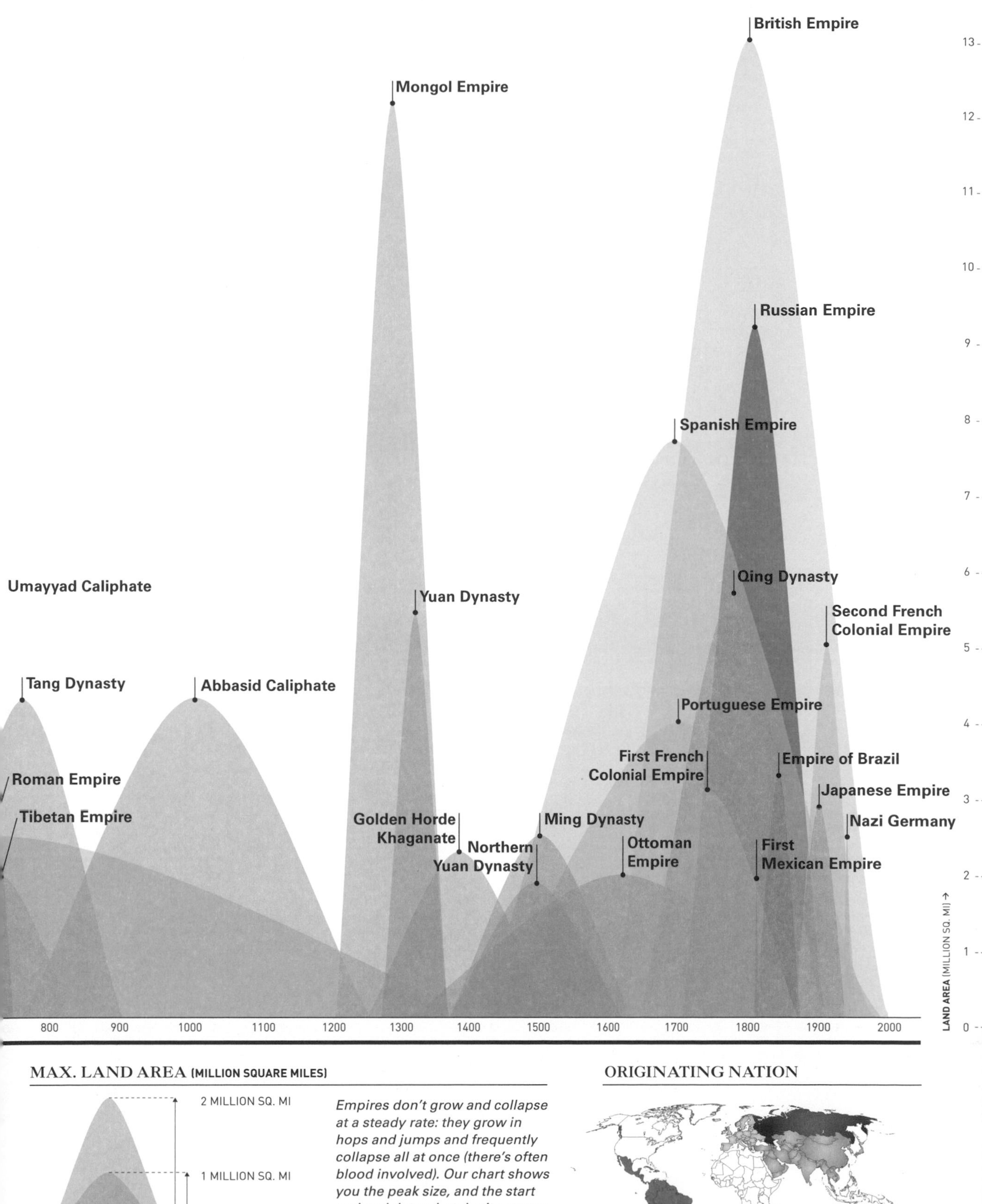

Empires don't grow and collapse at a steady rate: they grow in hops and jumps and frequently collapse all at once (there's often blood involved). Our chart shows you the peak size, and the start and end dates, but don't assume it grew, peaked or shrank like we show!

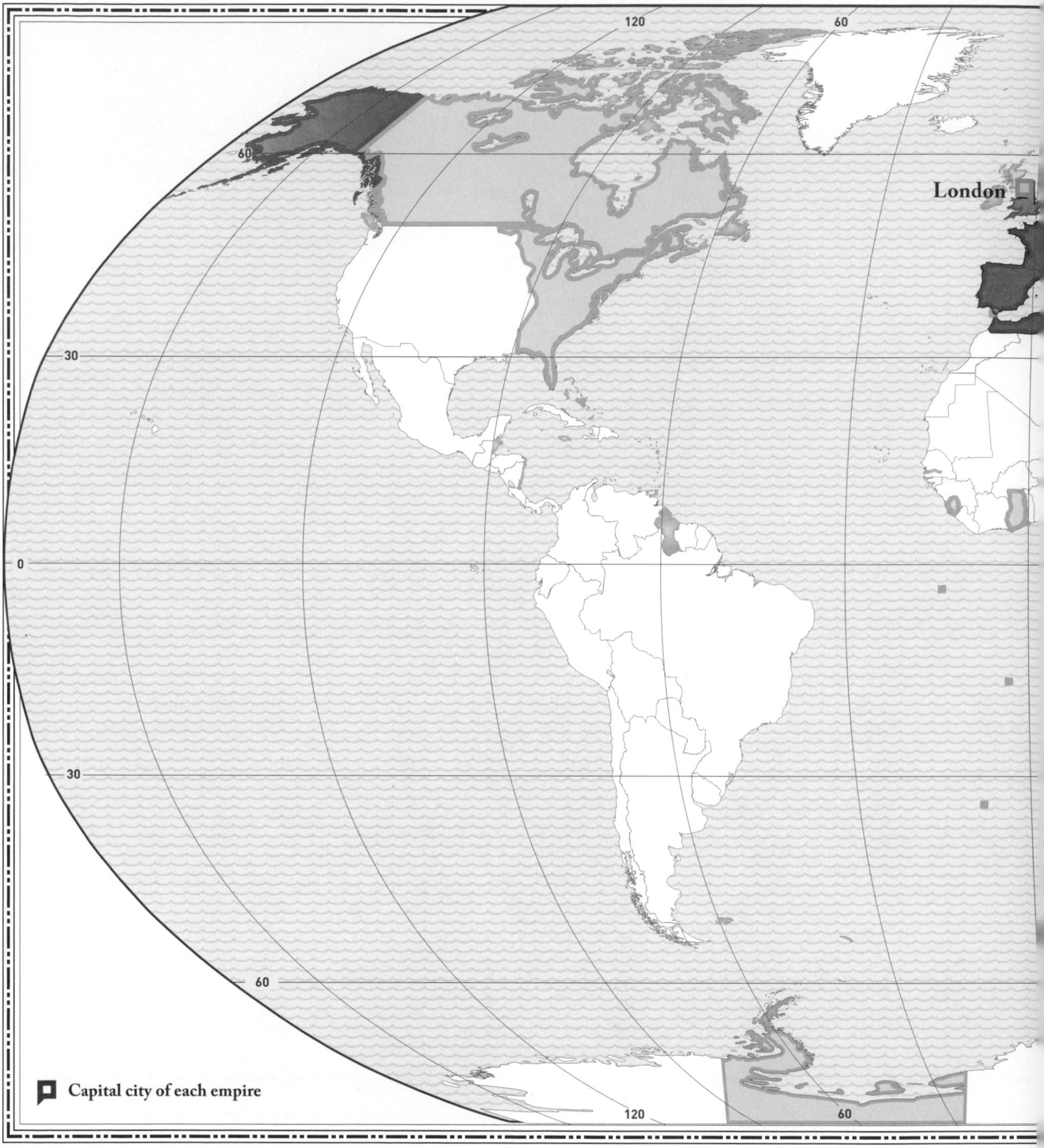

120
60
60
London
30
0
30
60
Capital city of each empire
120
60

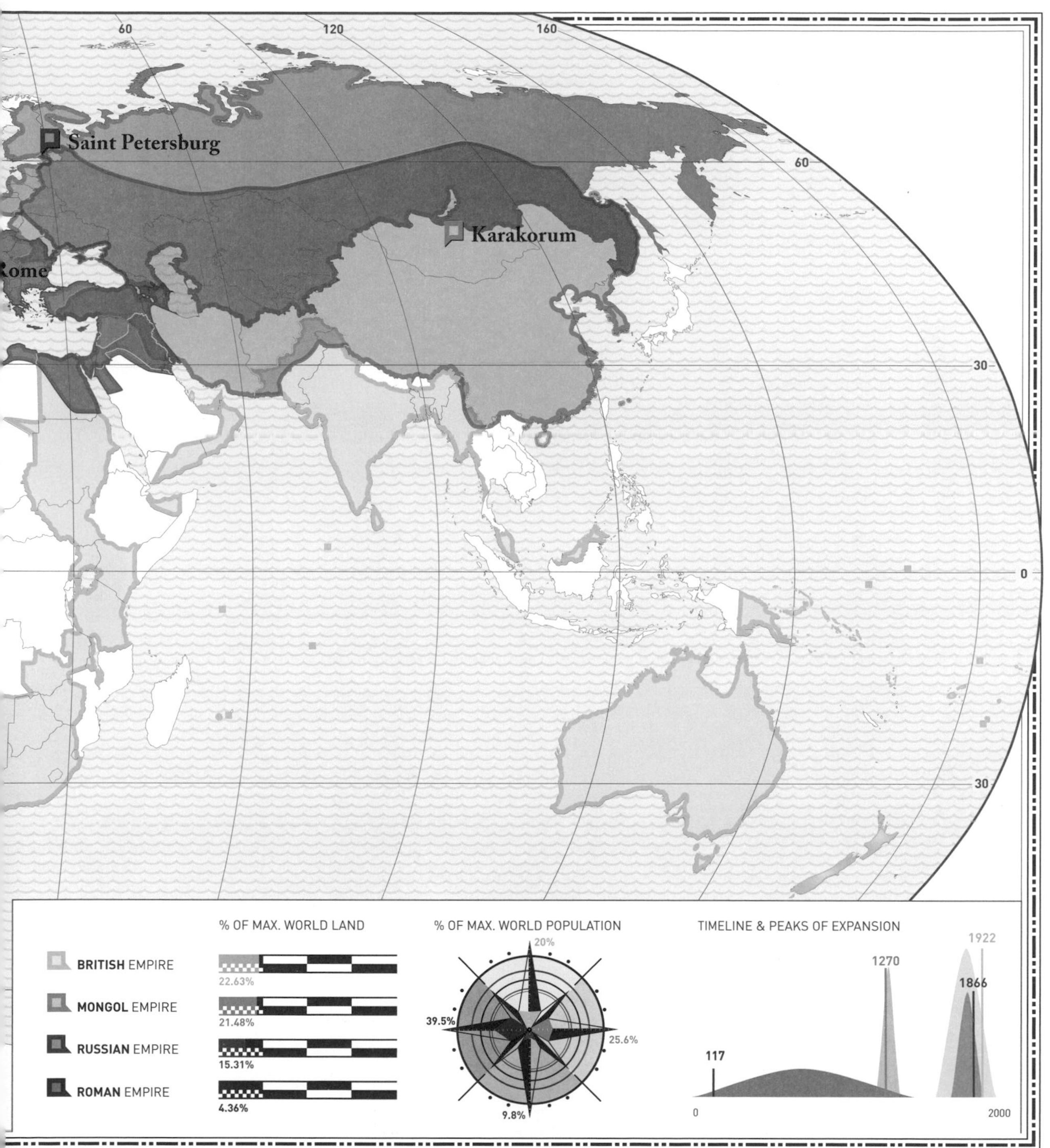

The Roman Empire is arguably history's most famous empire, but it was nowhere near the biggest, as this side-by-side shows. The British Empire distinguishes itself not just by sheer size, but also by virtue of being scattered across all corners of the globe – a result mainly of its more recent origins.

SCALE OF EMPIRES

Anatomy of a legion

The Roman Empire has been something of a gift to smart alecks – or those with a classical education – for centuries, not least because of Latin: an easy way for ruling elites through the ages to keep plebs out of the corridors of power.

But the quirks of the Empire's armies are enough to catch out the unwary in any battle of trivia, so here are a few mistakes to avoid. For one, despite everything your instincts might tell you, within the Roman military a century was not 100 men: it was nearer 80. Six centuries made a cohort and nine of these, plus various officers, cavalry and engineers, would make up a legion.

A second misapprehension to avoid is this: most people in the Roman army were not Romans. At the time of Hadrian, a reign immortalized by his efforts to wall off England from Scotland, the Roman army was made up of 28 **legions {■}** – about 154,000 troops, supported by more than 215,000 **auxiliaries {■}**, mostly from conquered lands.

It was a dauntingly large military, but perhaps not unreasonably so, even by modern standards. Including the elite **Praetorian Guard {■}**, the total size of Hadrian's military was around 380,000 men. Conservative estimates of the population of the Roman Empire at the time place it at around 65 million (around one in five of all living people).

DIVISIONS	ARMY PYRA-	TYPE OF SOLDIER

9,200
Praetorian Guards

154,000
Legionaries

217,920
Auxiliaries

EQUITES SINGULARES

PRAETORIAN GUARDS

CAVALRYMEN

ENGINEERS & OFFICER

LEGIONARIES

AUXILIA CAVALRYMEN

AUXILIA INFANTRYME

The number of soldiers in the Roman Army under Hadrian (ca. 130 CE), represented by the height of each soldiers' part of the pyramid.

MILITARY STRUCTURE (From the smallest → To the biggest organized unit)

✖ = 1 unit

2,000 CAVALRYMEN

CONTUBERNIUM

MADE UP OF:
8 Praetorian Guards

CENTURIA

MADE UP OF:
10 Contubernia
(80 Praetorian Guards)

DOUBLE COHORT

MADE UP OF:
10 Centuriae
(800 Praetorian Guards)

9 DOUBLE COHORTS

TOTAL: **7,200 Praetorian Guards**

CAVALRY ATTACHMENT

TOTAL: **120 Cavalrymen**

OFFICERS UNIT

TOTAL: **260 Engineers & officers**

CONTUBERNIUM

MADE UP OF:
8 Legionaries

CENTURIA

MADE UP OF:
10 Contubernia
(80 Legionaries)

DOUBLE COHORT

MADE UP OF:
10 Centuriae
(800 Legionaries)

COHORT

MADE UP OF:
6 Centuriae
(480 Legionaries)

LEGION

1 Cavalry Attachment

1 Officers Unit

1 Double Cohort
(800 Legionaries)

9 Cohorts
(4,320 Legionaries)

MADE UP OF:
5,500 Legionaries

28 LEGIONS

TOTAL:
154,000 Legionaries

TURMA

MADE UP OF:
32 Cavalrymen

ALA

MADE UP OF:
30 Turmae
(960 Cavalrymen)

88 ALAE

TOTAL: **84,480 Auxilia Cavalrymen**

CONTUBERNIUM

MADE UP OF:
8 Infantrymen

CENTURIA

MADE UP OF:
10 Contubernia
(80 Infantrymen)

COHORT

MADE UP OF:
6 Centuriae
(480 Infantrymen)

278 COHORTS

TOTAL: **133,440 Auxilia Infantrymen**

HOW DOES THE ROMAN ARMY COMPARE WITH THE UK'S TODAY?

ca.130 BCE

HADRIAN'S ARMED FORCES

381,120
personnel

Praetorian Guards	9,200
Legionaries	154,000
Auxiliaries	217,920

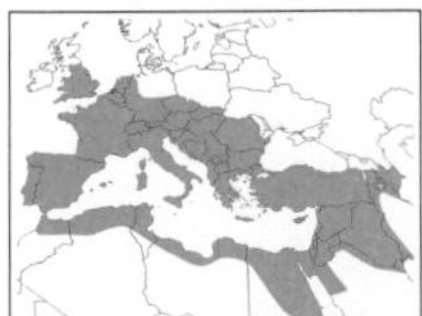

Population ca. 65 million

The population of Hadrian's empire was, roughly speaking, the size of the United Kingdom's population today. How do the militaries stack up? The active armed forces are considerably smaller, at around 180,000 troops – but the UK also has a further 220,000 or so reservists and volunteers – making the readily available complement larger today than in Roman times.
The news for Hadrian just keeps getting worse: turns out the UK has assault rifles, jets and nuclear weapons. And it's difficult to make a hasty retreat when you're wearing sandals...

2012

HER MAJESTY'S ARMED FORCES

402,070
personnel

36,160	Volunteers
184,160	**Active soldiers**
181,720	**Reservists**

62.6 million **Population**

✖ / ✚ Each symbol represents ca. 110 soldiers

3,450 ✖ =	381,120	Total personnel		3,650 ✚ =	402,070	Total personnel
83 ✖ =	9,200	Praetorian Guards		329 ✚ =	36,160	Volunteers
1,394 ✖ =	154,000	Legionaries		1,672 ✚ =	184,160	Active soldiers
1,973 ✖ =	217,920	Auxiliaries		1,650 ✚ =	181,720	Reservists

WHAT WAS THE DAILY ROUTINE IN THE MIDDLE AGES?

The medieval day

History tends to pay more attention to the ruling classes than to those further down the social ladder. There's no shortage of reasons for this – the documentation is better, their actions had greater ramifications, and they often lived (and died) in grisly and colorful ways. But even if the lives of peasants were thoroughly documented, they'd probably still not get all that much attention – as much of their lives was pretty monotonous.

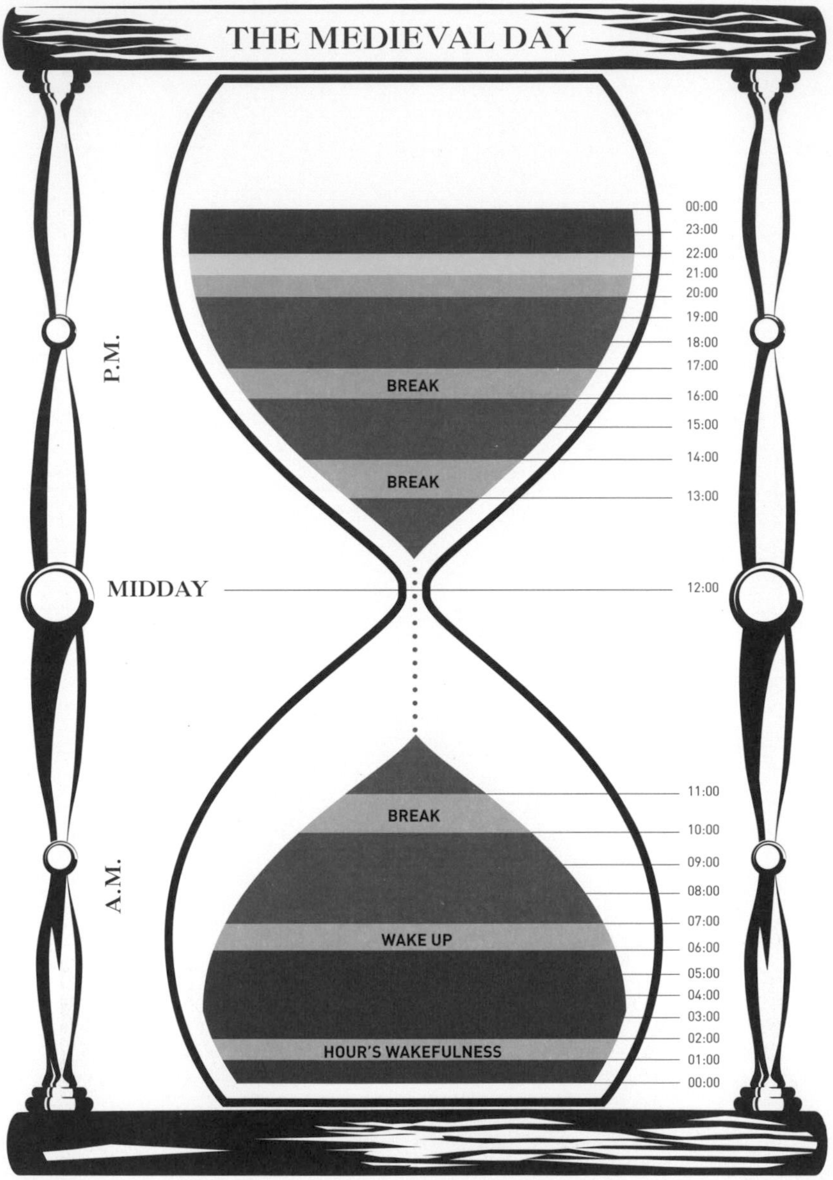

THE MEDIEVAL DAY

P.M.

00:00
23:00
22:00
21:00
20:00
19:00
18:00
17:00
BREAK
16:00
15:00
14:00
BREAK
13:00

MIDDAY 12:00

A.M.

11:00
BREAK
10:00
09:00
08:00
07:00
WAKE UP
06:00
05:00
04:00
03:00
02:00
HOUR'S WAKEFULNESS
01:00
00:00

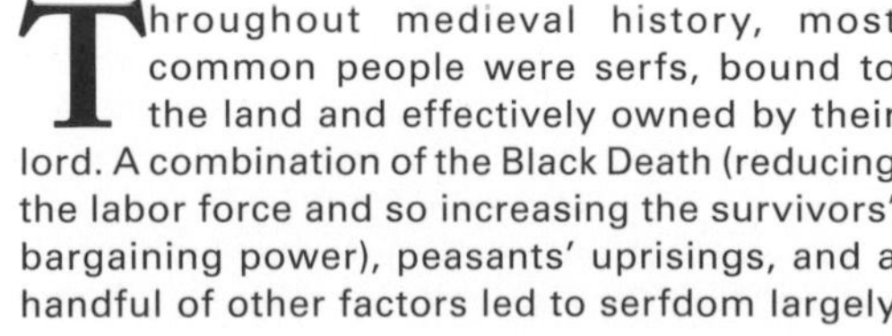

Throughout medieval history, most common people were serfs, bound to the land and effectively owned by their lord. A combination of the Black Death (reducing the labor force and so increasing the survivors' bargaining power), peasants' uprisings, and a handful of other factors led to serfdom largely dying out in England. But free or not, a laborer's day was tough (though in those more religious times, up to 100 days a year qualified as holy days or public holidays).

In summer, he'd be awake by 6 a.m. and working by 7 a.m. (in winter, when light was scant, sleeping in until 8 a.m. or so was common).

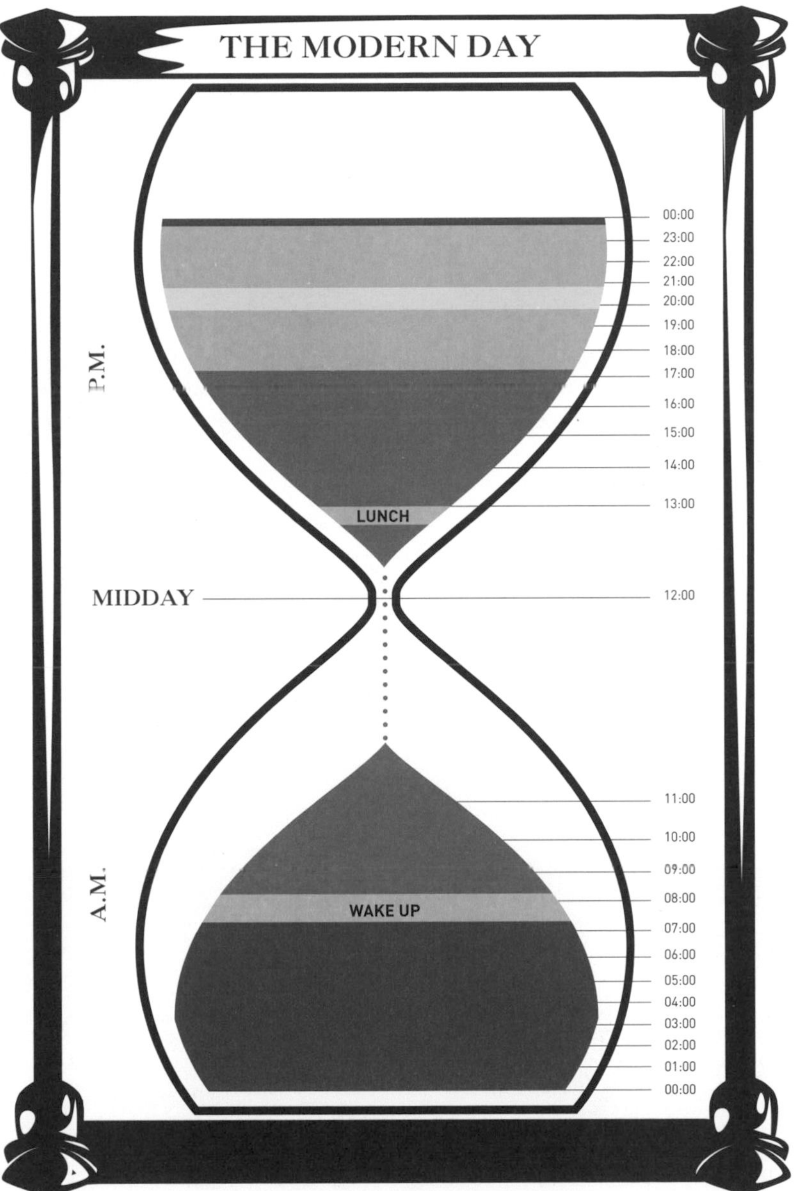

ACTIVITIES

- WORKING
- SLEEPING
- DINNER
- OTHER ACTIVITIES (eating, resting, etc.)

While the pattern of modern life – work, sleep and play – might not differ from the medieval ones, the balance is much different: in the modern world, we rise later, and thanks to cheap artificial light, go to bed far later too. But the big bonus of the 21st century? Much more free time.

From 7 a.m. until close to dusk – 8 p.m. or so – he'd be working the fields, with breaks perhaps at 10 a.m., 1 p.m. and 4 p.m., to get some respite from the physical labor.

Nighttime, though, held a curiosity by modern standards: our peasant and his family would probably not sleep all night. Typically, at some point in the night – let's say 1 a.m. – the house would be awake. A time used for, ah, intimate moments, quiet contemplation, or even, on occasion, to eat. This two-sleep cycle was common for perhaps most of our history, and only really died out with cheap and abundant artificial light. Who knows? Maybe we're missing out.

CRUSADES:

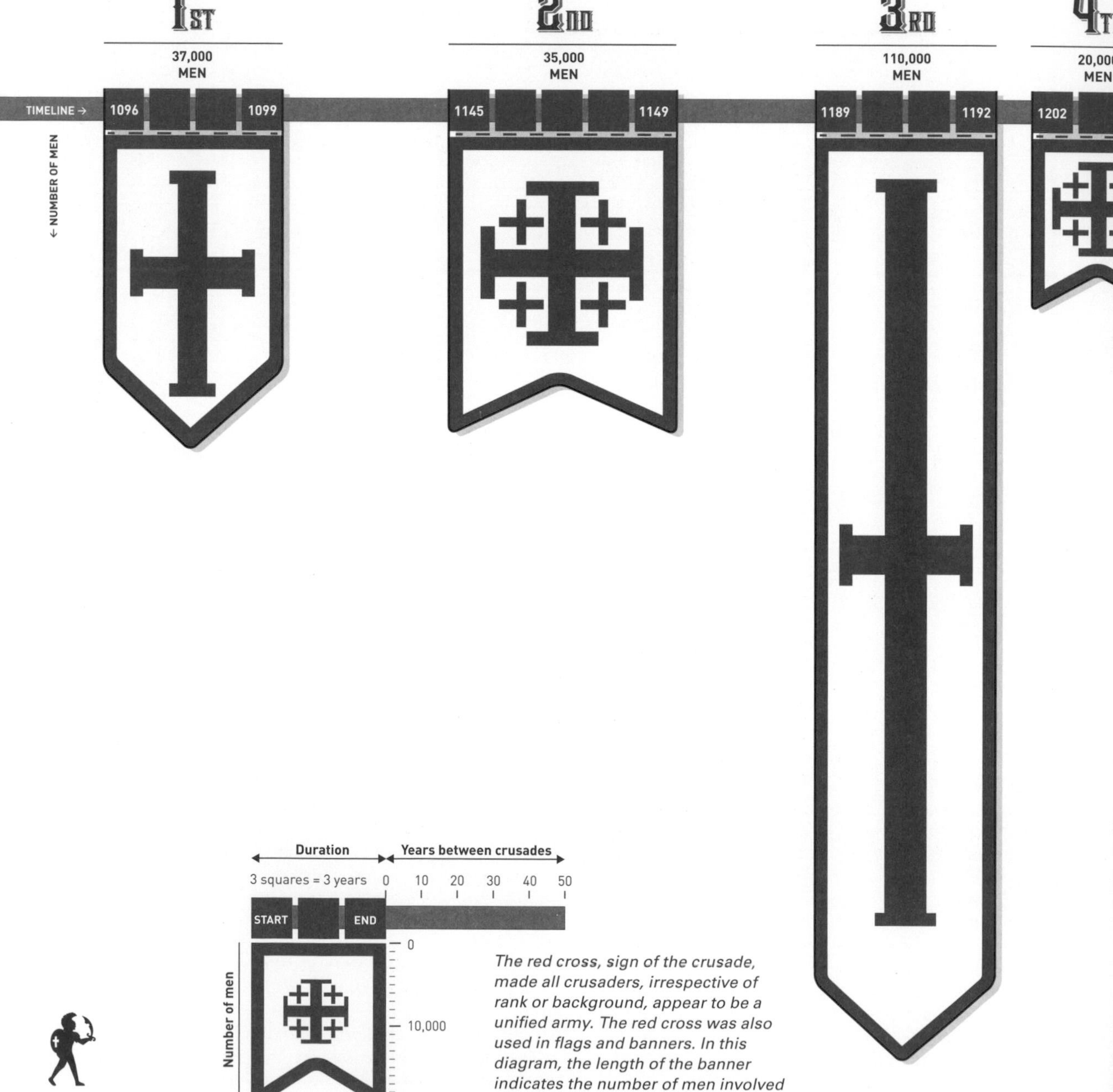

The red cross, sign of the crusade, made all crusaders, irrespective of rank or background, appear to be a unified army. The red cross was also used in flags and banners. In this diagram, the length of the banner indicates the number of men involved and its width represents the duration.

Going crusading

Once you invade the Middle East, it seems, it's difficult to stop – perhaps never more so than in the Middle Ages, during which the kingdoms of Christendom invaded the Holy Land not once, not twice, but nine times (and that's excluding the minor clashes).

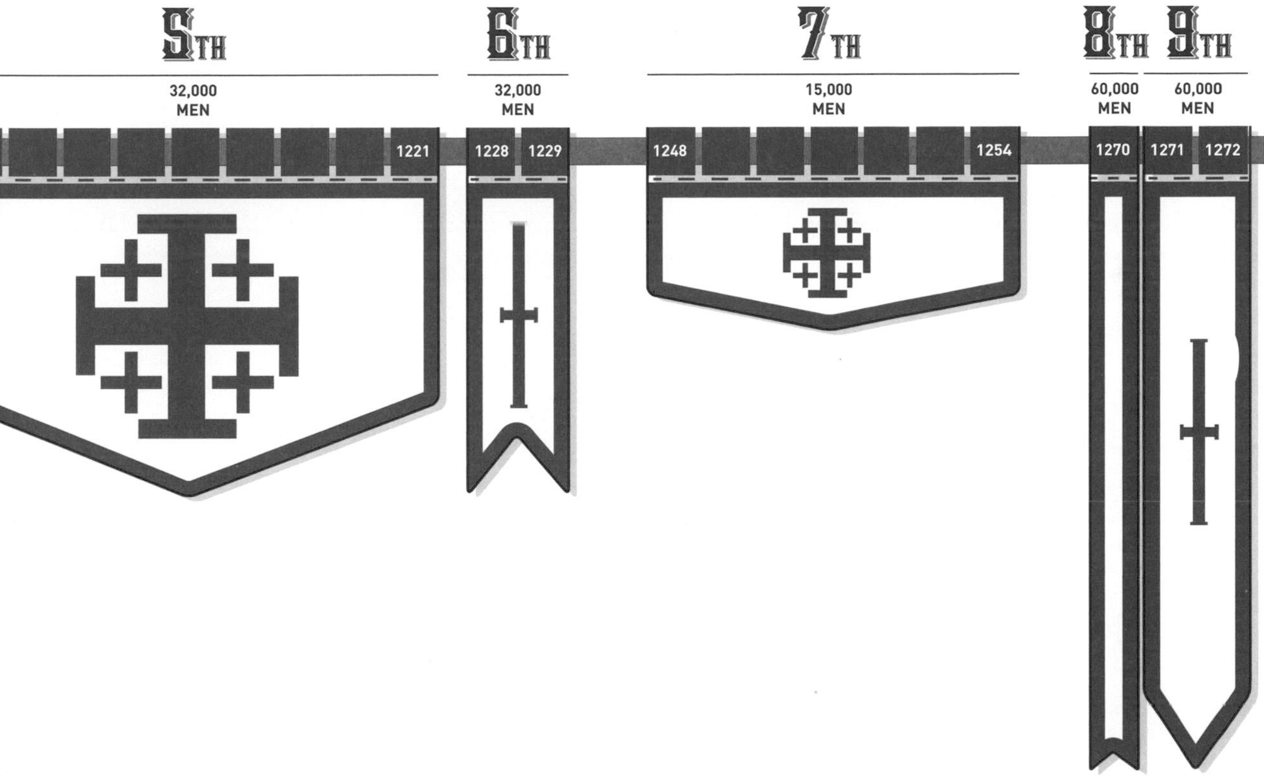

Perhaps the problem was that everything started so well. Pope Urban II announced a crusade in order to assist Byzantine allies in the East. Having managed that, the previously secondary goal of "retaking" Jerusalem came into view, and was accomplished after a bloody conflict. The conquering armies set up new nations in the Middle East and celebrated.

All went well for a surprisingly long while, but around 40 years later some of the new countries were recaptured, and a second crusade beckoned. These were just the beginnings of a string of conflicts over the next two centuries stretching from the Balkans to the Middle East, and even included wars against the Byzantines – the allies the West had originally sought to help.

The **Third Crusade** has a special place in English history as the one the generously named Richard the Lionheart bankrupted the treasury (and brought the country to the brink of civil war) to fight. His habit of getting kidnapped and ransomed along the way didn't help his reputation or the cause a great deal either.

One hundred and seventy-six years after the **First Crusade** began, the **Ninth Crusade** ended – in all, the conflicts had filled 28 of the intervening years. It took another 32 years for the final bit of territory the Christians had won to be recaptured, which left everyone more or less where they started.

Still, at least it was a lesson learned – you'd never find a Western superpower foolhardily charging into a Middle Eastern nation in the 21st century ... would you?

WHO WERE THE GREAT EXPLORERS AND WHAT DID THEY FIND?

The age of exploration

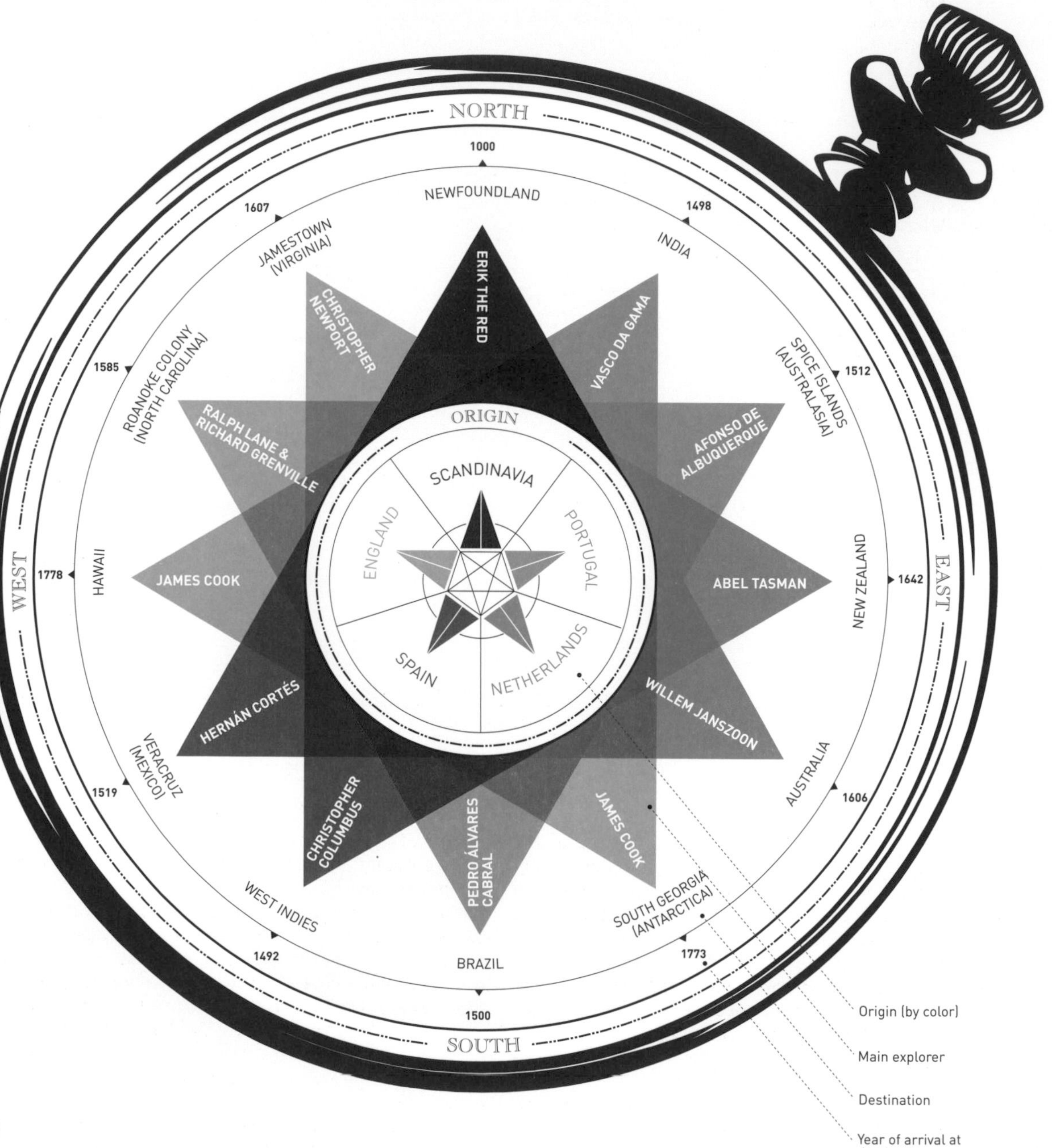

NORTH

1000

NEWFOUNDLAND

ERIK THE RED

1498

INDIA

VASCO DA GAMA

1512

SPICE ISLANDS (AUSTRALASIA)

AFONSO DE ALBUQUERQUE

EAST

1642

NEW ZEALAND

ABEL TASMAN

1606

AUSTRALIA

WILLEM JANSZOON

1773

SOUTH GEORGIA (ANTARCTICA)

JAMES COOK

SOUTH

1500

BRAZIL

PEDRO ÁLVARES CABRAL

1492

WEST INDIES

CHRISTOPHER COLUMBUS

1519

VERACRUZ (MEXICO)

HERNÁN CORTÉS

WEST

1778

HAWAII

JAMES COOK

1585

ROANOKE COLONY (NORTH CAROLINA)

RALPH LANE & RICHARD GRENVILLE

1607

JAMESTOWN (VIRGINIA)

CHRISTOPHER NEWPORT

ORIGIN

SCANDINAVIA

PORTUGAL

NETHERLANDS

SPAIN

ENGLAND

Origin (by color)

Main explorer

Destination

Year of arrival at destination

YEAR	MAIN EXPORER	DISCOVERY	ON BEHALF OF	ROUTE
1000	**Erik the Red**	Newfoundland	Vikings	1
1492	**Christopher Columbus**	West Indies	Ferdinand and Isabella	2
1498	**Vasco da Gama**	India	Manuel I	3
1500	**Pedro Álvares Cabral**	Brazil	Manuel I	4
1512	**Afonso de Albuquerque**	Spice Islands / Australasia	Manuel I	5
1519	**Hernán Cortés**	Veracruz (Mexico)	Charles V	6
1585	**Ralph Lane and Richard Grenville**	Roanoke Colony (North Carolina)	Sir Walter Raleigh	7
1606	**Willem Janszoon**	Australia	East India Company	8
1607	**Christopher Newport**	Jamestown (Virginia)	James I	9
1642	**Abel Tasman**	New Zealand	East India Company	10
1773	**James Cook**	South Georgia (Antarctica)	George III	11
1778	**James Cook**	Hawaii	George III	12

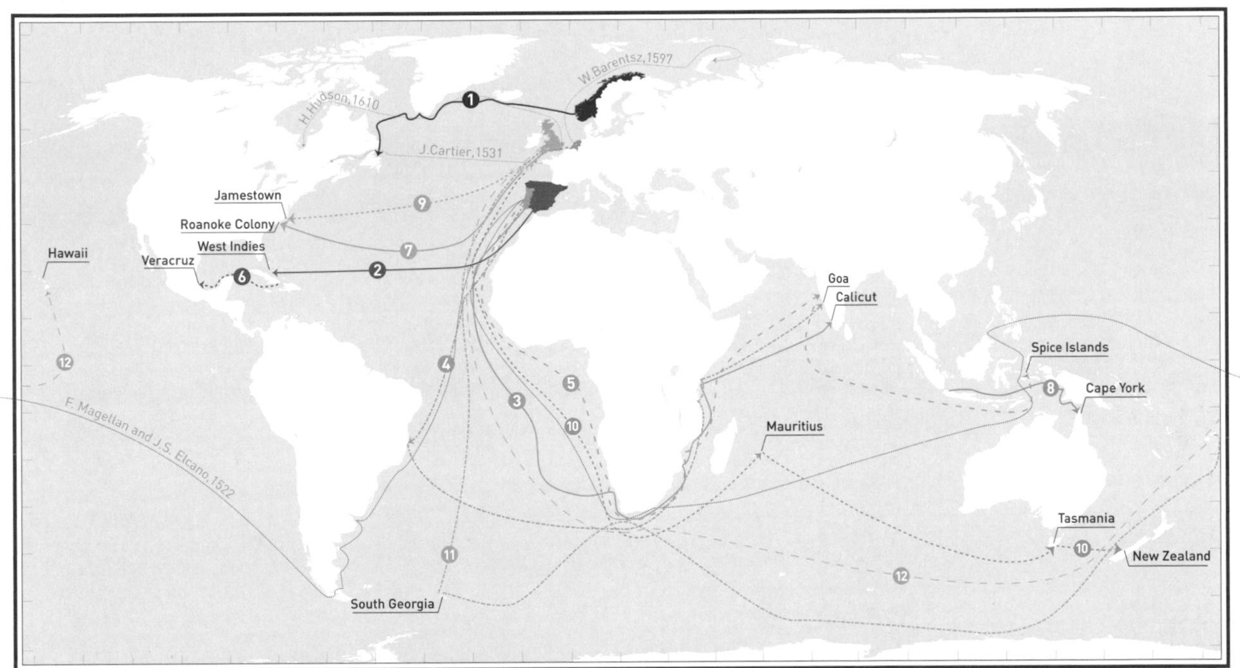

The Vikings should probably have sacked their PR manager. They're well known for the whole looting, pillaging and burning routine, but they were also pretty impressive explorers: they discovered and settled Newfoundland around 1000 CE, well before most Western explorers had decided to go and have a look around.

Exploration really kicked off in earnest through the late fifteenth century to early in the seventeenth, and like most things in life, was driven mainly by economic factors. The spirit of discovery is a wonderful thing, but it rarely inspires the money men needed to fund such trips.

The rise of the Ottoman Empire severed some key land trade routes to Asia, leading financiers to bankroll daring trips to find new, naval, trade routes. New landmasses were almost incidental (but the gold and exotic crop finds were certainly well appreciated). **Spain { ■ }** and **Portugal { ■ }** dominated exploration and settlement in the earlier stages of the age of exploration, but **England { ■ }** caught up eventually – though had several false starts in settling North America.

Exciting exploration might be, but safe it was not. Thanks to disease, accidents, privateers and violence with natives, the mortality rate among ships' crews was somewhere between 15% and 35% according to historical records. This often dampened achievements. The Portuguese explorer Ferdinand Magellan discovered the Strait of Magellan (who knew?) and his expedition was the first to circumnavigate the globe – but not until sixteen months after he died in action.

Still, the sacrifices were hardly inconsequential, giving birth to the interconnected world we know today, and bringing with it new crops and innovations. Plus, it's no coincidence that English and Spanish are both in the top three most spoken languages across the world. Muy bien!

WHERE DID THE COLONIAL EMPIRES GO TO TRADE?

Rule Britannia

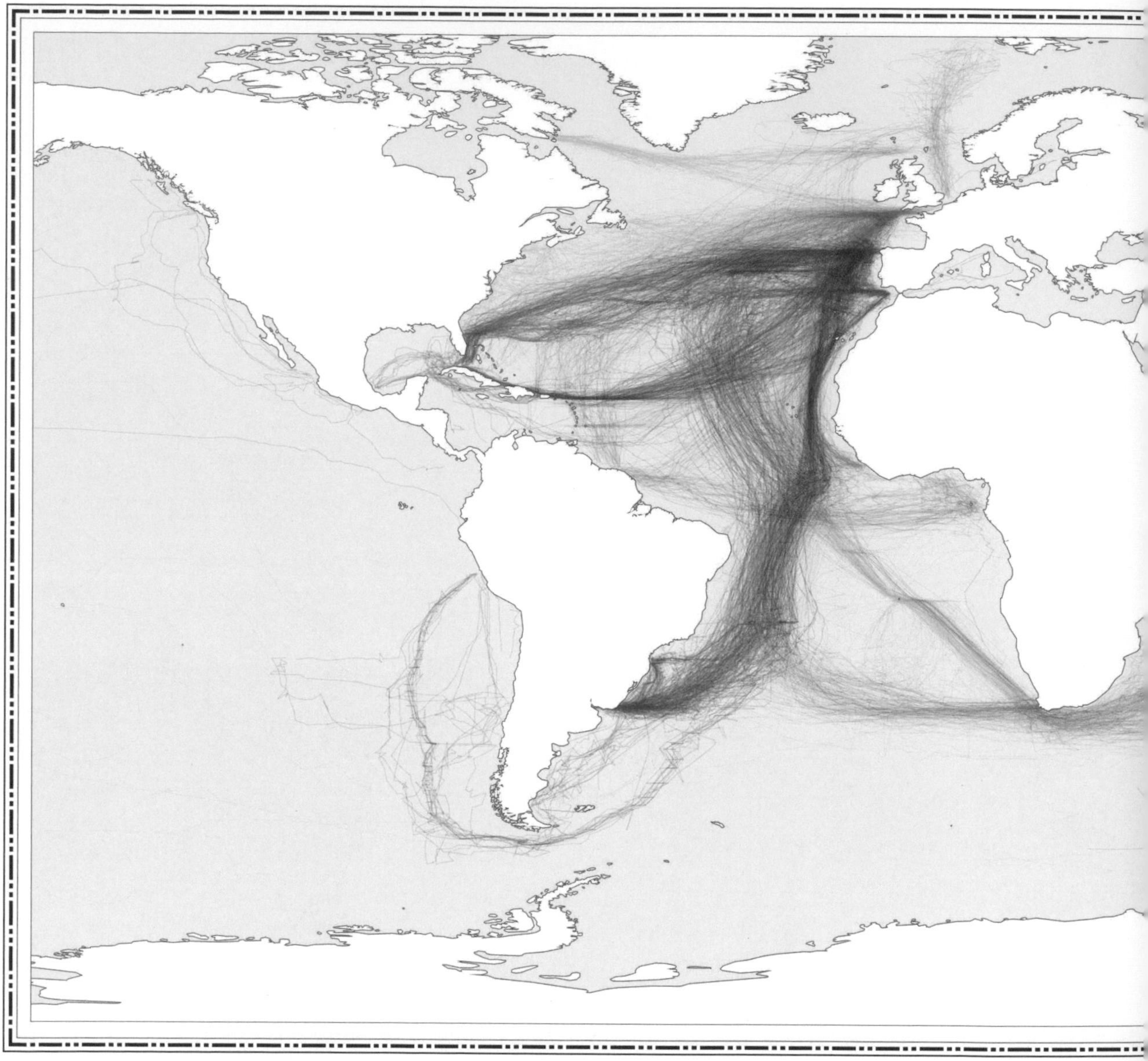

There's a jingoistic song that remains a faintly guilty pleasure for millions of Brits – "Rule Britannia, Britannia rules the waves." Thanks to pesky modern-day budget cuts, though, it's sadly no longer true: the United States has a much bigger navy.

However, if we jump back to the 18th century, when the song was written, the claim had a good case for being taken not as a boast, but as a simple statement of fact. And it's one backed up by an amazing dataset.

A project looking at climate change in the world's oceans gathered an array of location information from the logbooks of **British {■}**, **Spanish {■}** and **Dutch {■}** ships between 1750 and 1850 – and James Cheshire of University College, London, assembled the first 50 years of that information into this amazing graphic. It tells us that all three nations were eager and frequent travellers between the old and new worlds for

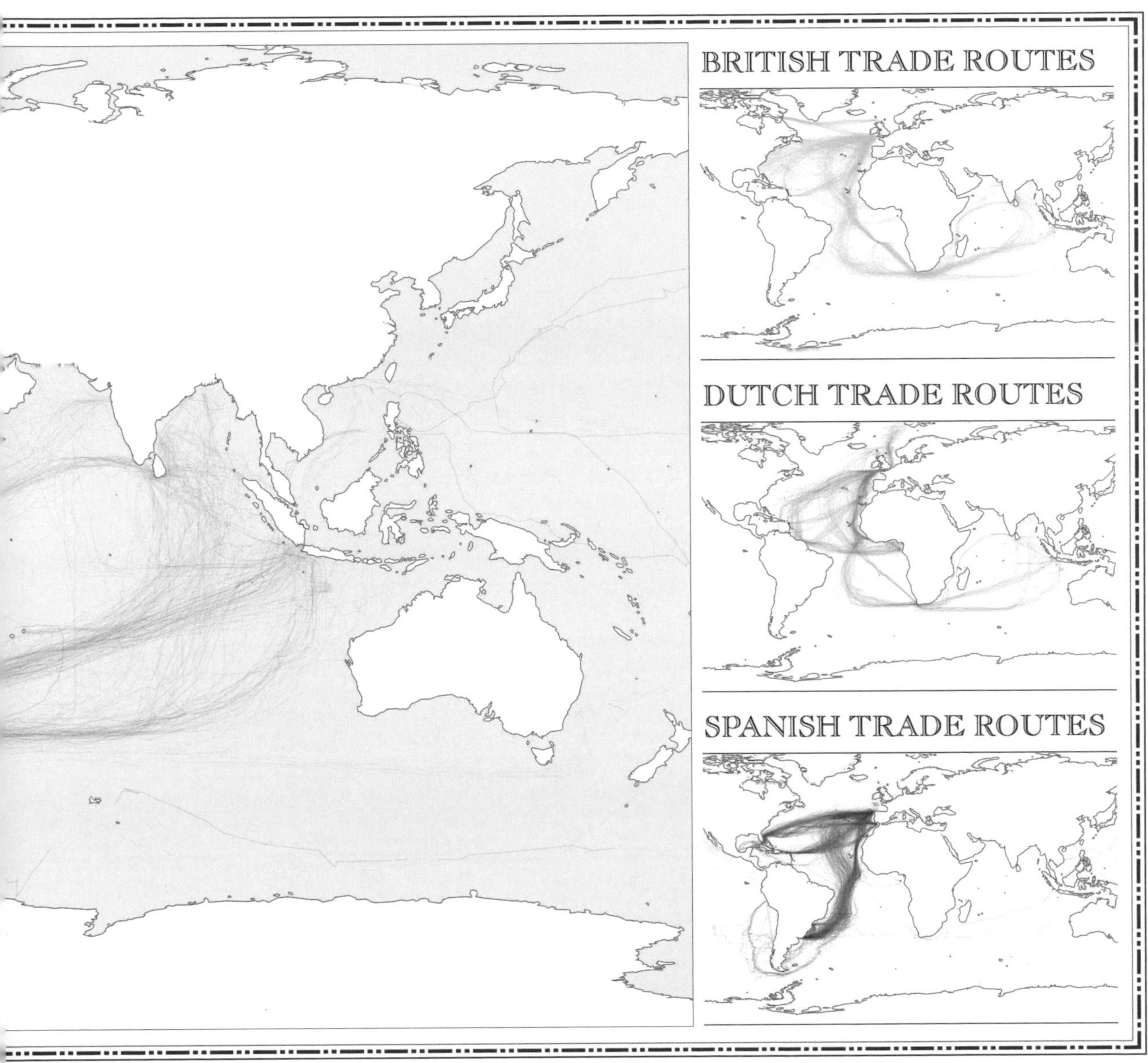

trade, but while Spain frequented both North and South America, the Dutch stuck largely to the South (and the Caribbean), and the British focused far more on the North.

The Brits were also the only one of the three great trading nations to bother making the trip to Canada all that often (maybe not a surprise given that a large chunk of Canada was a British colony). When it came to traversing the Cape of Good Hope for the perilous trip to Asia, the Brits won out again. Though numerous Dutch vessels plied their trade through these waters (the Spaniards never much bothered), British vessels dominated here too.

Whether Britain's naval dominance fuelled its trading empire or vice versa, the United Kingdom certainly had a good thing going. Jolly unfair that someone had to go and invent powered flight, and ruin the whole thing, really.

WHICH RULERS HAVE BEEN IN POWER THE LONGEST?

Long to reign o'er us

The U.K. enjoyed an outburst of good-natured patriotism to mark the Diamond Jubilee of **Queen Elizabeth** in 2012, lining the streets with lashings of bunting to congratulate the country's monarch on not dying (or getting deposed) for 60 years. And long may it continue – but how impressive is a 60-year reign as a national leader? How does it rank in history?

The first trick to staying on top for a long time is being born into it: comparing a list of the top 10 royal reigns with the top 10 non-royals (with verifiable dates) is telling. The top 10 monarchs have a total reign of 715 years – knocking the non-royals' 417 years into the dust. God, it seems, is in no rush to meet his anointed rulers on Earth.

The longest-ruling non-royal in history, at present, is **Fidel Castro**. Castro's 52-year tenure would place him just 134th in the royal rankings. The only thing worse for a long rule than not being a royal is being a democrat; all of the longest-lasting rulers tended, at the very least, towards the authoritarian. Several met a grisly end (just ask **Colonel Gaddafi** – if you've got a good medium).

So how does Queen Elizabeth rank? Not too badly; she's the 62nd-longest-reigning monarch in history, and at the time of writing, the second-longest-reigning living monarch, about five and a half years behind **Rama IX of Thailand**. Nice work, ma'am.

TERM	COUNTRY	ROYAL
82 years, 254 days	Swaziland	**Sobhuza II**
81 years, 234 days	Lippe (Holy Roman Empire)	**Bernhard VII**
78 years, 243 days	Henneberg-Schleusingen (HRE)	**Wilhelm IV**
77 years, 103 days	Reuss-Obergreiz (HRE)	**Heinrich XI**
75 years, 253 days	Palatinate-Sulzbach (HRE)	**Christian August**
74 years, 315 days	Phaltan (India)	**Muhoji IV Rao**
74 years, 87 days	Gondal state (India)	**Bhagvatsingh Sahib**
73 years, 282 days	Schaumburg-Lippe	**Georg Wilhelm**
73 years, 29 days	Baden	**Karl Friedrich**
72 years, 228 days	Nassau-Saarbrücken (HRE)	**John Louis**

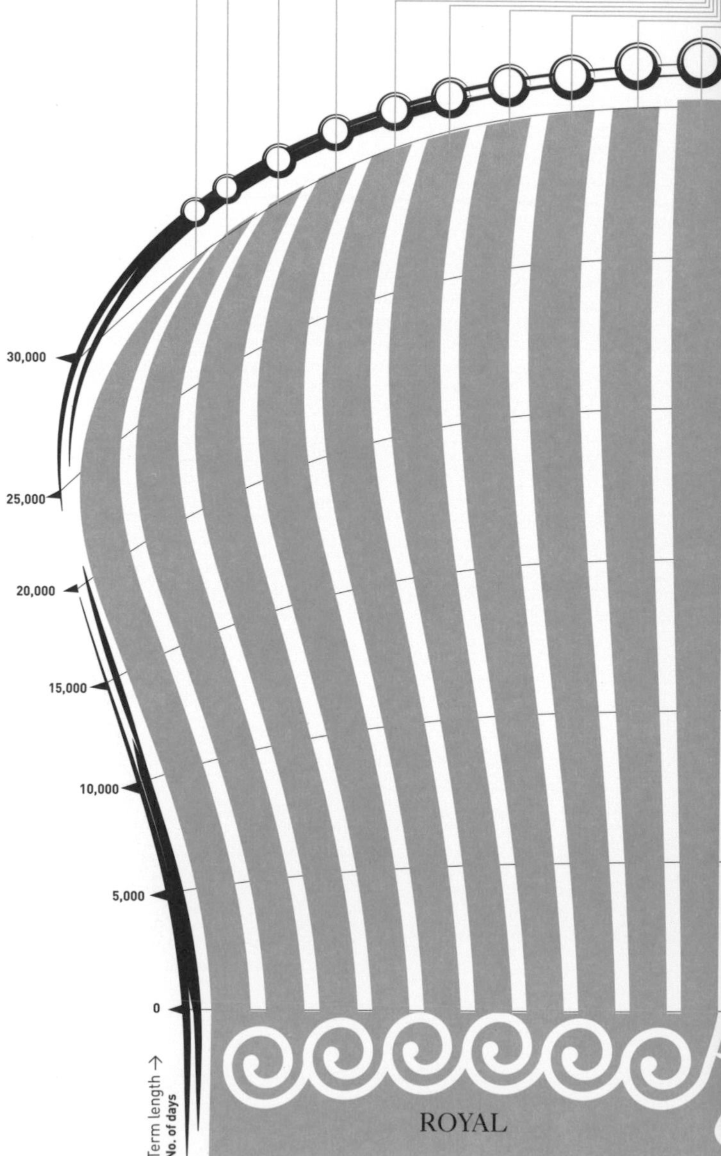

NON-ROYAL	COUNTRY	TERM
Fidel Castro	Cuba	52 years, 62 days
Kim Il-sung	North Korea	45 years, 302 days
Chiang Kai-shek	Republic of China	45 years, 57 days
Muammar Gaddafi	Libyan Arab Republic	42 years, 49 days
Omar Bongo	Gabon	41 years, 155 days
Enver Hoxha	Albania	40 years, 171 days
Francisco Franco	Spain	39 years, 50 days
Gnassingbé Eyadéma	Togo	37 years, 297 days
Josip Broz Tito	Yugoslavia	36 years, 157 days
António de Oliveira Salazar	Portugal	36 years, 82 days

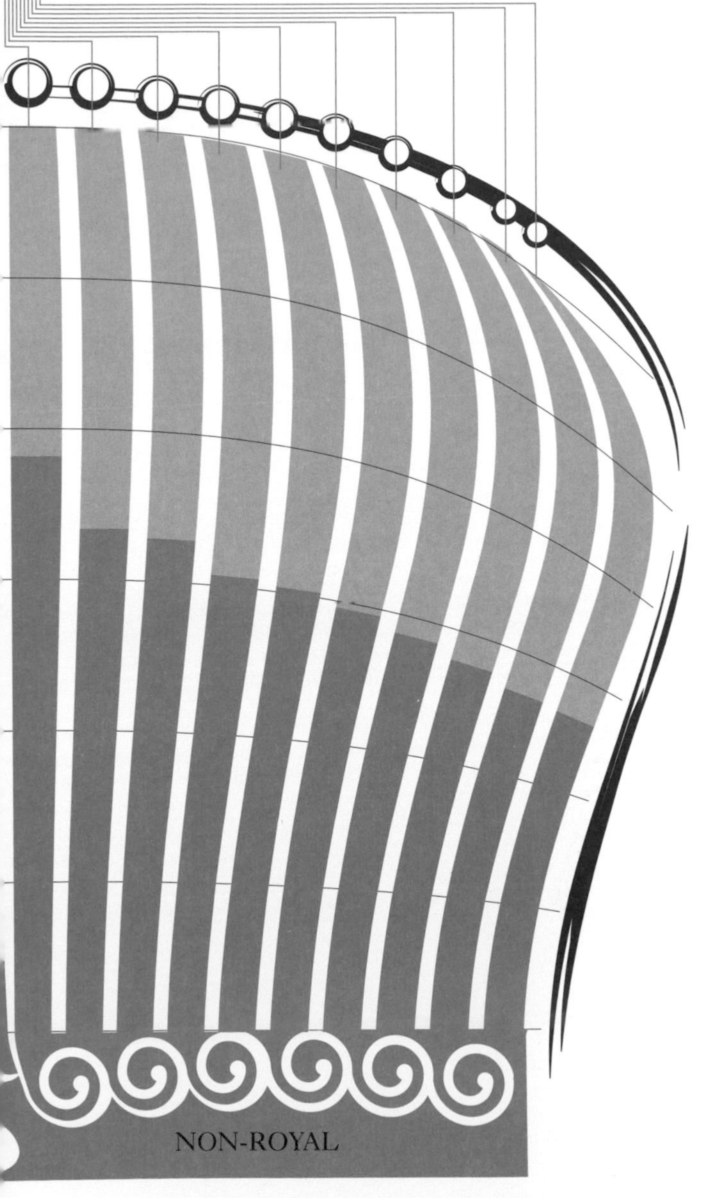

Rama IX
Thailand
66 years, 185 days

Elizabeth II
Commonwealth realms
60 years, 309 days

Abdul Halim
Kedah (Malaysia)
54 years, 149 days

Paul Biya
Cameroon
37 years, 161 days

Mohamed Abdelaziz
Sahrawi Republic
36 years, 100 days

T. Obiang Nguema Mbasogo
Equatorial Guinea
33 years, 127 days

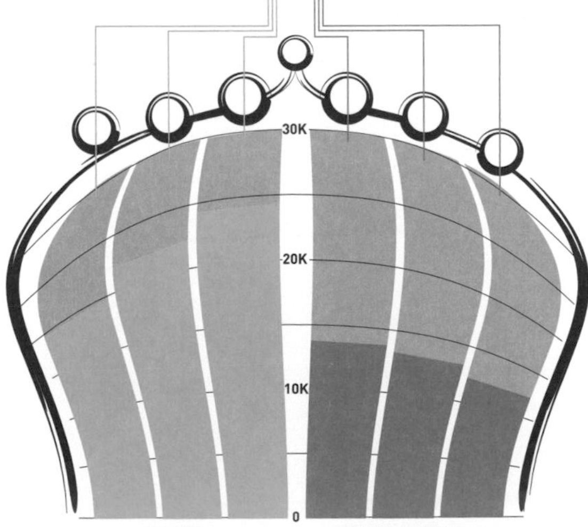

CURRENTLY RULING

Comparison of the longest royal and non-royal living tenures.

All about the money

It's easy (and fun!) to ignore the benefits of modern society. Frozen food tastes terrible, cities are soulless and devoid of nature, and we constantly hear about the miseries of sweatshops and evils of globalization. Frankly, the Industrial Revolution has got a lot to answer for.

Or does it? A fascinating set of figures – the life's work of the recently departed British economist Angus Maddison – suggests otherwise. He gathered figures for the size of the global economy from 1 CE to the present day. We're assuming they're estimates, because if he had a time machine, he kept it very cleverly under wraps.

The results are pretty stark. Correcting (approximately) for inflation and purchasing power, the world got roughly **three times** {x3} richer between year one and 1600.

To repeat that task – getting three times richer again – took about 270 years, taking us to 1870. By around the 1920s – a little over 50 years – the world's wealth had tripled again. Since then, that's happened two more times.

In short, after stagnating for almost two millennia, we've had an amazing economic boom, one that almost has to be seen to be believed. Lucky this is an infographics book, huh?

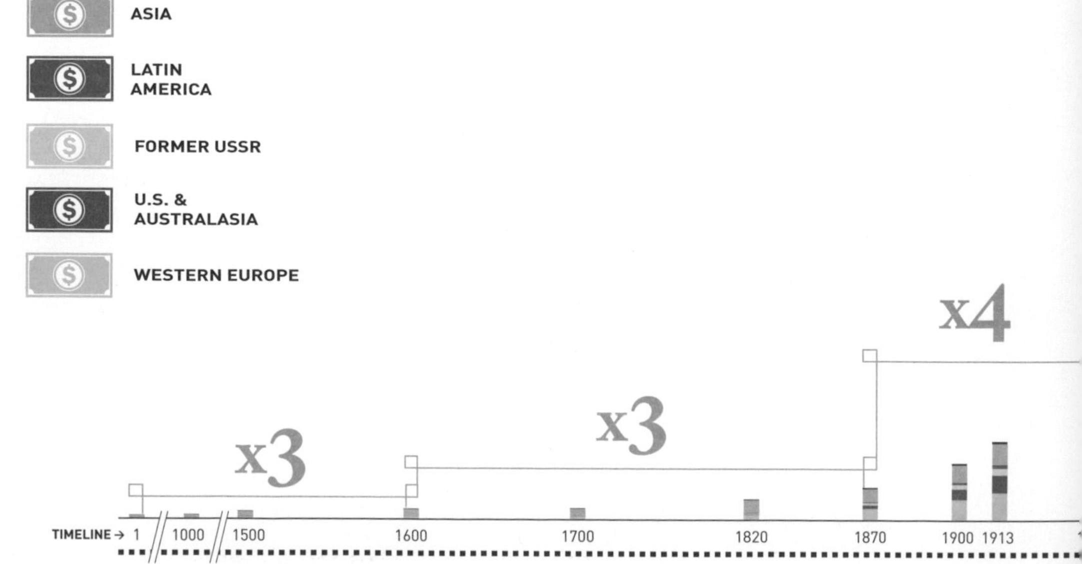

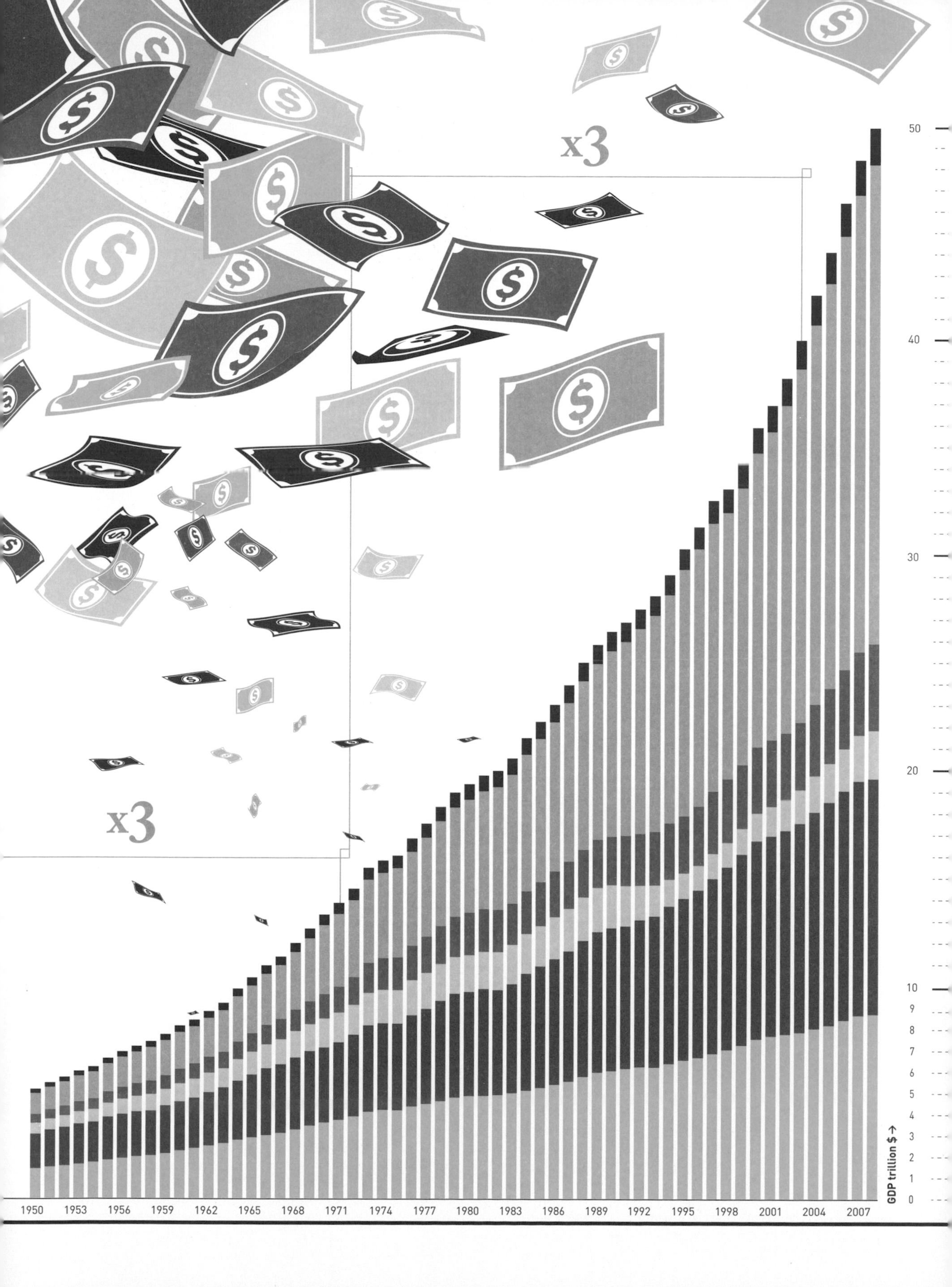
x3
x3
1950
1953
1956
1959
1962
1965
1968
1971
1974
1977
1980
1983
1986
1989
1992
1995
1998
2001
2004
2007
GDP trillion $ →
50
40
30
20
10
9
8
7
6
5
4
3
2
1
0

WHICH PARTS OF THE WORLD ARE WEALTHIEST?

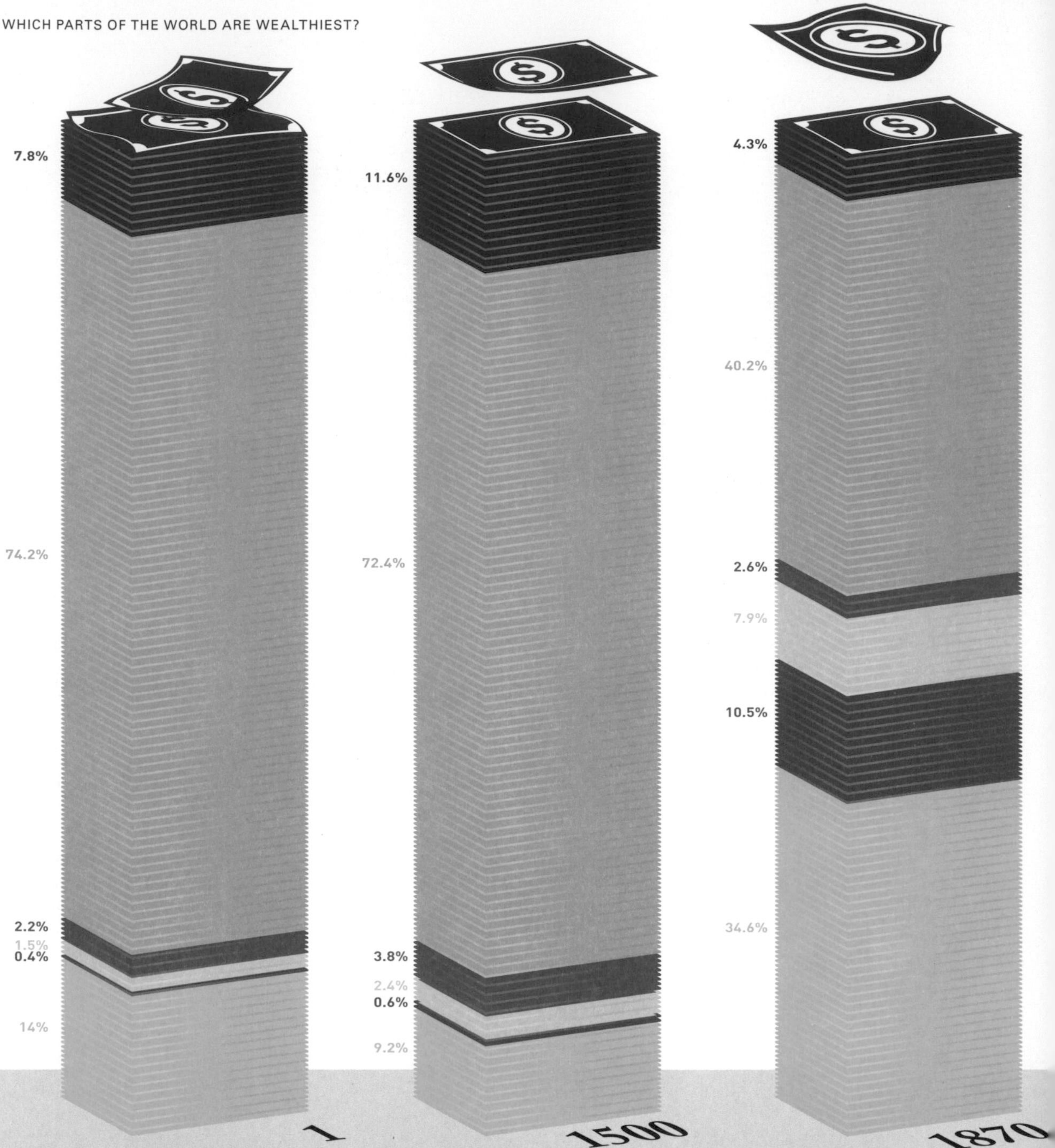

The long view also adds a little bit of context to one of the narratives of our times. The era of **U.S. { ■ }** dominance, we're told, is drawing to an end. At the time of writing, the U.S. economy was growing at about 1.5% a year – while China's growth is more than 7%. Forecasts suggest China's GDP will overtake that of the U.S. in the next decade.

Yet Maddison's research suggests that's less a new phenomenon than a return to what's happened throughout most of history. Prior to 1900, **Asia { ■ }** was the indisputable economic superpower. Perhaps we're just seeing history reassert itself.

Sadly, there's little sign of the same being true for **Africa { ■ }**. Once, the continent made up more than 10% of the world economy. For the last 60 years, it's never managed to top 4% – despite holding a huge trove of the world's raw materials.

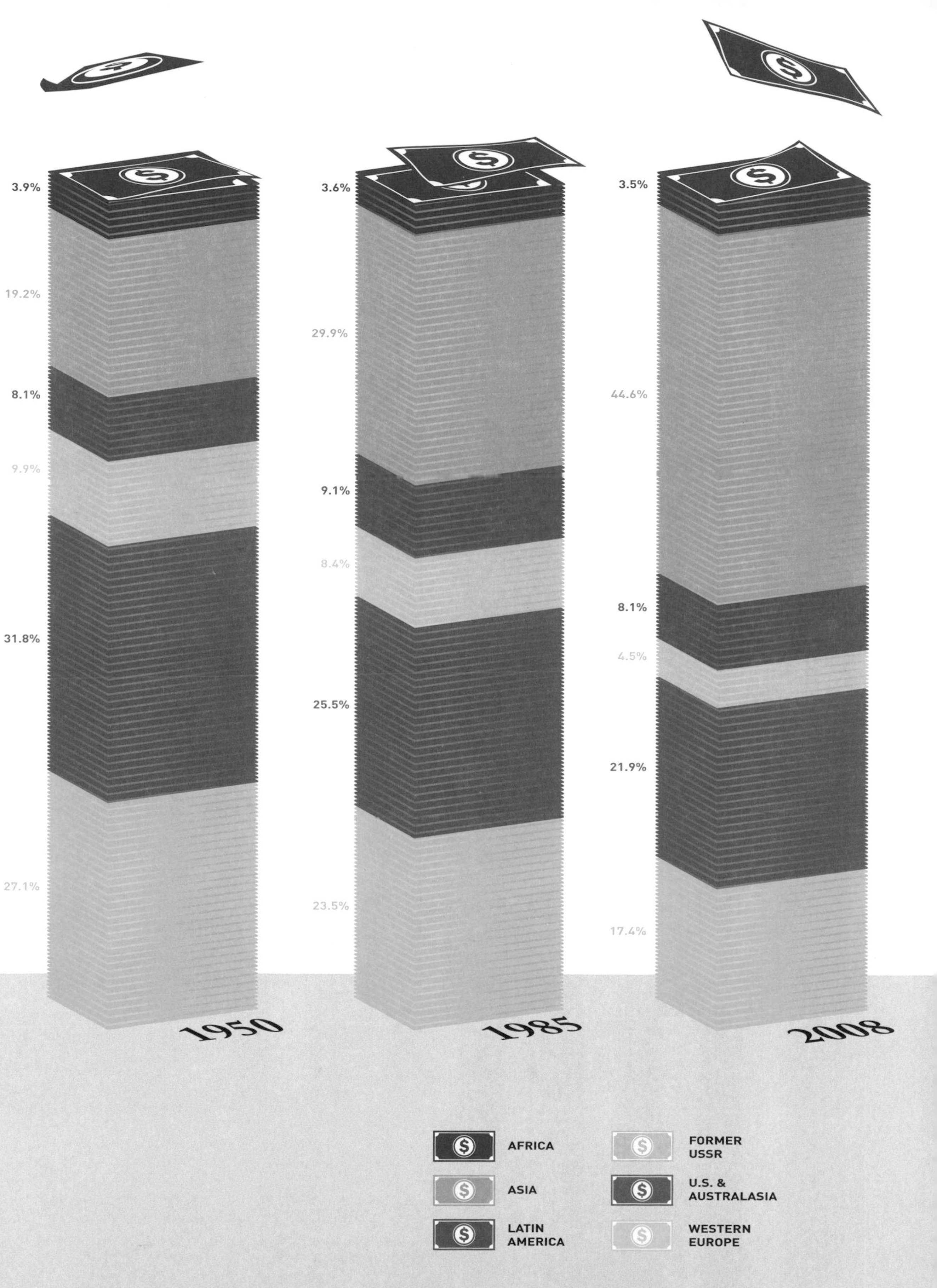

3.9%
19.2%
8.1%
9.9%
31.8%
27.1%
1950
3.6%
29.9%
9.1%
8.4%
25.5%
23.5%
1985
3.5%
44.6%
8.1%
4.5%
21.9%
17.4%
2008
AFRICA
ASIA
LATIN AMERICA
FORMER USSR
U.S. & AUSTRALASIA
WESTERN EUROPE

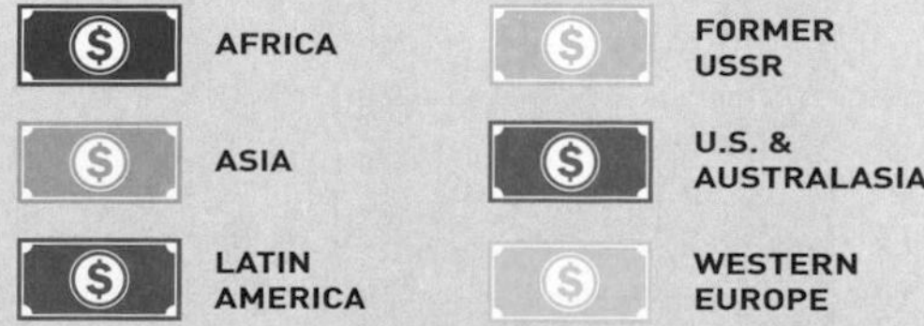

A rough guide to conflict

When we think about 20th-century wars, the two World Wars jump immediately to mind. What comes next depends on our generation, and our nation. For some, Vietnam would be the first candidate, for others, Korea – and for many under thirty, Iraq or Afghanistan would be the obvious candidates.

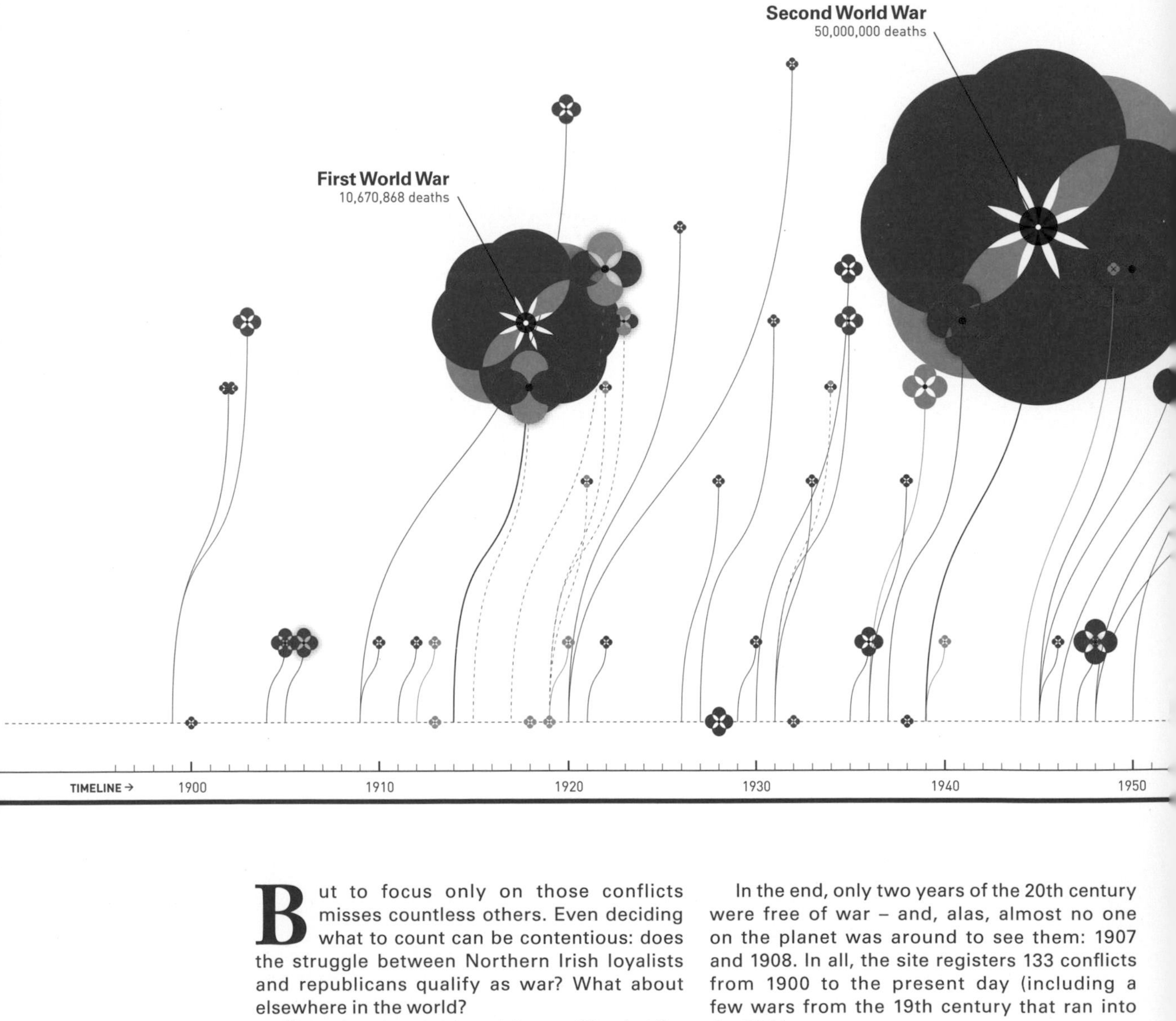

Second World War
50,000,000 deaths

First World War
10,670,868 deaths

TIMELINE → 1900 1910 1920 1930 1940 1950

But to focus only on those conflicts misses countless others. Even deciding what to count can be contentious: does the struggle between Northern Irish loyalists and republicans qualify as war? What about elsewhere in the world?

One attempt to chronicle conflict is The Polynational War Memorial website. Its results are sobering: even taking only those wars and disturbances that claimed at least 10,000 lives, looking for conflict-free years is a tough task.

In the end, only two years of the 20th century were free of war – and, alas, almost no one on the planet was around to see them: 1907 and 1908. In all, the site registers 133 conflicts from 1900 to the present day (including a few wars from the 19th century that ran into the 20th).

More chillingly still, the site keeps a tally of estimates of direct deaths due to those wars. At present, it stands at more than 95 million.

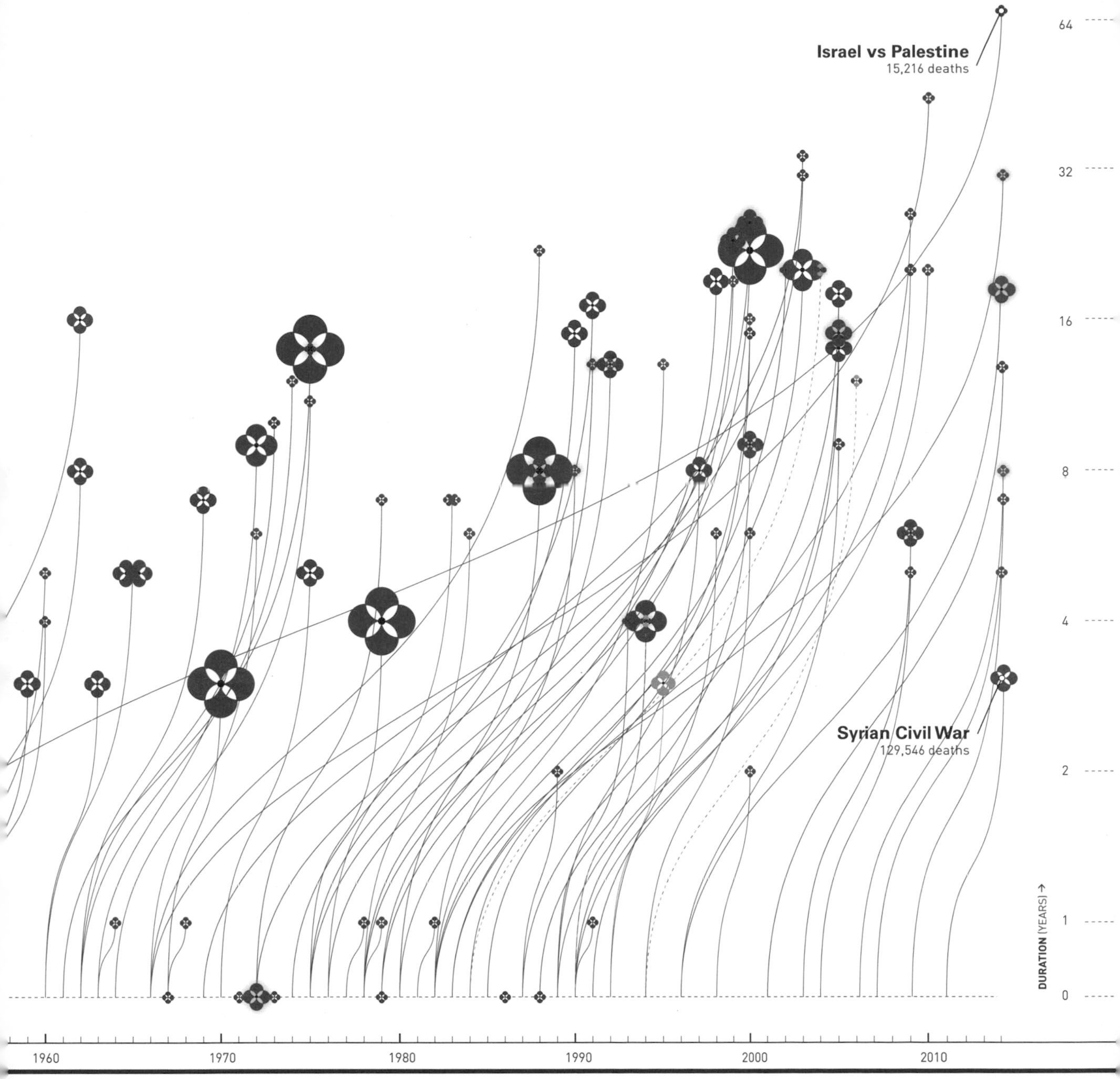

Israel vs Palestine
15,216 deaths
Syrian Civil War
129,546 deaths
64
32
16
8
4
2
1
0
DURATION (YEARS) →
1960
1970
1980
1990
2000
2010

POPPY DIAGRAM

Start
End
1
0
DURATION
(No. of years)
TIMELINE

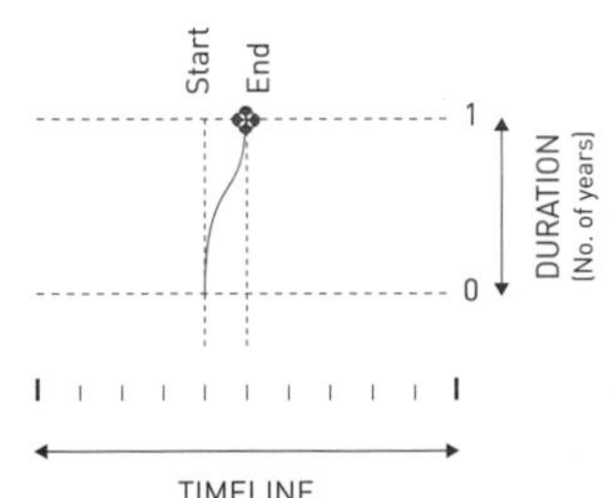

The remembrance poppy commemorates soldiers who have died in war. Each poppy in the diagram depicts a war of the last century (with more than 10,000 deaths). The stem grows from the year when the war started. The poppy flowers in the year the war ended. Its size shows the number of deaths.

NUMBER OF DEATHS (POPPY'S SIZE)

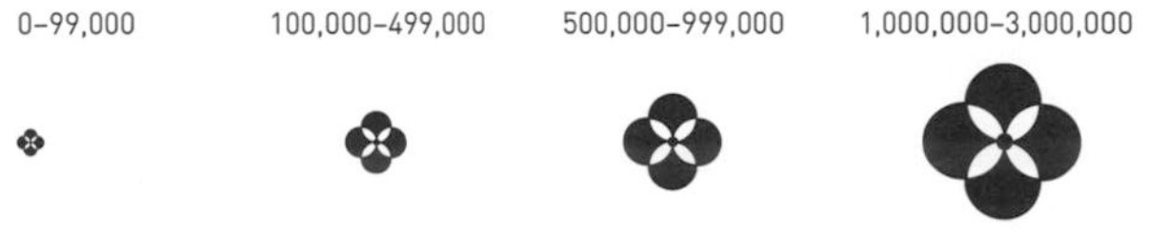

0–99,000
100,000–499,000
500,000–999,000
1,000,000–3,000,000

REGIONS INVOLVED IN WARS (POPPY'S COLOR)

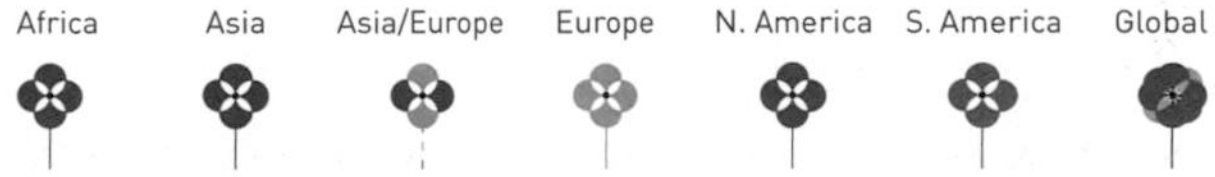

Africa
Asia
Asia/Europe
Europe
N. America
S. America
Global

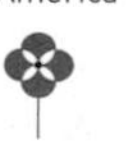

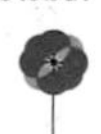

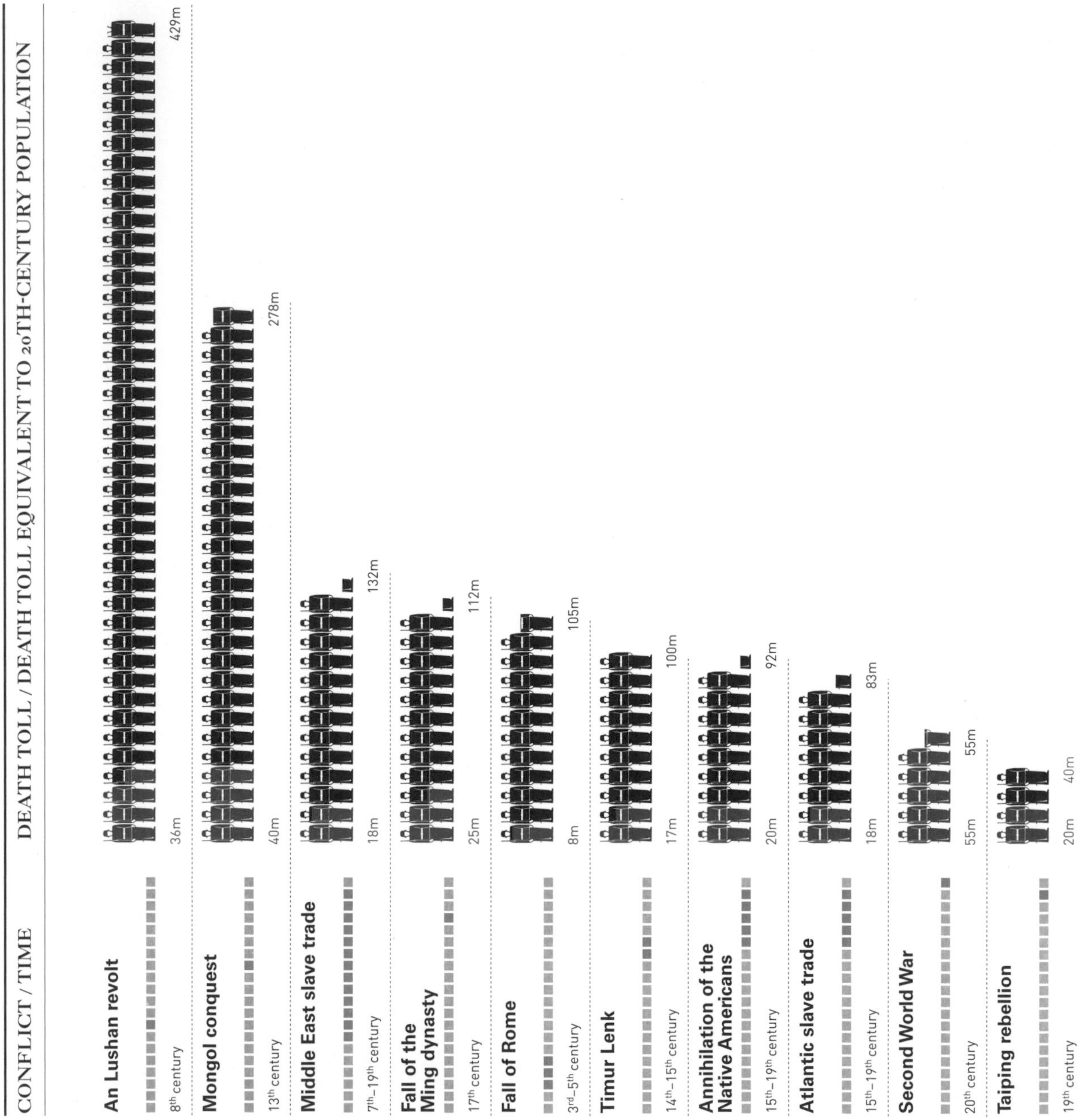

CONFLICT / TIME		DEATH TOLL / DEATH TOLL EQUIVALENT TO 20TH-CENTURY POPULATION	
An Lushan revolt	8th century	36m	429m
Mongol conquest	13th century	40m	278m
Middle East slave trade	7th–19th century	18m	132m
Fall of the Ming dynasty	17th century	25m	112m
Fall of Rome	3rd–5th century	8m	105m
Timur Lenk	14th–15th century	17m	100m
Annihilation of the Native Americans	15th–19th century	20m	92m
Atlantic slave trade	15th–19th century	18m	83m
Second World War	20th century	55m	55m
Taiping rebellion	19th century	20m	40m

To end all wars

The Second World War is often described as the deadliest in the world's history, with a terrible toll of 55 million dead over its six-year course.

No other conflict or man-made catastrophe has killed more than that, but simple numbers alone are not the only way to think about war. Take the US, which suffered the loss of 450,000 lives – second only to the **Civil War's** total of 620,000 dead across both sides.

Yet the population of the U.S. was four times higher in 1940 than 1860 – meaning the relative loss during the Civil War was even worse. The Civil War killed around one in 50 Americans, while the **Second World War** killed around one 1 in 300.

Both were terrible, but the scale of the losses relative to the size of the population was different by orders of magnitude. This is the principle behind work by Harvard professor Stephen Pinker into violence through the ages. He took 21 of history's worst atrocities, and rescaled them relative to the 20th-century population.

The results are displayed on this page. The heartening conclusion amid the grim body counts? The 20th century was not as bad as it first seemed: only one of the 10 worst atrocities happened in the last 100 years. We are, it seems, getting less, not more, violent with time.

As silver linings go, that's not a bad one.

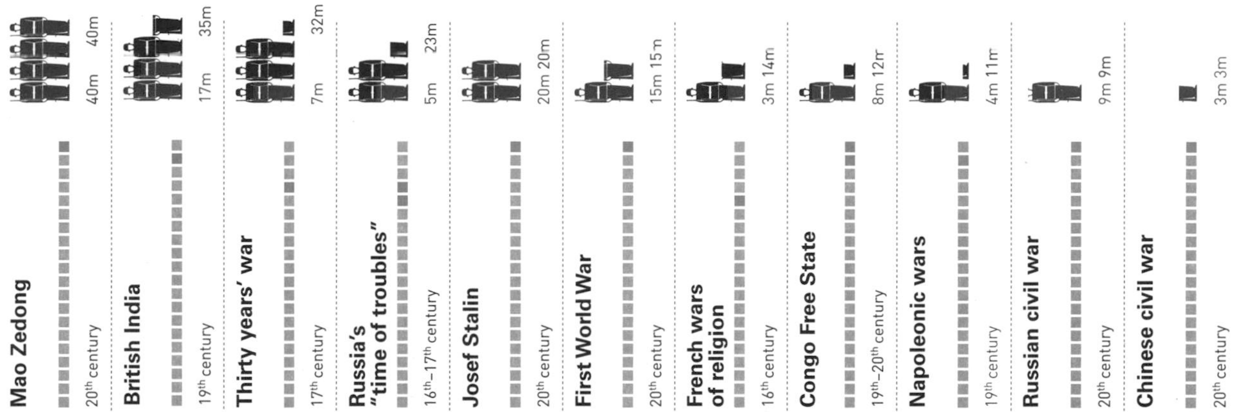

TIMELINE

1st 4th 8th 12th 16th 20th

1 SQUARE FOR 1 CENTURY

NUMBER OF DEATHS

1m 2m 3m 4m 5m 6m 7m 8m 9m 10m

1 MAN FOR 10 MILLION DEATHS

MODERN POPULATION COMPARISON

Death toll Death toll (Equivalent to 20th-century population)

COLOR INDEX

WHEN WERE THE GREAT ARTISTS AT WORK?

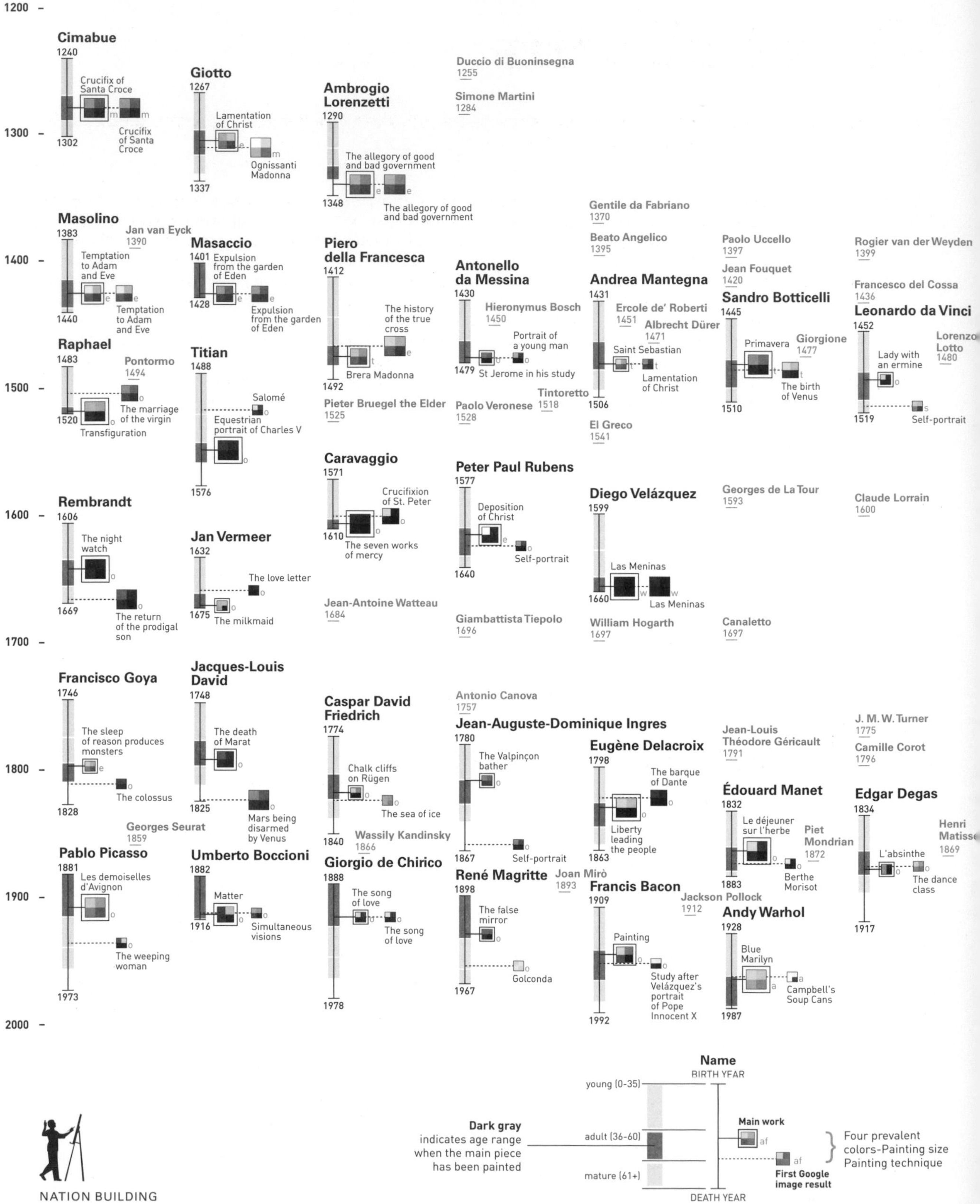

1200 –

Cimabue
1240
Crucifix of Santa Croce m
Crucifix of Santa Croce m
1302

Giotto
1267
Lamentation of Christ e
Ognissanti Madonna m
1337

Ambrogio Lorenzetti
1290
The allegory of good and bad government e
The allegory of good and bad government e
1348

Duccio di Buoninsegna
1255

Simone Martini
1284

1300 –

Gentile da Fabriano
1370

Masolino
1383
Temptation to Adam and Eve e
Temptation to Adam and Eve e
1440

Jan van Eyck
1390

Masaccio
1401
Expulsion from the garden of Eden e
Expulsion from the garden of Eden e
1428

Piero della Francesca
1412
The history of the true cross e
Brera Madonna t
1492

Antonello da Messina
1430
Portrait of a young man o
St Jerome in his study o
1479

Hieronymus Bosch
1450

Beato Angelico
1395

Andrea Mantegna
1431
Saint Sebastian t
Lamentation of Christ t
1506

Ercole de' Roberti
1451

Albrecht Dürer
1471

Paolo Uccello
1397

Jean Fouquet
1420

Sandro Botticelli
1445
Primavera t
The birth of Venus t
1510

Giorgione
1477

Rogier van der Weyden
1399

Francesco del Cossa
1436

Leonardo da Vinci
1452
Lady with an ermine o
Self-portrait s
1519

Lorenzo Lotto
1480

1400 –

Raphael
1483
The marriage of the virgin o
Transfiguration o
1520

Pontormo
1494

Titian
1488
Salomé o
Equestrian portrait of Charles V o
1576

Pieter Bruegel the Elder
1525

Paolo Veronese
1528

Tintoretto
1518

El Greco
1541

1500 –

Caravaggio
1571
Crucifixion of St. Peter o
The seven works of mercy o
1610

Peter Paul Rubens
1577
Deposition of Christ e
Self-portrait o
1640

Diego Velázquez
1599
Las Meninas w
Las Meninas w
1660

Georges de La Tour
1593

Claude Lorrain
1600

Rembrandt
1606
The night watch o
The return of the prodigal son o
1669

Jan Vermeer
1632
The love letter o
The milkmaid o
1675

Jean-Antoine Watteau
1684

Giambattista Tiepolo
1696

William Hogarth
1697

Canaletto
1697

1600 –

1700 –

Francisco Goya
1746
The sleep of reason produces monsters e
The colossus o
1828

Jacques-Louis David
1748
The death of Marat o
Mars being disarmed by Venus o
1825

Caspar David Friedrich
1774
Chalk cliffs on Rügen o
The sea of ice o
1840

Antonio Canova
1757

Jean-Auguste-Dominique Ingres
1780
The Valpinçon bather o
Self-portrait o
1867

Eugène Delacroix
1798
The barque of Dante o
Liberty leading the people o
1863

Jean-Louis Théodore Géricault
1791

Édouard Manet
1832
Le déjeuner sur l'herbe o
Berthe Morisot o
1883

J. M. W. Turner
1775

Camille Corot
1796

Edgar Degas
1834
L'absinthe o
The dance class o
1917

Georges Seurat
1859

Wassily Kandinsky
1866

Piet Mondrian
1872

Henri Matisse
1869

1800 –

Pablo Picasso
1881
Les demoiselles d'Avignon o
The weeping woman o
1973

Umberto Boccioni
1882
Matter o
Simultaneous visions o
1916

Giorgio de Chirico
1888
The song of love o
The song of love o
1978

René Magritte
1898
The false mirror o
Golconda o
1967

Joan Mirò
1893

Francis Bacon
1909
Painting o
Study after Velázquez's portrait of Pope Innocent X o
1992

Jackson Pollock
1912

Andy Warhol
1928
Blue Marilyn a
Campbell's Soup Cans a
1987

1900 –

2000 –

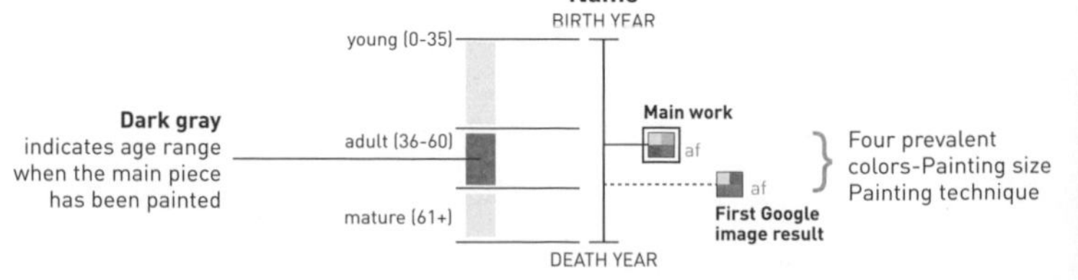

An artistic streak

The art world is really quite complicated, but we won't allow ourselves to go for the classic and easy cop-out: 'I don't know much about art, but I know what I like.'

The trouble is just how much there is to remember: which artists are associated with what style? When were they alive (and when were they painting)? What is their most famous work? And there's the small matter of what medium they painted with too...

Thankfully, a great visualization by Giorgia Lupi, adapted here, is a one-stop cheat sheet. It's a thing of elegance: not only does it give you a handy timeline of who's who in art, it tells you all the important facts, along with their top Google result (a neat 21st- century twist), and even the size of their most famous painting.

So the next time you're asked for your favorite 14th-century artwork – a question that I'm sure is put to you on an almost daily basis – rather than wearing an expression of baffled incomprehension, you can eloquently respond that it's probably Giotto's fresco of the Lamentation of Christ. Follow this up by remarking (whilst staring wistfully into the middle distance) that you've always wanted to see it in Padua's Scrovegni chapel. You'll have everyone convinced.

This chart should see you all the way through to the present day, covering Renaissance, Baroque, Romantic and even the birth of Modern art. You're very welcome.

One tip though: it's probably worth remembering a few of the highlights. Stylish as this book is, whipping it out for reference when in conversation at the gallery might just mark you as a bit of a cheat.

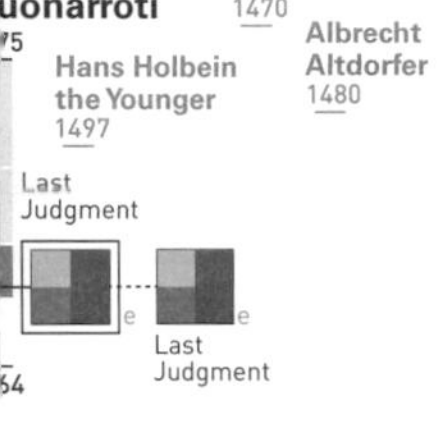

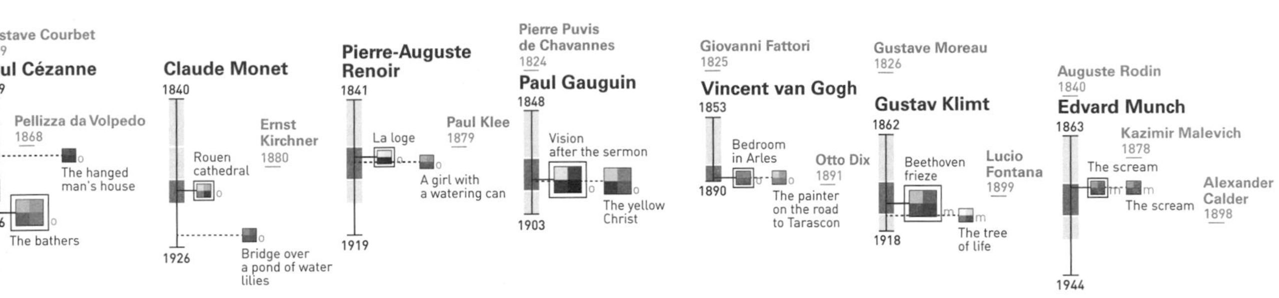

PAINTING SIZE (SQ M)

- **little** (up to 1)
- **medium** (from 1 to 4.5)
- **big** (from 4.5 to 14)
- **out of scale** (over 14)

PAINTING TECHNIQUE

a	**acrylic**	m	**mixed technique**
ena	**enamel**	o	**oil**
en	**engraving**	r	**ready-made**
e	**etching**	s	**sanguine**
f	**fresco**	t	**tempera**
i	**ink**	w	**watercolor**

The visualization shows 90 of the most important painters of the last eight centuries, 38 of whom are represented through their main pieces. The age range has been adjusted according to the life expectancy in each century, the main work is attributed according to the Le Garzantine *encyclopaedia* Arte*, and the Google image result is based on the first result for author's name and surname.*

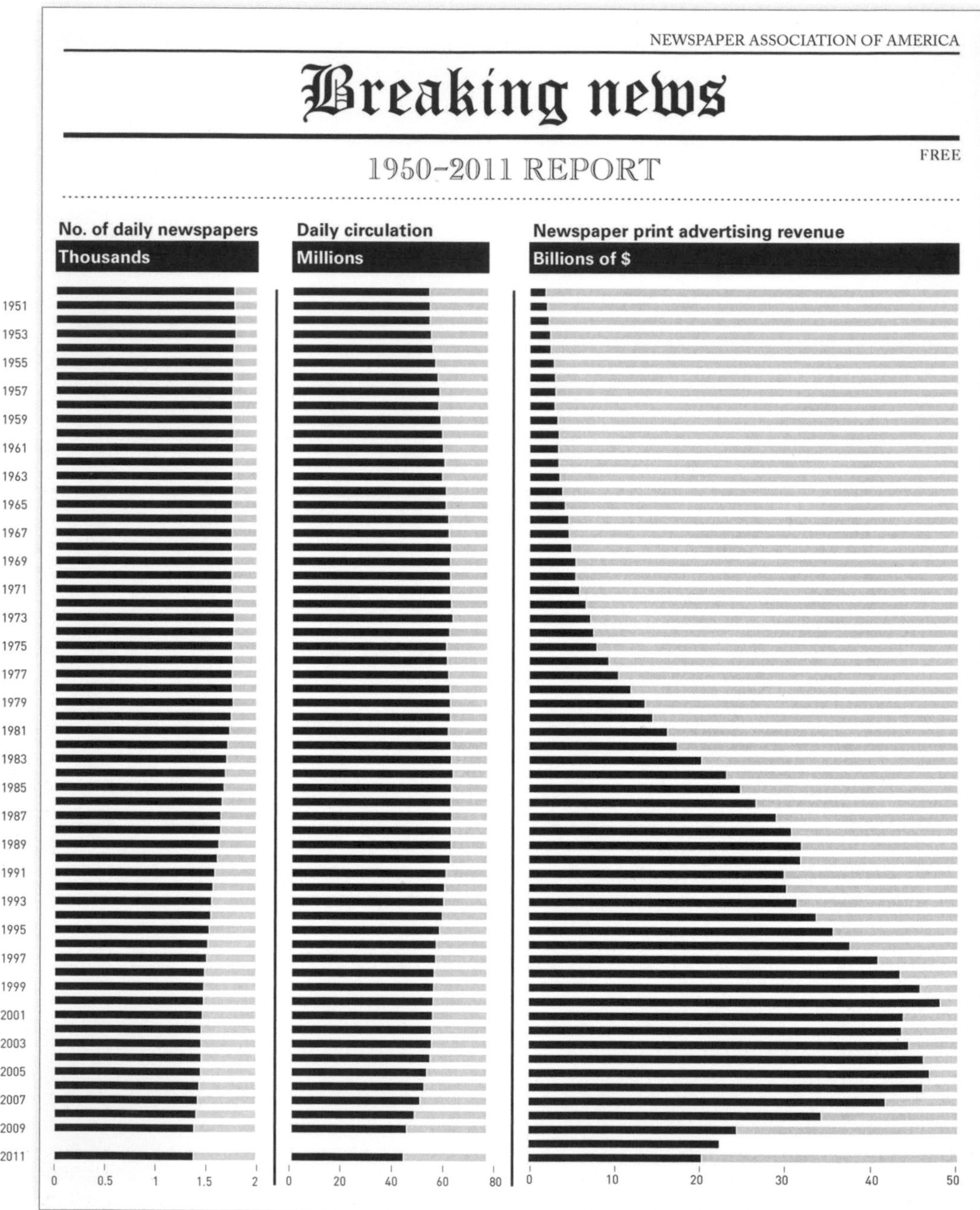
NEWSPAPER ASSOCIATION OF AMERICA
Breaking news
1950–2011 REPORT
FREE
No. of daily newspapers
Thousands
Daily circulation
Millions
Newspaper print advertising revenue
Billions of $
1951
1953
1955
1957
1959
1961
1963
1965
1967
1969
1971
1973
1975
1977
1979
1981
1983
1985
1987
1989
1991
1993
1995
1997
1999
2001
2003
2005
2007
2009
2011
0 0.5 1 1.5 2
0 20 40 60 80
0 10 20 30 40 50

Read all about it

If you've ever despaired of anything you've read in the newspapers – tabloid sleaze, phone hacking, smears or bias – the man who's probably ultimately more to blame than any other is Johannes Gutenberg.

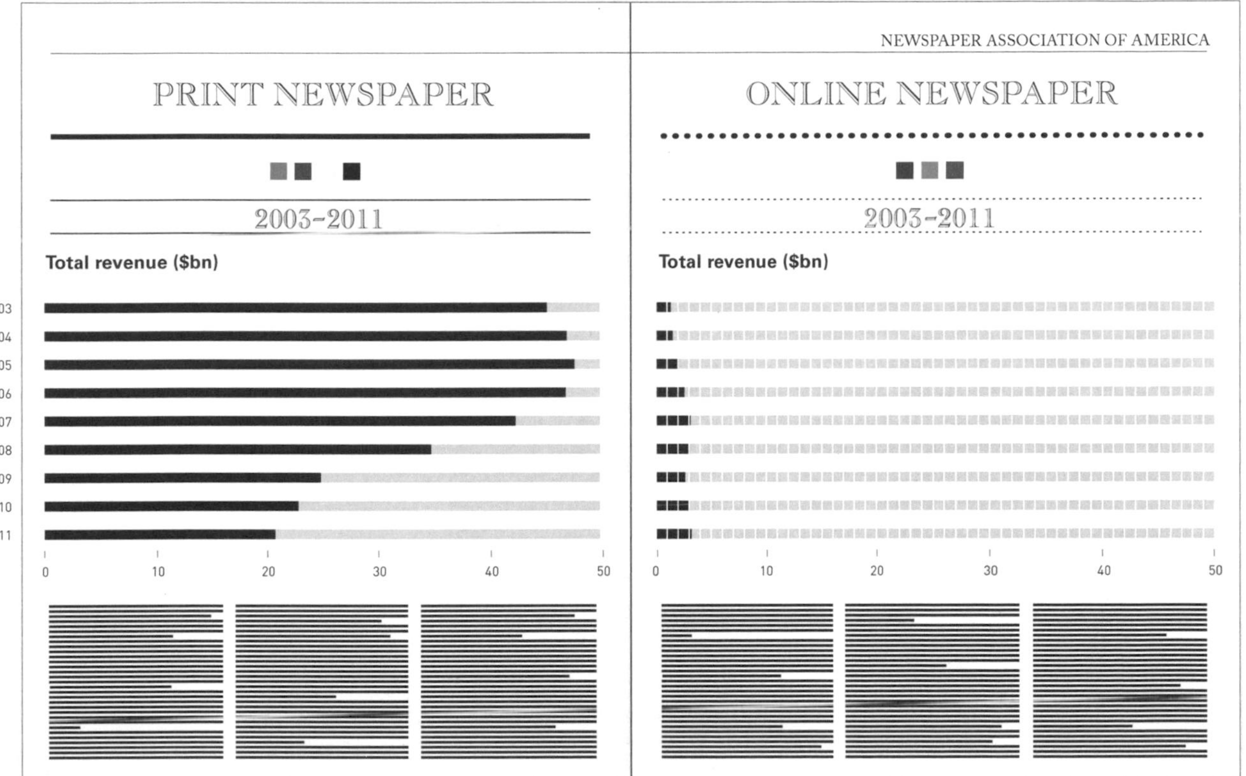

The good news for Gutenberg is he needn't worry about being summoned in front of Lord Leveson's inquiry into the British media. The bad news for him is that's because he's been dead for over 500 years.

But it was Gutenberg's invention of a printing press with movable type around the year 1439 that made possible the entire newspaper industry.

The first newspaper, which had grown out of newsletters and pamphlets, was published in Germany in 1605, while the oldest surviving paper in the world, the Swedish *Post-och Inrikes Tidningar*, began publishing in 1645. These days, it's online-only.

Looking at the economics of newspapers, it's not too hard to see why: the thing that's always driven their bottom line isn't the cash handed over by readers – it's the money received from advertisers. As classified ads and more have moved online, the papers have found themselves facing a serious problem.

The U.S. has the best data on this, but it's the same story around the world. In 1950, the U.S. had 1,772 daily papers. By 2011, this had plummeted to 1,382. Circulation rose between 1950 and 1990 from 53 million to more than 62 million. Then the internet arrived and it sank to 44 million.

The ad numbers are scarier still. In 2003, U.S. print advertising in papers was worth $44bn a year. By 2011, it was less than $21bn – and new online ads only filled $3bn of the gap.

Amid the gloom about the internet, there's one fact worth remembering: more people read the papers than ever. Take the *Guardian*: fewer than 250,000 people a day pick up a printed copy, but every month more than 68 million people worldwide read it online.

Truly, papers live in interesting times...

REVOLUTIONS
Number of deaths
Duration
Outcome
War of Independence
MEXICO
1810–1821
23,000
French Revolution
FRANCE
1789–1799
210,000
American Revolution
UNITED STATES
1775–1783
70,000
Glorious Revolution
ENGLAND
1688–1689
none
English Civil War
ENGLAND
1642–1651
190,000
Russian Civil War
RUSSIA
1917–1922
1,400,000
Chinese Civil War
CHINA
1927–1950
3,200,000
Spanish Civil War
SPAIN
1936–1939
Cuban Revolution
CUBA
1953–1959
Iranian Revolution
IRAN
1978–1979
3,000

Working men of the world, unite!

"Working men of the world, unite! You have nothing to lose but your chains" was Marx and Engels' plea to the proletariat. Had they been entirely truthful, they might have added "and maybe a limb or two, possibly your freedom, and maybe your life," but it pays to be positive when recruiting for the cause.

The reality is that revolutions are no picnic: not only do they tend to be violent in themselves, but they're often followed up by some pretty nasty atrocities. It's enough to lead a cynical man to ponder the word: a revolution of a wheel, after all, leaves you pretty much back where you started.

But still, such events have changed the world for the better and shaped many of our modern nations, so here we've compared a couple of the more significant revolutions and civil wars. Death counts have been kept to the duration of the revolution – not any subsequent actions of the new governments.

One revolution isn't quite like the others: England's **Glorious Revolution**. The elites, unhappy with their monarch, politely invited a foreign ruler to invade, and discouraged opposition. As he was helpfully married to the current monarch's daughter, once the unpopular king (James II) had fled the royal line could continue largely uninterrupted. A very British coup indeed (and largely bloodless, though it did spark other conflicts).

Others were less fortunate: 19th-century revolutions had body counts in the hundreds of thousands, and in the 20th century they numbered in the millions. Whether the triumphant revolutionaries felt their new rulers were worth the trouble is largely, alas, unknowable...

Number of deaths

■ 2,000 DEATHS

Duration

■ 1 YEAR

Outcome

COMMUNISM

FASCISM

INDEPENDENCE

NEW MONARCH

 REPUBLICANISM

 THEOCRACY

Give me freedom!

Slavery, you'll be pleased to hear, was abolished in 250 BCE. The Indian ruler of the time banned the trade and urged the good treatment of the remaining slaves – which lasted, for a time.

It was, in reality, the first of dozens upon dozens of futile attempts to do away with the trade that is still the blight of many Western nations' history, and which was the driving factor behind the United States' seismic civil war.

Britain made numerous attempts to outlaw the practice: London first outlawed slaves and serfdom in 1102, and Magna Carta (which was used as a basis for anti-slavery laws) was signed in 1205.

English courts and politicians regularly stressed the trade's illegality from the 16th century onward – and yet it became the core of an empire. In almost every country around the world, slavery is notionally illegal. Saudi Arabia abolished the practice in 1962, as did Yemen, with the United Arab Emirates following suit the next year.

But still the practice persists, and campaigners say there are more slaves alive today than ever before, at 21 million. They're distributed around the world, often hidden, and not necessarily doing what you might think. Only around 2 million are believed to be doing state-mandated forced labor. Despite the focus on the horrors of human trafficking and the sex trade, these people are estimated to be just 4.5 million of the total. The rest – 14.2 million – are working as forced laborers, often indentured for debt repayments they can't afford.

Perhaps the most jarring estimate is this: in modern currency, a slave in the American South would trade for around $40,000. In parts of the world today, the value of a slave – as they're much easier to find and keep – has fallen to just $90.

The chain shows the distribution of modern-day slaves by geographical region.

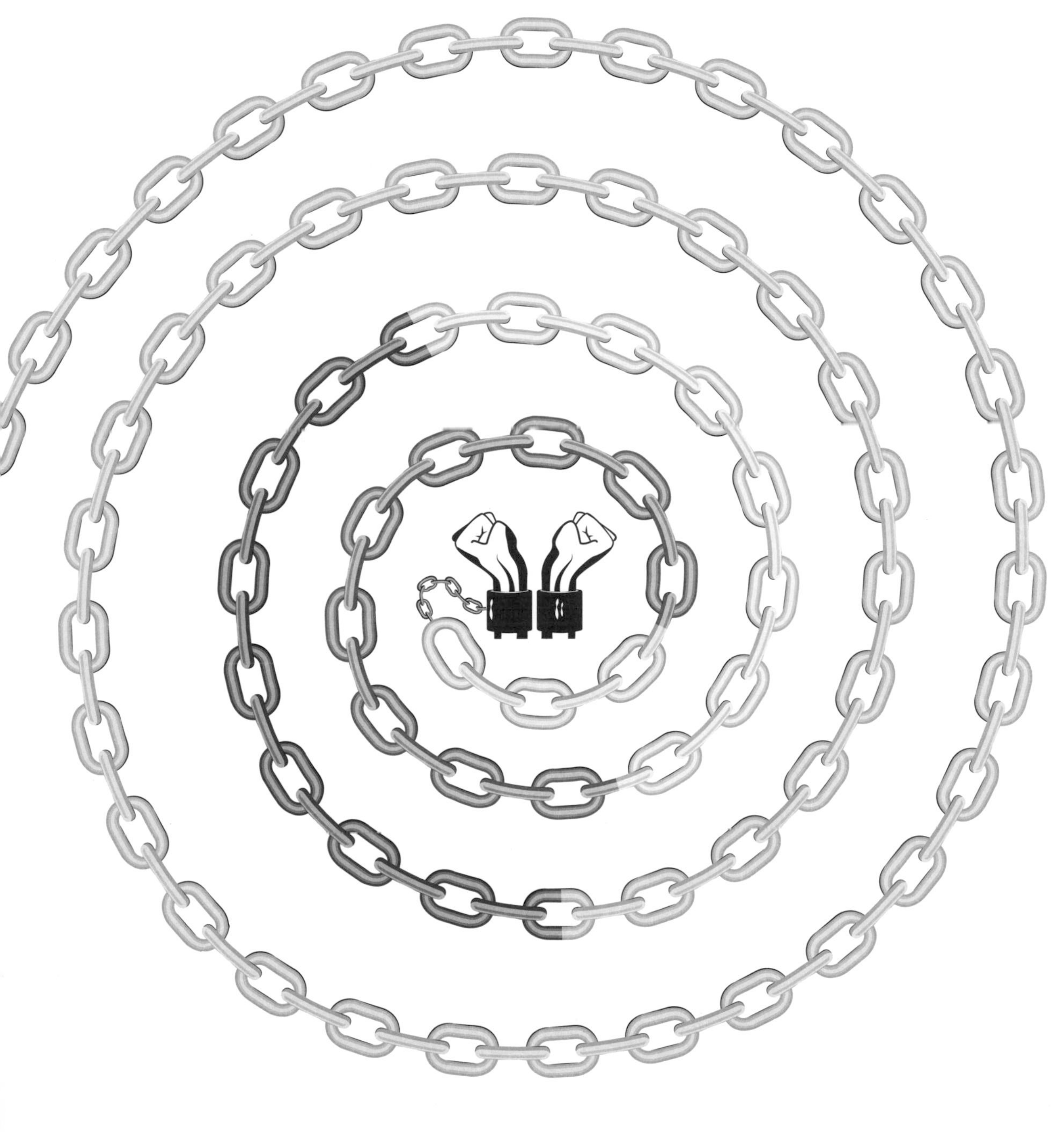

FORCED LABOR BY REGION (Number of people in millions)

- **3.7** AFRICA
- **11.7** ASIA-PACIFIC
- **1.6** CENTRAL AND SOUTH-EASTERN EUROPE AND CIS [Eastern Europe/transition states]
- **1.5** DEVELOPED ECONOMIES AND EUROPEAN UNION
- **1.8** LATIN AMERICA AND THE CARIBBEAN
- **0.6** MIDDLE EAST

WHICH GOODS AND COUNTRIES USE FORCED LABOR?

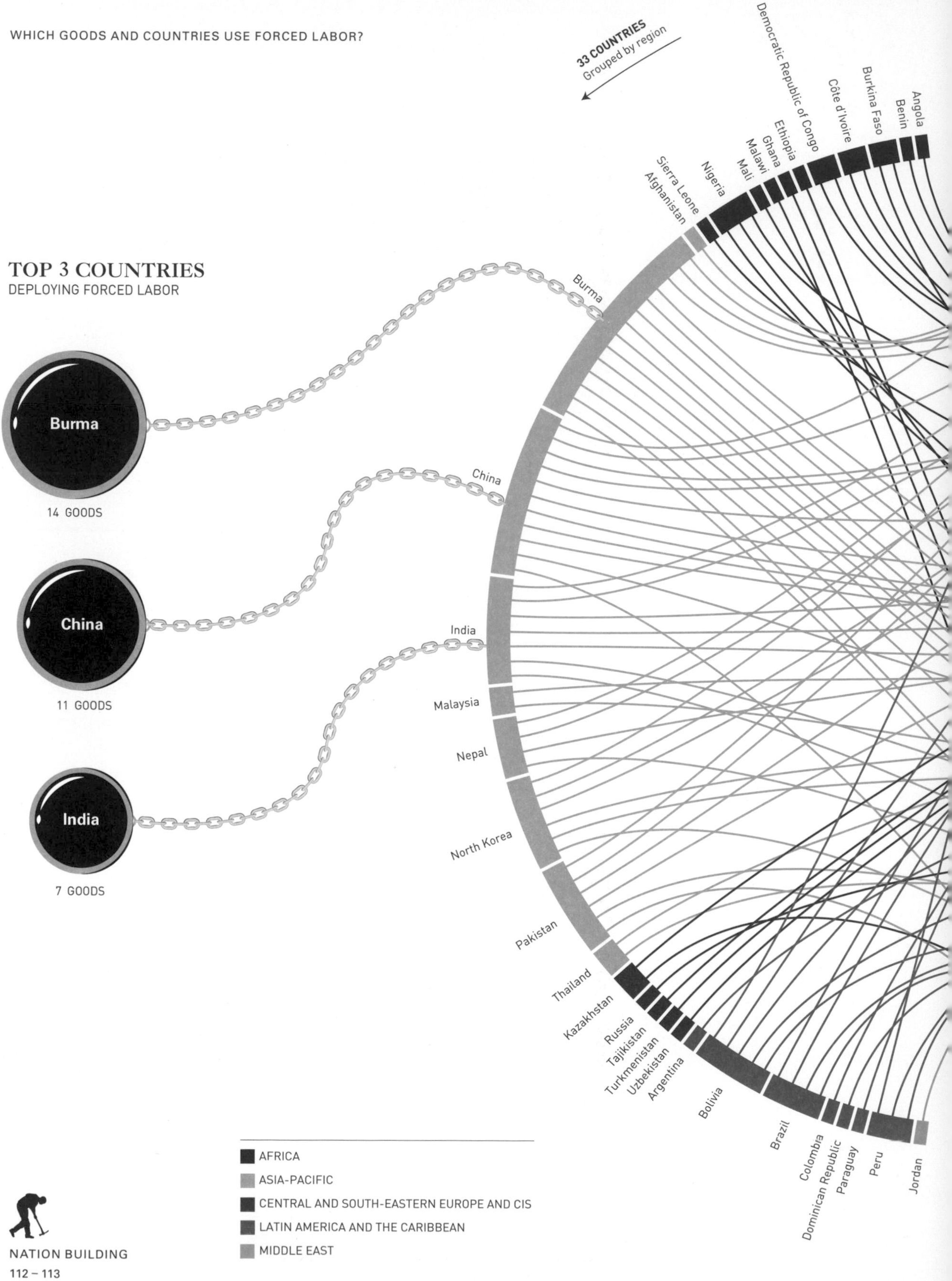

33 COUNTRIES
Grouped by region

Angola
Benin
Burkina Faso
Côte d'Ivoire
Democratic Republic of Congo
Ethiopia
Ghana
Malawi
Mali
Nigeria
Sierra Leone
Afghanistan
Burma
China
India
Malaysia
Nepal
North Korea
Pakistan
Thailand
Kazakhstan
Russia
Tajikistan
Turkmenistan
Uzbekistan
Argentina
Bolivia
Brazil
Colombia
Dominican Republic
Paraguay
Peru
Jordan

TOP 3 COUNTRIES
DEPLOYING FORCED LABOR

Burma
14 GOODS

China
11 GOODS

India
7 GOODS

AFRICA
ASIA-PACIFIC
CENTRAL AND SOUTH-EASTERN EUROPE AND CIS
LATIN AMERICA AND THE CARIBBEAN
MIDDLE EAST

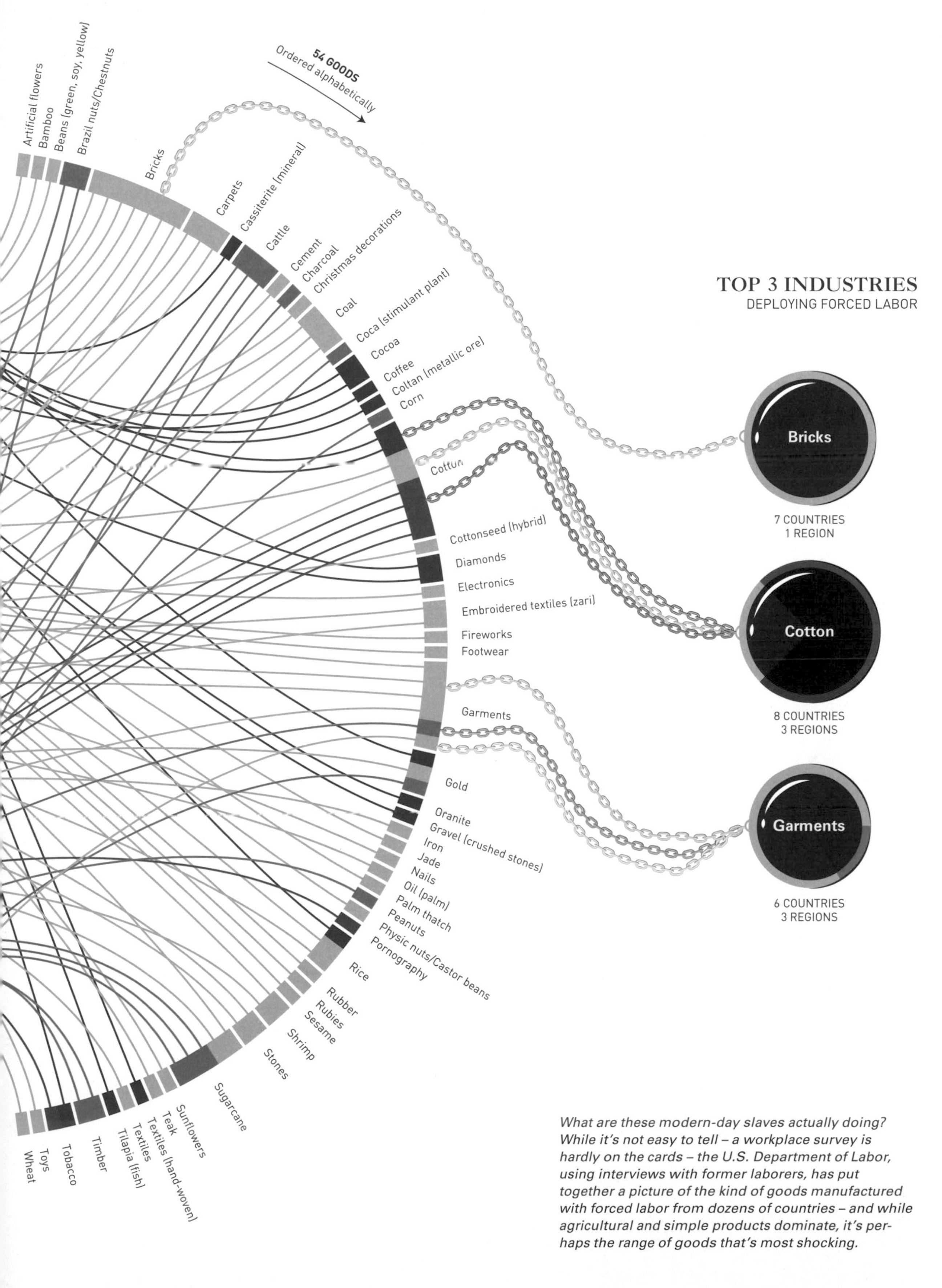

What are these modern-day slaves actually doing? While it's not easy to tell – a workplace survey is hardly on the cards – the U.S. Department of Labor, using interviews with former laborers, has put together a picture of the kind of goods manufactured with forced labor from dozens of countries – and while agricultural and simple products dominate, it's perhaps the range of goods that's most shocking.

A different kind of revolution

It might have lacked the drama of a more traditional revolution, but the Industrial Revolution – in which Britain led the way – was perhaps the most significant step toward the modern era of anything in this book.

The Industrial Revolution was, on one level, perhaps a more sedate affair than its name suggests, with a first phase from around 1760 to 1830, which revolutionized the textile industry and led to the growth of factories and the decline of homework. A second phase was powered by a host of new technologies like the combustion engine and electricity.

What made the results so special was the symbiosis: advances in machinery (starting with better textile machines like the Spinning Jenny in 1764) led to shifts in how people worked, especially as looms leaped to industrial scale, requiring more capital than a house-worker could provide. These led to the growth of factories, and economies of scale – incentivizing the building of new, yet larger machines. The results were extraordinary. After centuries of only marginal increases in wealth or production, Britain skyrocketed. Industrial production increased 25-fold between 1780–90 and 1905–13. In 1780–90, the U.K. produced just 69,000 tonnes of **pig iron {■}**. By 1875, it was making almost 6.5 million.

It was hardly a paradise, though. Skilled craftsmen bitterly mourned the death of their trades, children were sent to work at a very young age in brutal and dangerous workplaces, and workers rights, holidays, and health and safety all took decades to secure.

But over the course of just a few decades, virtually every comfort and convenience of the modern era – along with many of its ills too – were born.

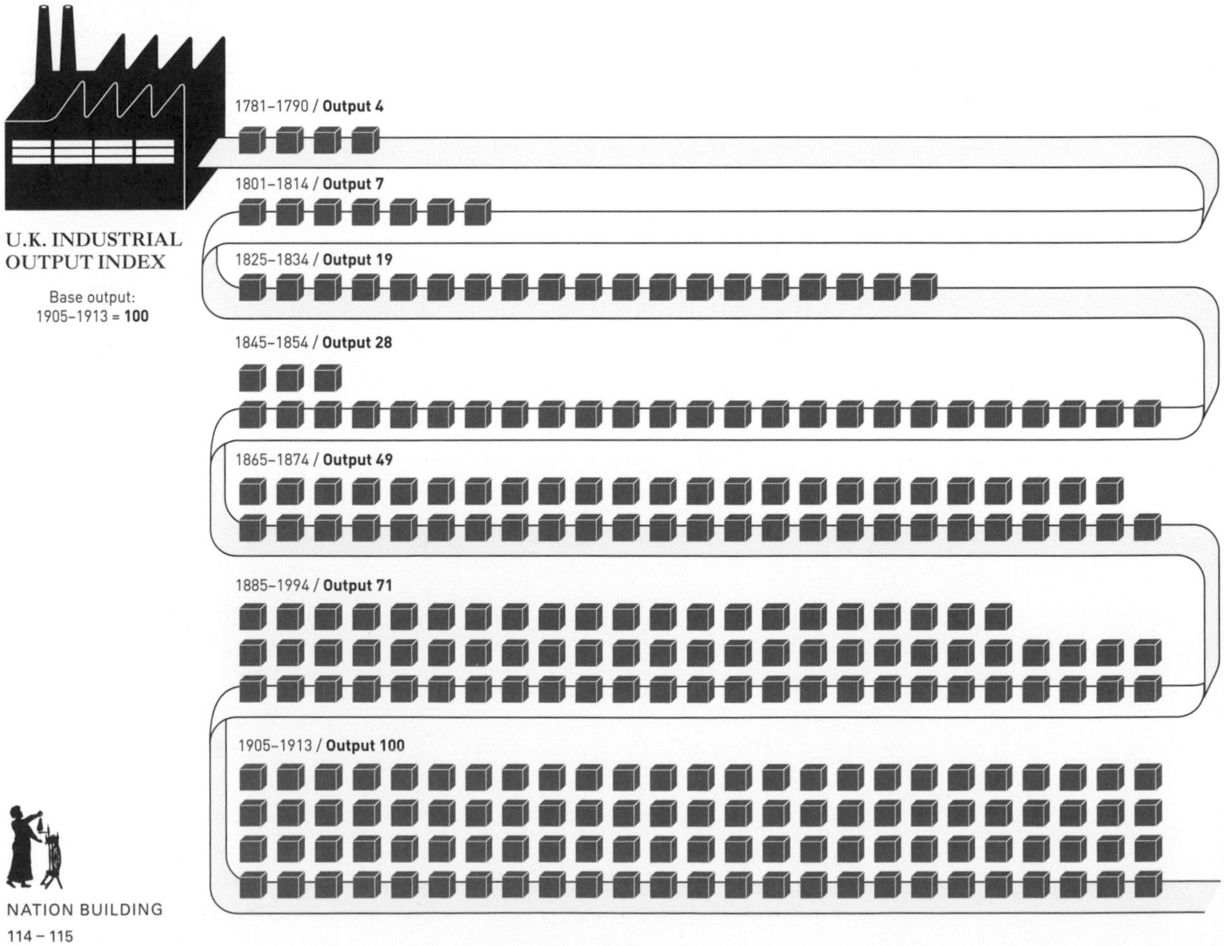

U.K. INDUSTRIAL OUTPUT INDEX

Base output: 1905–1913 = **100**

1781–1790 / **Output 4**

1801–1814 / **Output 7**

1825–1834 / **Output 19**

1845–1854 / **Output 28**

1865–1874 / **Output 49**

1885–1994 / **Output 71**

1905–1913 / **Output 100**

COAL AND LIGNITE

1 unit = 20 million tonnes

1820–1824 **17.7 million tonnes**

1840–1844 **34.2 million tonnes**

1860–1864 **86.3 million tonnes**

1880–1884 **158.9 million tonnes**

1900–1904 **230.4 million tonnes**

PIG IRON

1 unit = 200 thousand tonnes

1781–1790 **69k tonnes**

1825–1829 **669k tonnes**

1855–1859 **3,583k tonnes**

1875–1879 **6,484k tonnes**

1900–1914 **8,778k tonnes**

COTTON SPINDLES

1 unit = 1 million spindles

1834 **10 million spindles**

1877 **39.5 million spindles**

1913 **55.7 million spindles**

RAILWAY

1 unit = 1,000 miles

1840 **1.5k miles**

1860 **9.1k miles**

1880 **15.7k miles**

1900 **18.8k miles**

U.K. PRODUCTION GROWTH

A bunch of bankers

Those working in finance aren't the most popular people in the world right now, and so it's illuminating to get a sense of the history of banks. One of the most fascinating stories is that of the **Bank of England**: the U.K.'s national bank, and the oldest national bank in the world.

The Bank, which was originally privately owned by a consortium of commercial banks, was created in 1694 because the government wanted to borrow more money, and couldn't find people willing to lend it (sound at all familiar to anyone?).

The Bank offered depositors generous interest rates, and then lent the money on to the government at a still-higher rate. An easy route to profit, you might think, but it quickly ran into trouble. Bank notes, at the time, were convertible to gold at any time, and the Bank had over-lent, or "leveraged." When word of this got around, one of the first bank runs in history took place as frantic depositors tried to withdraw their cash.

What happened next might also sound familiar: the government stepped in. In need of a reliable source of funds, it stopped the Bank's depositors' right to cash in their investments for gold, but assured them the Bank was backed by the state and wouldn't be allowed to fail.

It worked, and as a result, the U.K. government has had a stable way of borrowing and a national bank for more than three centuries.

Worryingly, in that time, **net debt {■}** has grown from around £6 million (in today's money) in 1694 to more than £900 billion today. Yikes!

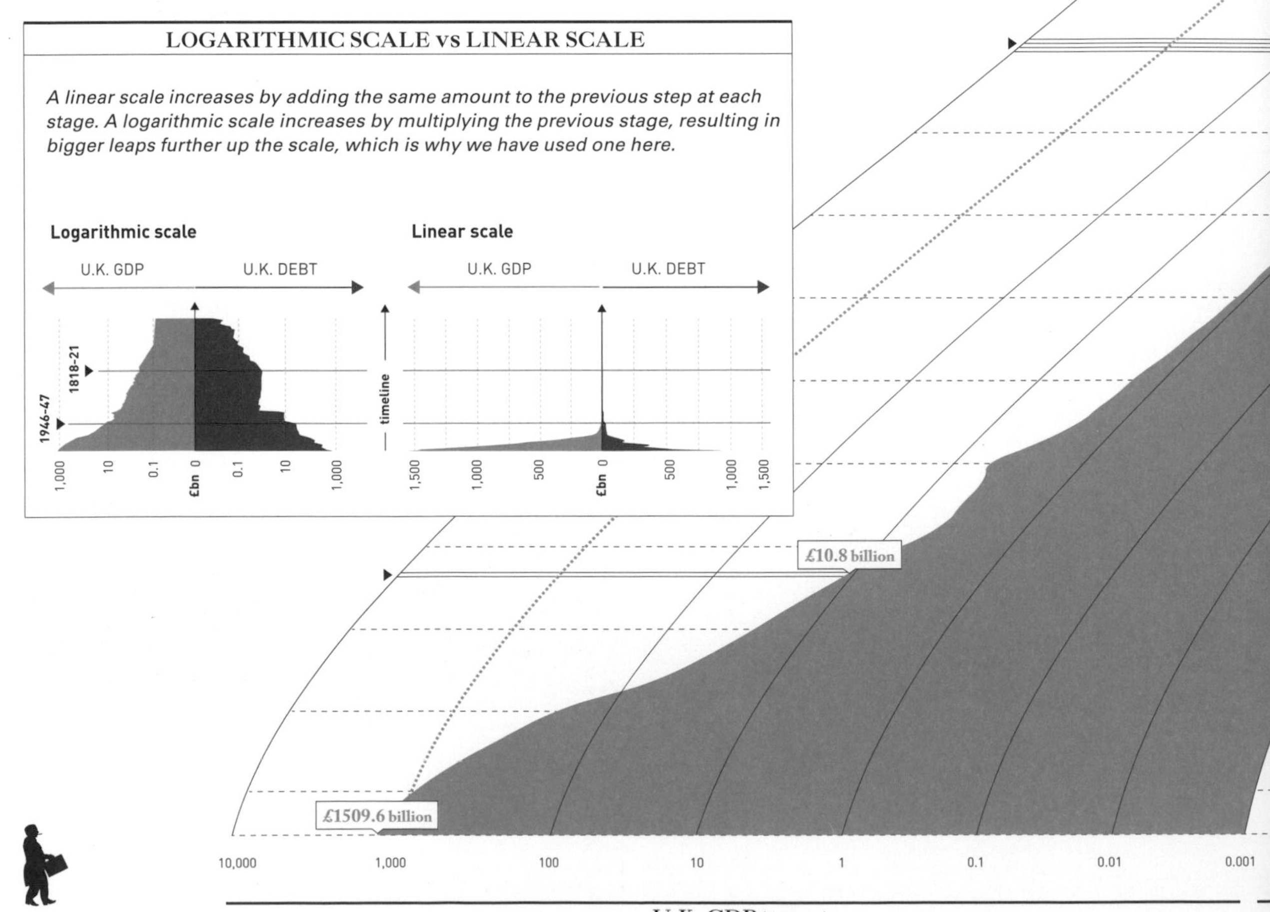

THE BANK OF ENGLAND

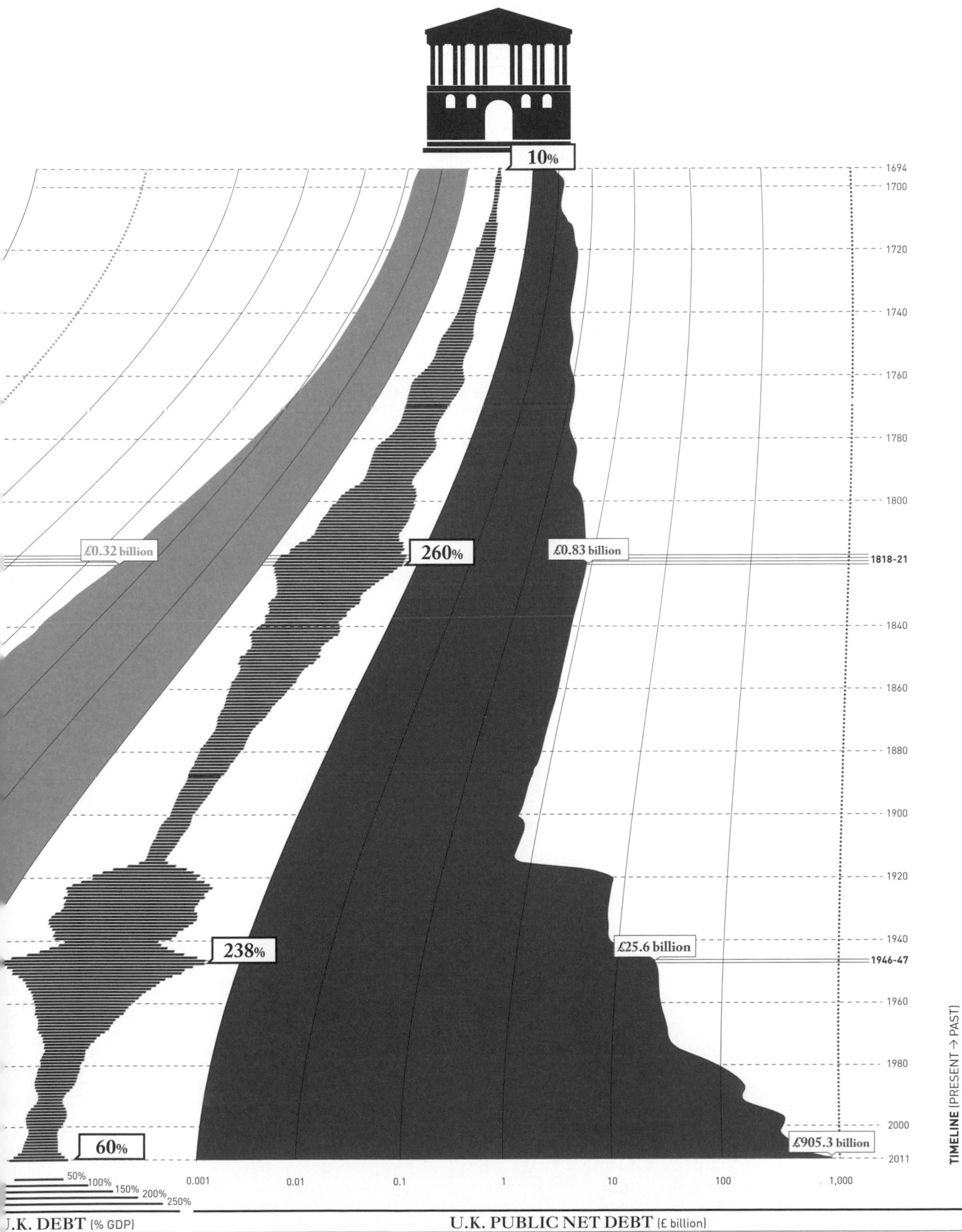

Cash and the crisis

We're not sure if you've noticed, but there was a little bit of an economic upset a couple of years ago. Nothing too bad – a couple of shaky banks ... and countries ... and, okay, perhaps a bit of a recession spanning more or less the whole of the Western world.

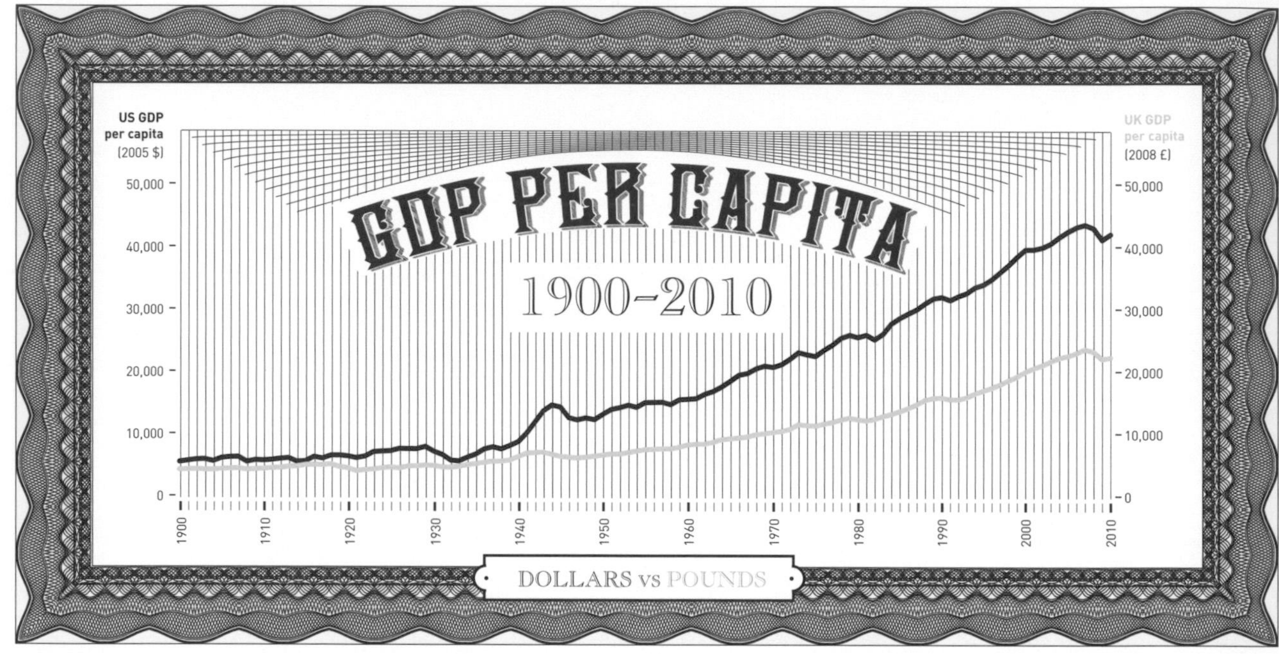

Flippancy aside, there was no missing the economic crash and the resulting economic meltdown. But trying to work out what it all really meant, and how it compared historically, are difficult tasks.

For one thing, some people believe that, for the UK at least, the recession following 2008 was more serious than the **Great Depression** of the 1930s. And in many ways, they were right: while the economy crashed further in the early 1930s, it recovered within three to five years. It took the UK economy seven years to reclaim 2007-levels of productivity, while the US economy recovered one year earlier in 2014.

So why doesn't it feel as bad as we always hear the Great Depression was? This historical data from the **U.S. {■}** and **UK {■}** helps show why – and the short answer is that we're much, much richer than we used to be. It's much easier to cope with knocks when you're relatively better off – and better-off economies have better safety nets, such as welfare systems and the like.

What else does the data show? For one, the Great Depression was a lot easier on the UK than the U.S. While the UK economy, by this measure, had got back to its original size within five years, it took the U.S. a decade. But the data doesn't always tell the full story: America's GDP just after the **Second World War** fell precipitously because the huge war spending dried up, but unemployment stayed low and the economy shifted to peace-time. Britain's GDP held up better, but the misery of rationing and rebuilding lasted for years. Sometimes, it's not only about what's in your wallet.

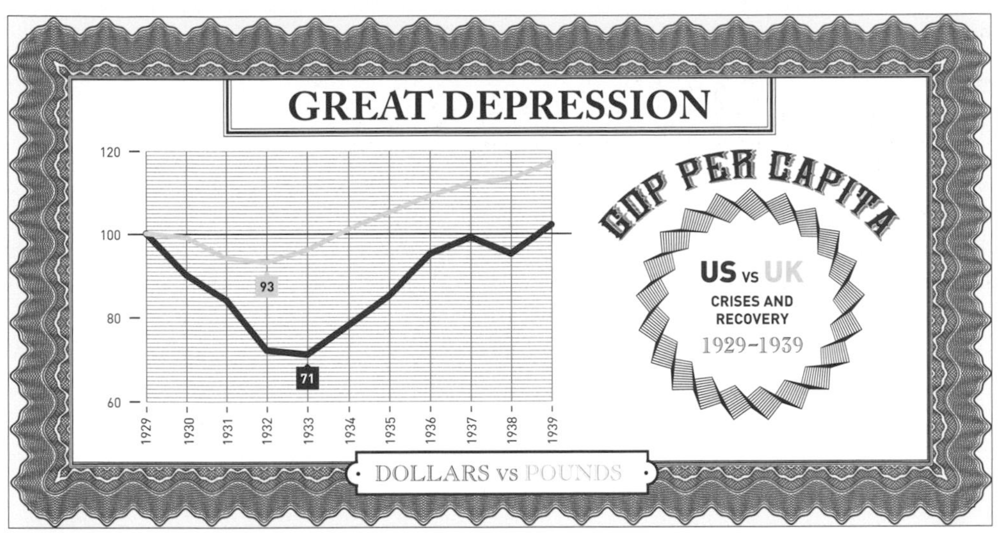

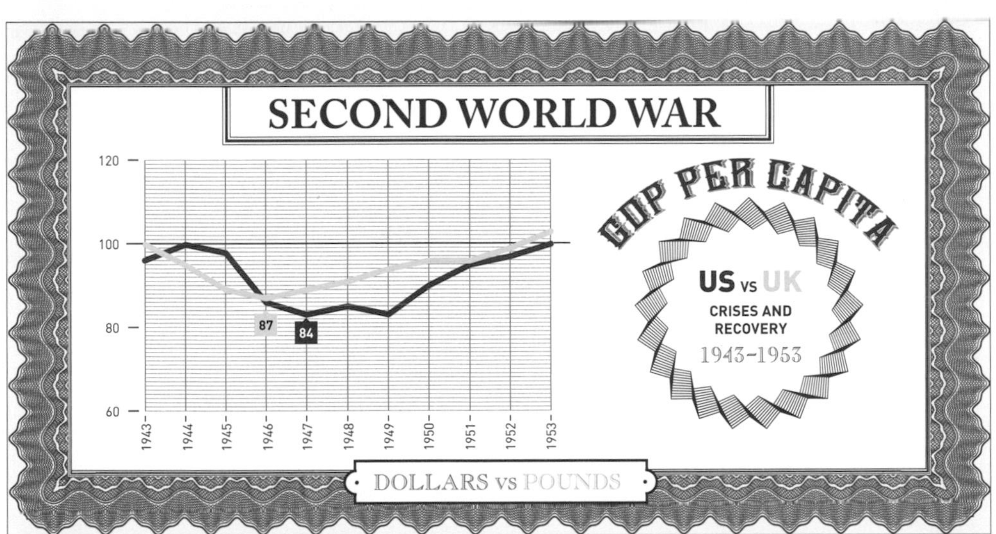

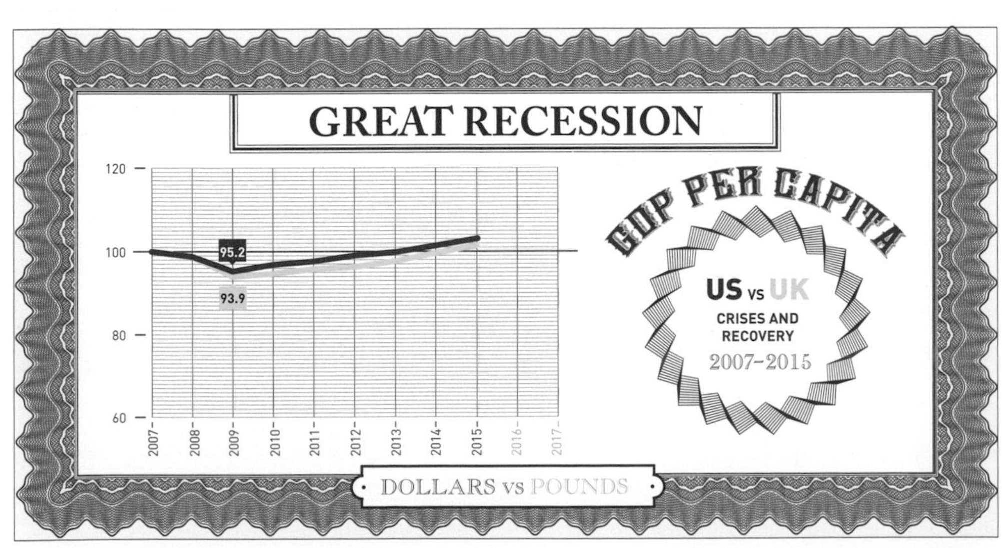

Each diagram shows a GDP per capita comparison between the U.S. and UK economies in the decades of three recession eras: ***Great Depression****, the* ***Second World War****, and the recent* ***Great Recession****. The GDP trends are indexed based on actual GDP output in the peak years preceeding each downturn.*

A question of faith

For many people in England, religion is more of a social club than a burning fervor – but the same isn't true everywhere. Thanks to the growing population of the planet, there are more religious people across the world today than there ever were.

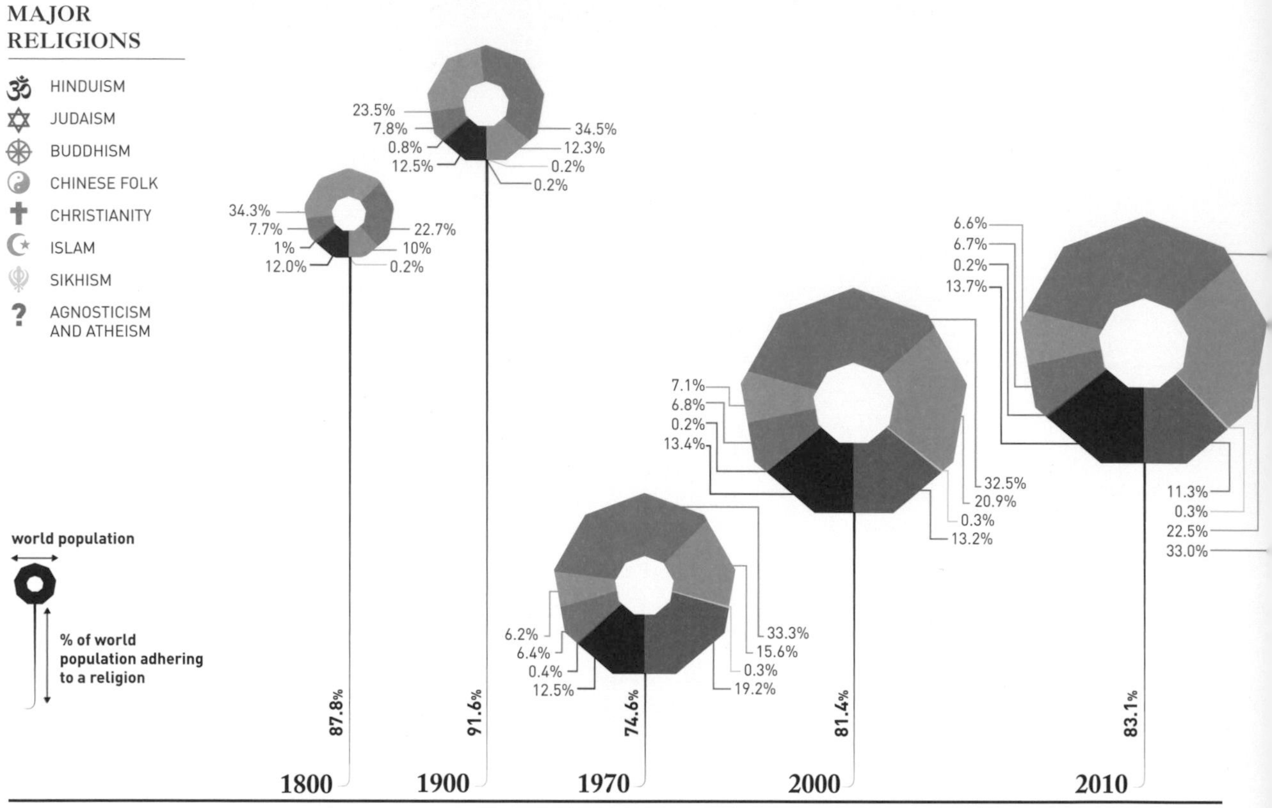

MAJOR RELIGIONS

- HINDUISM
- JUDAISM
- BUDDHISM
- CHINESE FOLK
- CHRISTIANITY
- ISLAM
- SIKHISM
- AGNOSTICISM AND ATHEISM

world population

% of world population adhering to a religion

23.5%
7.8%
0.8%
12.5%
34.5%
12.3%
0.2%
0.2%

34.3%
7.7%
1%
12.0%
22.7%
10%
0.2%

6.6%
6.7%
0.2%
13.7%

7.1%
6.8%
0.2%
13.4%

32.5%
20.9%
0.3%
13.2%

11.3%
0.3%
22.5%
33.0%

6.2%
6.4%
0.4%
12.5%

33.3%
15.6%
0.3%
19.2%

87.8%
91.6%
74.6%
81.4%
83.1%

	1800	1900	1970	2000	2010
WORLD POPULATION:	903,650,000	1,619,625,000	3,696,189,000	6,122,770,000	7,052,132,000

The world's oldest major religions – **Hinduism {■}** and **Judaism {■}** – have been going for almost three millennia, but they (and the other major religions) are still going strong: in 1800, almost 88% of the world's population belonged to one of the major faiths. In 2012, it's still a respectable 83%.

Of the major faiths, **Islam {■}** is the runaway success. Two centuries ago, around one in ten people on earth were Muslims. That's doubled over two centuries to more than one in five. **Christianity {■}** is still growing, too: from making up a fifth of the planet to more than a third.

Other religions aren't keeping pace: both **Buddhism {■}** and Judaism make up less of the world than once they did, despite there being more adherents of both religions now than in 1800.

Still, it shouldn't come as a shock to hear that one group is overtaking all of the above at an ungodly pace: the non-religious.

Now that religion is optional across large swathes of the planet, **agnostics and atheists {■}** have emerged from the woodwork: estimates have soared from fewer than a million in 1800 to about 3.5 million at the turn of the century, and today stand at over 800 million.

Not a bad development for a new century: a whole new way to disagree over God. What could be better?

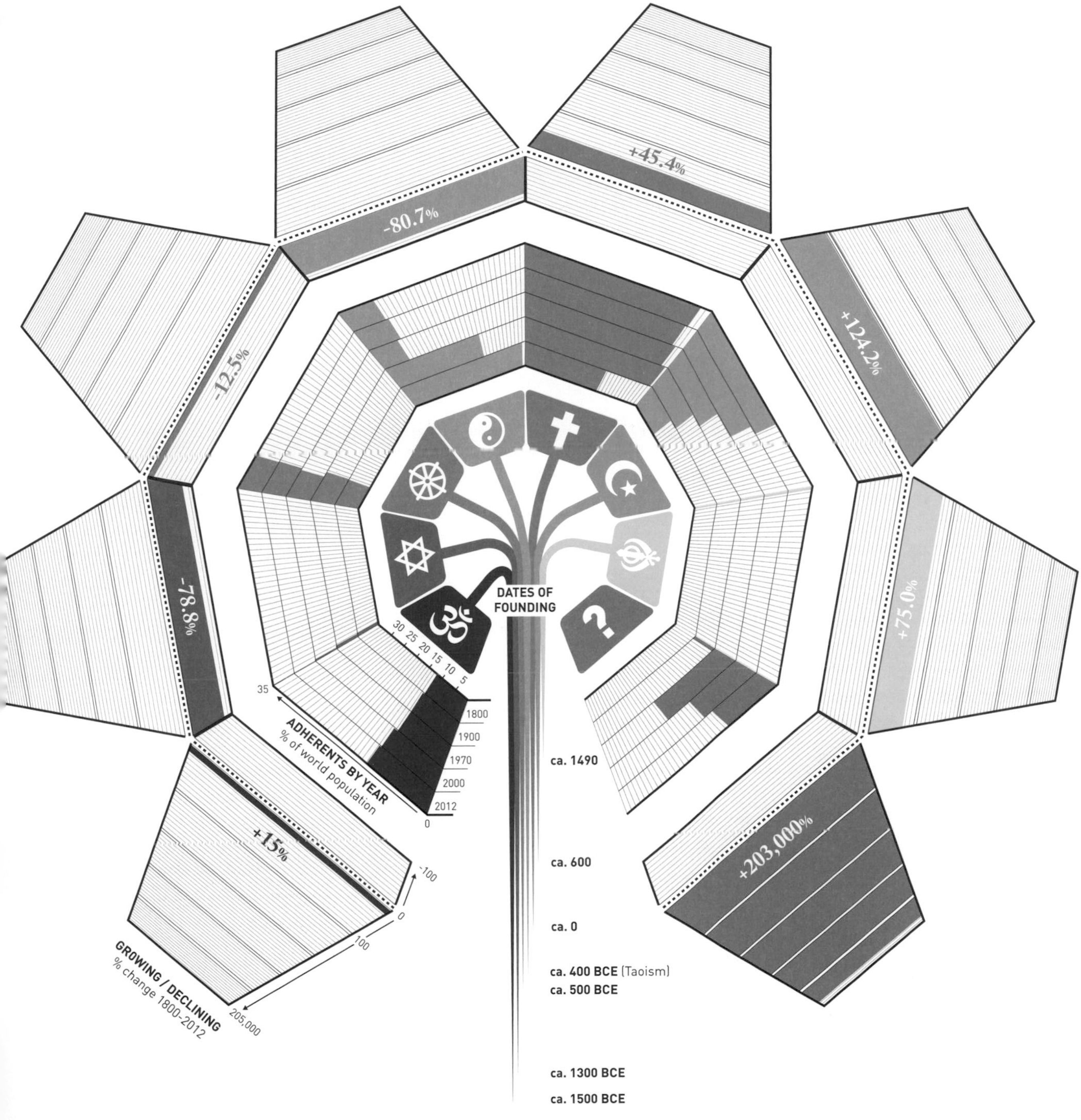

-80.7%

+45.4%

-12.5%

+124.2%

-78.8%

+75.0%

+15%

+203,000%

DATES OF FOUNDING

ADHERENTS BY YEAR
% of world population

35 30 25 20 15 10 5 0

1800
1900
1970
2000
2012

ca. 1490

ca. 600

ca. 0

ca. 400 BCE (Taoism)
ca. 500 BCE

ca. 1300 BCE
ca. 1500 BCE

GROWING / DECLINING
% change 1800-2012

-100
0
100
205,000

Main religions

Dates of founding

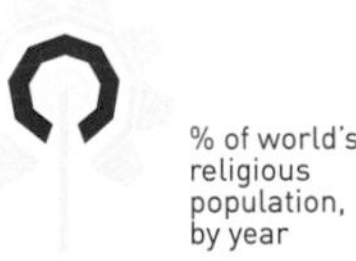
% of world's religious population, by year

% of religions' growth/decline

I get around

Transport historians probably don't give enough credit to the humble horse – the supreme form of transport for more than 6,000 years of civilization.

How long would it take you to run around the world?
Assuming you can run nonstop at full pelt, without rest, you could do it in just under 80 days. Of course, in reality if you tried that, you'd be dead. We tried the same with a horse, too (not really, hardly any animals were harmed in the making of this book). Some more practical methods of crossing the world are over on the next page.

SPEED (MILES PER HOUR) 0 5 10 15 20 25 30

5 mph WALKING

13 mph RUNNING

12.5 mph WALKING

30 mph GALLOPING

The horse's dominance is testimony to how long it took us to get much above our running speed. A fit human can **run {■}** at around 13 miles per hour (though not all day, of course), while a horse traveling long-distance goes at more or less the same rate, even if he can **gallop {■}** twice as fast.

About halfway through the 19th century, we finally managed to beat the horse. And then for about 100 years, it was left to eat our dust. In 1850, the fastest thing going traveled at 60 miles per hour. By 1900, it was 100 miles per hour. By 1960, you could travel at 1,500 miles per hour, in an F-106 interceptor.

That's 25 times faster in around a century, after 6,000 years of stagnation. But the journey wouldn't be a comfortable one, or a long one: the F-106 was a fighter jet, with a maximum range of around 1,700 miles.

We peaked just 10 years later, with the rockets used in the Apollo program generating an amazing 24,790 miles per hour. Traveling on the surface, that would take a traveler around the world in just one hour.

Most of us would never experience such cutting-edge travel technology, of course. Speedy consumer travel perhaps peaked with Concorde's 1,350 miles per hour transatlantic flights. But Concorde was retired in 2003, and few people expect mass supersonic flight to come back. For now, it seems, we've hit our peak, and have been going backward ever since.

Bummer.

They say a lie can travel around the world before the truth's got its boots on, but it still hasn't caught on as a form of transport. Here, we show ***how far around the world you can get in one day*** *in some of history's notable vehicles. We've ignored fuel, maximum range, oceans and other constraints for simplicity, so these are for illustrative purposes only (i.e. don't try to drive across any oceans. Please.).*

TASK: **travelling around the world**

EQUATOR: **24,900 miles**

TRANSPORTATION:

- STEAM LOCOMOTIVE
- ELECTRIC TRAIN
- CAR
- AIRPLANE
- ROCKET

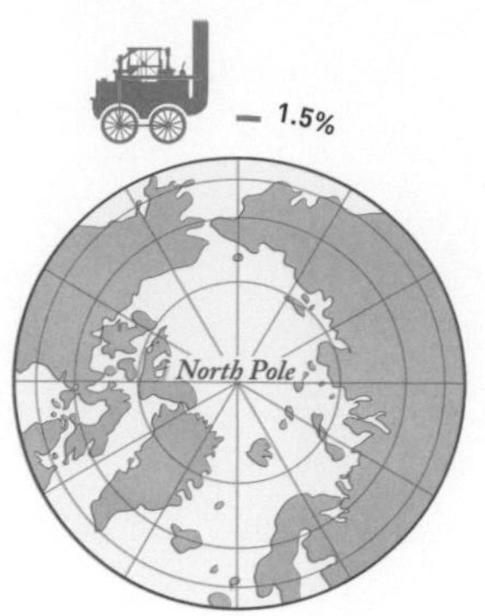

Locomotion No.1

1825 | SPEED: **15 mph** TASK TIME: **69d 4h** COUNTRY: **UK**

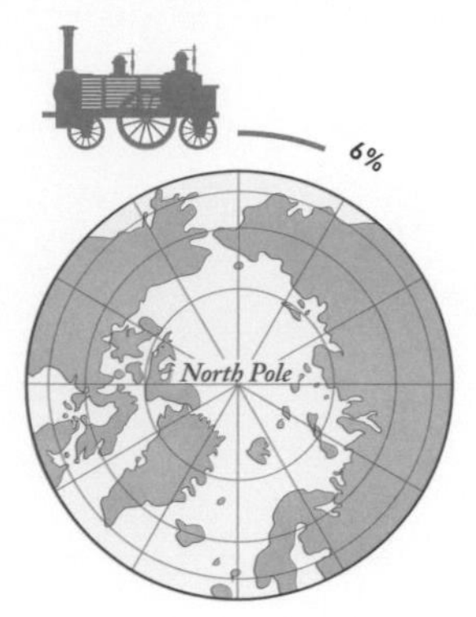

The Antelope

1848 | SPEED: **60 mph** TASK TIME: **17d 7h** COUNTRY: **U.S.**

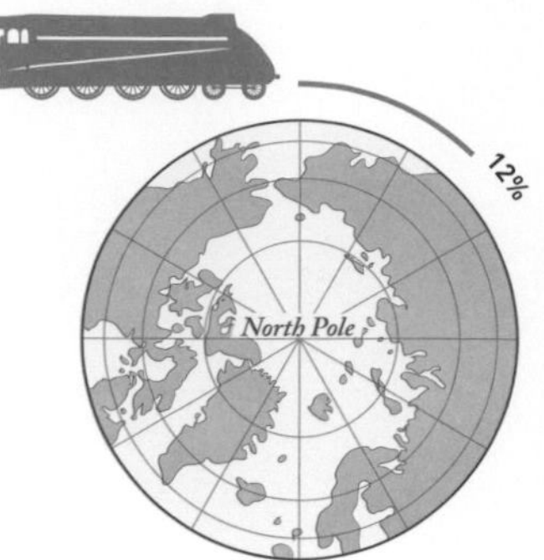

Mallard

1938 | SPEED: **126 mph** TASK TIME: **8d 5h 36m** COUNTRY: **UK**

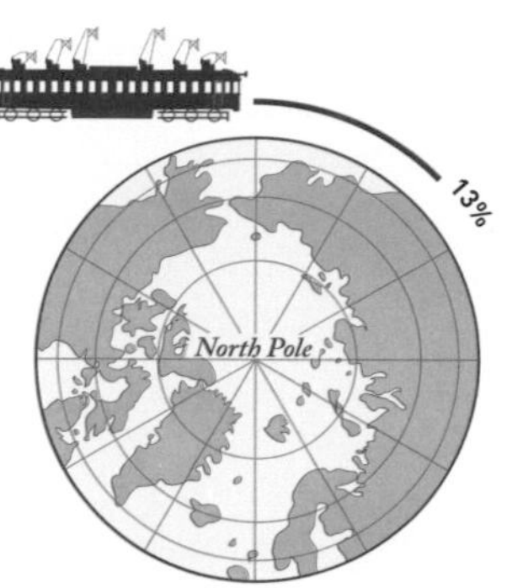

AEG Drehstrom-Triebwagen

1903 | SPEED: **131 mph** TASK TIME: **7d 22h 6m** COUNTRY: **Germany**

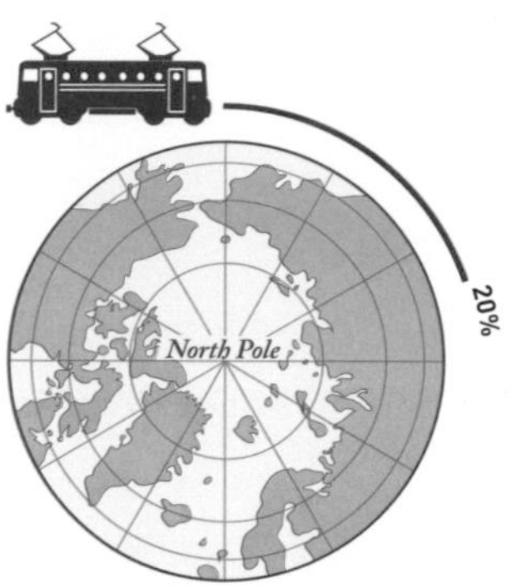

Jeumont-Schneider BB 9004

1955 | SPEED: **206 mph** TASK TIME: **5d 9h 30m** COUNTRY: **France**

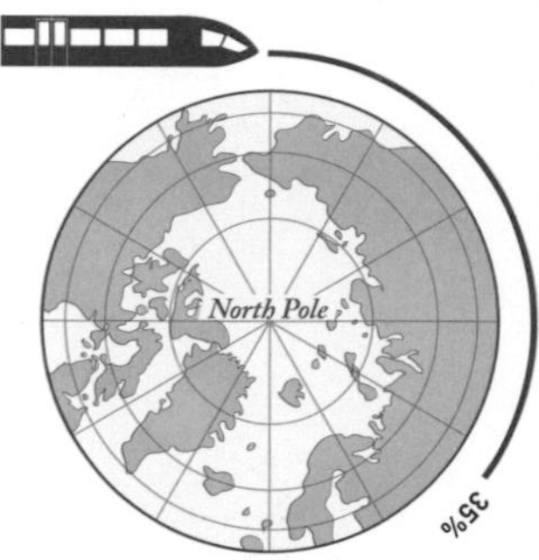

MLX01 Maglev

2003 | SPEED: **361 mph** TASK TIME: **2d 21h** COUNTRY: **Japan**

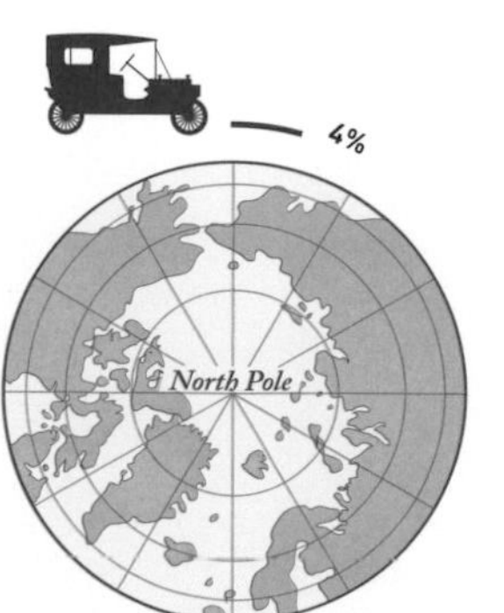

Ford Model T

1908 | SPEED: **45 mph** TASK TIME: **23d 1h 24m** COUNTRY: **U.S.**

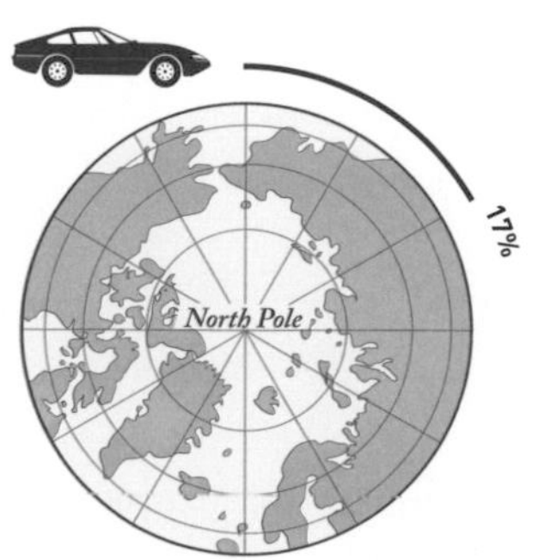

Ferrari 365 Daytona

1968 | SPEED: **174 mph** TASK TIME: **5d 23h** COUNTRY: **Italy**

27%

North Pole

Bugatti Veyron

2005 | SPEED: **284 mph** TASK TIME: **3d 15h 36m** COUNTRY: **France**

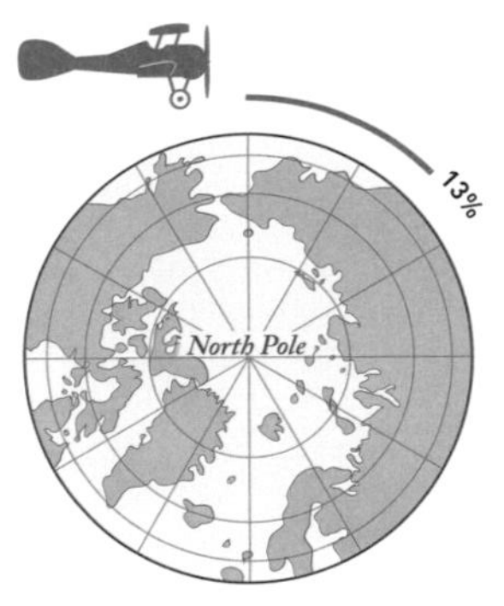

RAF S.E.4

1914 | SPEED: **134 mph**
TASK TIME: **7d 17h 48m**
COUNTRY: **UK**

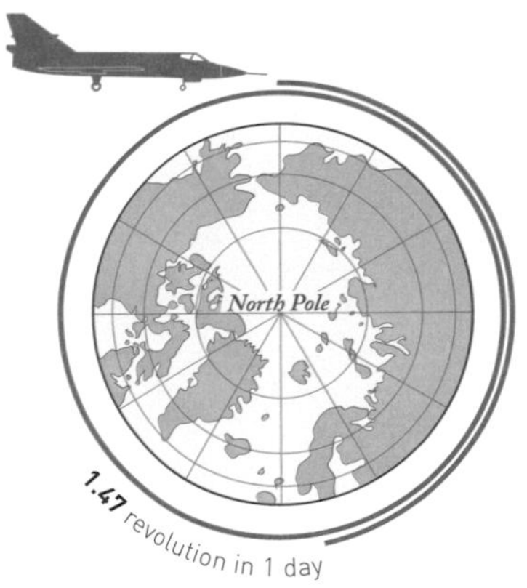

Convair F-106 Delta Dart

1959 | SPEED: **1,526 mph**
TASK TIME: **16h 18m**
COUNTRY: **U.S.**

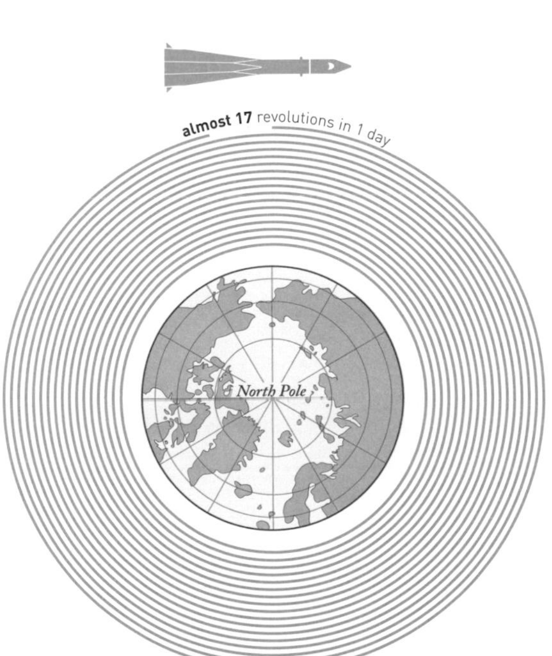

Vostok1

1961 | SPEED: **17,600 mph**
TASK TIME: **1h 24m**
COUNTRY: **USSR**

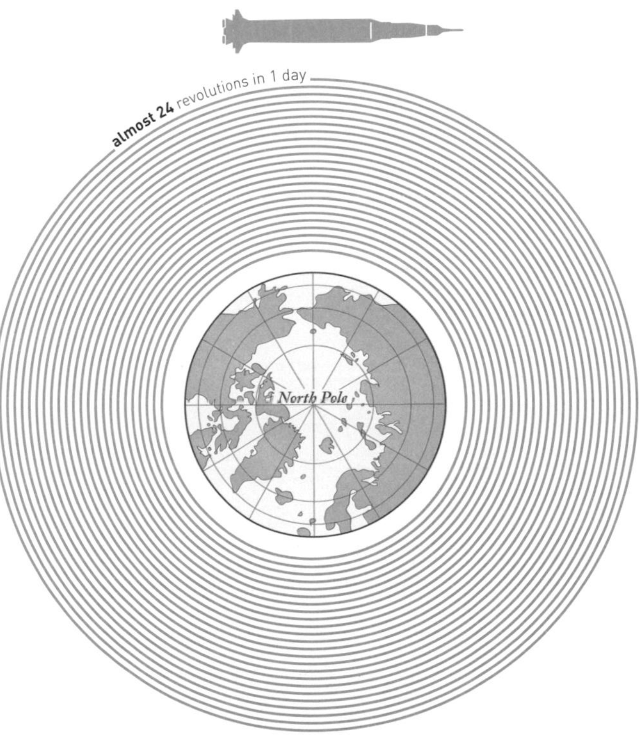

Apollo10

1969 | SPEED: **24,790 mph**
TASK TIME: **1h**
COUNTRY: **U.S.**

Who's in charge here?

This is not your average history book; we wanted to avoid getting too hung up on kings, queens, dates and all that stuff. But we'd be sorely letting you down if we didn't at least give you enough to bluff some knowledge of the basic history of some of the world's most significant countries.

So here, across two short pages, is 1,000 years of history of five of the world's most powerful nations:

England *is pretty straightforward: the Normans walk in and take over in 1066, and then different royal families take their turn through to 1649, when Charles I's head is forcibly removed. After trying eleven years of being a republic, England goes back to royal succession (William of Orange excepted) right through to the present day.*

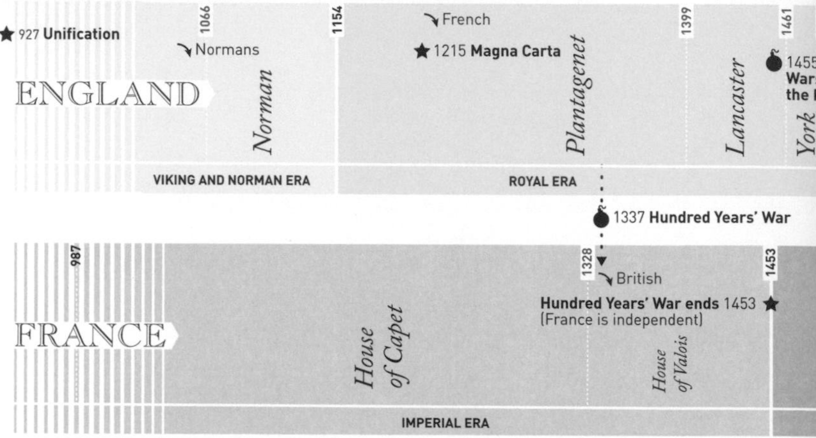

France *was happy enough with its monarchs until 1792, after which followed a rather indecisive patch: from republic, to empire, to monarchy, back to republic, then empire, then republic. Then, to further confuse matters, Nazi Germany invaded and set up a vassal state. Since then, France has managed to only go through two further republics. Nice work!*

China *enjoys a pretty straightforward 640 years with just three different ruling dynasties – but then things get more complicated: phase one of the country's revolution introduces the Republic of China. After an on-again-off-again civil war, this regime is replaced (except in Taiwan) by the People's Republic of China, and communist rule, which continues to this day.*

Japan *has been ceremonially ruled by the same royal family for longer than any other nation – the current emperor is the 125th in his line. But between 1192 and 1867 the real power lay with the military (bar three years). Since then, democracy has asserted itself, with the emperors continuing in an increasingly ceremonial role.*

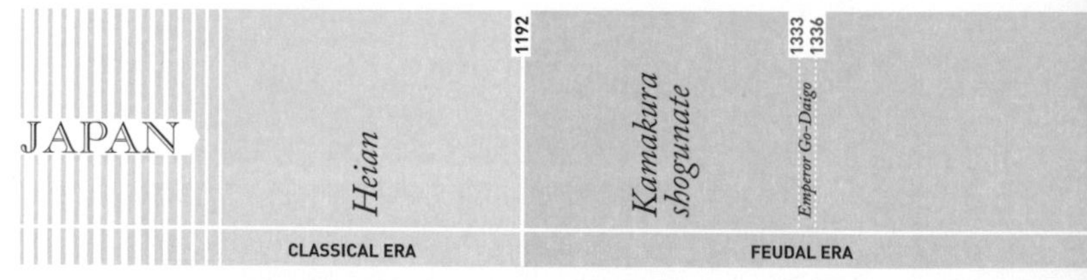

The ***United States*** *was the disputed turf of numerous colonial powers from the founding of Jamestown in 1607 to Britain finally kicking France off the territory in 1760. But just sixteen years later, a revolutionary war began. The presidency was established in 1789, and since 1853 has bounced back and forth between the same two parties.*

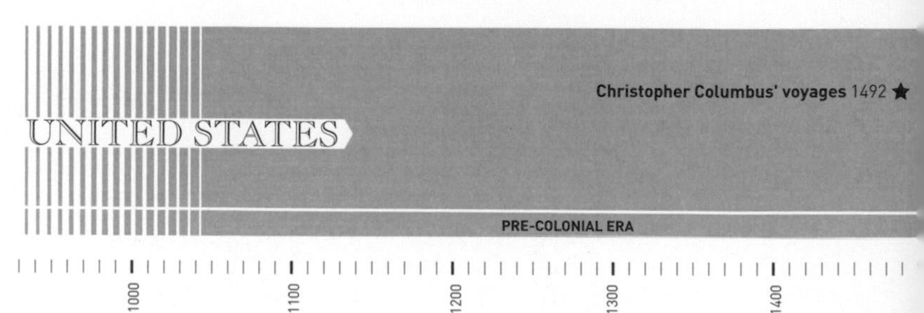

INVASION · MAJOR WAR · MAJOR EVENT · INTERNATIONAL CONFLICT

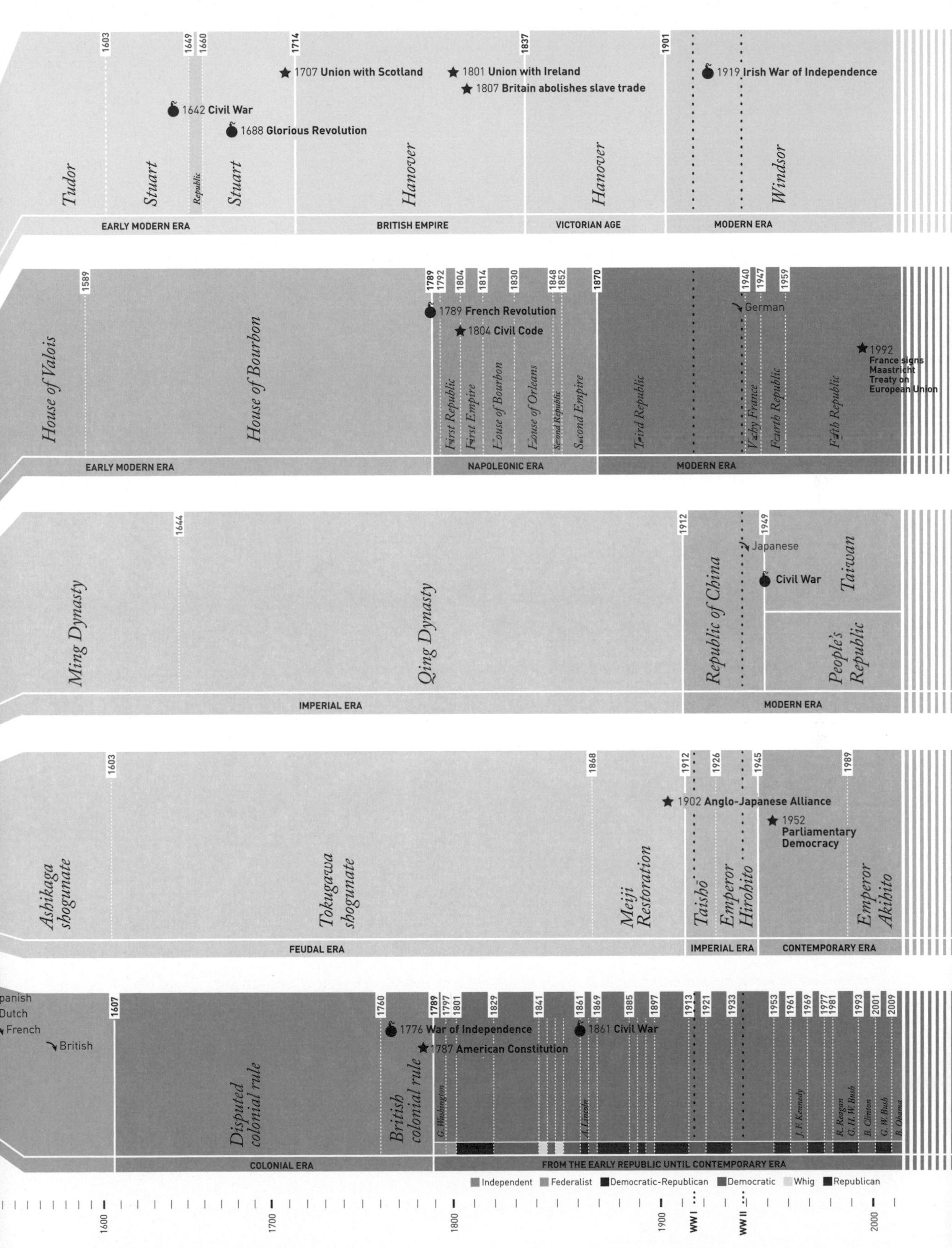

1603
1649
1660
1714
1837
1901
1707 Union with Scotland
1801 Union with Ireland
1807 Britain abolishes slave trade
1919 Irish War of Independence
1642 Civil War
1688 Glorious Revolution
Tudor
Stuart
Republic
Stuart
Hanover
Hanover
Windsor
EARLY MODERN ERA
BRITISH EMPIRE
VICTORIAN AGE
MODERN ERA
1589
1789
1792
1804
1814
1830
1848
1852
1870
1940
1947
1959
1789 French Revolution
1804 Civil Code
German
1992 France signs Maastricht Treaty on European Union
House of Valois
House of Bourbon
First Republic
First Empire
House of Bourbon
House of Orleans
Second Republic
Second Empire
Third Republic
Vichy France
Fourth Republic
Fifth Republic
EARLY MODERN ERA
NAPOLEONIC ERA
MODERN ERA
1644
1912
1949
Japanese
Civil War
Ming Dynasty
Qing Dynasty
Republic of China
Taiwan
People's Republic
IMPERIAL ERA
MODERN ERA
1603
1868
1912
1926
1945
1989
1902 Anglo-Japanese Alliance
1952 Parliamentary Democracy
Ashikaga shogunate
Tokugawa shogunate
Meiji Restoration
Taishō
Emperor Hirohito
Emperor Akihito
FEUDAL ERA
IMPERIAL ERA
CONTEMPORARY ERA
Spanish
Dutch
French
British
1607
1760
1789
1797
1801
1829
1841
1861
1869
1885
1897
1913
1921
1933
1953
1961
1969
1977
1981
1993
2001
2009
1776 War of Independence
1787 American Constitution
1861 Civil War
Disputed colonial rule
British colonial rule
G. Washington
A. Lincoln
J. F. Kennedy
R. Reagan
G. H. W. Bush
B. Clinton
G. W. Bush
B. Obama
COLONIAL ERA
FROM THE EARLY REPUBLIC UNTIL CONTEMPORARY ERA
Independent
Federalist
Democratic-Republican
Democratic
Whig
Republican
1600
1700
1800
1900
WW I
WW II
2000

The Modern World

Ancient civilization's all well and good, but now we're finally getting to the part we all secretly know is most interesting: ourselves. More people, more connections, more transport, more countries. The 20th century – and the start of the 21st – have everything the other eras did, but, well, more of it.

And thanks to more technology, more data and, frankly, more living witnesses, we've got a much better idea of what's gone on – so there's an embarrassment of riches here.

What could be better?

Let's start with the basics: where we're being born and what we're dying of. Between those two milestones, we look at how rich (or poor) we all are, how we live and work, and what we do with the rest of our time.

Culture's not left out either: what we read (obviously the top priority), listen to and what we do online. There's also – just because we can – information on information overload, the race for invention, and an attempt to make sense of the entirely separate universe that is the online world.

Last but not least, we also look at some of the big issues of the day: climate change, obesity, gendercide and gun crime.

If it's going on out there and it's been counted, you'll find something about it in here.

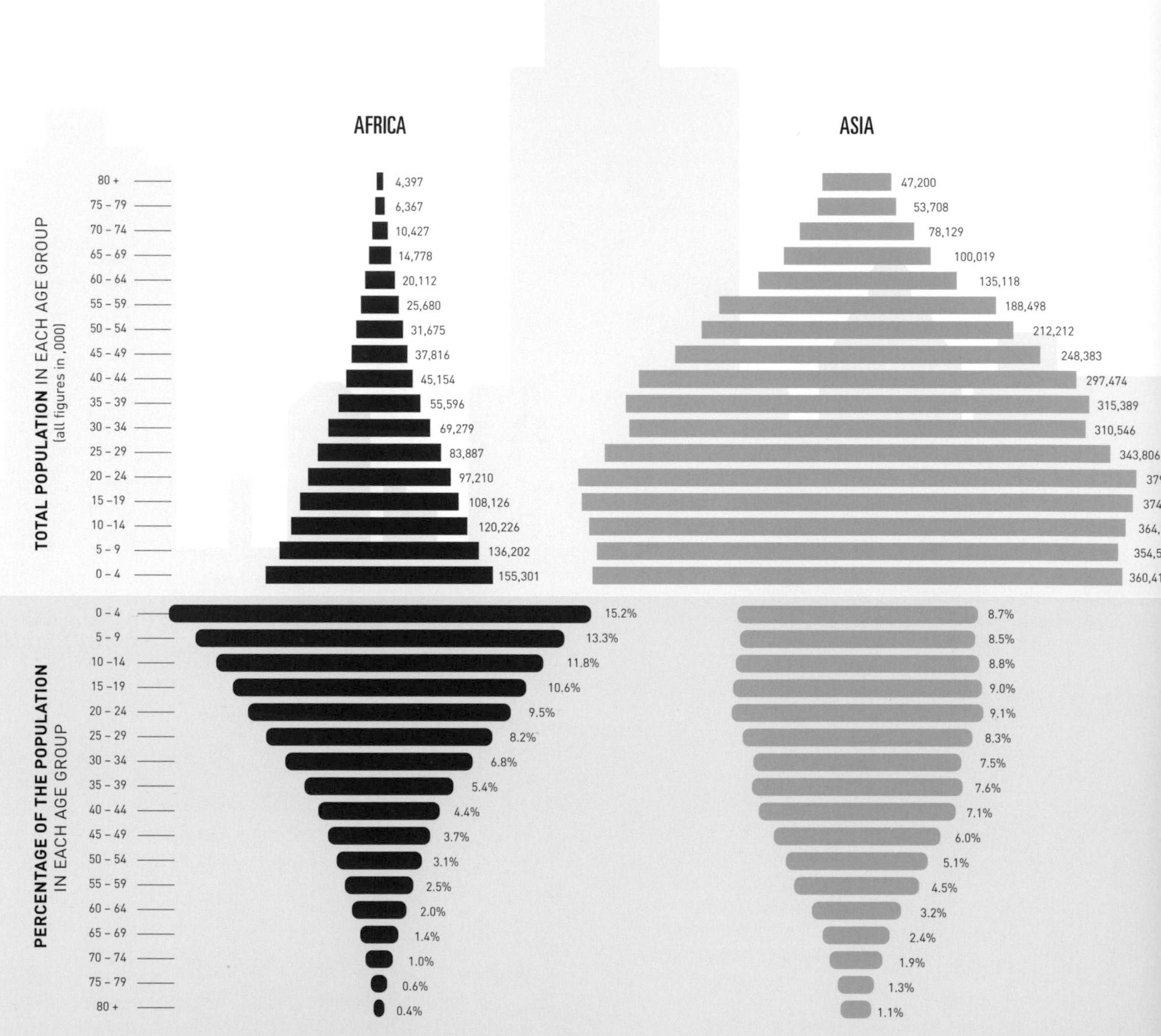
AFRICA
ASIA
TOTAL POPULATION IN EACH AGE GROUP
(all figures in ,000)
80 + 4,397 47,200
75 – 79 6,367 53,708
70 – 74 10,427 78,129
65 – 69 14,778 100,019
60 – 64 20,112 135,118
55 – 59 25,680 188,498
50 – 54 31,675 212,212
45 – 49 37,816 248,383
40 – 44 45,154 297,474
35 – 39 55,596 315,389
30 – 34 69,279 310,546
25 – 29 83,887 343,806
20 – 24 97,210 37
15 –19 108,126 374
10 –14 120,226 364,
5 – 9 136,202 354,5
0 – 4 155,301 360,41
PERCENTAGE OF THE POPULATION
IN EACH AGE GROUP
0 – 4 15.2% 8.7%
5 – 9 13.3% 8.5%
10 –14 11.8% 8.8%
15 –19 10.6% 9.0%
20 – 24 9.5% 9.1%
25 – 29 8.2% 8.3%
30 – 34 6.8% 7.5%
35 – 39 5.4% 7.6%
40 – 44 4.4% 7.1%
45 – 49 3.7% 6.0%
50 – 54 3.1% 5.1%
55 – 59 2.5% 4.5%
60 – 64 2.0% 3.2%
65 – 69 1.4% 2.4%
70 – 74 1.0% 1.9%
75 – 79 0.6% 1.3%
80 + 0.4% 1.1%

Population pyramids

Infographics can be deceptive things: a small circle on one chart can mark something innocuous like government spending. On another chart, it can mark thousands of deaths. One of the most traditional subjects is demographics – particularly the famous population pyramid.

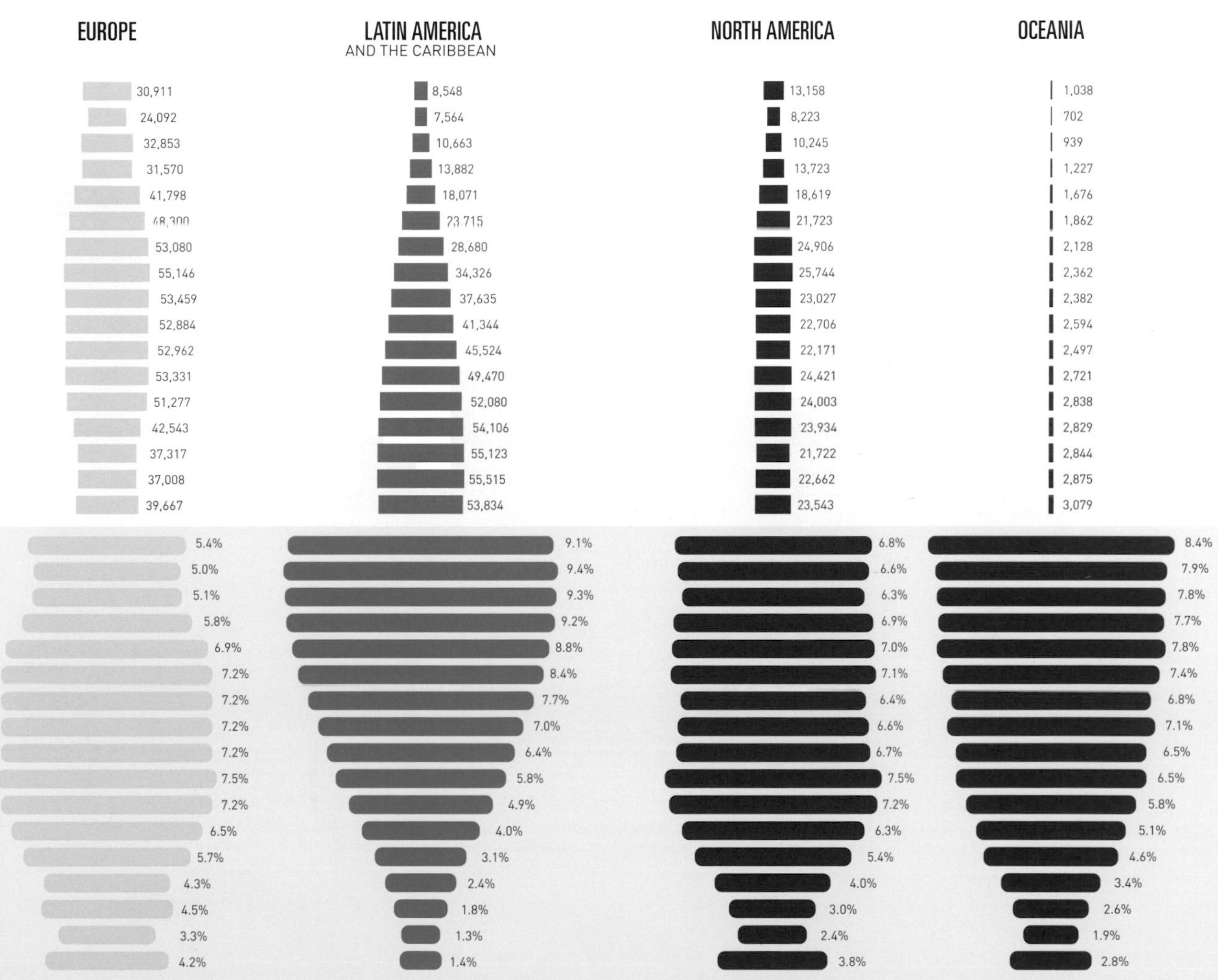

The idea's simple: 0–4-year-olds go at the bottom, then 5–9s, and so on, all the way up to centenarians. But the shape tells you a huge amount about a society. The classical shape, as you might predict, is a pyramid. Each step gets smaller than the one before.

But think about what that implies: at each step along the way, people are dying. A pyramid with a wide base – like the one on the African continent today – shows childhood mortality is still high. **Africa {■}** has more than 155 million infants, but fewer than 100 million people aged 20–24: serious signs of youth mortality.

But other shapes have significance too. The charts for **Europe { }** show a huge generation moving through the age brackets – with a smaller group coming along behind it. That has its own important consequences, too: not least for pensions.

A review of global population composition from 1950 and 2000, alongside official projections for 2050 and 2100, tell a dramatic story about where we're headed.

It's almost startling, but our planet's human population is expected to surpass eleven billion by 2100. This is characterized by dramatic growth in Africa, which will account for one quarter of the world's population in 2050 and nearly 40 percent in 2100.

Two of the primary drivers of these overall population shifts are declining fertility and improving longevity. The result is a narrowing nearer the bottom (fewer youngsters) and a widening nearer the top (more elders). The fastest growing segment of the population will be those aged 60+. In fact, by 2100, there will be more people aged 65 or over than the total living population in 1950.

THE FUTURE AND PAST OF GLOBAL POPULATION
TOTAL NUMBERS BY EACH AGE GROUP
(all figures in ,000)

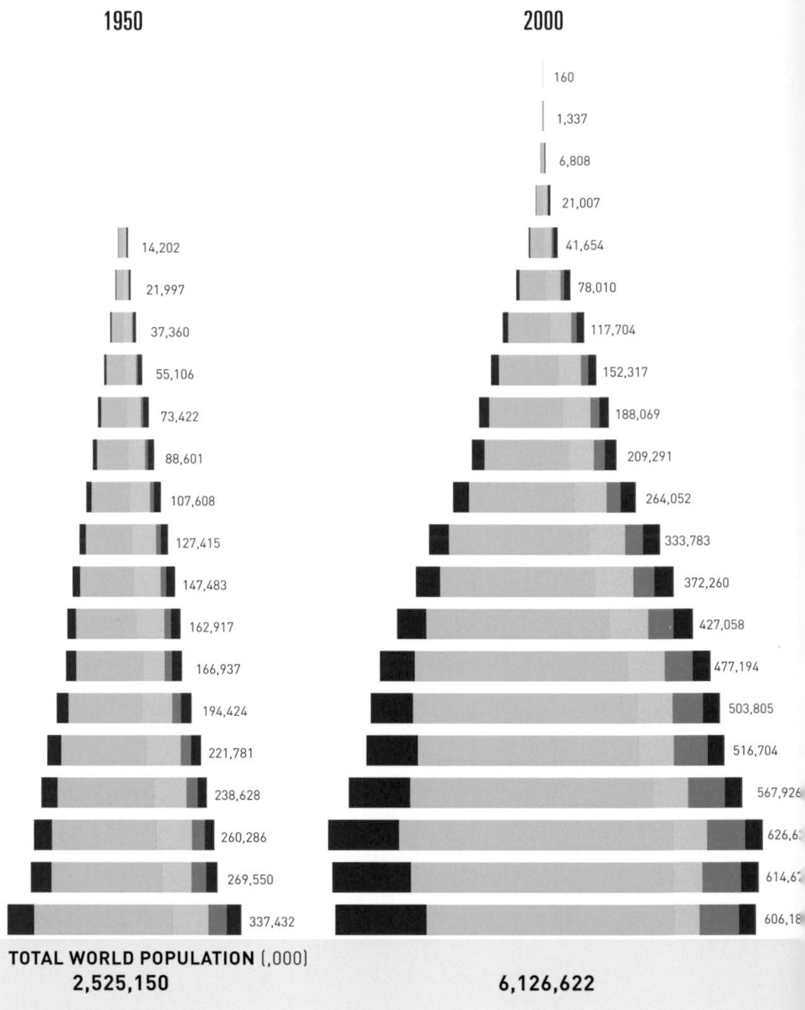

TOTAL WORLD POPULATION (,000)
2,525,150 **6,126,622**

SHARE BY REGION
% OF GLOBAL POPULATION

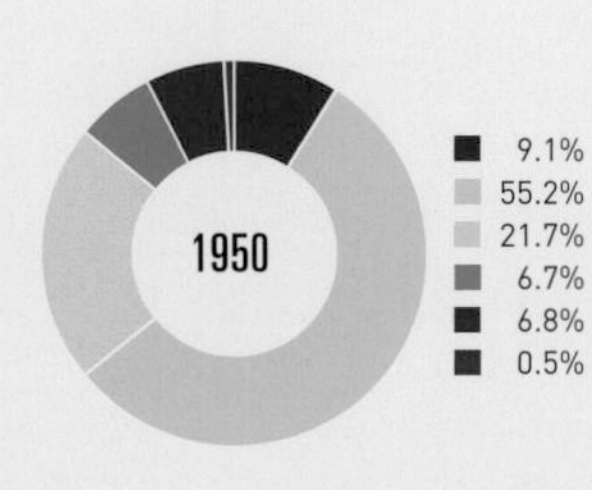

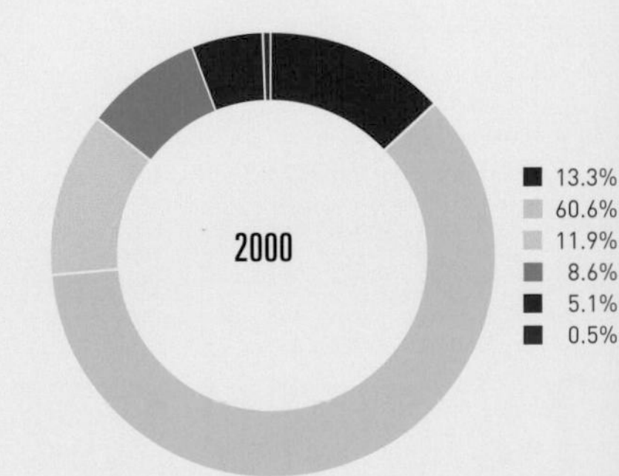

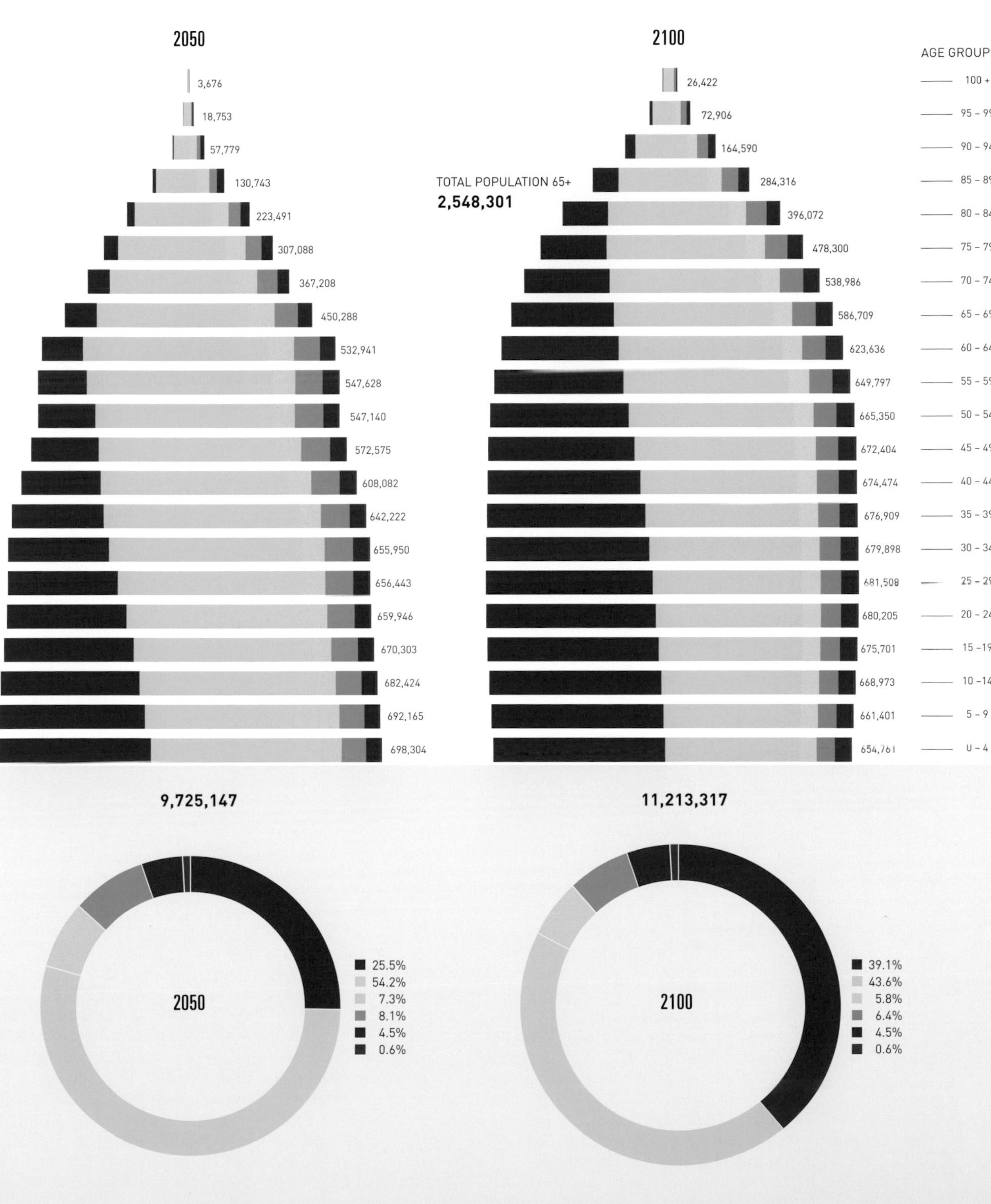
2050
2100
AGE GROUPS
3,676
18,753
57,779
130,743
223,491
307,088
367,208
450,288
532,941
547,628
547,140
572,575
608,082
642,222
655,950
656,443
659,946
670,303
682,424
692,165
698,304
TOTAL POPULATION 65+
2,548,301
26,422
72,906
164,590
284,316
396,072
478,300
538,986
586,709
623,636
649,797
665,350
672,404
674,474
676,909
679,898
681,508
680,205
675,701
668,973
661,401
654,761
100 +
95 – 99
90 – 94
85 – 89
80 – 84
75 – 79
70 – 74
65 – 69
60 – 64
55 – 59
50 – 54
45 – 49
40 – 44
35 – 39
30 – 34
25 – 29
20 – 24
15 –19
10 –14
5 – 9
0 – 4
9,725,147
11,213,317
2050
25.5%
54.2%
7.3%
8.1%
4.5%
0.6%
2100
39.1%
43.6%
5.8%
6.4%
4.5%
0.6%
REGIONS
AFRICA
ASIA
EUROPE
LATIN AMERICA AND THE CARIBBEAN
NORTH AMERICA
OCEANIA

How we die

As aphorisms go, "Life's a bitch and then you die" is a strong contender for the least inspiring. It's always nice to be able to inject some reality into this pessimism with the deployment of some cold, hard facts. One of those facts is that year-for-year, we're dying less.

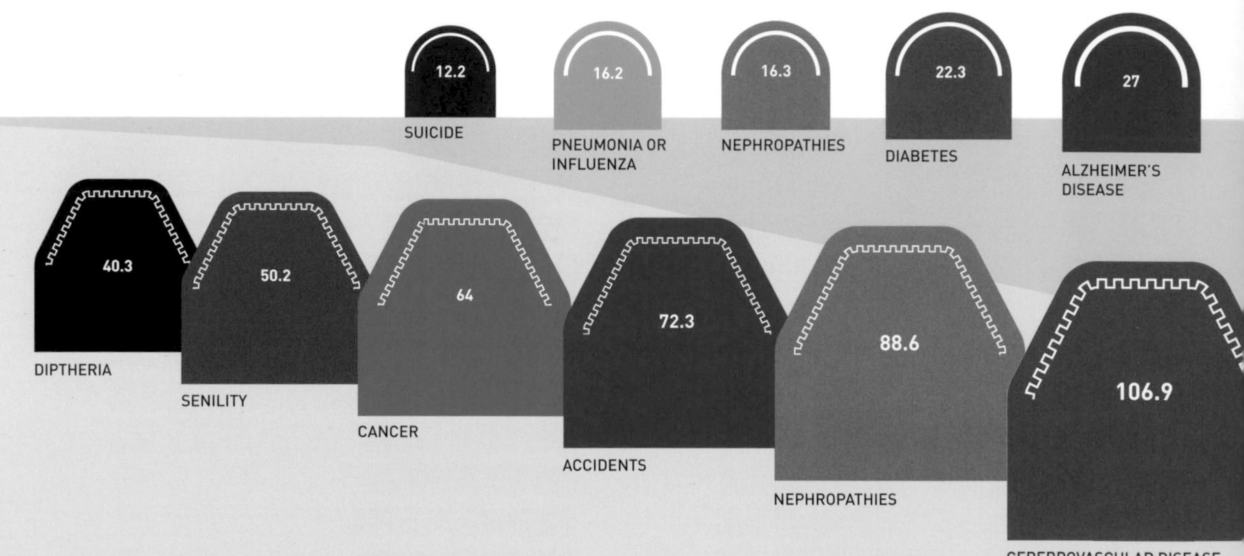

A study by the *New England Journal of Medicine* paints the picture nicely. It compares life and death for an imaginary group of 100,000 people in 1900 with a group of the same size in 2010. While it's still true that none of us is immortal, longer lifespans, lower child mortality and advances in medicine mean that in any given year far fewer of us die than was once the case.

In 1900, over the course of the year, 1,719 of our 100,000 would die. In 2010, this had dropped by more than half, to just 799. What's killing us is dramatically different too: **pneumonia and influenza** {■} were the leading cause of death in 1900, claiming 202 of our group. By 2010, this had dropped vastly, to just 16. **Tuberculosis** {■} and **gastrointestinal infections** {■}, the second- and third-largest causes of death, dropped dramatically too.

But not everything is rosy, of course: in the modern era, there are two great killers left: **cancer** {■} and **heart disease** {■}. These two ailments collectively account for almost half of all modern deaths. Other leading causes of death are the flipside of increased longevity and affluence: **diabetes** {■} and **Alzheimer's** {■}, the price we pay for prosperity.

One major cause of death can strike at any time – and though it has dropped since 1900 it is still pretty significant. It's accidents, most of which occur around the home. So, hey, walk carefully, tie up your shoelaces and watch where you're going...

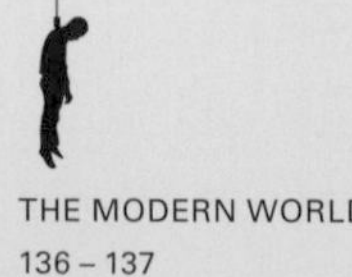

TOTAL MORTALITY

per 100,000 people per year

CAUSES OF DEATH

per 100,000 people per year

Gendercide

The world is missing a lot of women because their parents didn't want them. It's a stark-but-true fact, in large part made possible by advances in technology. In many countries around the world, parents prefer a male child to a female one because boys will produce a better income, keep the family name or are simply more valued in the culture. The graphics speak for themselves:

*The pink/blue split shows the **gender ratio** of each nation, and the figures show the number of missing girls each year. India's high birth rate means despite not having the highest ratio, it's second only to China for the number of missing girls.*

The result is parents that are aborting girls. All else being equal, around 105 boys will be born for every 100 girls (this naturally compensates for higher death rates among males). In **China**, where the one-child policy also exerts an effect, there are 119 boys born for every 100 girls. But China is not alone: in India it's 108, and for parents having second or third children, the ratio can jump as high as 200. Sex-selective abortion is illegal in most of the world (including China) but continues apace.

The phenomenon was dubbed "**Gendercide**" by Mary Anne Warren in 1985, and is still going strong. We combined the World Bank data with UN birth rates – and found that in 2010 alone there were more than one million missing baby girls, and more than 350,000 missing in **India**.

As the *Economist* noted in a groundbreaking article on the topic, the phenomenon is testament to the law of unintended consequences. Since its invention the ultrasound machine has spread an immense amount of good by helping spot birth problems, letting parents know if they are having twins, and more – but by allowing parents to spot the gender of their fetus easily and cheaply, this technology has had a more insidious influence.

More starkly still: gender ratios in affected countries often worsen between birth and the age of five. This could have multiple causes, but hints at an older and darker practice: sex-selective infanticide.

The good news, of sorts, is that gendercide is slowing: after years of increasing ratios, both China and India are stabilizing. Perhaps soon it will be a historical relic.

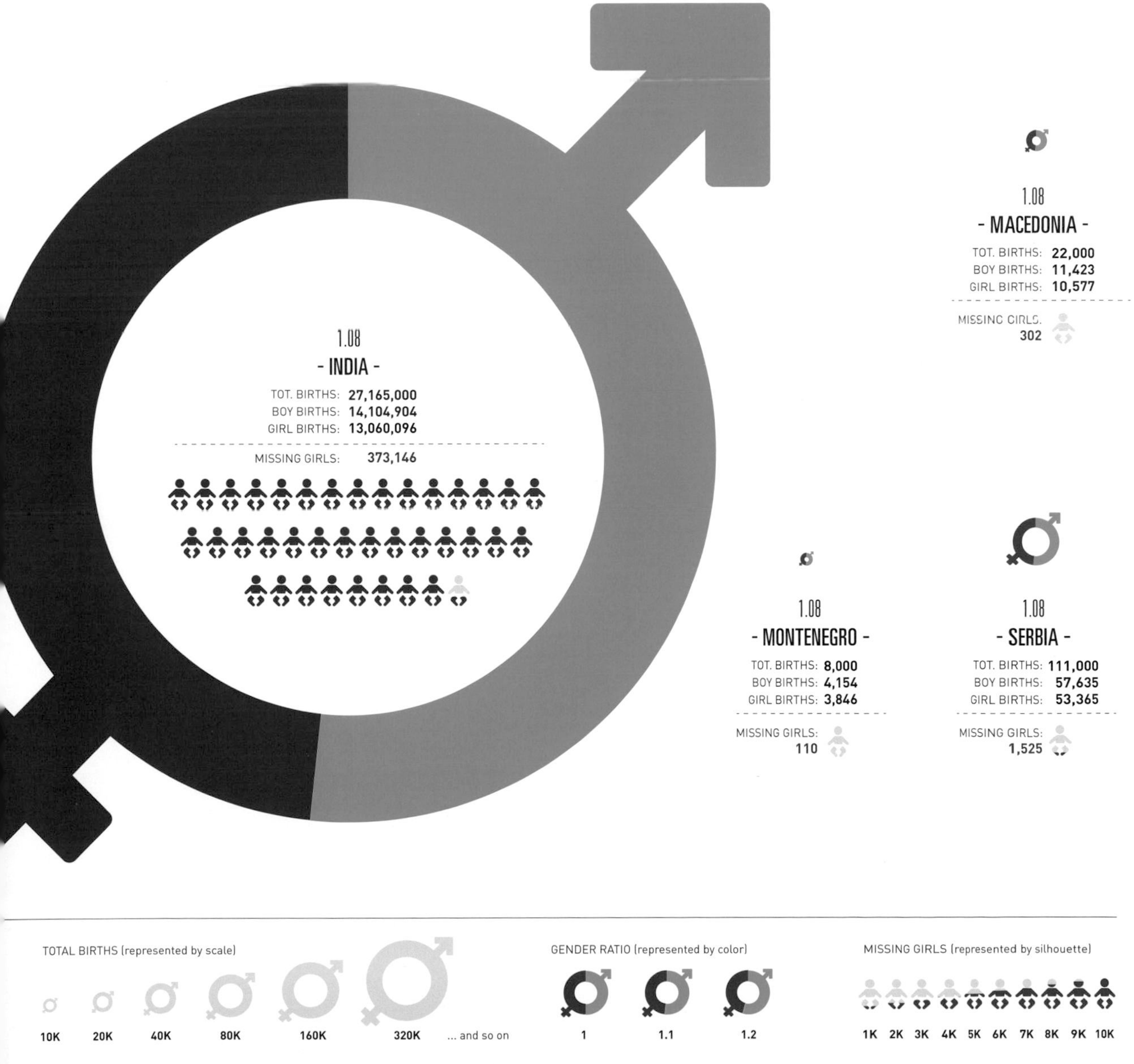

1.08
- INDIA -
TOT. BIRTHS: **27,165,000**
BOY BIRTHS: **14,104,904**
GIRL BIRTHS: **13,060,096**
MISSING GIRLS: **373,146**

1.08
- MACEDONIA -
TOT. BIRTHS: **22,000**
BOY BIRTHS: **11,423**
GIRL BIRTHS: **10,577**
MISSING GIRLS: **302**

1.08
- MONTENEGRO -
TOT. BIRTHS: **8,000**
BOY BIRTHS: **4,154**
GIRL BIRTHS: **3,846**
MISSING GIRLS: **110**

1.08
- SERBIA -
TOT. BIRTHS: **111,000**
BOY BIRTHS: **57,635**
GIRL BIRTHS: **53,365**
MISSING GIRLS: **1,525**

TOTAL BIRTHS (represented by scale)

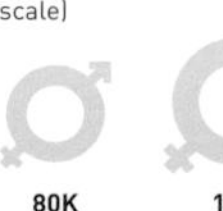

10K **20K** **40K** **80K** **160K** **320K** ... and so on

GENDER RATIO (represented by color)

1 **1.1** **1.2**

MISSING GIRLS (represented by silhouette)

1K 2K 3K 4K 5K 6K 7K 8K 9K 10K

WHAT'S THE WAGE GAP BETWEEN THE SEXES?

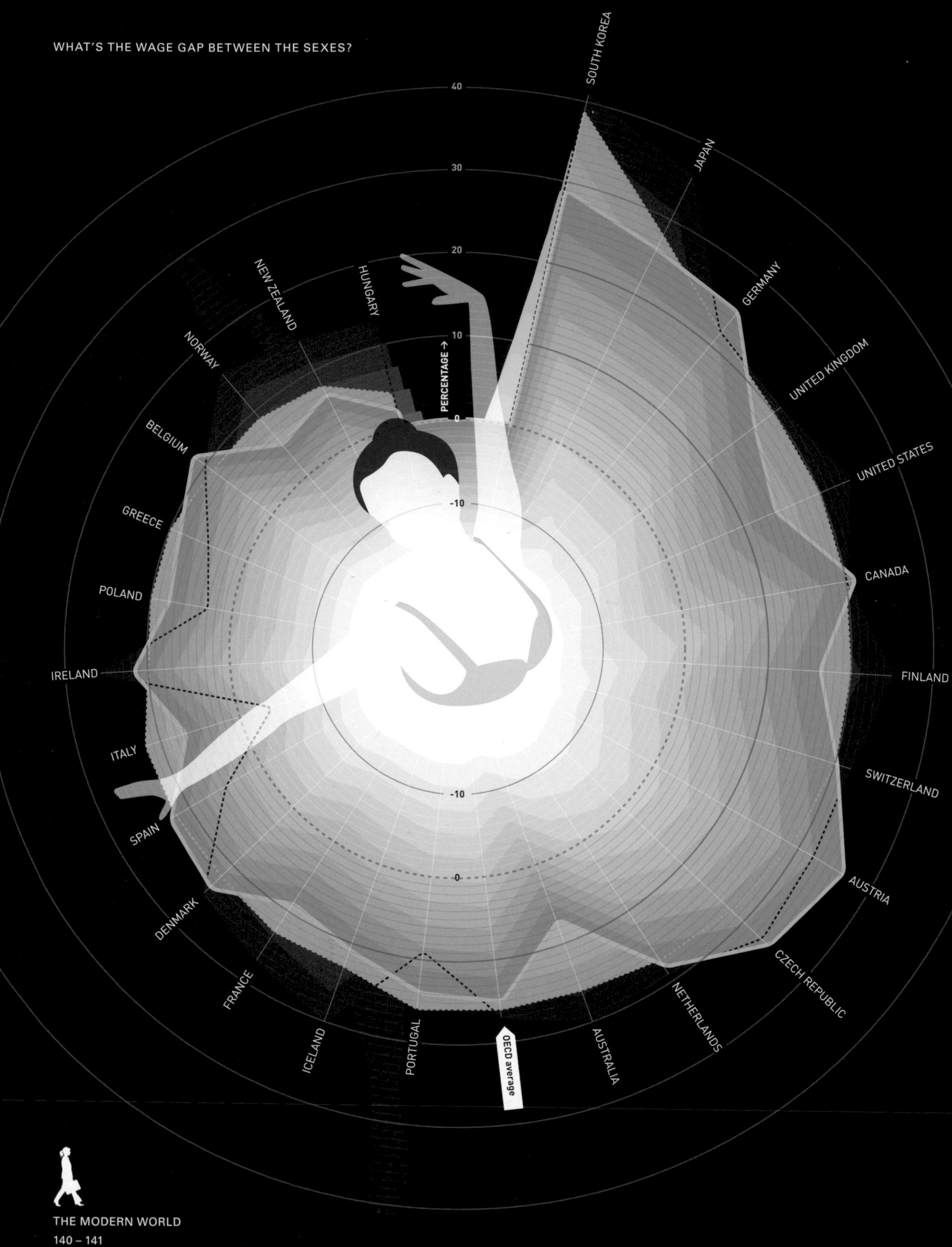

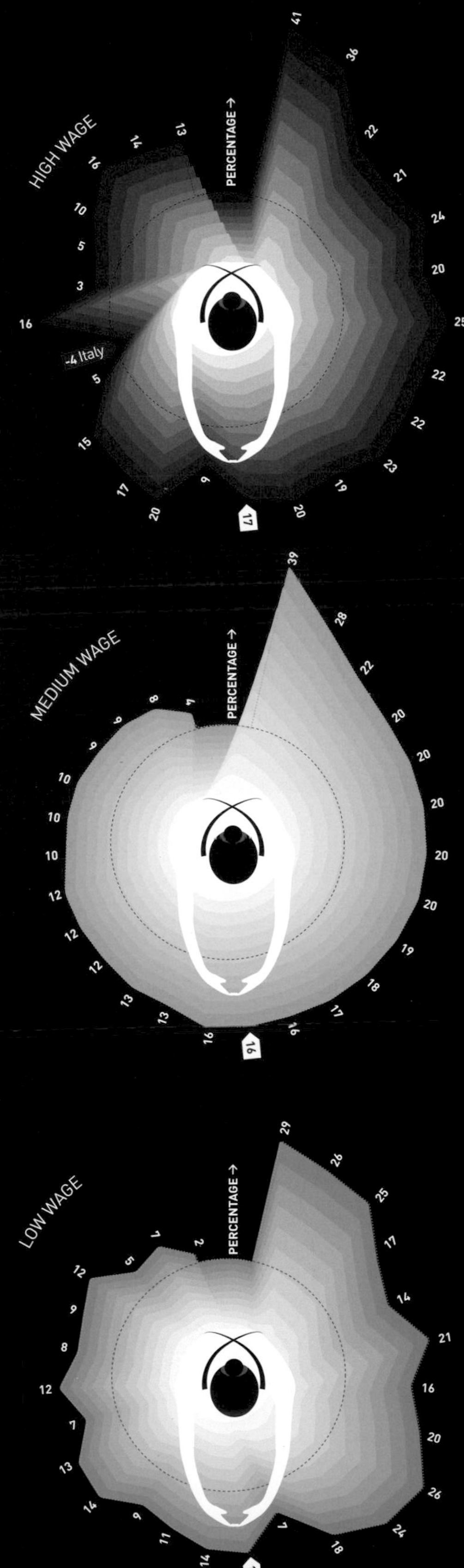

This woman's work

"Sometimes, it's hard to be a woman," Tammy Wynette was wont to sing – and we think she was probably right. But, just maybe, for the wrong reasons.

As difficult as she made "giving all your love to just one man" sound, it doesn't seem to be the toughest challenge facing lots of women today. One contender is doing the same job as "just one man," and for every dollar he gets, receiving just 61 cents. *That* sounds pretty crummy. But that's the real situation today for the average woman working in **South Korea**, which has the worst gender pay gap in the modern world.

Given that lots of countries have a whole plethora of laws trying to fix this problem, it's worth noting that it's complex: rather than just simply being paid less for identical roles (though this still happens), women either choose or are directed to different types of work, or have careers that suffer due to the expectation that they'll be the main caregivers for children.

Every country in the **OECD** has some kind of pay gap: South Korea's is the worst by far, at 39%, while **Hungary's** tops the table at just 4%. Neither the **U.K.** nor the **U.S.** does all that well, really, ranking 4th and 5th worst respectively.

But there is one easy thing a woman can do to make her pay nearer to a comparable man – but it might not be all that fun: take a low-paid job. In almost every country, inequality was far lower at the bottom of the pay scale than at the top.

In the States for example, women in the bottom fifth of female earners got 14% less than men. In the top fifth this surged to 24%. **Italy** provided the one rogue example: despite women on average earning less than men, high-earning women out-earn their male counterparts, by a slim 4%.

Wynette's economic analysis was, essentially, spot on: "You'll have bad times," she sighed, "and he'll have good times." Forty-four years on, seems like she's still right. Unless you're Italian.

GENDER GAP

The diagram shows how much less women earn than men, as a percentage. The greater the distance from the center, the greater the inequality. The countries are arranged in descending order of gender gap based on median wage.

The patent race

If invention's a race, it's one that's only getting faster.

AVERAGE NUMBER OF PATENTS ISSUED BY DECADE (1836–2011)

The current U.S. patent system began in 1836, when 109 patents were granted, and that number has increased ever since. By 1899, when patent commissioner Charles H. Dowell apocryphally said, "Everything that can be invented has been invented," more than 23,000 new patents were issued. In 2011, that total had shot to more than 220,000.

The biggest lull in mankind's creativity over last century was war, with the years following the **Second World War {■}** seeing a huge drop-off in inventions, with less than half the patents of the years just before the biggest conflict the world has ever known.

Paths to patent don't often run smoothly: Alexander Graham Bell's patent for the telephone, perhaps the most valuable ever granted, was issued in 1876, thirty years after the concept of a telephone was first mooted. The first patent for a mobile phone was issued less than a century later, in 1969. Another of the world's most important patents – for the production of penicillin – lies not with its discoverer Alexander Fleming, but with the man who found how to mass-produce the chemical, Andrew Moyer, who was granted it in 1948. Some wonder whether the patent system is broken. The year 2010 saw 60,000 more patents than the year before – many for tiny developments in software – as they shift from being a form of protection to a weapon of legal war between the world's biggest technology giants, who file, purchase and barter over thousands at a time. In 175 years the U.S. has issued 8 million patents. At the current rate it would take fewer than 36 years to issue that many again.

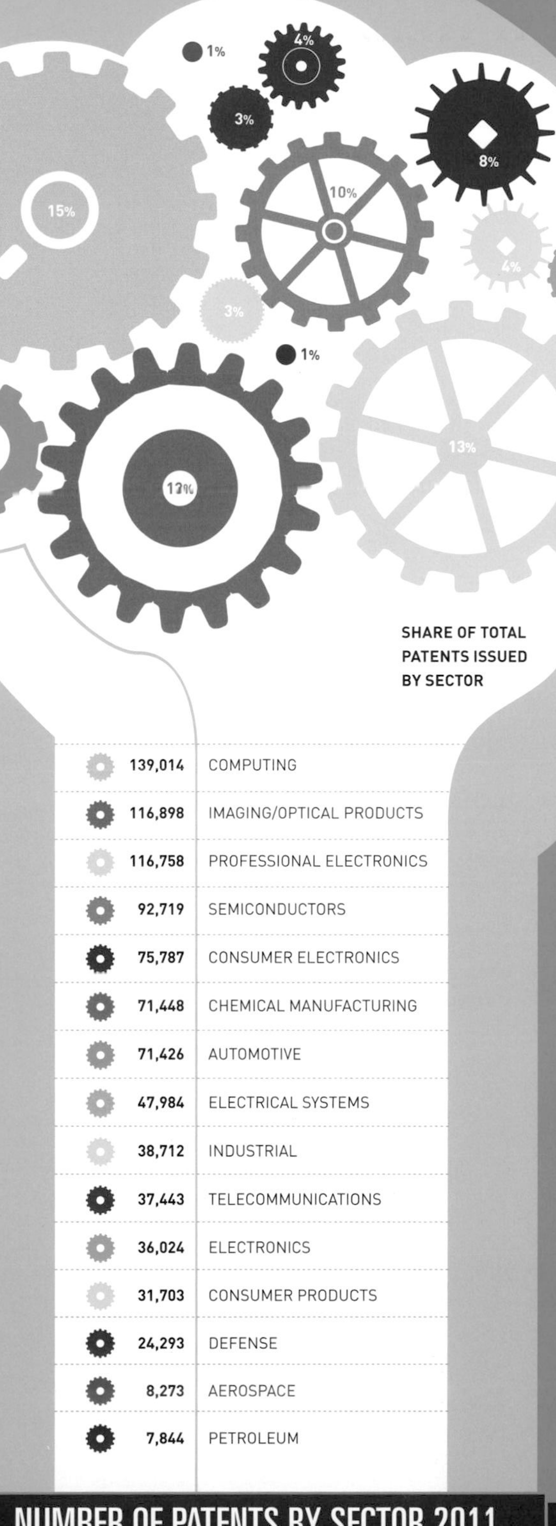

NUMBER OF PATENTS BY SECTOR 2011

Invention comprehension

How long has the stuff all about us been around? Is the **fridge** 40 years old? 80? Or 120? Which came first – the **car** or the **motorcycle**? We might appreciate all the conveniences of modern life, but generally we have almost no idea how long most of them have been around.

That's where we step in to help out, with 60 recent (and not-so-recent) inventions, which throw up more than a few oddities: did you know the **submarine** predates the **steam train** by 19 years? Or that the first working **electric car** was demonstrated in 1881? Or that the first **email** was sent in 1971, just two years after the first prototype of the **internet** was assembled? There's all that and plenty more – what else can you spot?

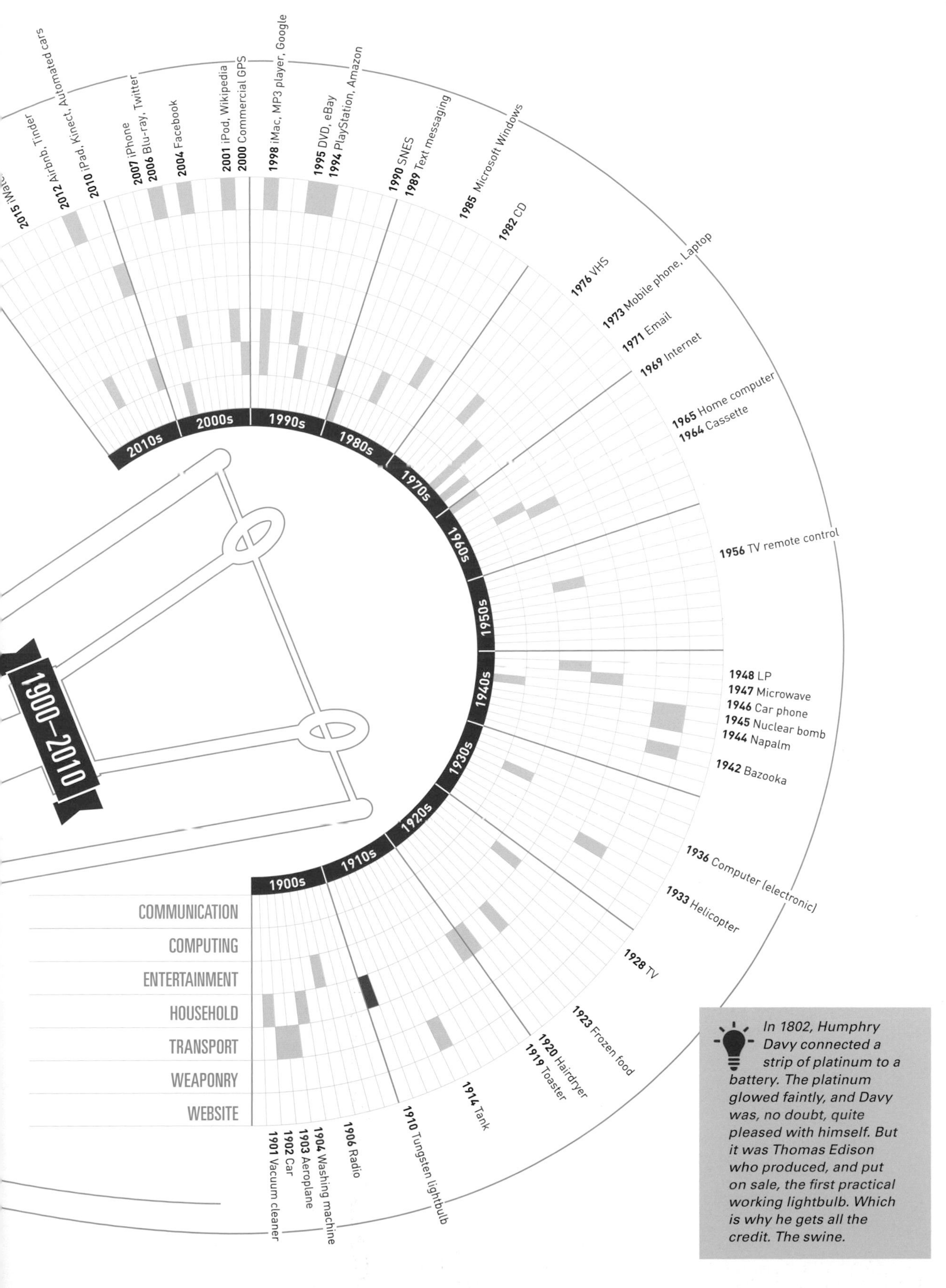

In 1802, Humphry Davy connected a strip of platinum to a battery. The platinum glowed faintly, and Davy was, no doubt, quite pleased with himself. But it was Thomas Edison who produced, and put on sale, the first practical working lightbulb. Which is why he gets all the credit. The swine.

Written in a book that I've read

What's in a good book? Given that this particular book is all about data, we've got to let the figures speak for themselves. So here are the top 20 bestselling books in the U.K. since 1998 – and wow, there's a lot of Harry Potter.

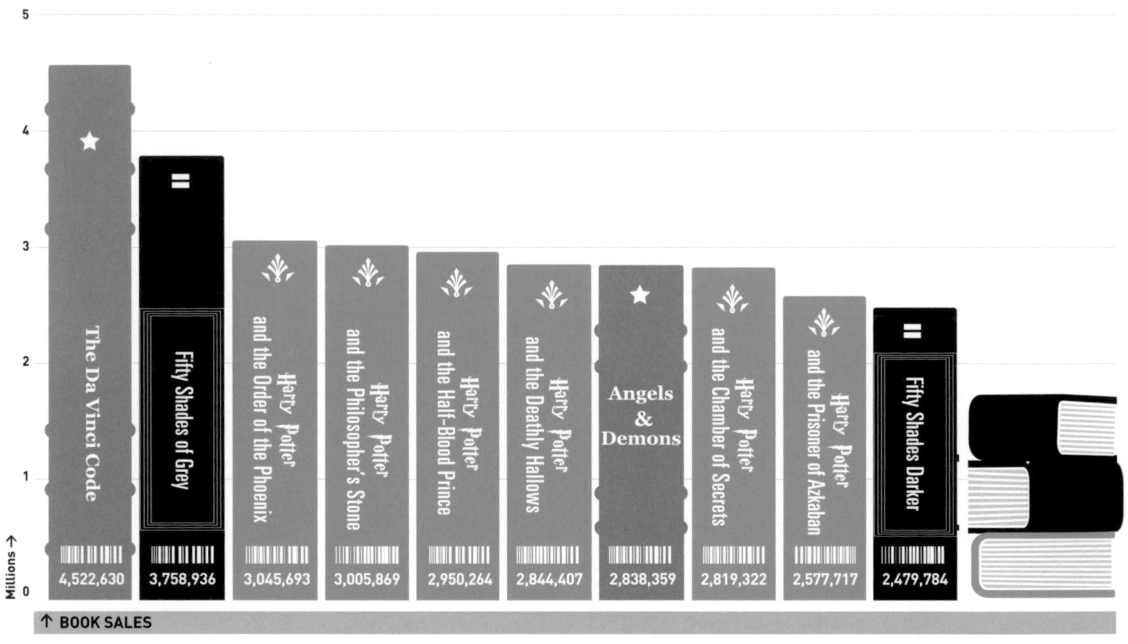

BOOK GENRES

- CRIME, THRILLER & ADVENTURE
- ROMANCE & SAGAS
- CHILDREN'S FICTION
- YOUNG ADULT FICTION
- FOOD & DRINK
- GENERAL & LITERARY FICTION

AUTHORS

- BROWN, D.
- JAMES, E. L.
- ROWLING, J. K.
- MEYER, S.
- OLIVER, J.
- SEBOLD, A.
- LARSSON, S.

2002–2012

BOOK SALES
DECLINE

0% —23%
taking inflation into account

$15 billion $15 billion

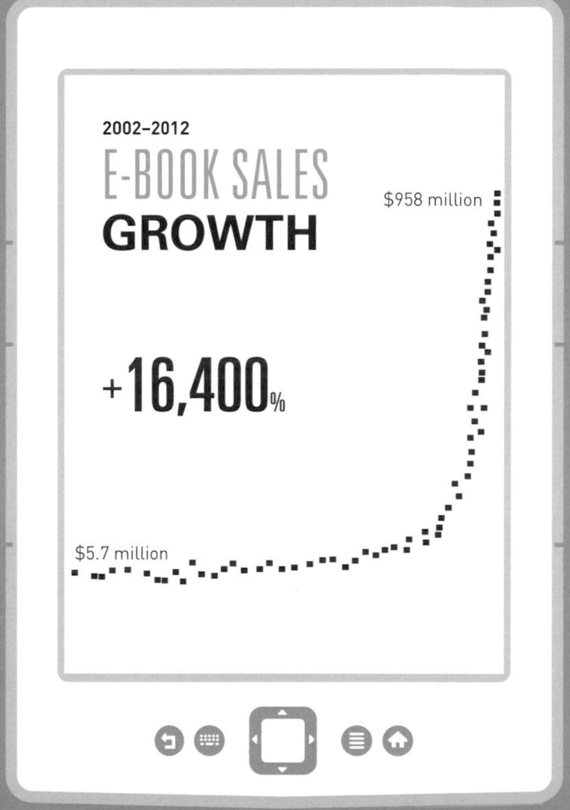

In fact, we'd say the results are pretty clear: any book with a boy-wizard or a detective-journalist investigating massive conspiracies with a female hacker companion simply cannot fail. Especially if there are vampires involved.

Now that we've crafted the perfect bestseller, will anyone buy it? Conventional wisdom dictates book sales are declining as we all turn our short attention spans to TV, video games, Twitter and ... stuff.

Thankfully (given this is, y'know, a book), some U.S. data suggests things might not be as bad as you might think.

The U.S. Census Bureau doesn't make great reading for U.S. bookstores: data from the last full year, 2011, show sales have fallen back to levels last seen in 2002 – which after inflation suggests they're selling almost 25% fewer books than they used to.

But these figures miss out a couple of little booksellers, including one or two you might have heard of: Walmart and Amazon. Big box retailers and online shops aren't included – and industry estimates suggest these could add around $10 billion a year to the figures. Much healthier.

E-book sales are also changing the game. Ten years ago, less than $2 million of e-books were sold each quarter. By the end of 2011 this hit more than $230 million. Early 2012 data suggest monthly sales are topping $100 million – even if anecdotal evidence indicates that's almost entirely women enjoying an illicit read of **Fifty Shades of Grey** {■} during their morning commute.

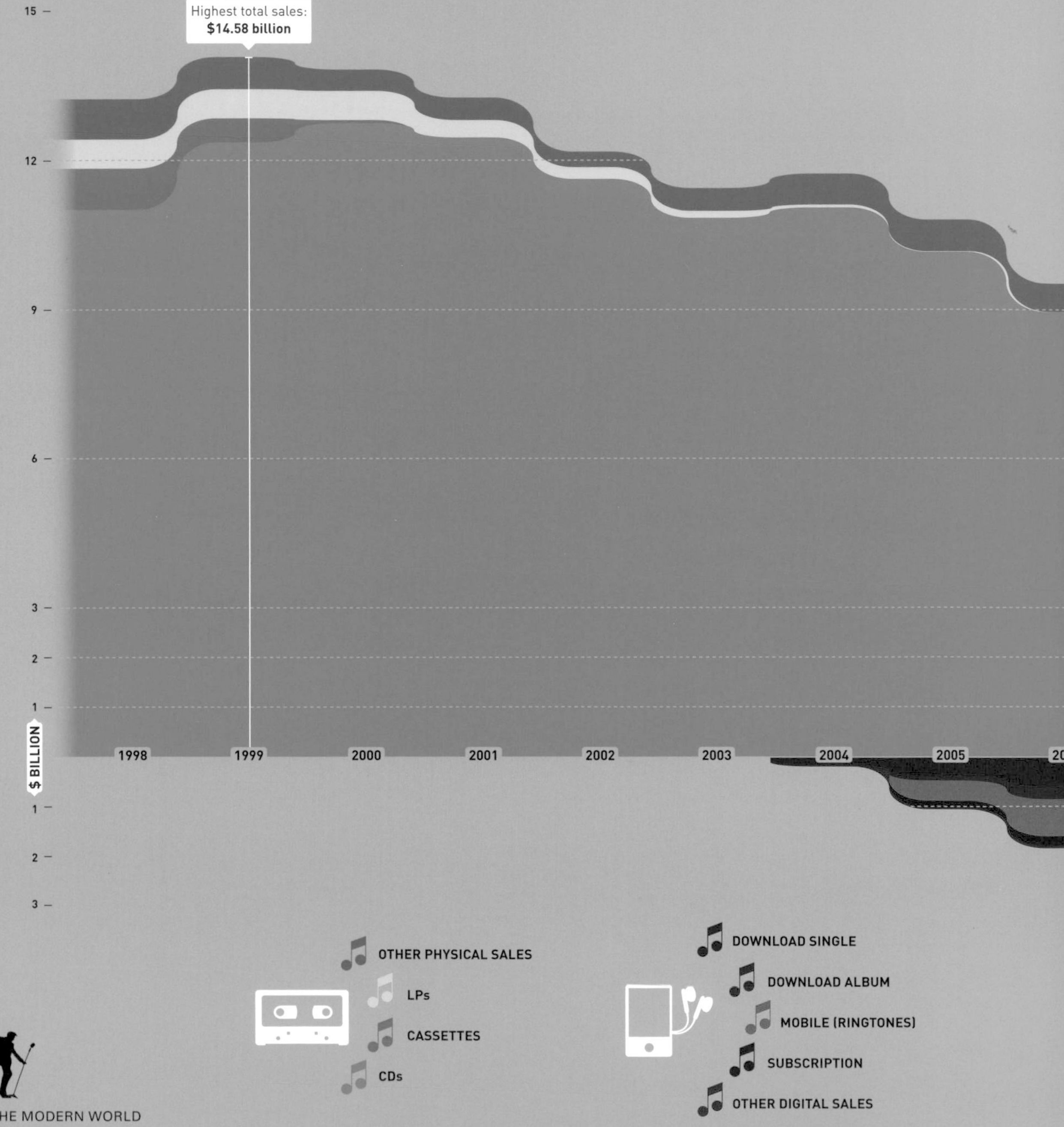
15
12
9
6
3
2
1
$ BILLION
1
2
3
Highest total sales:
$14.58 billion
1998
1999
2000
2001
2002
2003
2004
2005
OTHER PHYSICAL SALES
LPs
CASSETTES
CDs
DOWNLOAD SINGLE
DOWNLOAD ALBUM
MOBILE (RINGTONES)
SUBSCRIPTION
OTHER DIGITAL SALES

Makin' music

"Home Taping Is Killing Music!" – to a certain generation, this dire warning about the ills of using a cassette recorder to bootleg tracks from the radio provokes a nostalgic, wry smile. As any star from the CD era will testify, music – and the music industry – survived home taping just fine.

Today, the bogeyman threatening the music business is online piracy – but here, maybe, the numbers are a bit scarier. According to figures on U.S. sales published by the RIAA, in 1998 the U.S. recorded-music business was selling $13.7 billion dollars of songs. Nice. But by 2010, this wasn't looking quite so healthy, at a mere $7 billion – a fall of almost half in just 12 years. But painful though that is, pinning all of the blame on piracy might just prove premature. There's so much more going on.

For one, formats were born, and formats died. **Cassette tapes { }**, after failing in their bid to murder music, died off themselves, dropping from $1.4 billion sales in '98 to absolutely zilch by 2009. Thanks to hipsters – yes, you did read those three words correctly – **LPs { }** were spared a similar fate. Sales slumped to a low of just $14 million in 2005, but then sprang back to a hefty $119 million six years later, raising the potentially troubling prospect that there are more hipsters than you might hope.

Another strange boom was **ringtones { }**, which rose, supernova-like, only to collapse. In 2008, the market for these travesties was worth $977 million. By 2011, it was less than a third of that. In your irritating little FACE, Crazy Frog.

But it's **digital sales** – numbering only 2% of the total in 2004, but climbing to 52% in 2011 – that really unpick the mystery. Yes, sales have grown more slowly than **CD { }** sales have fallen. But piracy might only be one factor. Another is the rise of the single, as people pick-and-mix their playlists.

CD albums always vastly outsold singles. In the digital era, sales of singles are comfortably more than double those of albums. It's a whole new world, but there seems to be plenty of life left in music – downloaded, live, or even on LP. Anything, frankly, except tapes.

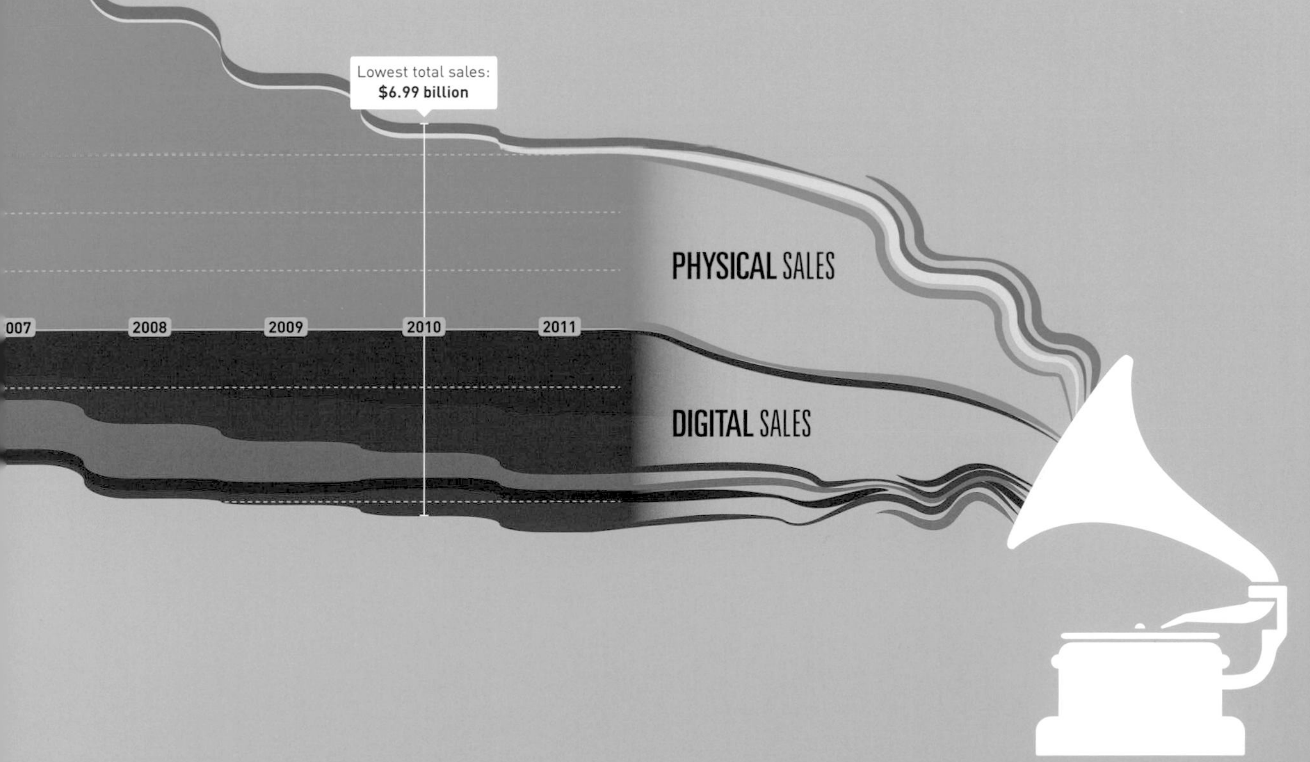

And just in case you're curious, here are the artists whose records have made up those untold billions of dollars' sales over the years: the **top-selling artists** of all time by confirmed sales in markets across the globe.

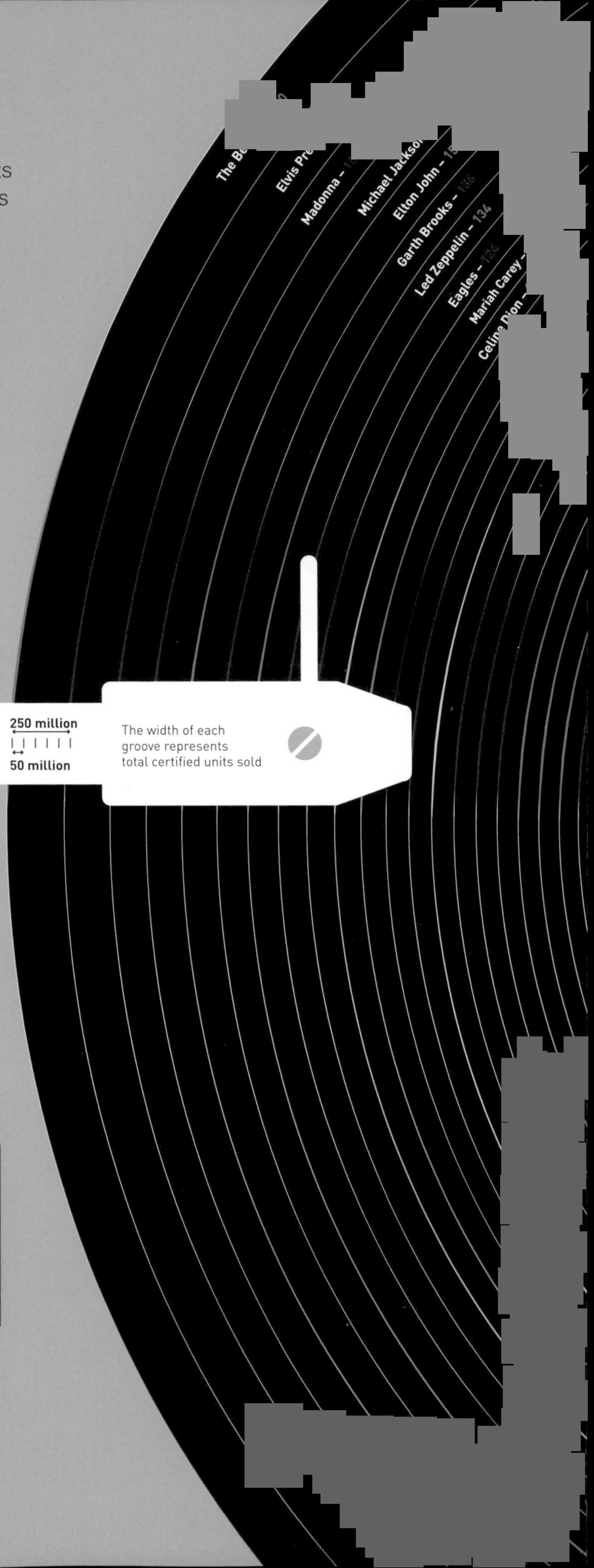
Madonna -
Elton John -
Garth Brooks -
Led Zeppelin - 134
Eagles -
Mariah Carey -
250 million
50 million
The width of each groove represents total certified units sold

TOP 50 BESTSELLERS

TOTAL CERTIFIED UNITS (MILLIONS) BY COUNTRY OF ORIGIN

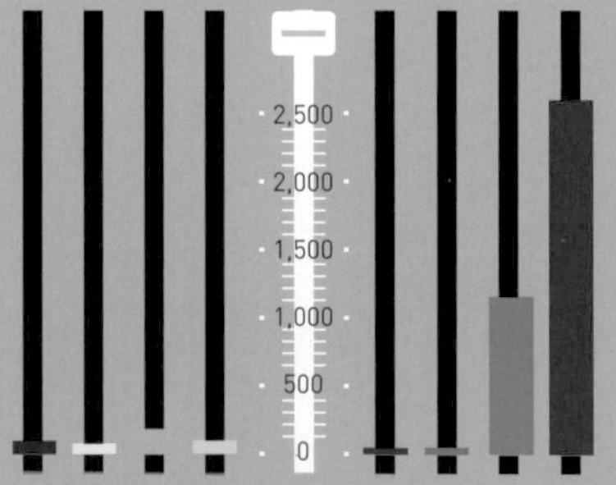
2,500
2,000
1,500
1,000
500
0

AUSTRALIA
BARBADOS
CANADA
IRELAND
JAPAN
SWEDEN
U.K.
U.S.

Pink Floyd – 110
AC/DC – 100
Whitney Houston – 100
U2 – 98
Billy Joel – 98
Barbra Streisand – 93
Bruce Springsteen – 93
Queen – 91
The Rolling Stones – 90
Phil Collins – 82
Metallica – 82
Aerosmith – 79
Rihanna – 77
Eminem – 75
Shania Twain – 71
George Strait – 71
Fleetwood Mac – 70
Rod Stewart – 68
Backstreet Boys – 67
Britney Spears – 67
Bon Jovi – 64
Bee Gees – 64
Neil Diamond – 63
Van Halen – 63
Guns N' Roses – 62
Prince – 60
Santana – 60
Kenny Rogers – 58
ABBA – 55
Journey – 55
Kenny G – 51
R. Kelly – 50
B'z – 50
Taylor Swift – 50
The Black Eyed Peas – 49
Beyoncé
Red Hot Chili Peppers – 49
Adele – 49
Janet Jackson – 48
Lady Gaga – 48
TOP 50
1 → 50
50 ← 1
BESTSELLERS

Who are the 1%?

The Occupy movement came virtually out of nowhere at the height of the economic crisis, campaigning against economic inequality and injustice. Their most famous dividing line was pitching "us" – the 99% – against a rich elite: the 1%. But who, exactly, are that 1%?

The divide is most startling when you look at wealth, the total value of what we own, rather than income (what we earn). The Forbes rich list shows wealth extraordinary enough to make even Mother Teresa green with envy: the world's wealthiest man is worth $69 billion. The top hundred are worth $1,716 billion – enough to clear the U.K.'s national debt overnight.

But when we start to look a little bit more widely, the lives of the world's **top 1% { }** might not look quite so lavish. To be in the world's top 1% in 2011, you need to be worth at least $712,000 – a heck of a lot more than most of us have, but hardly private-jet territory. Anyone who owns a half-decent property in London, Tokyo, Moscow or New York is probably part of the 1%.

If that's you – congratulations! But what about the rest of us? Well, $10,000 of assets is enough to place someone among the richest 25% of adults across the world. In the western world, that's more or less anyone who owns a fairly new car.

If you're carless, fear not. To be in the wealthiest half of the planet's adults, the total value of your worldly possessions has to top $4,200. Got a laptop and a decent record collection? You're in!

But it's only in the aggregate that we get to see the end result of these inequalities. There are **30 million (dollar) millionaires { }** on the planet. Between them, they're worth more than 11 times as much as the **poorest three billion { }**. Maybe, just maybe, those Occupy guys had a point.

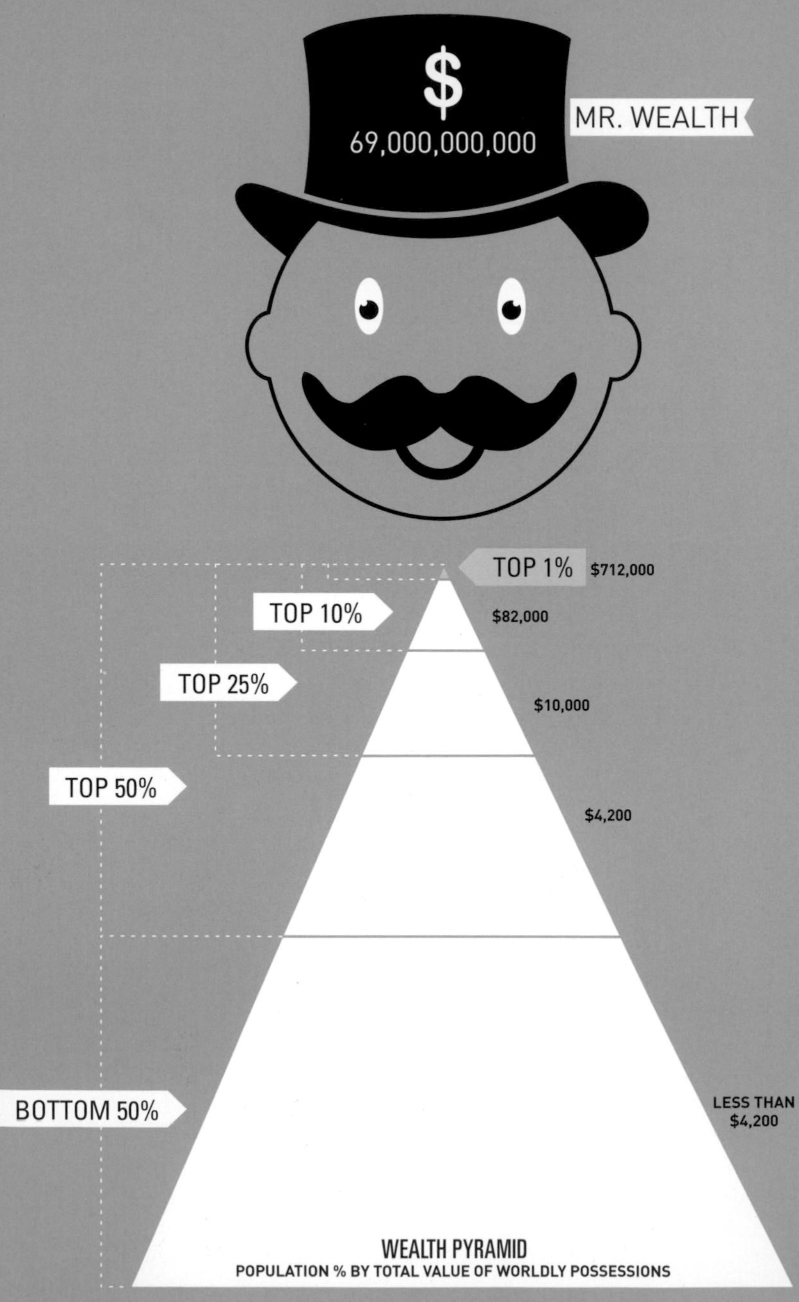

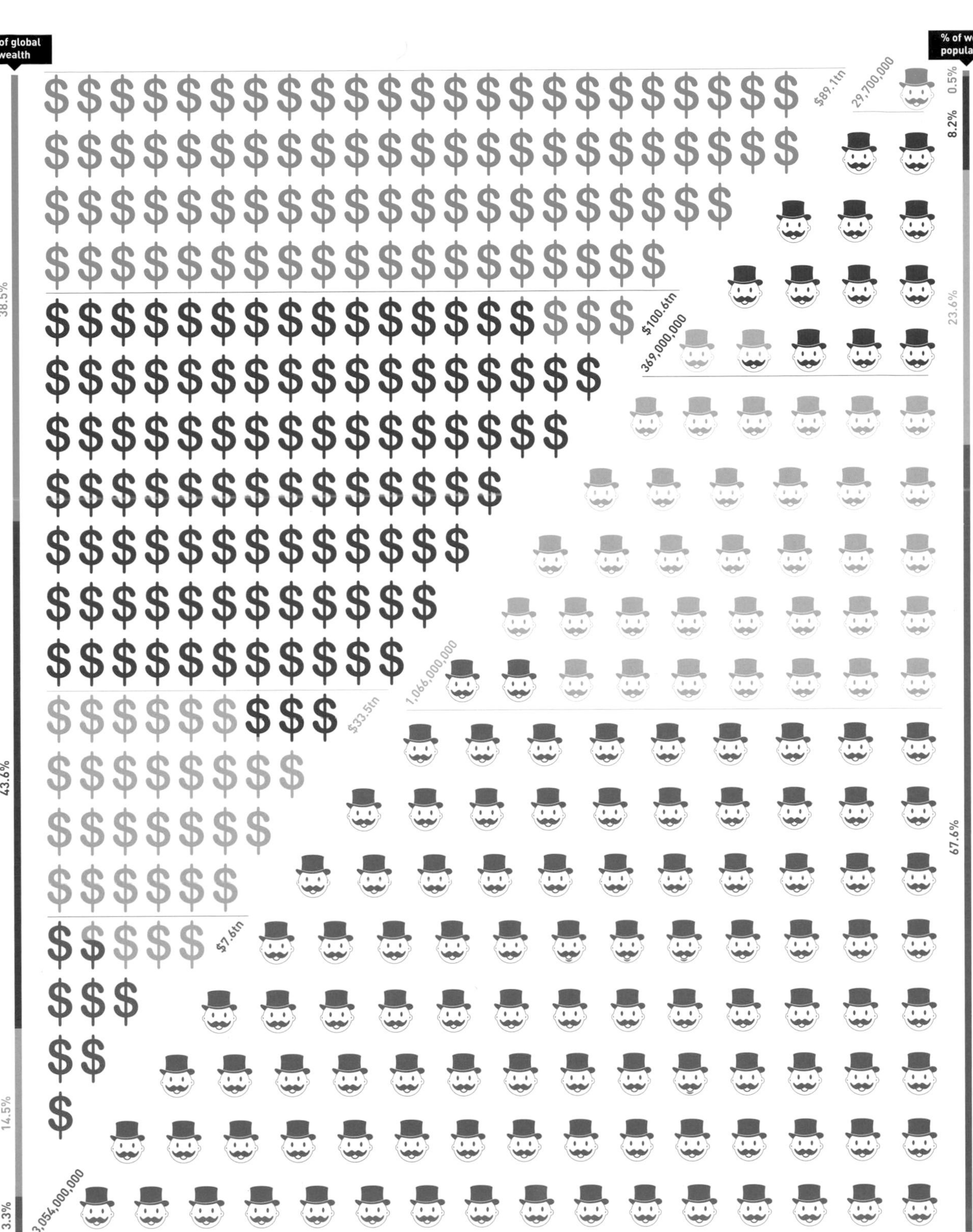

TOTAL WEALTH

$ = 1 TRILLION DOLLARS

TOTAL NUMBER OF PEOPLE

= 30 MILLION PEOPLE

WEALTH GROUPING

- $1MILLION +
- $100,000 – $1MILLION
- $10,000 – $100,000
- $0 – $10,000

Global gluttony

Charles Dickens got a lot right – and one thing particularly so: when the orphans of *Oliver!* sing "Food, glorious food! What wouldn't we give for that extra bit more?" they got right to the core of the issue.

Just about all of us know the deal: men are meant to eat about 2,500 calories a day, and women can chow down on 2,000. If we eat more, we're likely to get fat. Turns out to be advice a great deal of the world is ignoring.

But first: what, exactly, is a calorie? Almost no one knows. It turns out, what we usually refer to as a calorie is actually a kilocalorie (a thousand calories), and it's the amount of energy it takes to heat one liter of water by one degree Celsius. So each day a typical man should consume enough energy to heat a bath by around 30 degrees. Who knew?

Problem is, he's probably eating a lot more than that. The typical **U.S. citizen {■}**, according to UN data, is eating an amazing 3,750 calories a day (only **Austrians {■}** typically eat more). At that rate, you'd expect a man who doesn't exercise much to gain about 1 kg of extra fat every week. So maybe it's no surprise that 44.2% of U.S. adults are obese.

It's not just them, though. In more than 60 countries, adults typically eat more than 3,000 calories a day – and we're eating ever more. Across the world, an average person ate 180 calories more each day (roughly speaking, equivalent to a small bag of chips) in 2006–08 than they did in 1990–92.

There are, of course, countries such as **Haiti {■}** and **Eritrea {■}**, in which people don't have enough to eat: in 14 nations the average person ate fewer than 2,200 calories a day – and many will have had far fewer than that. Worse still, nutrition isn't only about calories; far more will fail to get enough protein or vitamins in the little they do eat.

But it's the contrast that's most telling: people in the five countries that eat the least all ate less than half what the average Austrian does daily.

Obesity is a result of many factors. And generally, higher fat vs protein intake is common among nations with high rates of obesity. ***Egypt {■}*** *stands out with relatively high obesity (22% of adults) yet a low consumption of fat (just 53 g per day).*

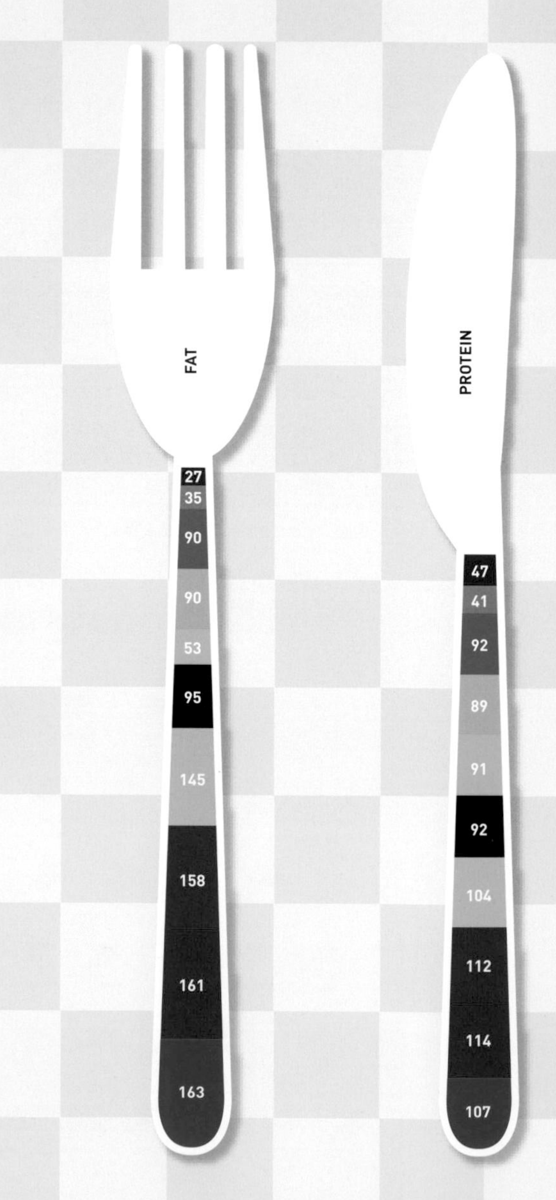

FAT & PROTEIN

DAILY INTAKE PER PERSON (g)

COUNTRIES

- ERITREA
- HAITI
- JAPAN
- CHINA
- EGYPT
- MEXICO
- UNITED KINGDOM
- ITALY
- UNITED STATES
- AUSTRIA

0
1.3
2.3
4.1
23.1
44.2
22
14.4
30.1
23.7
OBESITY (adult population %)

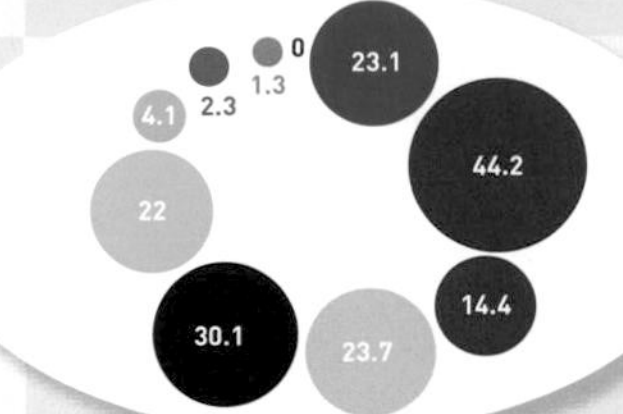

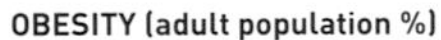

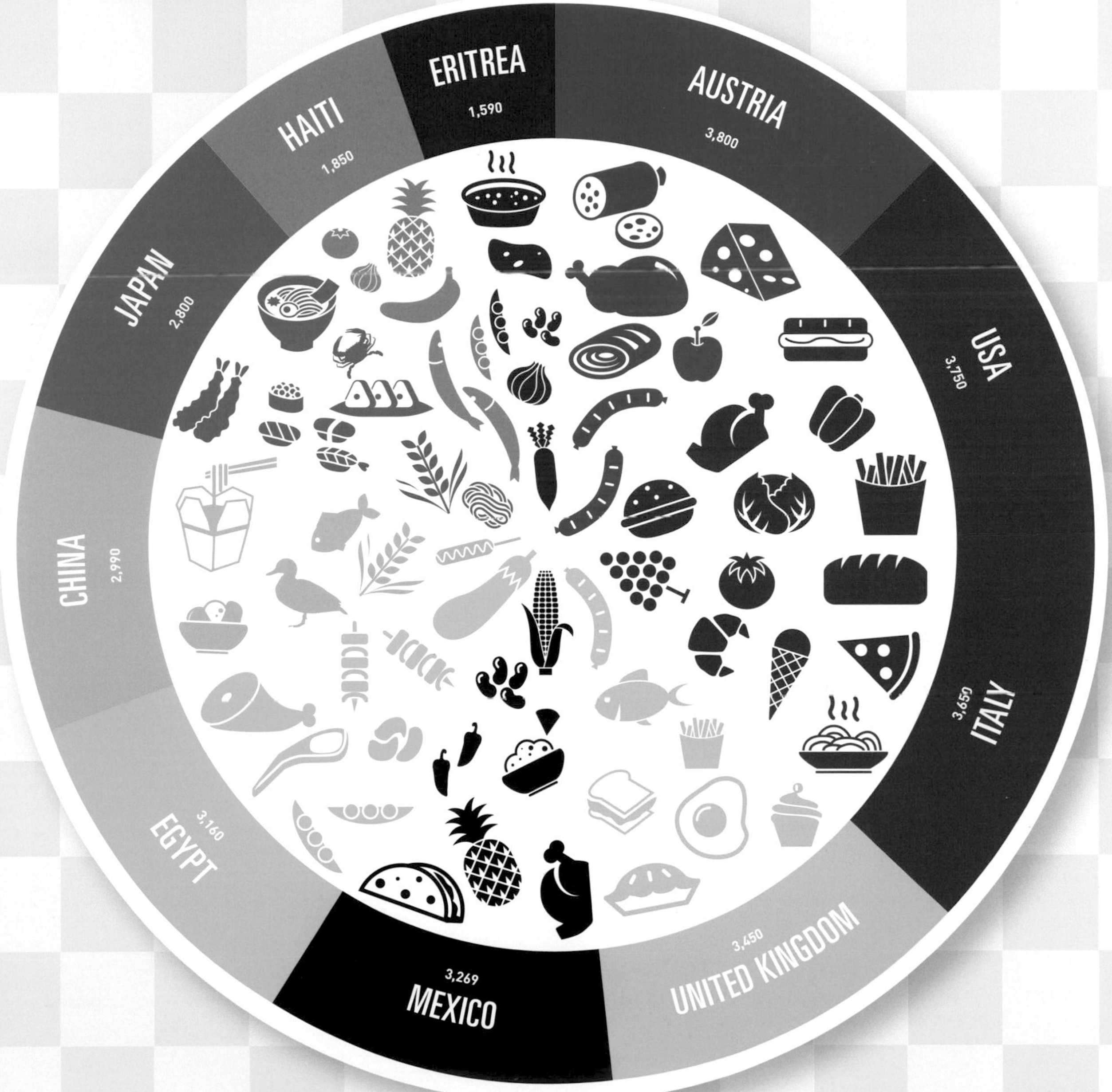

ERITREA
1,590
AUSTRIA
3,800
USA
3,750
ITALY
3,650
UNITED KINGDOM
3,450
MEXICO
3,269
EGYPT
3,160
CHINA
2,990
JAPAN
2,800
HAITI
1,850

CALORIES

DAILY INTAKE PER PERSON (kcal)

Hey, state spender

Big government, tax and spend, government handouts, and more – there are a lot of phrases describing spending by the state, and not many of them are all that positive. However, most governments have decided they want to play a pretty large role: only 24 out of 182 countries for which data is available spend less than 20% of GDP.

The country that has seen the biggest shift in government spending since the first publication of this book is a nation undergoing considerable change – **Burma**. Its public spending went from just 11.5% of its GDP in 2012 to almost 30% – or in cash terms – $1,207 more per person.

The government of the **Democratic Republic of Congo**, on the other hand, is still at the bottom of the table spending only 12.7% of its GDP and being a poor country, this means only $89 per person.

The countries at the top of the charts are perhaps not a shock: **East Timor**, **Kiribati**, **Libya** and – of course – **Cuba**, all of whose governments spend more than 65% of their GDP. The **UK**'s government spending is around 45% of GDP, while the **U.S.** government spends 39% – both considerably ahead of the nominally Communist government of **China**, where government spending is just 29% of GDP.

And, just in case there are any jetsetting welfare scroungers out there looking for where the government will lavish the most cash on them, the place to head turns out to be **Luxembourg**, where the state spends $40,133 for each person in the country. Not bad!

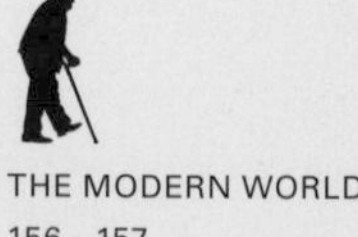

GOVERNMENT EXPENDITURE (Heritage Foundation 2016)

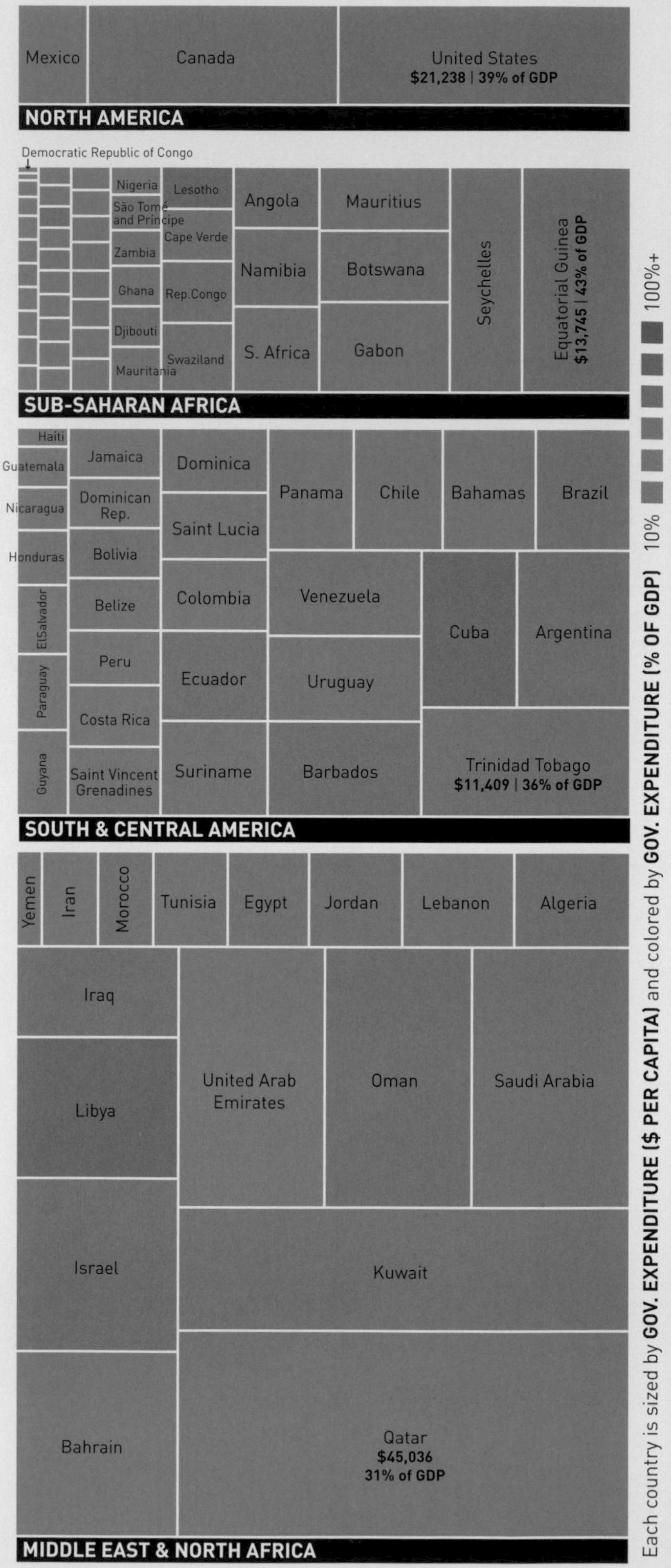

Mexico
Canada
United States
$21,238 | 39% of GDP
NORTH AMERICA

Democratic Republic of Congo
Nigeria
São Tomé and Principe
Zambia
Ghana
Djibouti
Mauritania
Lesotho
Cape Verde
Rep.Congo
Swaziland
Angola
Namibia
S. Africa
Mauritius
Botswana
Gabon
Seychelles
Equatorial Guinea
$13,745 | 43% of GDP
SUB-SAHARAN AFRICA

Haiti
Guatemala
Nicaragua
Honduras
ElSalvador
Paraguay
Guyana
Jamaica
Dominican Rep.
Bolivia
Belize
Peru
Costa Rica
Saint Vincent Grenadines
Dominica
Saint Lucia
Colombia
Ecuador
Suriname
Panama
Chile
Bahamas
Brazil
Venezuela
Uruguay
Barbados
Cuba
Argentina
Trinidad Tobago
$11,409 | 36% of GDP
SOUTH & CENTRAL AMERICA

Yemen
Iran
Morocco
Tunisia
Egypt
Jordan
Lebanon
Algeria
Iraq
Libya
Israel
Bahrain
United Arab Emirates
Oman
Saudi Arabia
Kuwait
Qatar
$45,036
31% of GDP
MIDDLE EAST & NORTH AFRICA

Each country is sized by **GOV. EXPENDITURE ($ PER CAPITA)** and colored by **GOV. EXPENDITURE (% OF GDP)**
10%
100%+

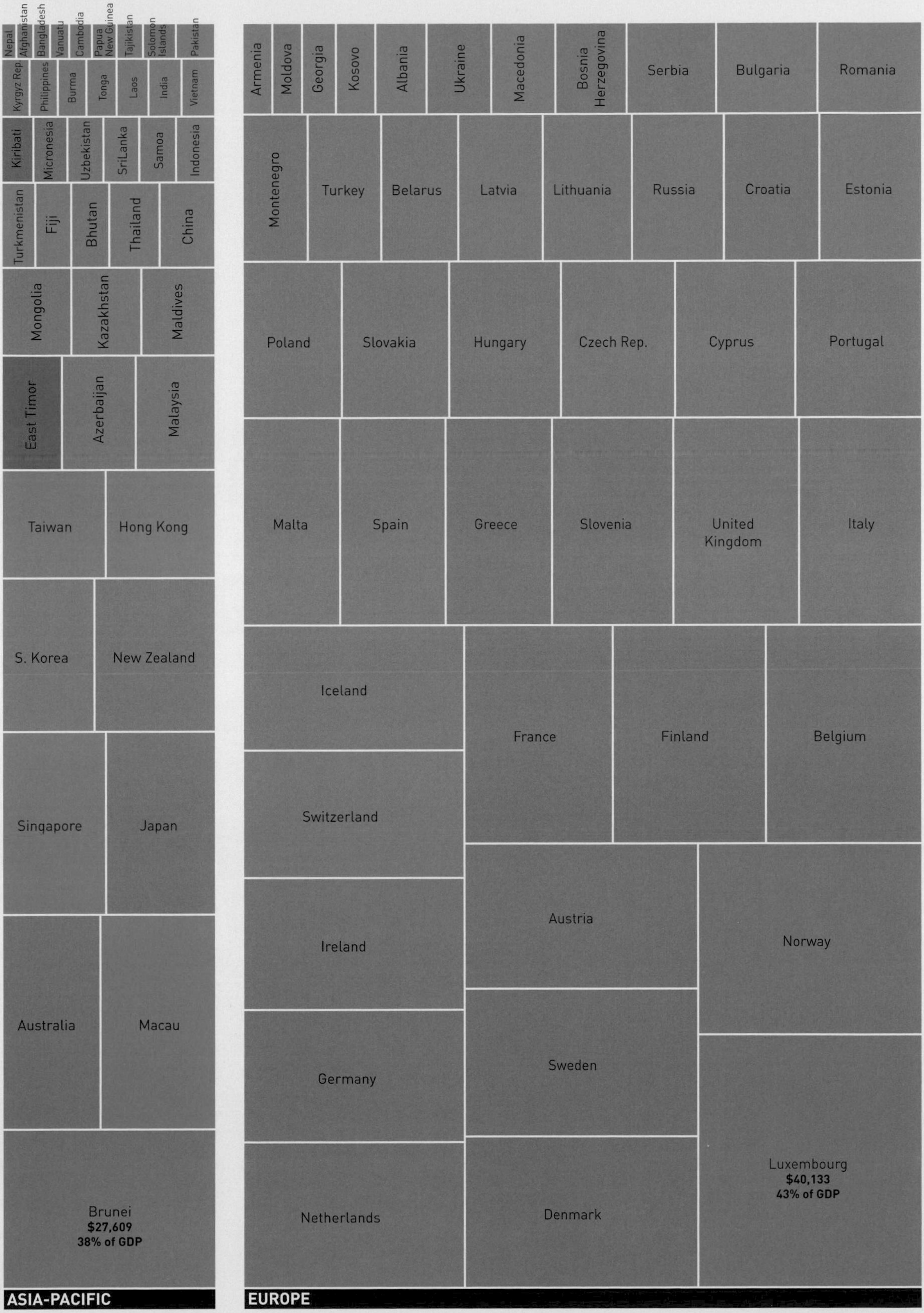

Nepal
Afghanistan
Bangladesh
Vanuatu
Cambodia
Papua New Guinea
Tajikistan
Solomon Islands
Pakistan
Kyrgyz Rep.
Philippines
Burma
Tonga
Laos
India
Vietnam
Kiribati
Micronesia
Uzbekistan
SriLanka
Samoa
Indonesia
Turkmenistan
Fiji
Bhutan
Thailand
China
Mongolia
Kazakhstan
Maldives
East Timor
Azerbaijan
Malaysia
Taiwan
Hong Kong
S. Korea
New Zealand
Singapore
Japan
Australia
Macau
Brunei
$27,609
38% of GDP

ASIA-PACIFIC

Armenia
Moldova
Georgia
Kosovo
Albania
Ukraine
Macedonia
Bosnia Herzegovina
Serbia
Bulgaria
Romania
Montenegro
Turkey
Belarus
Latvia
Lithuania
Russia
Croatia
Estonia
Poland
Slovakia
Hungary
Czech Rep.
Cyprus
Portugal
Malta
Spain
Greece
Slovenia
United Kingdom
Italy
Iceland
France
Finland
Belgium
Switzerland
Austria
Norway
Ireland
Sweden
Germany
Luxembourg
$40,133
43% of GDP
Netherlands
Denmark

EUROPE

Carbon sinks (and kitchens, cars, emails)

Climate change might be one of the biggest threats to our way of life, a challenge the world's governments meet regularly to discuss, and something set to make millions homeless – but it would make a terrible Bond villain.

The problem with stuff that acts slowly is that however serious it is (and all the evidence suggests climate change really is pretty grave), it doesn't really scare us all enough to make us change our ways.

Seeing as we don't all seem set to break down our cars for scrap, abandon electricity and move to eco-villages, we're left looking for other solutions to the problem, and some of these are looked at in the next few spreads. But just because we don't want to change our lifestyle doesn't mean there's nothing we can do.

The examples across this page show that oftentimes, it ain't what we do, it's the way that we do it that affects how much carbon we emit. **Washing your dishes {■}** under a running tap with scorching hot water will use about 8 kg of carbon dioxide. Doing it under cold water will leave you with a carbon footprint of zero. Sadly, it might also leave you with tired arms and yucky dishes (and consequently, probably pretty unhappy houseguests). A happy medium – using a dishwasher – uses less than 800 g.

Ditching milk from your tea {■} cuts its carbon footprint in half. **Talking less on your cell {■}** saves masses of energy – as does **cutting down on email attachments {■}** (so only send photos of cats if they're really hysterical. That's still allowed).

Maybe the coolest example – if it's cheating a bit – is how you use the money in your pocket. **A buck fifty spent on a bargain flight {■}** generates about 10 kg of CO_2. Spending it on a lawyer uses about 160 g. Or, put it in a really efficient rainforestry project, and you might save 330 kg.

Take a look opposite at what saves a lot, and what saves very little.

Carbon footprint – **TONS**

MANUFACTURING A NEW CAR	LAND ROVER DISCOVERY, top of the line
	FORD MONDEO, medium spec
	CITROËN C1, basic spec
USING A CELL PHONE	A YEAR AT 1 HOUR OF CALLS PER DAY
	A YEAR AT 30 MINS OF CALLS PER DAY
	A YEAR AT 10 MINS OF CALLS PER DAY

Carbon footprint – **KILOGRAMS**

SPENDING $1.50 ON TRAVEL	BUDGET FLIGHTS
	FLIGHTS
	GAS FOR YOUR CAR
WASHING DISHES	BY HAND, extravagant use of water
	DISHWASHER AT 55°C
	BY HAND, minimum water, not too hot
DOING A LOAD OF LAUNDRY	60°C, combine washer/dryer
	40°C, tumble-dried in vented dryer
	30°C, dried on the line
DRINKING A PINT OF BEER	EXTENSIVELY TRANSPORTED BOTTLED
	LOCAL BOTTLED BEER
	LOCALLY BREWED CASK ALE AT A PUB
READING A NEWSPAPER	DAILY MAIL, recycled
	SUN, recycled
	GUARDIAN, recycled
CYCLING A MILE	ENERGY FROM BACON
	ENERGY FROM CEREAL AND MILK
	ENERGY FROM BANANAS
HAVING A CUP OF TEA	WHITE, boiling twice the required water
	WHITE, boiling only required water
	BLACK, boiling only required water
DRYING YOUR HANDS	STANDARD ELECTRIC DRYER
	ONE PAPER TOWEL
	DYSON AIRBLADE DRYER
SENDING AN EMAIL	EMAIL WITH LARGE ATTACHMENT
	NORMAL EMAIL
	SPAM EMAIL

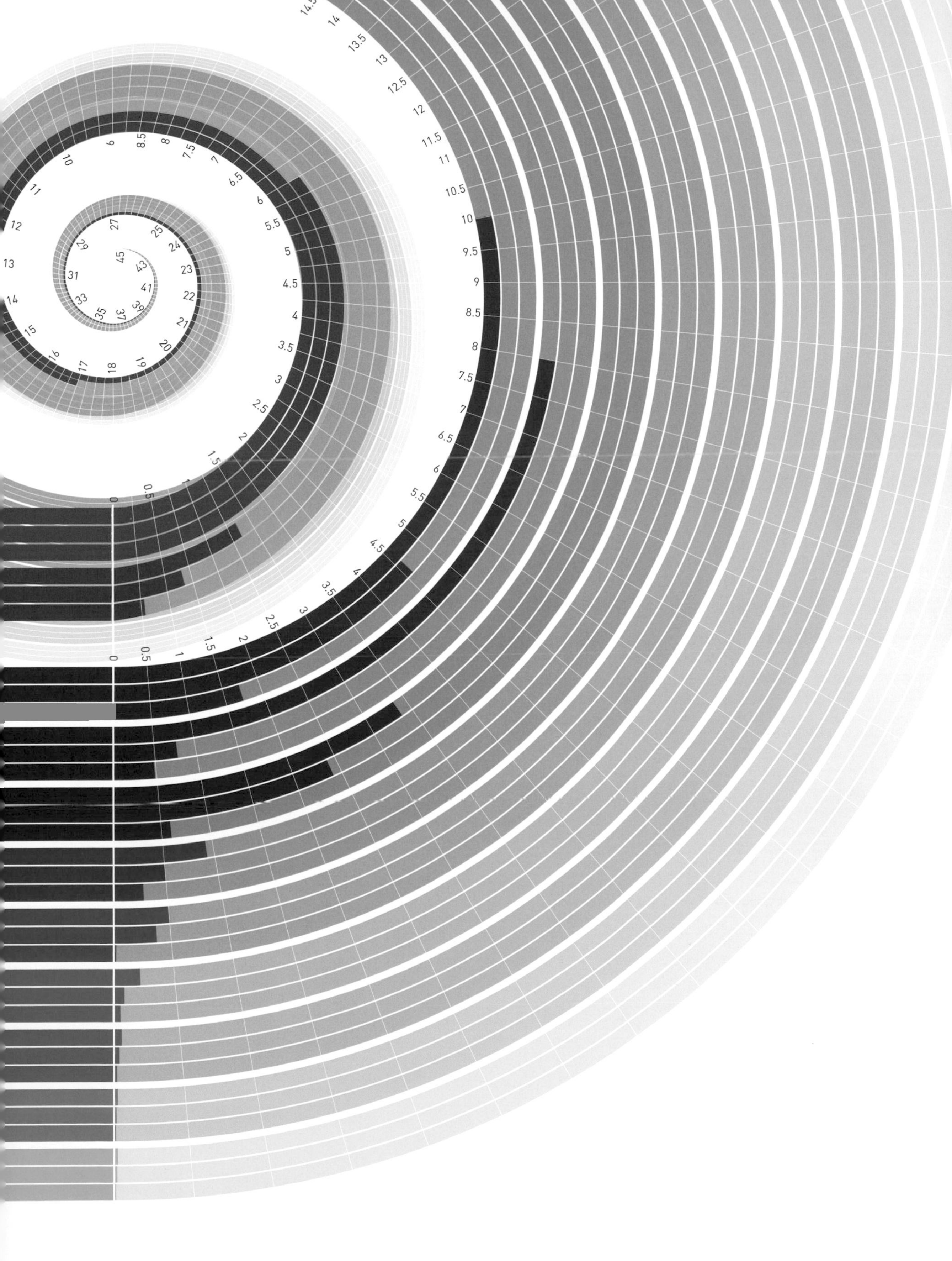

The world in carbon

It's rare for the world's leaders to agree on trivial issues, let alone something important – but in 1992, that's exactly what happened. Most of the world's major economies recognized climate change as a serious and pressing challenge to humanity, agreed greenhouse gas emissions had to be controlled, and even agreed to reduce them.

Sure, we know there's bound to have been hitches in the 20 years since that landmark conference, but given the gravity of the subject, surely some progress has been made.

In 1992, the world emitted an amazing 21.4 billion tonnes of carbon dioxide, according to the U.S. EIA. Surely, 20 years on, that figure looks dramatically different.

It does indeed. In 2010 – the last year for which data is available – the world emitted 31.8 billion tonnes of carbon dioxide. The amount of emissions is up almost 50% since the Kyoto protocols, having increased every year since 1992.

Tracking down the culprits is harder than it might seem. **China** is indisputably the biggest producer of greenhouse gases, responsible for 8.3 billion tonnes of emissions in 2010 – a billion more than just a year before. Not only does it emit vastly more than anyone else – the **U.S.** is second with 5.6 billion tonnes – but the amount is increasing massively each year.

But China is a relatively poor country whose population is finally starting to get richer at a fair rate: exactly the kind of development we hope for across the planet. They argue, as do other countries in a similar position, that they shouldn't have to pay the price for damage caused by the West.

They could also point out that each Chinese citizen is responsible for 6.3 tonnes of carbon dioxide a year – far less than the 18.1 tonnes for every U.S. citizen. Is it China's fault it's a big country?

The problem's a thorny one – but clearly not a Presidential priority: across six hours of Presidential and Vice-Presidential debates in 2012, climate change dominated a huge ... zero seconds of debate time. Oh dear.

DIAGRAM

The comparison between past and present carbon emissions – per geographical area and per person – is illustrated using the molecular structure of CO_2.

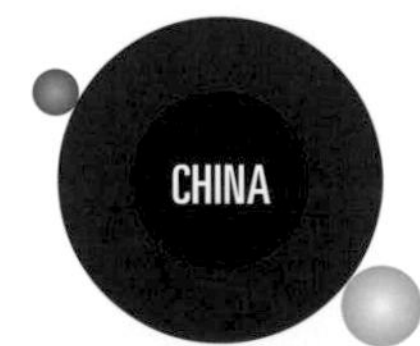

TOTAL EMISSIONS: **2,449.2 / 8,321** (1992/2010)
EMISSIONS PER PERSON: **2.1 / 6.3** (1992/2010)

TOTAL EMISSIONS: **5,093.6 / 5,610.1** (1992/2010)
EMISSIONS PER PERSON: **19.9 / 18.1** (1992/2010)

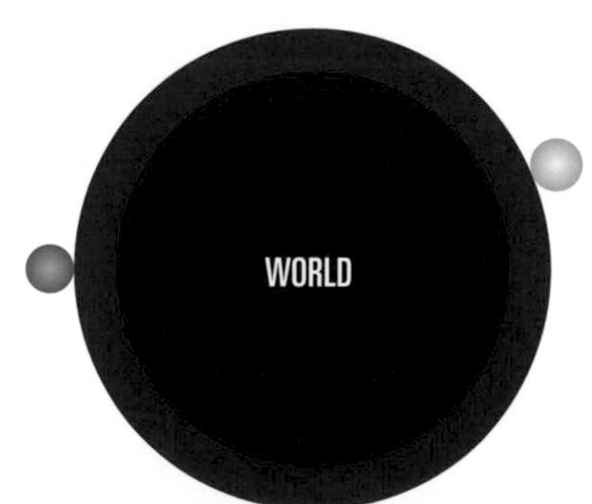

TOTAL EMISSIONS: **21,420.4 / 31,780.4** (1992/2010)
EMISSIONS PER PERSON: **3.9 / 4.6** (1992/2010)

CO_2 EMISSIONS PER AREA 1992 / 2010

INCREASING

DECREASING

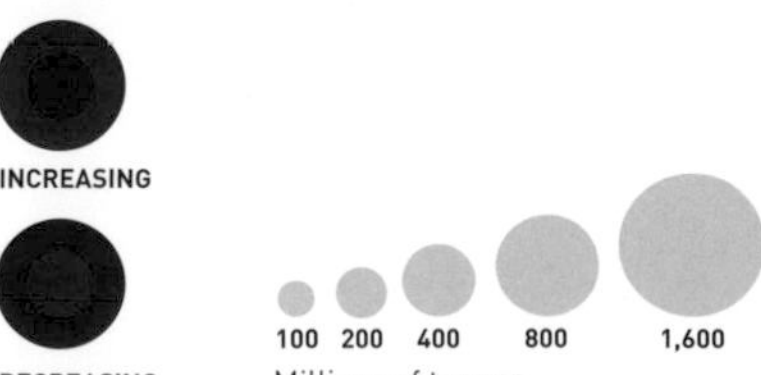

Millions of tonnes

CO_2 EMISSIONS PER PERSON 1992 / 2010

INCREASING

DECREASING

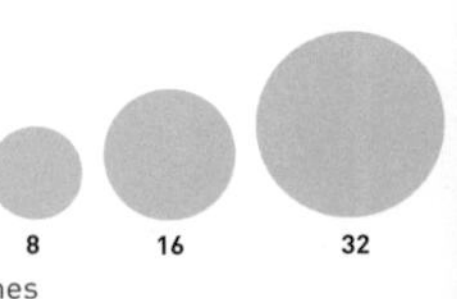

Millions of tonnes

CO2 EMISSION
PER MAIN GEOGRAPHIC AREAS
- NORTH AMERICA -
TOTAL EMISSIONS: 5,893.1 / 6,605.7
EMISSIONS PER PERSON: 15.8 / 14.5
- EUFOPE -
TOTAL EMISSIONS: 4,319.6 / 4,370.3
EMISSIONS PER PERSON: 7.7 / 7.2
- EURASIA -
TOTAL EMISSIONS: 3,213.4 / 2,454.1
EMISSIONS PER PERSON: 11 / 8.7
- MIDDLE EAST -
TOTAL EMISSIONS: 815 / 1,785.9
EMISSIONS PER PERSON: 5.7 / 8.4
- ASIA & OCEANIA -
TOTAL EMISSIONS: 5,675 / 14,161.4
EMISSIONS PER PERSON: 1.9 / 3.7
- AFRICA -
TOTAL EMISSIONS: 760.7 / 1,145.2
EMISSIONS PER PERSCN: 1.1 / 1.1
- CENTRAL & SOUTH AMERICA -
TOTAL EMISSIONS: 743.6 / 1,257.7
EMISSIONS PER PERSON: 2 / 2.6
TOTAL EMISSIONS: 1992 / 2010
EMISSIONS PER PERSON: 1992 / 2010

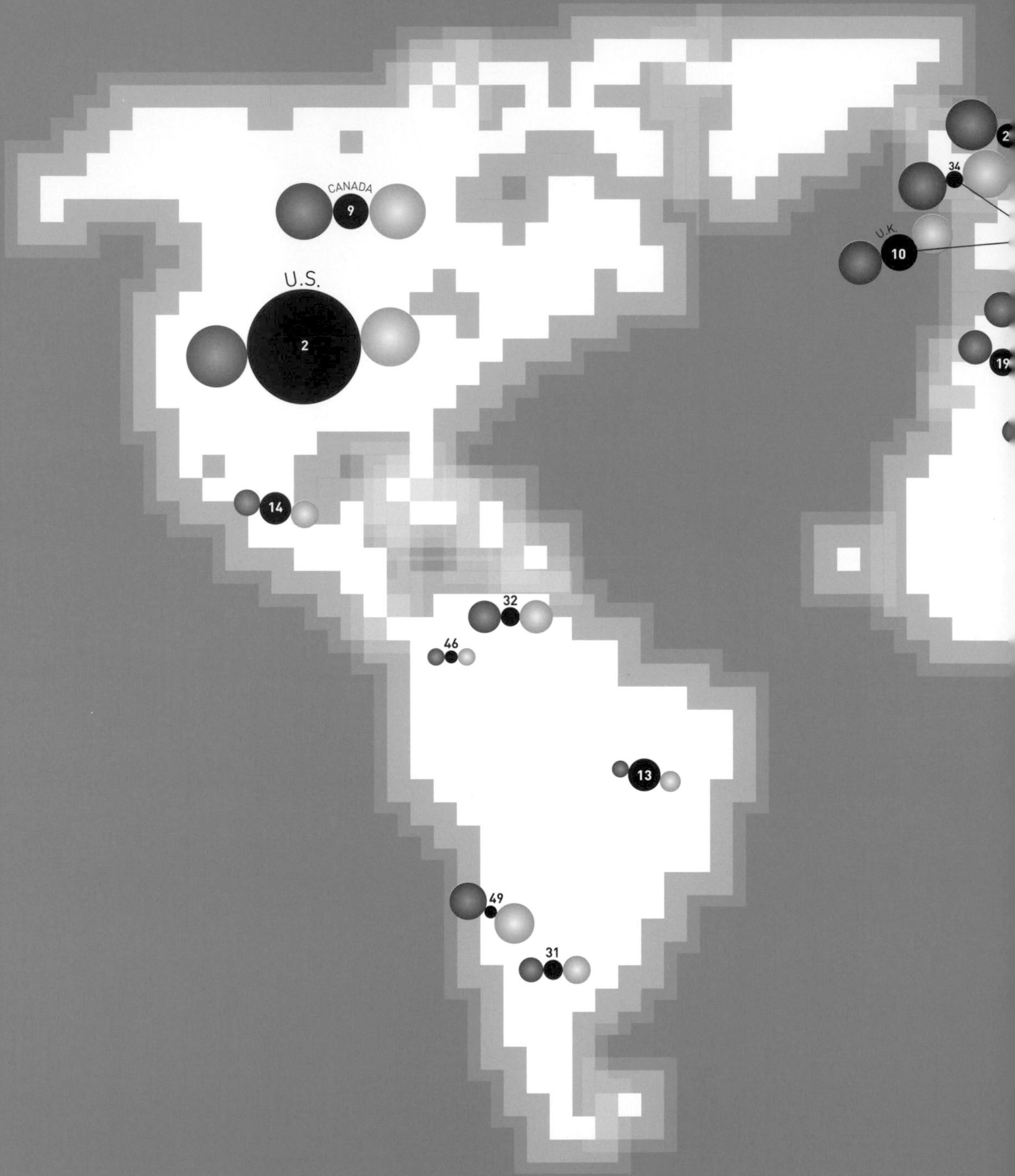

CANADA
9

U.S.
2

14

U.K.
10

34

19

32

46

13

49

31

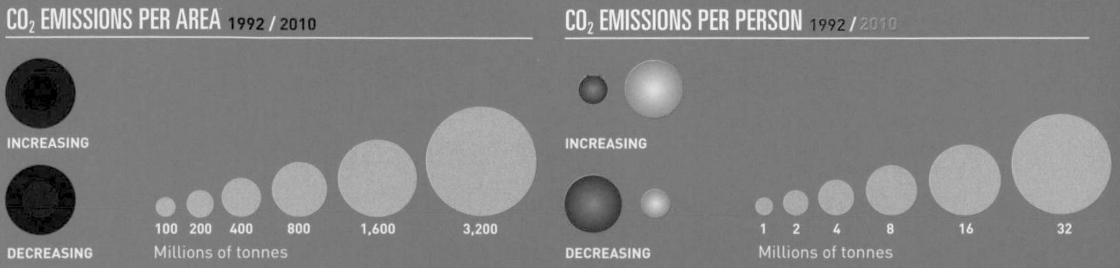

CO_2 EMISSIONS PER AREA 1992 / 2010

INCREASING

DECREASING

100 200 400 800 1,600 3,200
Millions of tonnes

CO_2 EMISSIONS PER PERSON 1992 / 2010

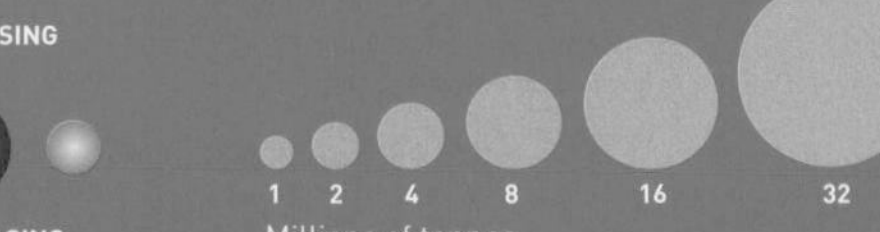

INCREASING

DECREASING

1 2 4 8 16 32
Millions of tonnes

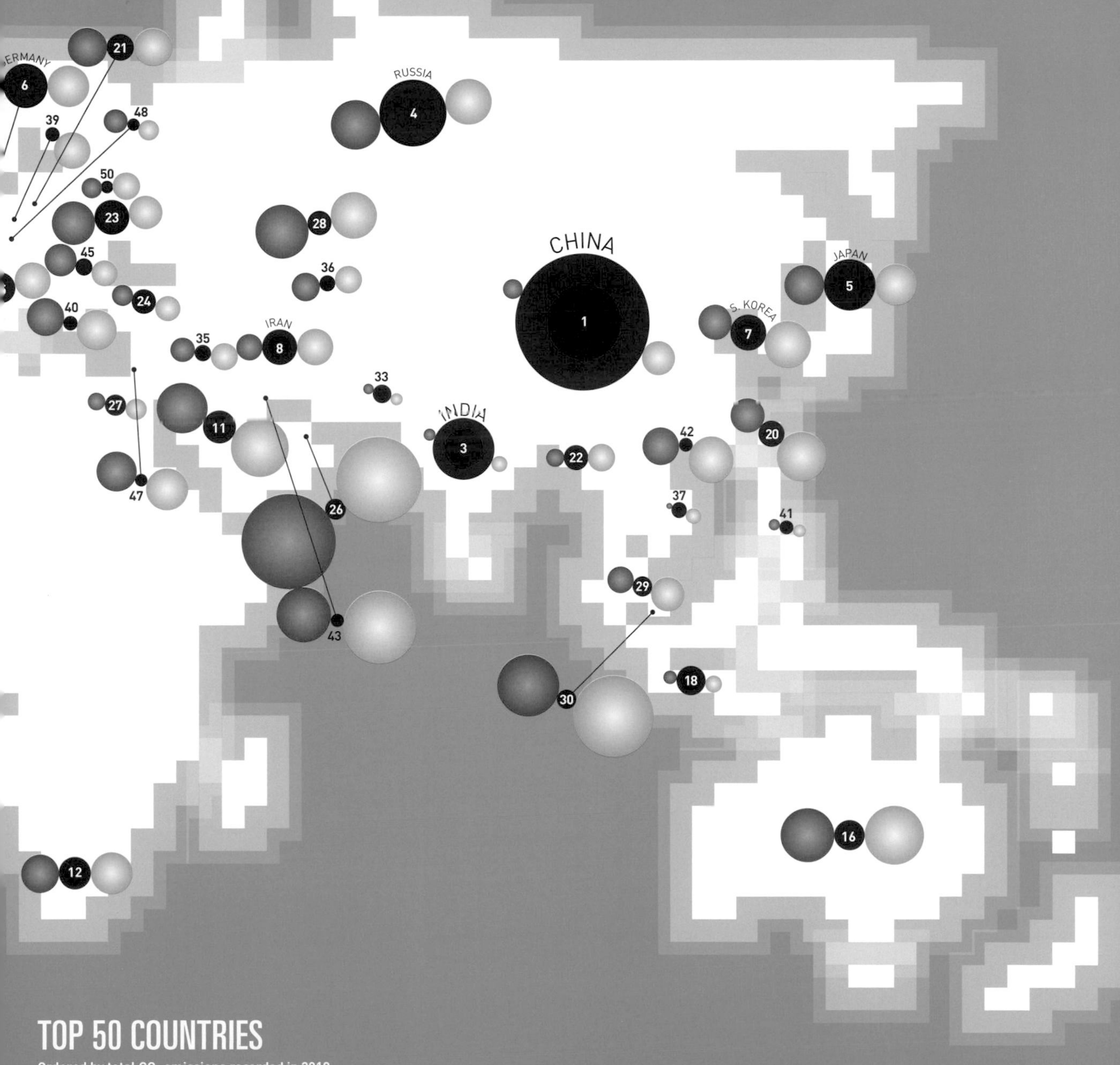

TOP 50 COUNTRIES

Ordered by total CO_2 emissions recorded in 2010

1 China
2 United States
3 India
4 Russia
5 Japan
6 Germany
7 South Korea
8 Iran
9 Canada
10 United Kingdom
11 Saudi Arabia
12 South Africa
13 Brazil
14 Mexico
15 Italy
16 Australia
17 France
18 Indonesia
19 Spain
20 Taiwan
21 Poland
22 Thailand
23 Ukraine
24 Turkey
25 Netherlands
26 United Arab Emirates
27 Egypt
28 Kazakhstan
29 Malaysia
30 Singapore
31 Argentina
32 Venezuela
33 Pakistan
34 Belgium
35 Iraq
36 Uzbekistan
37 Vietnam
38 Algeria
39 Czech Republic
40 Greece
41 Philippines
42 Hong Kong
43 Kuwait
44 Nigeria
45 Romania
46 Colombia
47 Israel
48 Austria
49 Chile
50 Belarus

The end of cash?

The fundamental way we buy stuff has barely changed in millennia: coins were invented in around 700 BCE, and we still use them today. Paper money took a bit longer – around 1,300 years to be precise – and has been in use since the 7th century in China.

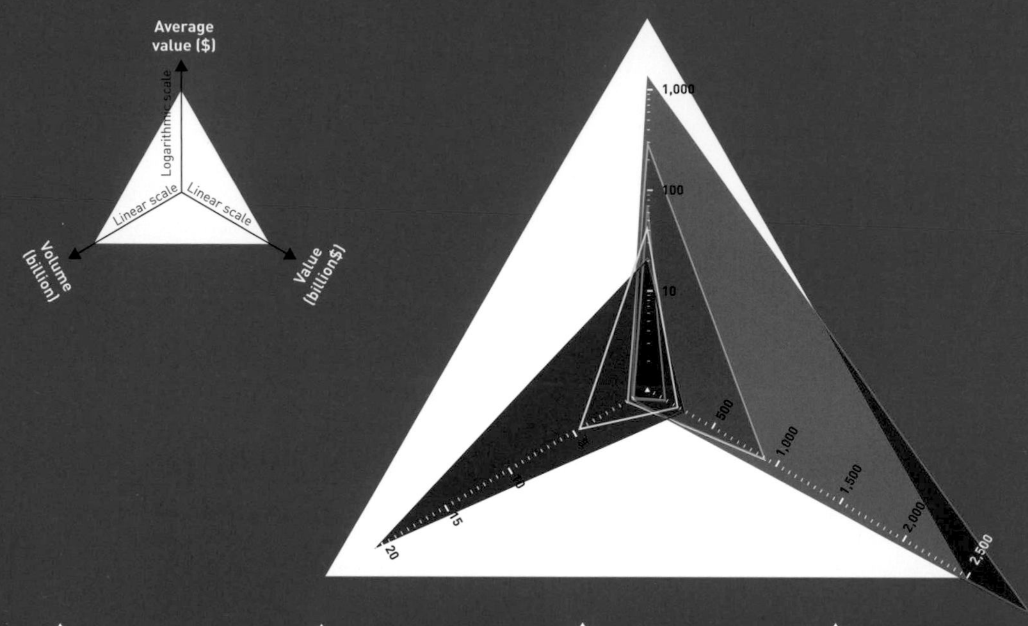

- CASH -

VOLUME: **22.6 billion**
VALUE: **$415 billion**
AVG VALUE: **$18.38**

- DIRECT DEBIT -

VOLUME: **3.1 billion**
VALUE: **$1,456 billion**
AVG VALUE: **$469.83**

- DEBIT CARDS -

VOLUME: **5.4 billion**
VALUE: **$375 billion**
AVG VALUE: **$69.48**

- DIRECT CREDITS -

VOLUME: **2.4 billion**
VALUE: **$4,673 billion**
AVG VALUE: **$1947.25**

- CREDIT CARDS -

VOLUME: **2 billion**
VALUE: **$216 billion**
AVG VALUE: **$108.27**

While it works as well today as ever it did, and with new anti-fraud features is more sophisticated than ever, for the first time in history the future of cash is under threat: it's no longer the easiest way to buy and sell. For many transactions, electronic is easier.

Data collected by the British Payments Council show the growing impact of cash's competitors: between them, electronic payment (**credit** and **debit cards, direct debit** and **electronic salary transfer**) made up around £4.2 trillion worth of transactions. **Cash {■}**, by contrast, totaled just £267 billion.

But there's another side of the story: we might not spend huge amounts (relatively speaking) with cash, but we use it much more often. The BPC tallied more than 22 billion cash transactions in 2008 (versus 25 billion in 1998). Electronic methods made up around 12.9 billion.

That small-but-frequent market shows up across the economy: only around 17% of the value of all travel payments (planes, trains, buses, etc.) are made in cash, but 83% by volume are done with money. It makes sense: you'd use cash for your many bus journeys, but not for your less-frequent plane fare.

Cash's electronic battle seems set to get tougher: with new "touch" and instant payments, its last bastion (small transactions) is under fire. Despite its 2,700-year pedigree, cash might soon just be a topic for the history books. Like this one.

WHERE WE SPEND CASH

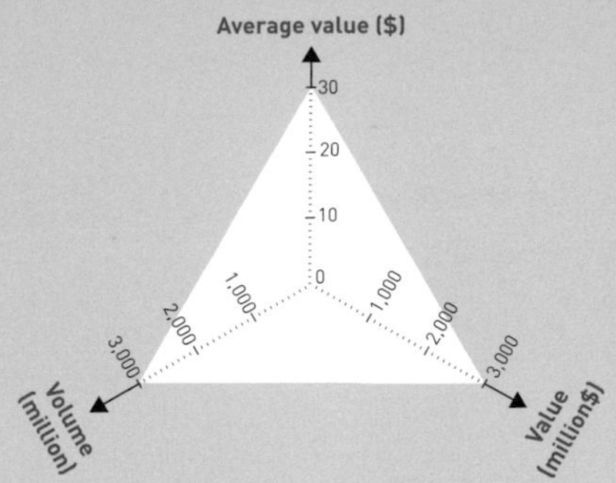

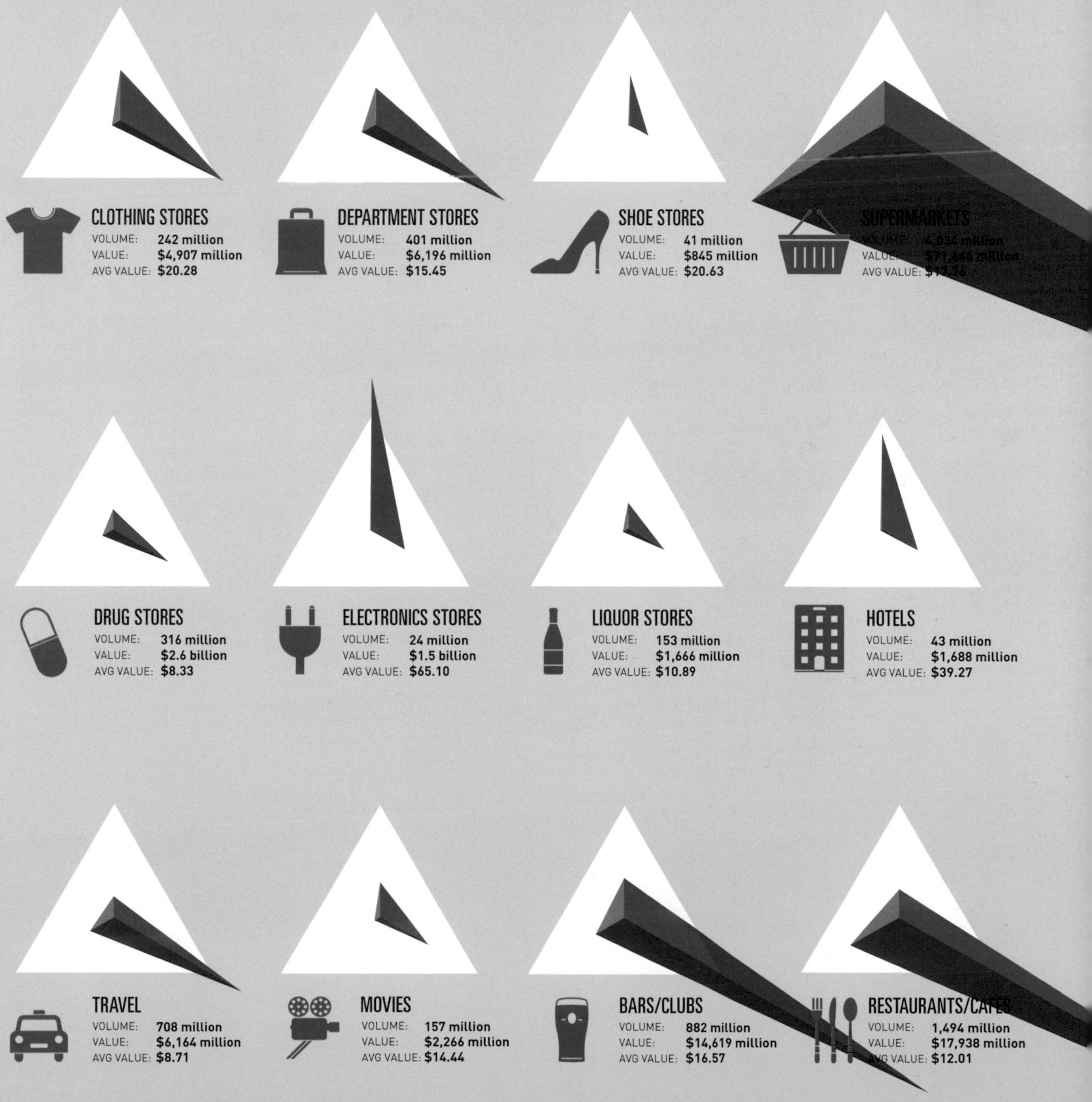

Average value ($)
30
20
10
0
1,000
2,000
3,000
1,000
2,000
3,000
Volume (million)
Value (million$)

CLOTHING STORES
VOLUME: 242 million
VALUE: $4,907 million
AVG VALUE: $20.28
DEPARTMENT STORES
VOLUME: 401 million
VALUE: $6,196 million
AVG VALUE: $15.45
SHOE STORES
VOLUME: 41 million
VALUE: $845 million
AVG VALUE: $20.63
SUPERMARKETS
VOLUME: 4,034 million
VALUE: $71,646 million
AVG VALUE: $17.76
DRUG STORES
VOLUME: 316 million
VALUE: $2.6 billion
AVG VALUE: $8.33
ELECTRONICS STORES
VOLUME: 24 million
VALUE: $1.5 billion
AVG VALUE: $65.10
LIQUOR STORES
VOLUME: 153 million
VALUE: $1,666 million
AVG VALUE: $10.89
HOTELS
VOLUME: 43 million
VALUE: $1,688 million
AVG VALUE: $39.27
TRAVEL
VOLUME: 708 million
VALUE: $6,164 million
AVG VALUE: $8.71
MOVIES
VOLUME: 157 million
VALUE: $2,266 million
AVG VALUE: $14.44
BARS/CLUBS
VOLUME: 882 million
VALUE: $14,619 million
AVG VALUE: $16.57
RESTAURANTS/CAFES
VOLUME: 1,494 million
VALUE: $17,938 million
AVG VALUE: $12.01

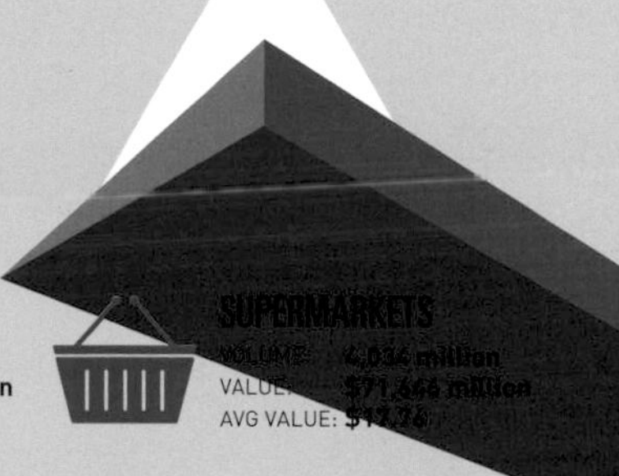

The drugs don't work, do they?

Media coverage about drugs tends to focus on people whose lives are torn apart by addiction or those who die on nights out. But what's it really like for drug users in the U.K.?

An annual survey by the *Guardian* and *MixMag* into their attitudes is illuminating. The risks are certainly real – but there are hundreds of thousands of people who regularly use drugs, legal or otherwise, and live pretty normally.

This survey was aimed at people who take drugs fairly regularly, and specifically asked about their drug use, so it's not giving stats on the actual prevalence of such habits. The data actually suggests that drug use is falling – figures published by the *Economist* suggest that only around 5% of 16–24-year-olds in the U.K. use recreational drugs.

Of the more pharmacologically inclined sample that took part in the survey, though, some results stand out. For one, people are more likely to have tried **cannabis {■}** (91.1%) than **tobacco {■}** (85.0%) or even **caffeine pills {■}** (47.3%).

WHAT DRUGS HAVE PEOPLE TRIED...

Each cell represents 1% of U.K. respondents. Colors indicate the type of drugs and the decimals are represented as below:

0.1%
0.2%
0.3%
0.4%
0.5%
0.6%
0.7%
0.8%
0.9%
1.0%

ALCOHOL 99.2%

CANNABIS 91.1%

TOBACCO 85%

MDMA 75.8%

COCAINE 69.4%

KETAMINE 47.8%

CAFFEINE PILLS 47.3%

CRACK 8.3%

HEROIN 7%

"STICK IT UP YER BUM"

Percentage of people who've tried drug X rectally

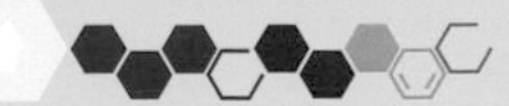

MDMA 3.5%
MEPHEDRONE 2%
COCAINE 1.8%
KETAMINE 0.5%

GETTING BUSTED...

Percentage of people who've been searched for drugs (by age)

...AND THE CONSEQUENCES

The end result of getting caught (% of users by type of drug)

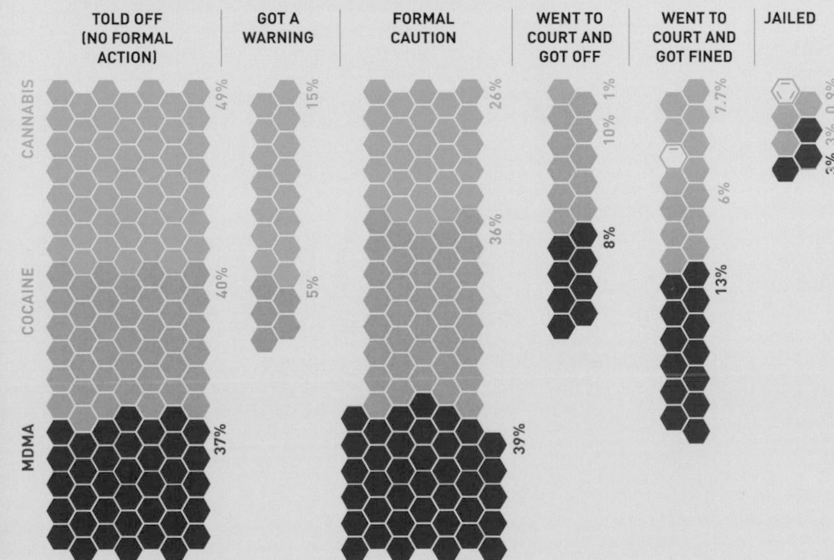

REALLY WORRYING...

Percentage of people who've taken a white powder without knowing or asking what it was (by age)

*Some get quite, well, creative about how they like to take their drugs: 3.5% have put **MDMA {■}** where the sun doesn't shine, and 2% have put **ketamine {■}** – a horse tranquilizer – there, too.*

More serious, perhaps, are the consequences. Here's the bad news (or, depending on your age, good news): the younger you are, the more likely you are to have been searched for drugs in the last year. A total of 24% of 18–19-year-olds said they'd been searched, versus just 4% of over-30s.

*The consequences if police caught you with drugs varied. Around a quarter of cannabis users got a formal caution (1% went to prison), versus 36% of people found with **cocaine {■}** and 39% with MDMA (in both cases 3% were jailed for possession).*

If the risk of people taking a particular drug worries you, then try not to think too much about this next statistic: that more than one in five of the 21- and 22-year-olds who took part in the survey admitted to having taken a "mystery" white powder without knowing or asking what it was. Reassuringly, the idea of drug roulette seems to become less attractive with age.

*One final twist: users of each substance were asked whether they'd like to cut down their use, or not. For **tobacco {■}**, 63% of users said they'd like to cut down. For **alcohol {■}**, 36% did – far more than wanted to cut **cannabis {■}** 20% or **MDMA {■}** 8%. Despite being legal, users said it was cigarettes and booze that were doing the harm.*

■ ALCOHOL
■ CANNABIS
■ TOBACCO
■ MDMA
■ COCAINE
■ KETAMINE
■ CAFFEINE PILLS
■ CRACK
■ HEROIN
■ MEPHEDRONE

CUTTING DOWN...

Which drug would you like to cut down on? (% of users)

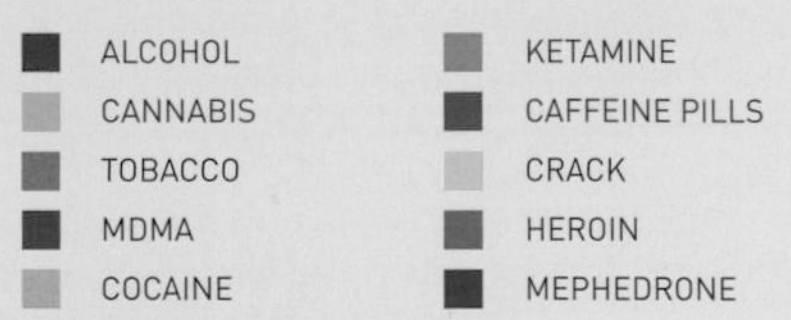

Ditched in the downturn

We usually count the cost of the economic crisis that began in 2008 in pounds, dollars and euros. But many people think we should look at unemployment too – particularly those who've lost their jobs.

The numbers paint a shocking picture of the effect of a financial crisis whose real impact is often hard to grasp.

We've taken figures from the International Labour Organization on some of the world's leading economies – ignoring Israel and Germany, who escaped a jobs crisis – and compared unemployment from their lowest levels before the crisis with their highest points after.

There's no mistaking the results: 26.8 million extra people were in the jobless line across 29 nations. Perhaps surprisingly, the data suggest men were hardest hit, at 16 million new jobless – but women who lose their jobs often disappear from the figures, becoming discouraged from looking for work at all.

More than nine million of the newly jobless were from the **U.S.** alone, as joblessness surged from a low of under 7 million, by the ILO measure, to almost 16 million in less than three years. Around 1.1 million unemployed were added to the **UK**'s roster.

But – just in case this is getting you down – it's not quite as bad as it looks. First, unemployment isn't a stagnant lump; lots of people get jobs and are replaced by newly unemployed people each month. Most unemployed people remain so for less than six months.

Second, in almost every country in this data set things have got better since the low point we measured.

Finally – for those in the U.S., at least – a (hopefully short) spell of unemployment is a great chance to catch up on Maury Povich. And everyone loves a good lie-detector test. Don't they?

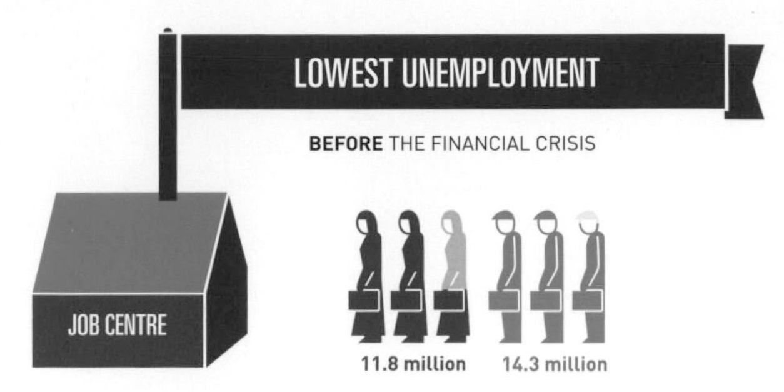

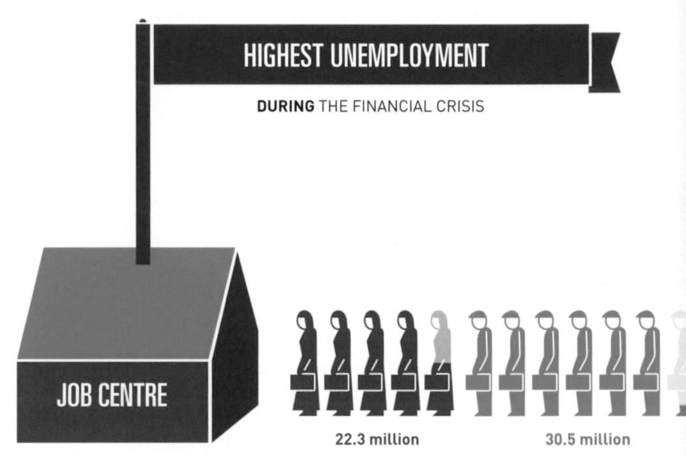

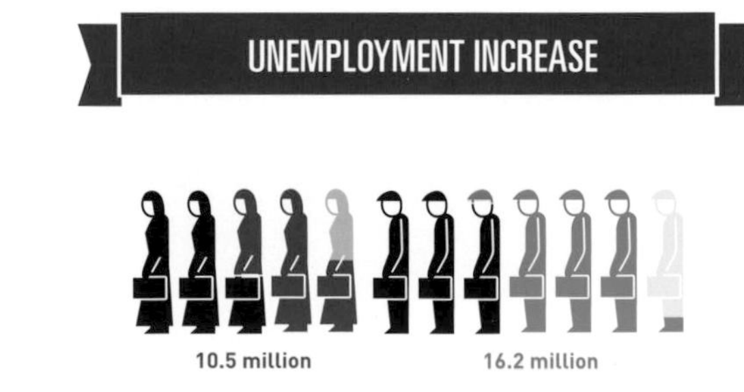

5 million UNEMPLOYED WOMEN

5 million UNEMPLOYED MEN

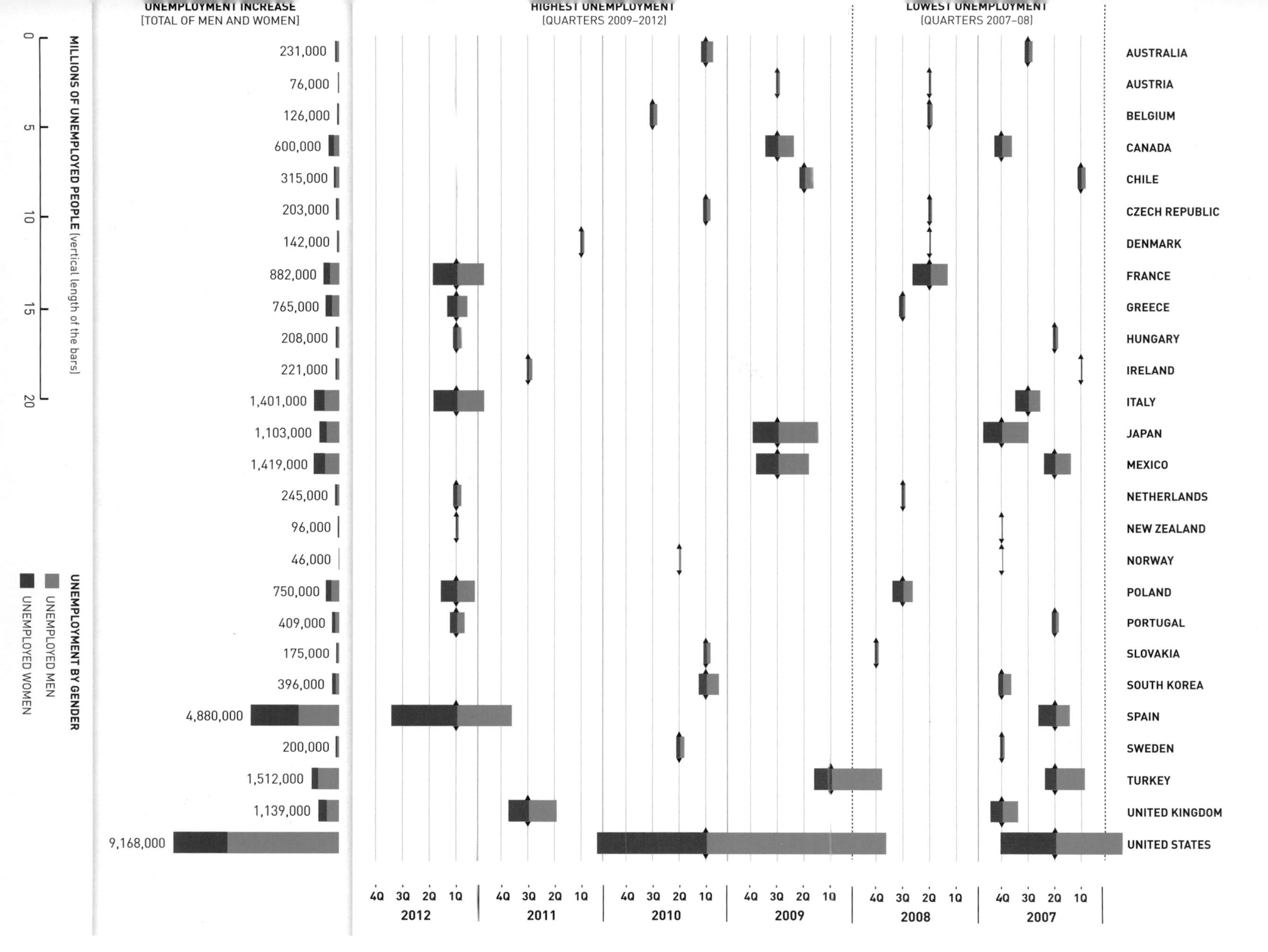

UNEMPLOYMENT INCREASE
[TOTAL OF MEN AND WOMEN]
HIGHEST UNEMPLOYMENT
[QUARTERS 2009–2012]
LOWEST UNEMPLOYMENT
[QUARTERS 2007–08]
231,000
76,000
126,000
600,000
315,000
203,000
142,000
882,000
765,000
208,000
221,000
1,401,000
1,103,000
1,419,000
245,000
96,000
46,000
750,000
409,000
175,000
396,000
4,880,000
200,000
1,512,000
1,139,000
9,168,000
AUSTRALIA
AUSTRIA
BELGIUM
CANADA
CHILE
CZECH REPUBLIC
DENMARK
FRANCE
GREECE
HUNGARY
IRELAND
ITALY
JAPAN
MEXICO
NETHERLANDS
NEW ZEALAND
NORWAY
POLAND
PORTUGAL
SLOVAKIA
SOUTH KOREA
SPAIN
SWEDEN
TURKEY
UNITED KINGDOM
UNITED STATES
4Q 3Q 2Q 1Q
2012
4Q 3Q 2Q 1Q
2011
4Q 3Q 2Q 1Q
2010
4Q 3Q 2Q 1Q
2009
4Q 3Q 2Q 1Q
2008
4Q 3Q 2Q 1Q
2007
MILLIONS OF UNEMPLOYED PEOPLE (vertical length of the bars)
0
5
10
15
20
UNEMPLOYMENT BY GENDER
UNEMPLOYED MEN
UNEMPLOYED WOMEN

Seeking refuge

Forced displacement has become a defining issue of the twenty-first century. From Syria to the Mediterranean to Calais, this plight and the pressure it applies on the global community are increasing. The current number of people displaced – by human rights violations, generalized violence, conflict or persecution – is the highest since the end of World War II.

The number of people displaced in 2015 increased by nearly six million – by the end of the year, more than 65 million people were displaced. To put this into perspective, this total is comparable to the populations of Thailand or the United Kingdom. The figure becomes even more heartbreaking when we realize that this means one in every 113 people globally is either seeking asylum, internally displaced or a refugee.

Refugees account for one-fourth of the total population of concern – and their numbers have nearly doubled since 2005. A vast majority of the world's refugees originated from only ten countries; more than half of them come from **Syria**, **Afghanistan** and **Somalia**.

Although individuals find safety in a variety of host countries, the pressure to manage this human movement rests primarily with a small number of neighboring nations. **Turkey** and **Pakistan** have accepted significantly more refugees than other nations. However, if we compare asylum seekers to native population, another story arises. Take a look at **Lebanon**, for example, where one-in-five is a refugee.

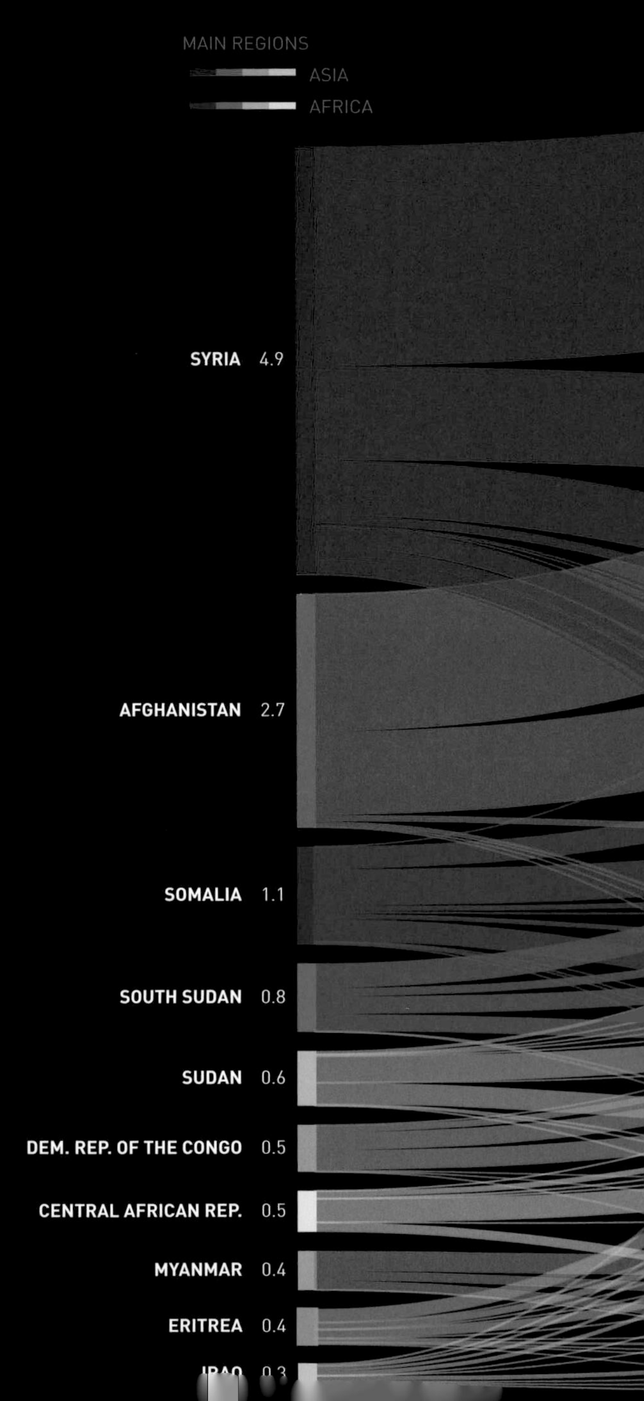

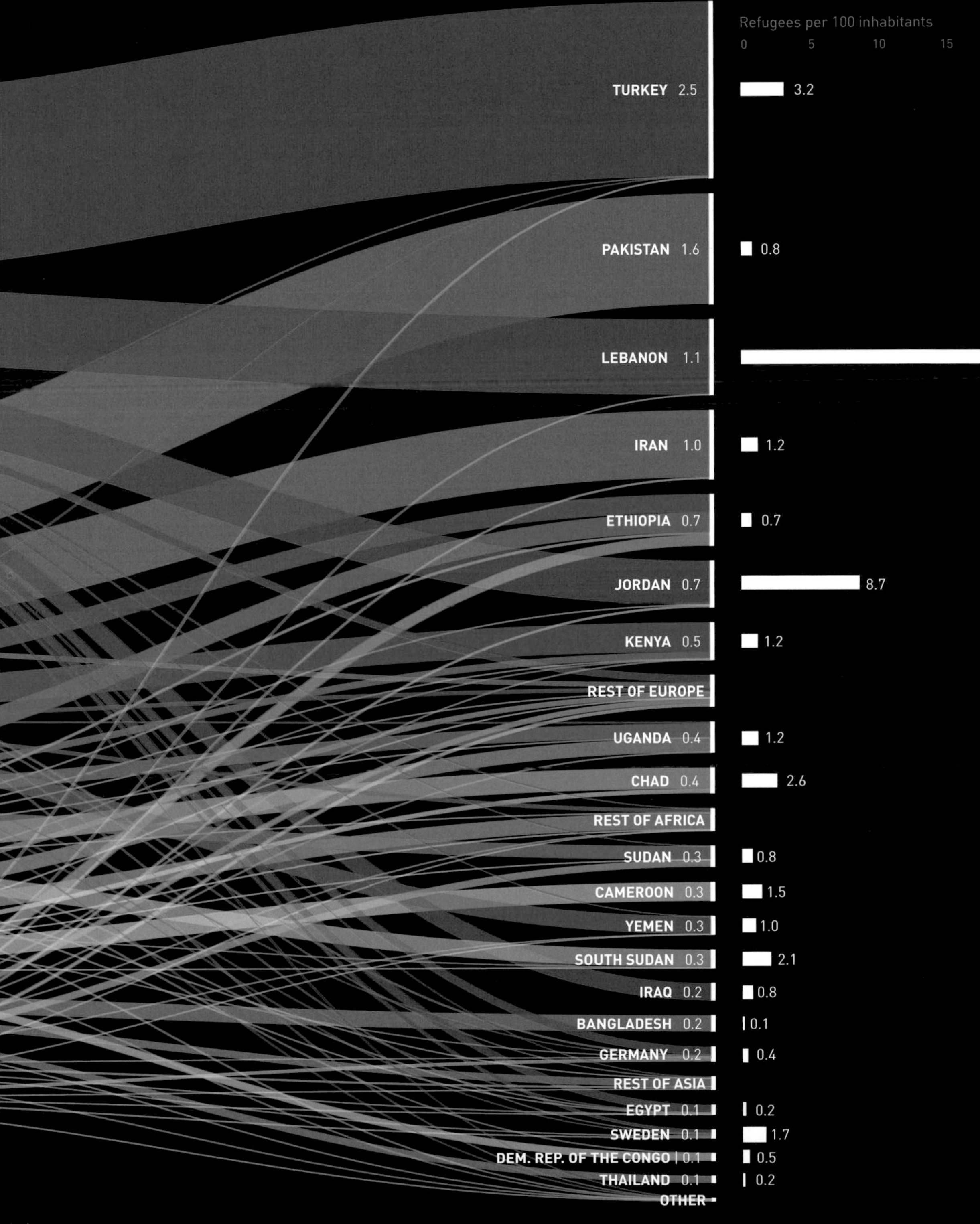

Refugees per 100 inhabitants
0
5
10
15
TURKEY 2.5
3.2
PAKISTAN 1.6
0.8
LEBANON 1.1
IRAN 1.0
1.2
ETHIOPIA 0.7
0.7
JORDAN 0.7
8.7
KENYA 0.5
1.2
REST OF EUROPE
UGANDA 0.4
1.2
CHAD 0.4
2.6
REST OF AFRICA
SUDAN 0.3
0.8
CAMEROON 0.3
1.5
YEMEN 0.3
1.0
SOUTH SUDAN 0.3
2.1
IRAQ 0.2
0.8
BANGLADESH 0.2
0.1
GERMANY 0.2
0.4
REST OF ASIA
EGYPT 0.1
0.2
SWEDEN 0.1
1.7
DEM. REP. OF THE CONGO 0.1
0.5
THAILAND 0.1
0.2
OTHER

Gotta get yourself connected

If you're living in the West, the true scale of the communications revolution over the last decade has almost certainly passed you by.

GLOBAL SUBSCRIPTIONS

No. of total world-wide subscriptions by communication medium.

REGIONAL SUBSCRIPTIONS

*No. of subscriptions for each communication medium split by geographical area **(in millions)**.*

SUBSCRIPTION RATE

*Subscriptions **per 100 inhabitants** within each region by different communication media.*

2.5 billion
2.2 billion
215 million
1 billion
10 30 559 64 273 291
87 85 834 166 550 459
1 80 2 66 66
17 25 344 27 278 316
2 12 2
9 27 8
15 23 2 9
23 60 1 10
46 92 11 46
33 52 8 36
Africa
Arab states
Asia & Pacific
Former Soviet states
Europe
The Americas
2005

Cell phones have changed our lives in so many ways, from the very important to the ridiculously trivial. But important as they've been for us, it's what cells have done for the rest of the world that is truly remarkable.

Imagine if rather than an extra convenience, cell phones represented the first time you'd had easy contact with the outside world. For hundreds of millions in **Africa {■}** and **Asia {■}**, this is exactly what's happened.

Landlines basically passed Africa by. In 2005, there were only 1.5 landline connections per 100 households – and by 2011 that had fallen, not risen (in Asia the same pattern's true, but higher – 15 per 100 in 2005, 14 per 100 today).

But what's happened with cell phones is startling: where there were 12.4 cell subscriptions per 100 Africans in 2005, just six years on there were 53.1. Given that in some African countries up to five people can share one cell phone account, this rate of growth is startling and unprecedented. **Europe {■}**, by contrast, has

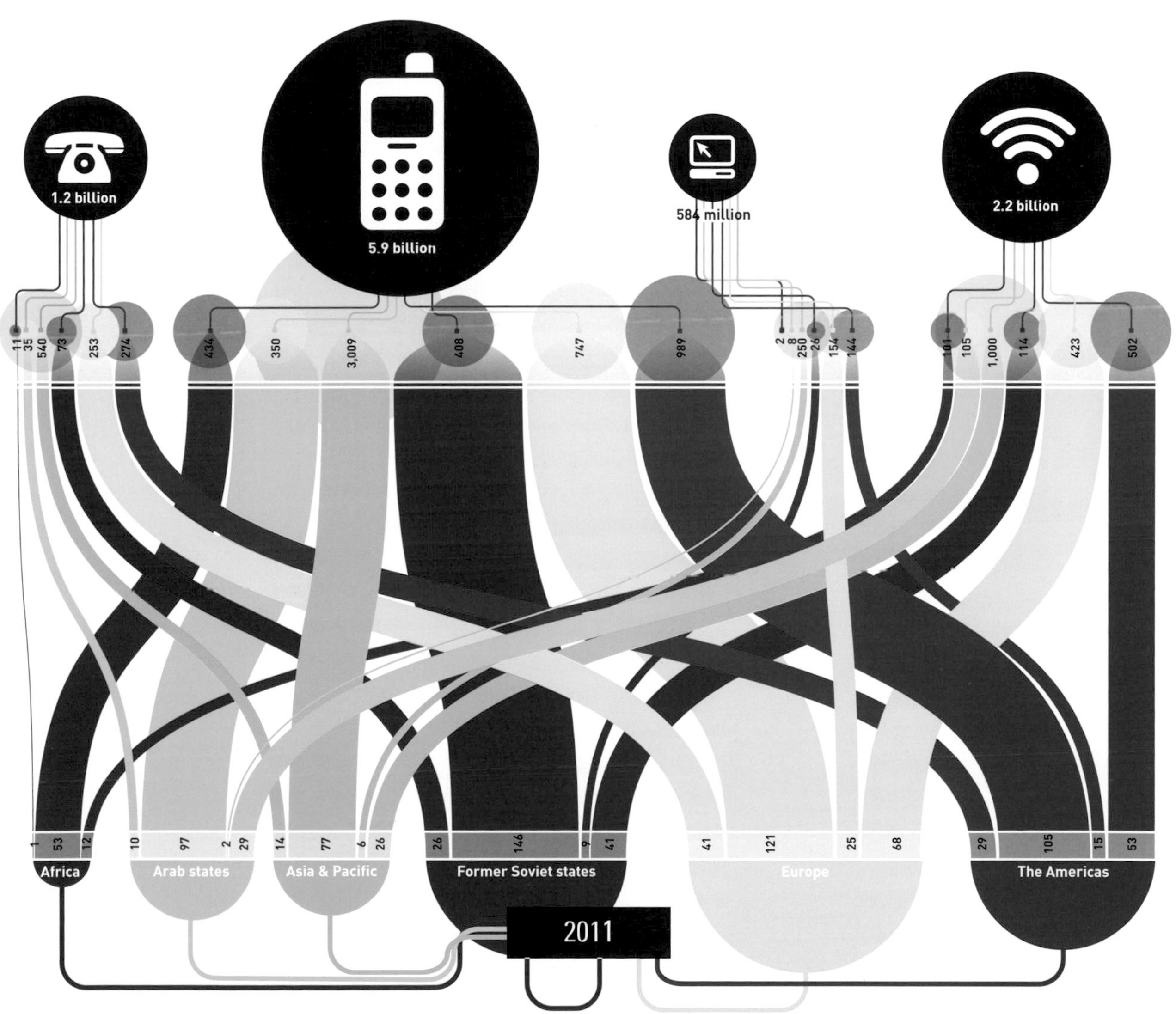

more cell phone accounts than people – 1.2 per person! The world is connected for the first time.

The effect is as remarkable elsewhere. Cells in Asia leapt from 22.6 per 100 people to 76.7. In the **Arab states {■}**, the jump was from 27.1 to a huge 96.9. Technological change has never happened so quickly.

The developing world's leapfrogging of a whole generation of expensive wired technology has had domino effects, too. The International Telecommunications Union estimated there were one billion people online in 2005. By 2011 it had grown to 2.2 billion. About 84 million of those come from Africa (despite only one household in 500 having wired broadband). Around 330 million come from Europe and **the Americas {■}**.

But an amazing 656 million new online subscribers come from Asia. The balance of the online world is shifting seismically every day, and the speed of that change is doing anything but slowing...

LANDLINE
CELL PHONES
FIXED (WIRED)-BROADBAND
INDIVIDUALS USING THE INTERNET

AFRICA
ARAB STATES
ASIA & PACIFIC
FORMER SOVIET STATES
EUROPE
THE AMERICAS

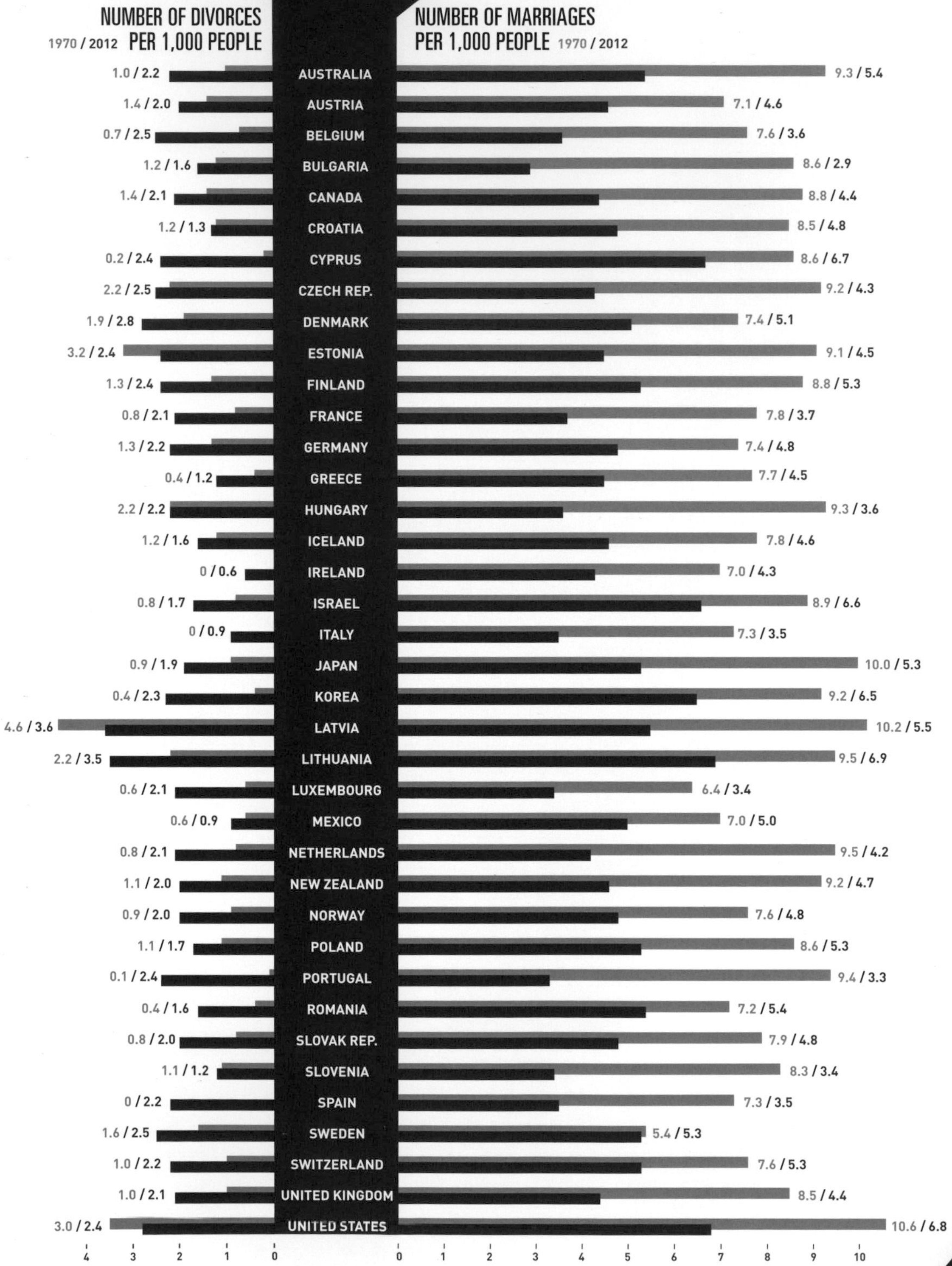

HOW DRAMATIC IS THE RISE IN DIVORCE?

NUMBER OF DIVORCES PER 1,000 PEOPLE 1970 / 2012		NUMBER OF MARRIAGES PER 1,000 PEOPLE 1970 / 2012
1.0 / 2.2	AUSTRALIA	9.3 / 5.4
1.4 / 2.0	AUSTRIA	7.1 / 4.6
0.7 / 2.5	BELGIUM	7.6 / 3.6
1.2 / 1.6	BULGARIA	8.6 / 2.9
1.4 / 2.1	CANADA	8.8 / 4.4
1.2 / 1.3	CROATIA	8.5 / 4.8
0.2 / 2.4	CYPRUS	8.6 / 6.7
2.2 / 2.5	CZECH REP.	9.2 / 4.3
1.9 / 2.8	DENMARK	7.4 / 5.1
3.2 / 2.4	ESTONIA	9.1 / 4.5
1.3 / 2.4	FINLAND	8.8 / 5.3
0.8 / 2.1	FRANCE	7.8 / 3.7
1.3 / 2.2	GERMANY	7.4 / 4.8
0.4 / 1.2	GREECE	7.7 / 4.5
2.2 / 2.2	HUNGARY	9.3 / 3.6
1.2 / 1.6	ICELAND	7.8 / 4.6
0 / 0.6	IRELAND	7.0 / 4.3
0.8 / 1.7	ISRAEL	8.9 / 6.6
0 / 0.9	ITALY	7.3 / 3.5
0.9 / 1.9	JAPAN	10.0 / 5.3
0.4 / 2.3	KOREA	9.2 / 6.5
4.6 / 3.6	LATVIA	10.2 / 5.5
2.2 / 3.5	LITHUANIA	9.5 / 6.9
0.6 / 2.1	LUXEMBOURG	6.4 / 3.4
0.6 / 0.9	MEXICO	7.0 / 5.0
0.8 / 2.1	NETHERLANDS	9.5 / 4.2
1.1 / 2.0	NEW ZEALAND	9.2 / 4.7
0.9 / 2.0	NORWAY	7.6 / 4.8
1.1 / 1.7	POLAND	8.6 / 5.3
0.1 / 2.4	PORTUGAL	9.4 / 3.3
0.4 / 1.6	ROMANIA	7.2 / 5.4
0.8 / 2.0	SLOVAK REP.	7.9 / 4.8
1.1 / 1.2	SLOVENIA	8.3 / 3.4
0 / 2.2	SPAIN	7.3 / 3.5
1.6 / 2.5	SWEDEN	5.4 / 5.3
1.0 / 2.2	SWITZERLAND	7.6 / 5.3
1.0 / 2.1	UNITED KINGDOM	8.5 / 4.4
3.0 / 2.4	UNITED STATES	10.6 / 6.8

4 3 2 1 0   0 1 2 3 4 5 6 7 8 9 10

Love and marriage (and, er, divorce)

'Love and marriage, love and marriage, go together like a horse and carriage.'

Frank Sinatra may have sung about the ideals of love and marriage, but when the song was released in 1956, he had already gone through the first of three divorces. That, along with the fact that you probably haven't seen a horse and carriage in a while, should be enough to convince you that times have changed pretty rapidly when it comes to marriage – and it hasn't been good news.

In a nutshell, that is the story of marriage over the last forty years. The marriage rate in the **UK** has almost halved, from 8.5 marriages per 1,000 people per year to 4.4. **Americans** remain much more inclined to wed – 6.8 weddings per 1,000 people – but even there the rate has fallen by around 36%. The same is true in almost every country in the **OECD**.

For the incurable romantics, the second half of this story makes for even more distressing reading – because as if the falling marriage rate wasn't enough, divorces have soared over the generation, as they've become legal or easier to access in countries across the world.

In Britain, we've doubled from one divorce per 1,000 people each year to 2.1. Spain and Portugal from almost none to 2.4, while only three countries saw a decline in divorce rate. However, to get the full picture of our new un-wed and re-wed way of life, the marriages-per-divorce figure is maybe the most telling.

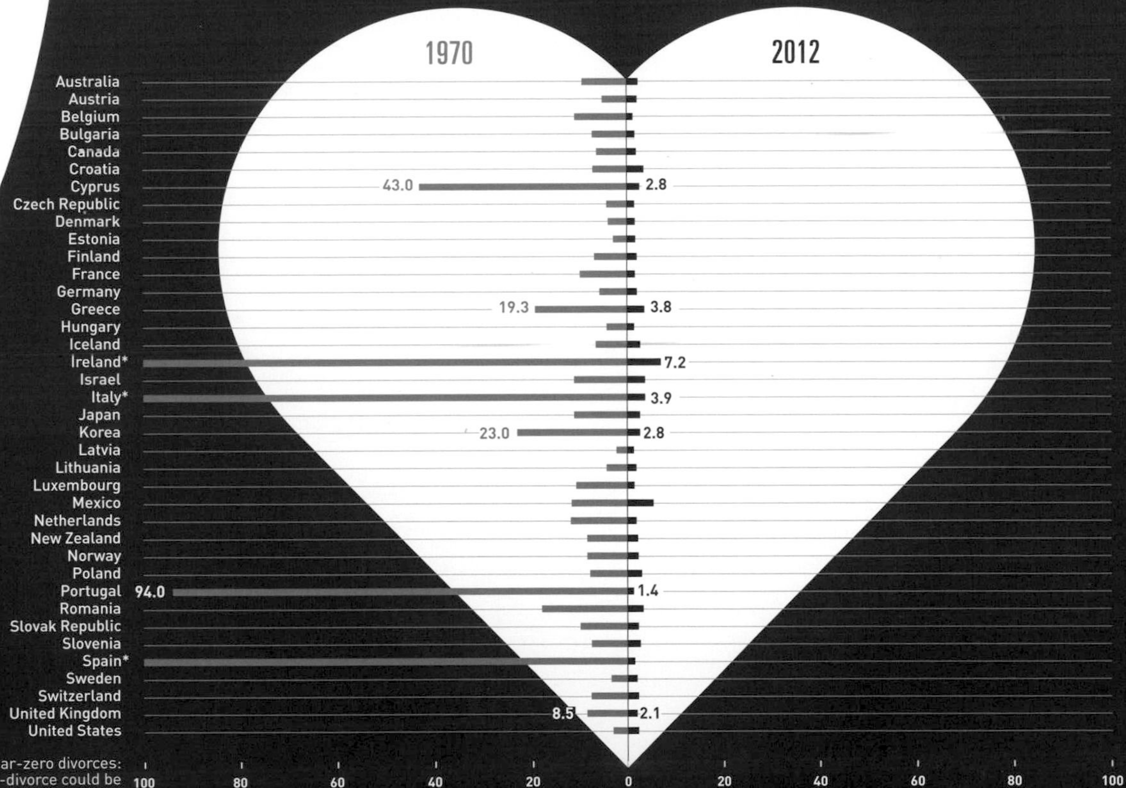

*Zero or near-zero divorces: marriages-per-divorce could be far higher still, but we're simplifying to 100.

*In the UK in 1970, we had eight weddings for every divorce. Now we have fewer than two. That's nothing compared to **Portugal**, though – there, in 1970, there were 94 weddings for every divorce each year. Now, there are just 1.6. Still, it's not necessarily all doom and gloom. In recent years, divorce rates across the OECD (including the UK) have dropped. Romantics suggest it's because as fewer people are getting married, they're now taking it much more seriously. Cynics say it's expensive to divorce, so fewer people split up in tough economic times. But as all good relationships are about compromise, we think it's fair to say that maybe both sides are right.*

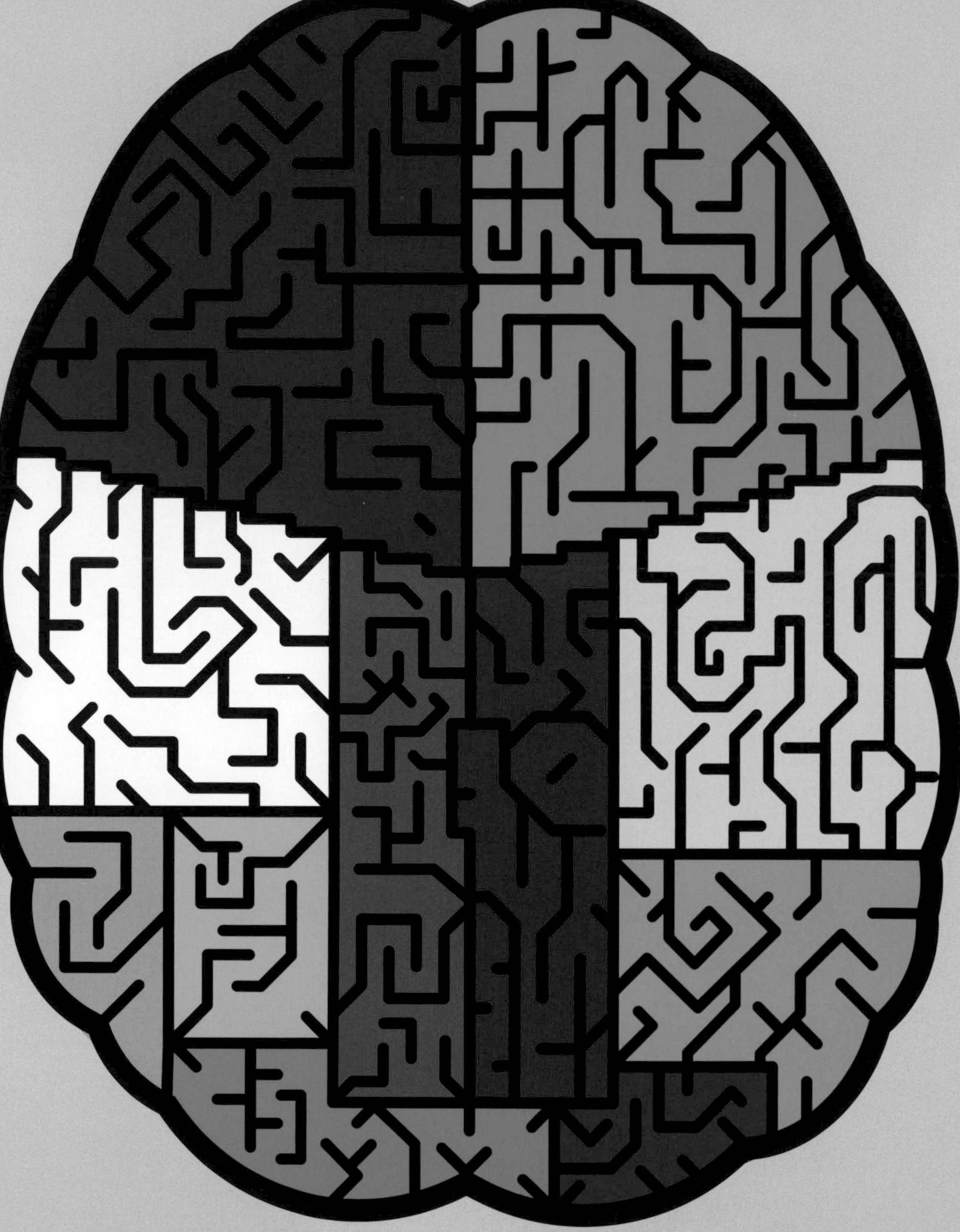

NUMBER OF ADULTS PER MENTAL DISORDER

Number	Disorder
15,000,000	SOCIAL ANXIETY DISORDER (SOCIAL PHOBIA)
14,800,000	MAJOR DEPRESSIVE DISORDER
7,700,000	POST-TRAUMATIC STRESS DISORDER
6,800,000	GENERALIZED ANXIETY DISORDER
6,000,000	PANIC DISORDER
5,700,000	BIPOLAR DISORDER
4,500,000	ALZHEIMER'S DISEASE
3,300,000	DSYTHYMIC DISORDER (CHRONIC MILD/MODERATE DEPRESSION)
2,400,000	SCHIZOPHRENIA
2,200,000	OBSESSIVE-COMPULSIVE DISORDER
1,800,000	AGORAPHOBIA

State of mind

Our treatment of people suffering from mental illness has hardly been one of the brightest facets of humanity's history – those with such conditions have been demonized as "possessed," as witches, left homeless, or thrown into asylums.

While the stigma of mental disorders has hardly been consigned to the past, treatment has improved immeasurably, and psychiatry is now a central part of modern medicine. As it so often is, the stigma is also unfounded – people with mental illnesses are not significantly more likely to perpetrate violence than those without, but are far more likely to be victims of violence.

The dissipation of stigma is just as well, as statistics suggest around a quarter of the population has some form of mental disorder: figures from the U.S. National Institute of Mental Health indicate that in any given year, 57 million adults have a mental disorder.

Major depressive disorder {■} is the biggest cause of disability in the U.S., experienced by more than 14 million adults (social phobia is more prevalent but less debilitating). **Obsessive-compulsive disorder {■}**, **schizophrenia {■}**, **post-traumatic stress disorder {■}** and **bipolar disorder {■}** all number millions more.

The huge increase in people diagnosed with mental disorders has prompted something of a backlash.

This is particularly strongly felt in the Church of Scientology, which believes that the psychiatric profession is an integral part of a conspiracy to create a one-world government.

The Scientologists are, of course, wrong. But the rise in the number of psychiatric conditions is undeniable. The psychiatric bible of the U.S. is the *Diagnostic and Statistical Manual of Mental Disorders*. Its first edition, released in 1952, detailed 106 conditions across 130 pages. The second edition in 1968 upped this to 182 (a reissue in 1974 removed **homosexuality** from the list). The current edition used by professionals today details 297 separate conditions across 943 pages.

Better research and diagnosis, a profession looking to expand its client base with ever-more disorders, or a bit of both? Something to think about...

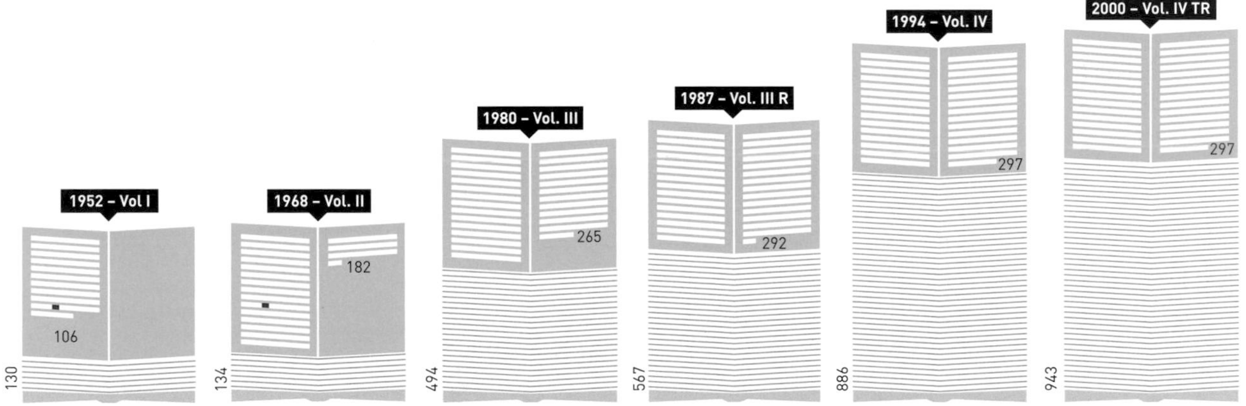

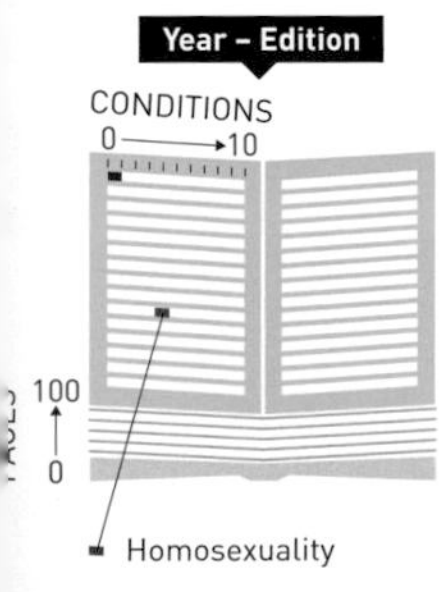

Each book represents – by number of conditions and number of pages – an edition of the Diagnostic and Statistical Manual of Mental Disorders.

Give me land, lots of land

It's a big world out there: the surface of the planet (including the oceans) is more than five billion square kilometers, and there are seven billion of us living on those bits of it that are located on dry land.

But just looking at a map gives less of a sense of how that land is divvied up between different countries than you'd think – and almost no information about who lives in each. **Russia** is the world's largest nation, with more than 16 million sq km of land (though given its climate, and mountains, not all of it is the kind of land you'd want to live on). That's around 12% of the world's real estate.

The next three nations, **China**, the **United States** and **Canada,** each have around 7% of the world's land, while fifth-place **Brazil** trails with just under 6.5%. That gives the world's five largest countries more than a third of all its land.

But when we look at number of people, things look very different: **Russia** might have 12% of the planet's floor space, but it's only got 2% of the population. China, by contrast, has more than 19% of the world's population sharing just 7% of the land. Between them, China and **India** make up 37% of all the seven billion people on Earth.

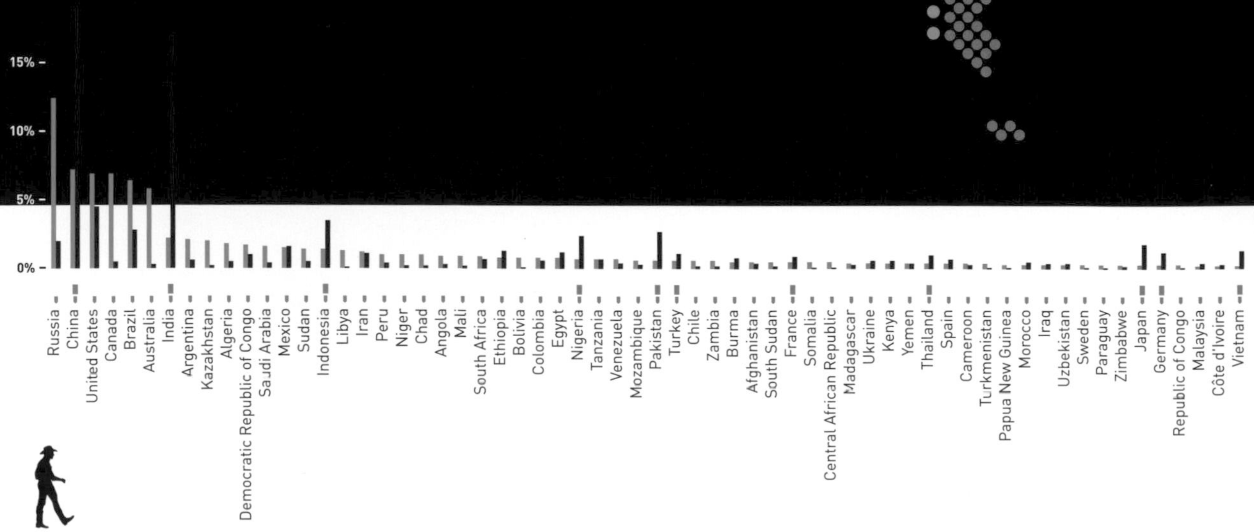

15% –
10% –
5% –
0% –

Russia
China
United States
Canada
Brazil
Australia
India
Argentina
Kazakhstan
Algeria
Democratic Republic of Congo
Saudi Arabia
Mexico
Sudan
Indonesia
Libya
Iran
Peru
Niger
Chad
Angola
Mali
South Africa
Ethiopia
Bolivia
Colombia
Egypt
Nigeria
Tanzania
Venezuela
Mozambique
Pakistan
Turkey
Chile
Zambia
Burma
Afghanistan
South Sudan
France
Somalia
Central African Republic
Madagascar
Ukraine
Kenya
Yemen
Thailand
Spain
Cameroon
Turkmenistan
Papua New Guinea
Morocco
Iraq
Uzbekistan
Sweden
Paraguay
Zimbabwe
Japan
Germany
Republic of Congo
Malaysia
Côte d'Ivoire
Vietnam

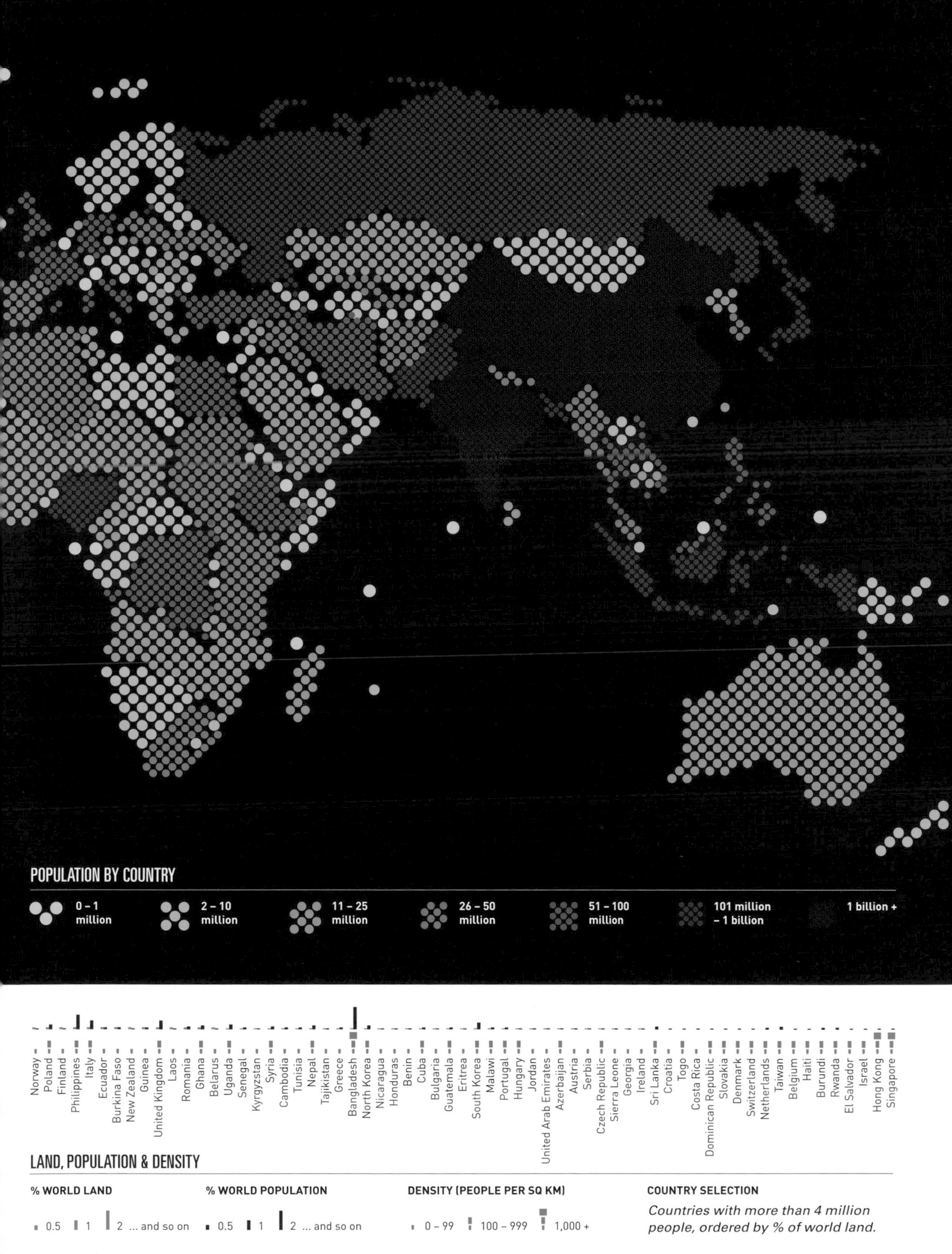

POPULATION BY COUNTRY
0 – 1 million
2 – 10 million
11 – 25 million
26 – 50 million
51 – 100 million
101 million – 1 billion
1 billion +
Norway
Poland
Finland
Philippines
Italy
Ecuador
Burkina Faso
New Zealand
Guinea
United Kingdom
Laos
Romania
Ghana
Belarus
Uganda
Senegal
Kyrgyzstan
Syria
Cambodia
Tunisia
Nepal
Tajikistan
Greece
Bangladesh
North Korea
Nicaragua
Honduras
Benin
Cuba
Bulgaria
Guatemala
Eritrea
South Korea
Malawi
Portugal
Hungary
Jordan
United Arab Emirates
Azerbaijan
Austria
Serbia
Czech Republic
Sierra Leone
Georgia
Ireland
Sri Lanka
Croatia
Togo
Costa Rica
Dominican Republic
Slovakia
Denmark
Switzerland
Netherlands
Taiwan
Belgium
Haiti
Burundi
Rwanda
El Salvador
Israel
Hong Kong
Singapore
LAND, POPULATION & DENSITY
% WORLD LAND
0.5
1
2 ... and so on
% WORLD POPULATION
0.5
1
2 ... and so on
DENSITY (PEOPLE PER SQ KM)
0 – 99
100 – 999
1,000 +
COUNTRY SELECTION
Countries with more than 4 million people, ordered by % of world land.

HOW MUCH SPACE DO WE ALL HAVE TO LIVE IN?

AREA PER PERSON

(in million square meters)

37.5

37.1

3.9

0.07

0.01

SHEEP PER SQ M

5 SHEEP

PEOPLE PER SQ M

1,000 PEOPLE

GREENLAND 37,543,739 SQ M PER PERSON

SVALBARD 31,494,924 SQ M PER PERSON

MACAU 49 SQ M PER PERSON

EQUIVALENT TO:

7m

single floor high

PEOPLE PER SQ M

20,497

SINGAPORE 128 SQ M PER PERSON

EQUIVALENT TO:

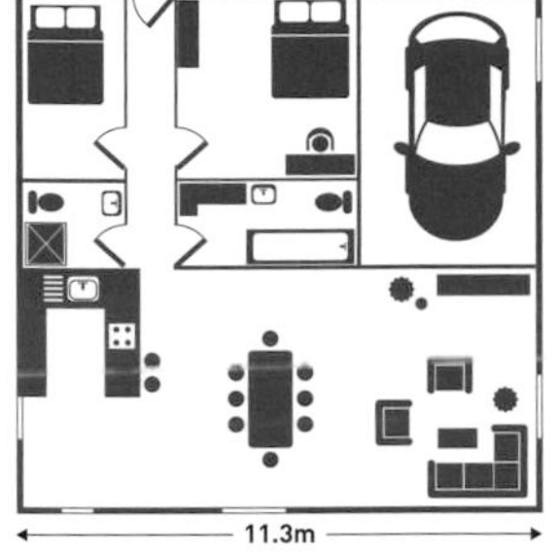

11.3m

single floor high

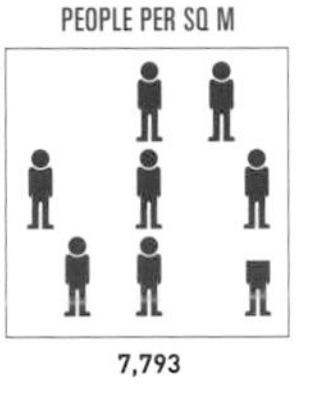

PEOPLE PER SQ M

7,793

UNITED KINGDOM 3,837 SQ M PER PERSON

EQUIVALENT TO:

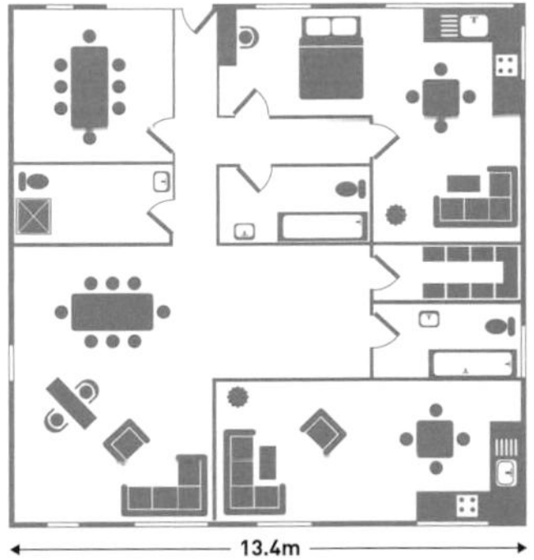

13.4m

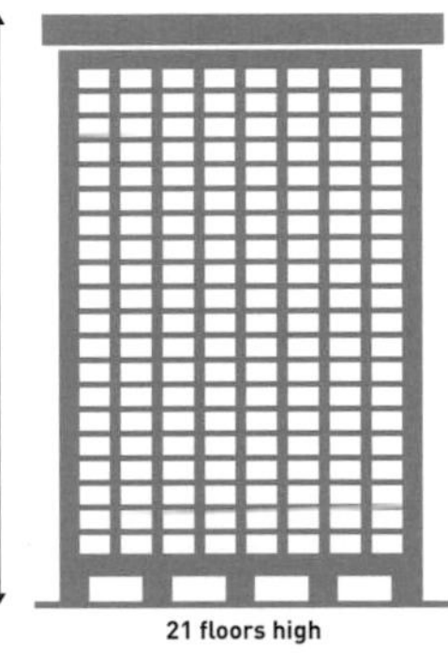

21 floors high

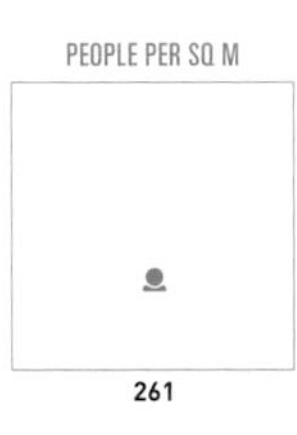

PEOPLE PER SQ M

261

UNITED STATES 29,192 SQ M PER PERSON

EQUIVALENT TO:

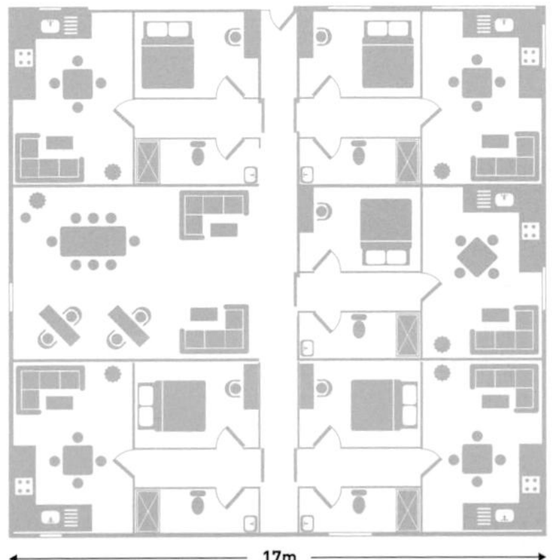

17m

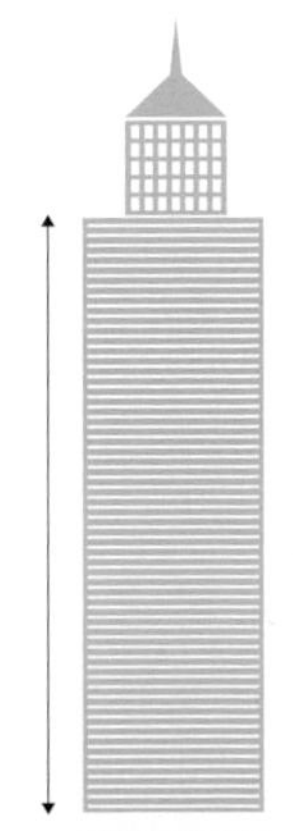

100 floors high

PEOPLE PER SQ M

34

What does that mean for how much room each of us has to stretch our legs? Let's imagine we decide to share out all the land in each country equally among its inhabitants. The communists among you will, no doubt, be thrilled.

The differences in the amount of land people would be allocated in such a scenario are pretty drastic. In **Macau {■}**, the world's most densely populated country, each person would get a patch of land measuring 49 square meters – about the size of a reasonably big living room. That's pretty crowded.

Over in the **U.K.** {■}, everyone would get a more substantial 3,837-square-meter patch of land. That's roughly an acre each. **Americans** {■} could expect about seven times more land, each receiving a patch measuring more than 29 thousand square meters.

If you really love your space (or really hate company) your best bet is **Greenland {■}**: here, you can expect a huge 37.5-million-square-meter patch all to yourself. Unfortunately, it's in Greenland.

For those who prefer a more temperate climate, there's always the **Falkland Islands {■}**, where there's a 3.9-million-square-meter plot of land for each person. Roomy – provided you like livestock: as the islands have 180,000 sheep, you can expect to be sharing your plot with at least 60 of them.

Synthetic disaster

What was the biggest man-made (accidental) disaster in history? And how bad was it? You'd think the answer would be straightforward – but it's not.

There are two big contenders. The first is the Bhopal disaster of 1984, a chemical leak in India that exposed hundreds of thousands of people to toxic gas. The second is the Chernobyl reactor breakdown in Ukraine in 1986.

Counting the toll of each is tricky, as long-term exposure to either toxic chemicals or radiation increases the risk of numerous cancers and health issues, without giving certainty of death.

The official counts for Bhopal place the death toll at a minimum of 3,300, but others argue the real long-term toll is in excess of 10,000. For Chernobyl, the long-term effects are still more contentious: 31 died in the immediate aftermath of the disaster, but anti-nuclear campaigners have suggested vast long-term death tolls, often challenged by expert scientific opinion. An official enquiry put the long-term death toll at around 4,000 – countering estimates of 60,000 or more put forward by other groups.

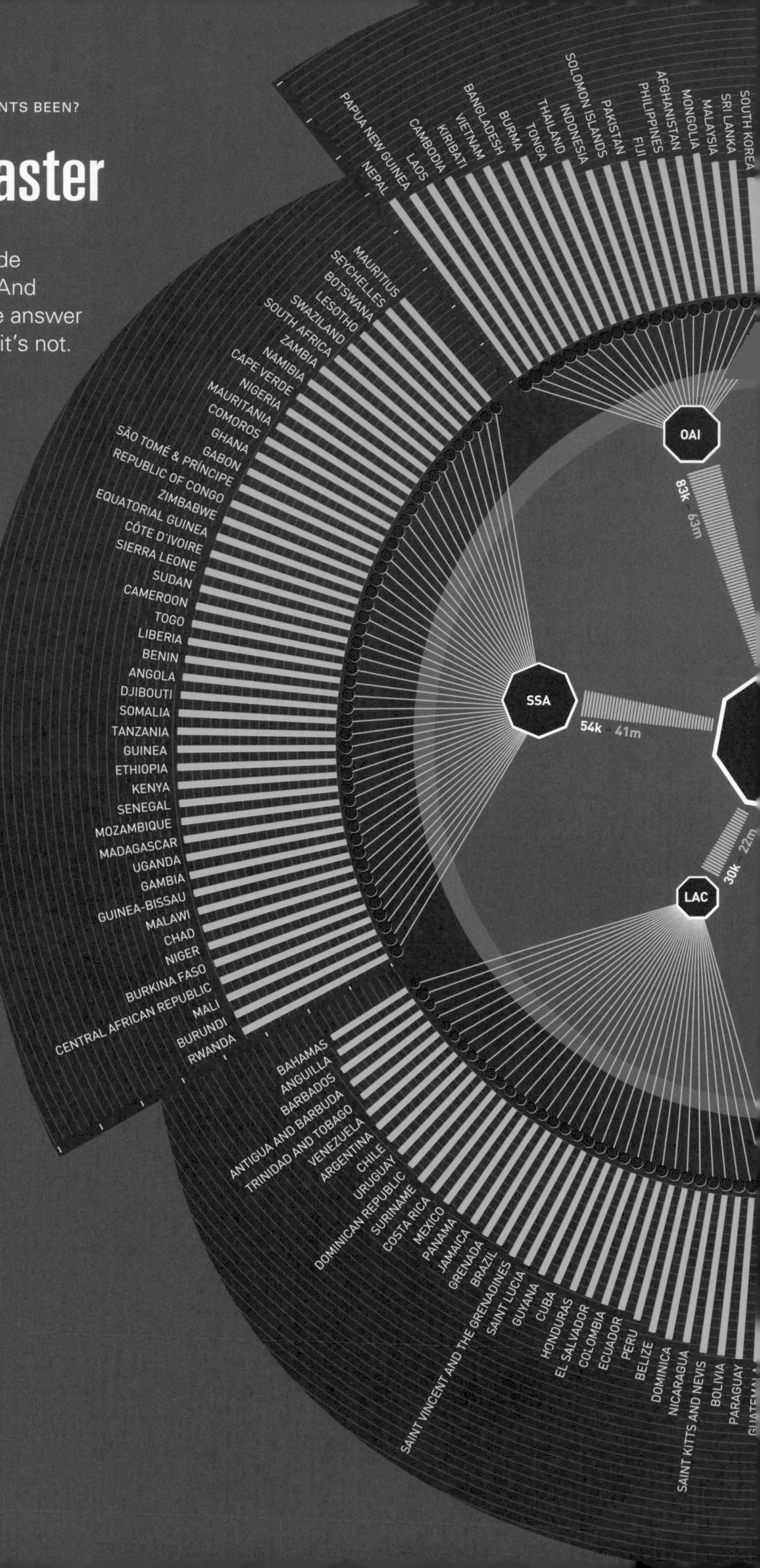

NEPAL
PAPUA NEW GUINEA
LAOS
CAMBODIA
KIRIBATI
VIETNAM
BANGLADESH
BURMA
TONGA
THAILAND
SOLOMON ISLANDS
INDONESIA
PAKISTAN
FIJI
PHILIPPINES
AFGHANISTAN
MONGOLIA
MALAYSIA
SRI LANKA
SOUTH KOREA
OAI
83k – 63m
MAURITIUS
SEYCHELLES
BOTSWANA
LESOTHO
SWAZILAND
SOUTH AFRICA
ZAMBIA
NAMIBIA
CAPE VERDE
NIGERIA
MAURITANIA
COMOROS
GHANA
GABON
SÃO TOMÉ & PRÍNCIPE
REPUBLIC OF CONGO
ZIMBABWE
EQUATORIAL GUINEA
CÔTE D'IVOIRE
SIERRA LEONE
SUDAN
CAMEROON
TOGO
LIBERIA
BENIN
ANGOLA
DJIBOUTI
SOMALIA
TANZANIA
GUINEA
ETHIOPIA
KENYA
SENEGAL
MOZAMBIQUE
MADAGASCAR
UGANDA
GAMBIA
GUINEA-BISSAU
MALAWI
CHAD
NIGER
BURKINA FASO
CENTRAL AFRICAN REPUBLIC
MALI
BURUNDI
RWANDA
SSA
54k – 41m
LAC
30k – 22m
BAHAMAS
ANGUILLA
BARBADOS
ANTIGUA AND BARBUDA
TRINIDAD AND TOBAGO
VENEZUELA
ARGENTINA
CHILE
URUGUAY
DOMINICAN REPUBLIC
SURINAME
COSTA RICA
MEXICO
PANAMA
JAMAICA
GRENADA
BRAZIL
SAINT VINCENT AND THE GRENADINES
SAINT LUCIA
GUYANA
CUBA
HONDURAS
EL SALVADOR
COLOMBIA
ECUADOR
PERU
BELIZE
DOMINICA
NICARAGUA
SAINT KITTS AND NEVIS
BOLIVIA
PARAGUAY

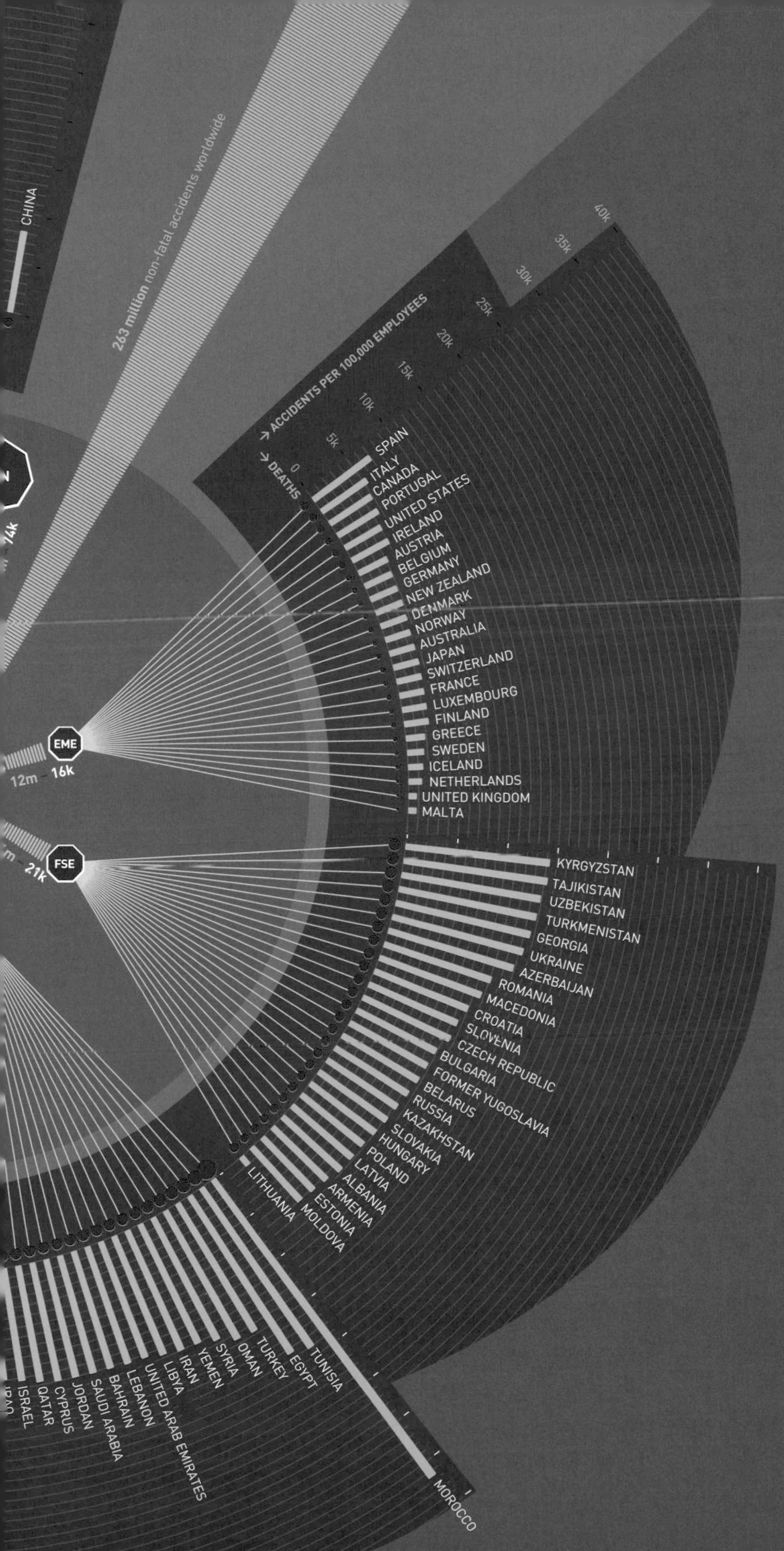

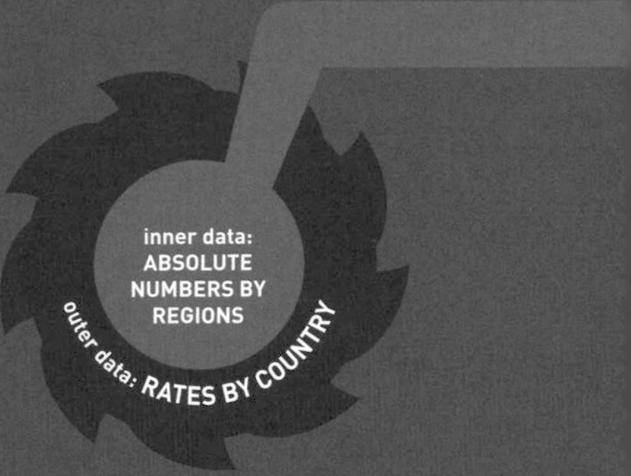

263 million non-fatal accidents worldwide

CHINA

→ ACCIDENTS PER 100,000 EMPLOYEES

→ DEATHS

0 5k 10k 15k 20k 25k 30k 35k 40k

EME 12m 16k

FSE 21k

SPAIN, ITALY, CANADA, PORTUGAL, UNITED STATES, IRELAND, AUSTRIA, BELGIUM, GERMANY, NEW ZEALAND, DENMARK, NORWAY, AUSTRALIA, JAPAN, SWITZERLAND, FRANCE, LUXEMBOURG, FINLAND, GREECE, SWEDEN, ICELAND, NETHERLANDS, UNITED KINGDOM, MALTA

KYRGYZSTAN, TAJIKISTAN, UZBEKISTAN, TURKMENISTAN, GEORGIA, UKRAINE, AZERBAIJAN, ROMANIA, MACEDONIA, CROATIA, SLOVENIA, CZECH REPUBLIC, BULGARIA, FORMER YUGOSLAVIA, BELARUS, RUSSIA, KAZAKHSTAN, SLOVAKIA, HUNGARY, POLAND, LATVIA, ALBANIA, ARMENIA, ESTONIA, MOLDOVA, LITHUANIA

MOROCCO, TUNISIA, EGYPT, TURKEY, OMAN, SYRIA, YEMEN, IRAN, LIBYA, UNITED ARAB EMIRATES, LEBANON, BAHRAIN, SAUDI ARABIA, JORDAN, CYPRUS, QATAR, ISRAEL

FATAL AND NON-FATAL ACCIDENTS BY REGION

10,000 deaths — 10,000,000 accidents

FATAL AND NON-FATAL ACCIDENTS BY COUNTRY

10 deaths per 100,000 employees — 1,000 accidents per 100,000 employees

REGIONS

EME: ESTABLISHED MARKET ECONOMIES
FSE: FORMERLY SOCIALIST ECONOMIES
IND: INDIA
CHN: CHINA
OAI: OTHER ASIA AND ISLANDS
SSA: SUB-SAHARAN AFRICA
LAC: LATIN AMERICA AND THE CARIBBEAN
MEC: MIDDLE EASTERN CRESCENT

Yet the real story of industrial trauma might not lie in these large-scale catastrophies.

Research carried out using the best available data from around the world on industrial accidents (often very bad data, as many countries are suspected of vast under-reporting) suggests that more than 345,000 people a year die in workplace accidents, while a further 260 million have an accident requiring at least three days off work.

Workers in the developing world are up to five times more likely – even on these under-reported figures – to die at work than those in the West.

Assuming workplaces were as safe in 1984 as in 2005, when the research was done (they were probably more dangerous), that's 11 million deaths at work since the Bhopal disaster – dwarfing even the highest estimates.

The real man-made disasters, maybe, aren't one-off huge events, but daily, unnoticed, small tragedies building to a horror – a little bit like what the IPCC and others keep saying about climate change...

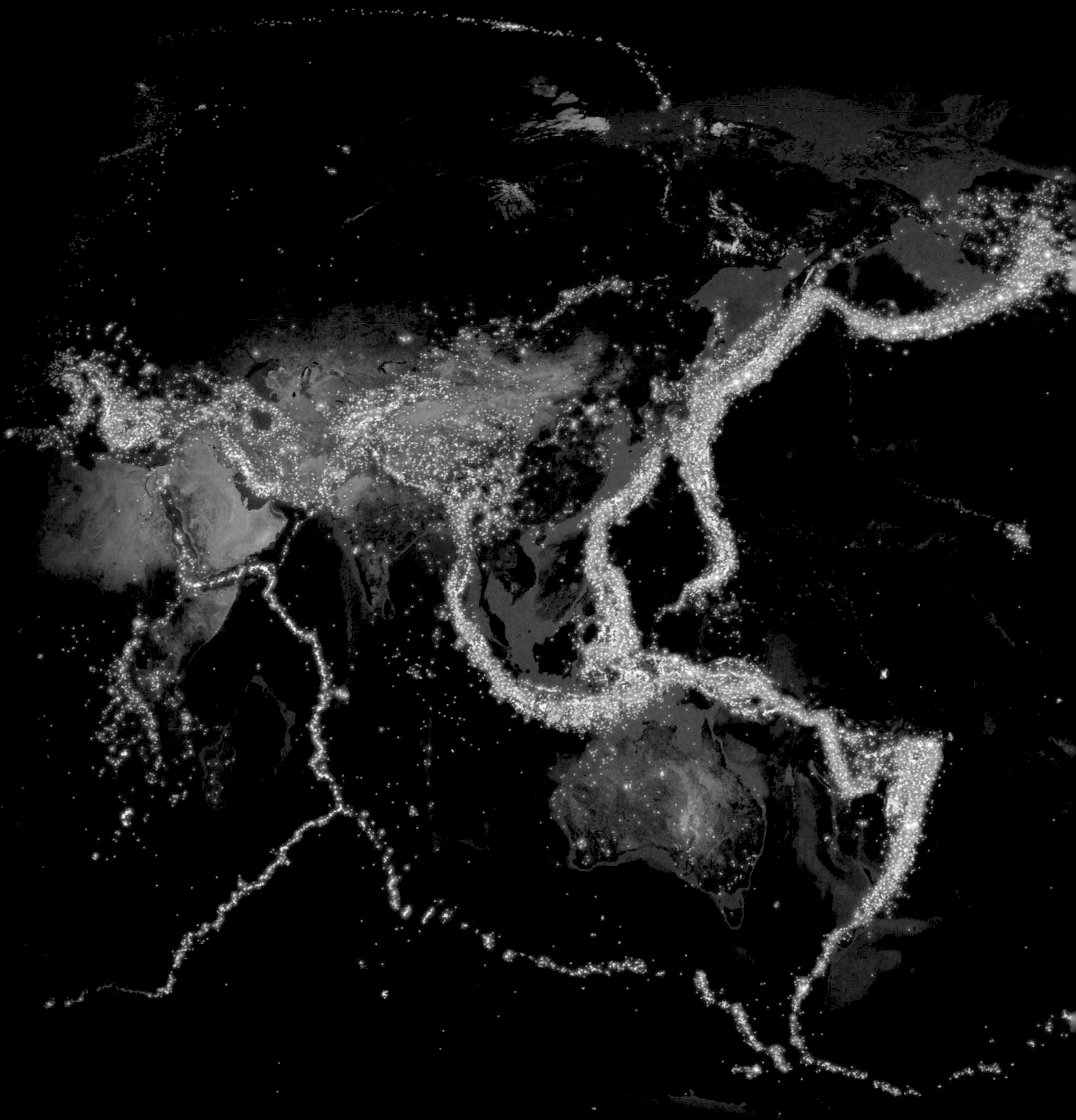

PERCENTAGE OF EARTHQUAKES AT MAGNITUDES 4-8

4

73.45%

Shake it out

If you live anywhere in England, earthquakes probably never cross your mind. If you're a resident of San Francisco – a city that could easily one day be plunged into the sea by a quake – they'll be more than a passing concern. And if you live in Japan, you'll be all too familiar with the terrifying destruction they can wreak.

Earthquakes are a strange phenomenon, particularly to those with a mathematical bent. They are at present – despite what cranks may tell you – completely impossible to predict. But for 50 years, we've been able to measure them precisely and easily. And they follow strangely regular patterns.

We typically measure earthquakes on a scale based on the Richter scale. This might not work exactly as you'd expect it to: an earthquake of magnitude 4.0 is ten times bigger than one at 3.0 – which is in turn ten times bigger than a 2.0 quake.

The energy released (we can use TNT as a handy equivalent) increases in a similar way: each point up the scale represents about 30 times more energy. So a 1.0 quake releases less energy than a stick of dynamite. A factor 6.0 quake approximates a 1945 nuclear bomb. Japan's horrendous 2011 quake was factor 9.0.

Thankfully, the likelihood of quakes follows a similar, regular pattern: we get over 1,000 factor 5.0 quakes a year, but only around 100 at 6.0, 10 at 7.0 or so, and we'd expect to see a factor 9.0 quake just once a decade.

The results of these strange, mathematically regular quakes have been projected onto a beautiful map by John Nelson at IDV Solutions. This shows every recorded earthquake since 1898 – and the intensity of the color represents the size of the quake. We might not be able to see what's coming, but a look at what's gone before is still pretty revelatory – and answers at least one question: did the Earth move for you?

5
24.63%
6
1.7%
7
0.21%
0.01%
8

Lock 'n' load

Guns don't kill people, advocates say, people kill people. But, as those opposed to firearms point out, people find it difficult to propel hot lead at speeds fast enough to kill someone without the help of a gun.

Whatever your view on the right to bear arms, the data on private firearm ownership – collated by the *Guardian* datablog – are startling. Across the world, there are more than 500 million firearms in private hands, and these weapons are responsible for around 126,000 homicides each year.

Beyond that, the data might tell you different things depending on what you think about guns. Anti-gun people might point out that the **U.S.** owns more guns than anyone else: for every 100 Americans there are 88 guns – and the country has more than 9,000 gun murders each year.

But the relationship between **guns { }** and **gun deaths {■}** is not nearly that simple:

TOP 20 GUNS PER 100 PEOPLE		TOP 20 GUN HOMICIDE RATE PER 100,000 PEOPLE	
1	UNITED STATES	1	HONDURAS
2	SWITZERLAND	2	EL SALVADOR
3	FINLAND	3	JAMAICA
4	SERBIA	4	VENEZUELA
5	CYPRUS	5	GUATEMALA
6	URUGUAY	6	TRINIDAD AND TOBAGO
7	SWEDEN	7	COLOMBIA
8	NORWAY	8	BELIZE
9	FRANCE	9	BRAZIL
10	CANADA	10	SOUTH AFRICA
11	AUSTRIA	11	DOMINICAN REPUBLIC
12	GERMANY	12	PANAMA
13	ICELAND	13	BAHAMAS
14	BAHRAIN	14	ECUADOR
15	MACEDONIA	15	GUYANA
16	NEW ZEALAND	16	MEXICO
17	GREECE	17	PHILIPPINES
18	NORTHERN IRELAND	18	PARAGUAY
19	PANAMA	19	NICARAGUA
20	CROATIA	20	ZIMBABWE

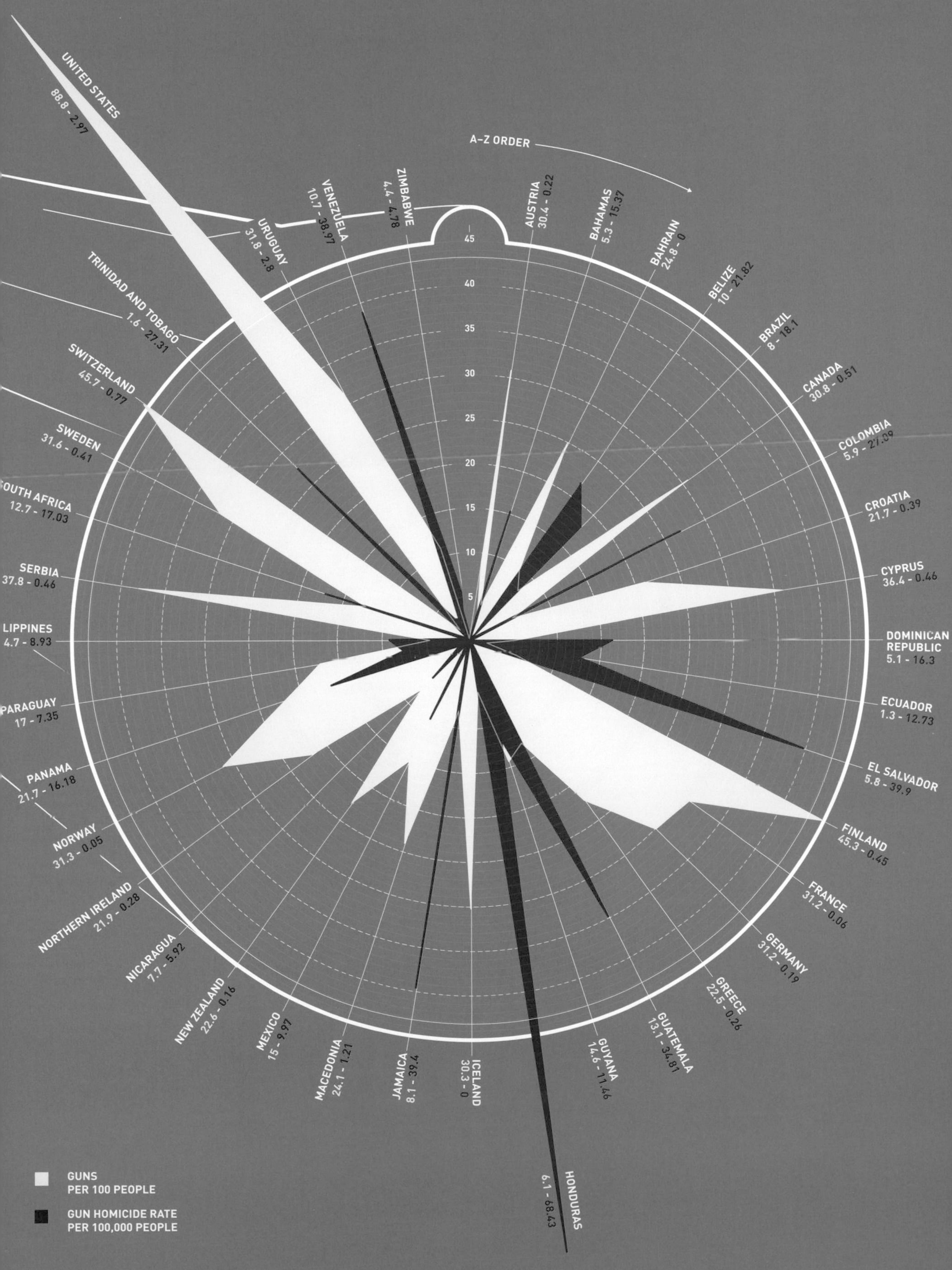

A–Z ORDER
AUSTRIA 30.4 - 0.22
BAHAMAS 5.3 - 15.37
BAHRAIN 24.8 - 0
BELIZE 10 - 21.82
BRAZIL 8 - 18.1
CANADA 30.8 - 0.51
COLOMBIA 5.9 - 27.09
CROATIA 21.7 - 0.39
CYPRUS 36.4 - 0.46
DOMINICAN REPUBLIC 5.1 - 16.3
ECUADOR 1.3 - 12.73
EL SALVADOR 5.8 - 39.9
FINLAND 45.3 - 0.45
FRANCE 31.2 - 0.06
GERMANY 31.2 - 0.19
GREECE 22.5 - 0.26
GUATEMALA 13.1 - 34.81
GUYANA 14.6 - 11.46
HONDURAS 6.1 - 68.43
ICELAND 30.3 - 0
JAMAICA 8.1 - 39.4
MACEDONIA 24.1 - 1.21
MEXICO 15 - 9.97
NEW ZEALAND 22.6 - 0.16
NICARAGUA 7.7 - 5.92
NORTHERN IRELAND 21.9 - 0.28
NORWAY 31.3 - 0.05
PANAMA 21.7 - 16.18
PARAGUAY 17 - 7.35
LIPPINES 4.7 - 8.93
SERBIA 37.8 - 0.46
OUTH AFRICA 12.7 - 17.03
SWEDEN 31.6 - 0.41
SWITZERLAND 45.7 - 0.77
TRINIDAD AND TOBAGO 1.6 - 27.31
URUGUAY 31.8 - 2.8
UNITED STATES 88.8 - 2.97
VENEZUELA 10.7 - 38.97
ZIMBABWE 4.4 - 4.78
45
40
35
30
25
20
15
10
5
GUNS PER 100 PEOPLE
GUN HOMICIDE RATE PER 100,000 PEOPLE

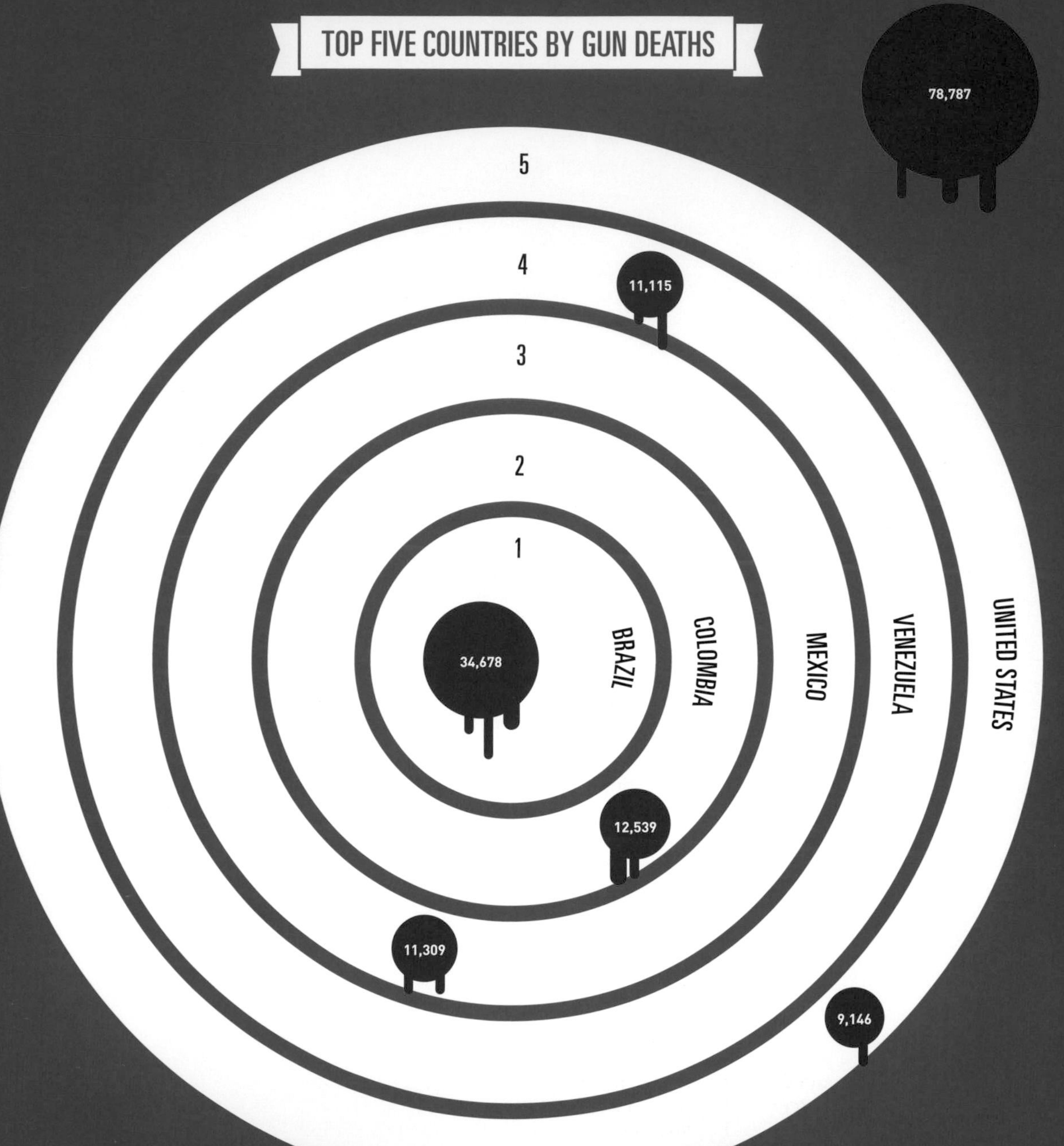

TOP FIVE COUNTRIES BY GUN DEATHS

78,787

5

4

11,115

3

2

1

34,678

BRAZIL

COLOMBIA

MEXICO

VENEZUELA

UNITED STATES

12,539

11,309

9,146

The top five of gun deaths is depressingly predictable: **Brazil**, **Colombia**, **Mexico**, **Venezuela** and the **United States**, with more than 78,000 between them.

= 10 PEOPLE

= 10 GUNS

GUNS PER 100 PEOPLE

- TRINIDAD AND TOBAGO -

1.6

- U.S. -

88.8

- FRANCE -

31.2

GUNS PER GUN HOMICIDE

- TRINIDAD AND TOBAGO -

58

- U.S. -

29,521

- FRANCE -

542,857

Other statistics from the data are less conclusive. For instance, the tiny country of **Trinidad and Tobago** has one gun murder for every 58 firearms owned. If the **U.S**. had that same rate, it would be looking at 4.6 million gun murders a year, rather than 9,000. In reality, there is only one gun murder for every 29,500 guns in U.S. hands.

In **France** the gun-ownership picture seems even more benign. The country has 19 million guns in private hands, but just 35 gun murders: that's one murder per 540,000 weapons.

Whether it's different weapons, different policing or different cultures, there's clearly more going on than just more guns = more murders.

But what? It seems as if – maybe – data doesn't solve mysteries. People solve mysteries.

The Olympic spirit

While the world anticipates the Rio 2016 Olympic games, it's worth reflecting on what transpired in London 2012. As host country, the UK not only invested £9.3bn and delivered an Olympics experience among the most successful in history, but team GB turned in its best official ranking since 1920. It will be interesting to see if Team Brazil can replicate this home nation performance in 2016.

The final medals tally also brought great news for the home nation: the **UK** came third in the official rankings with 29 gold medals – though the **U.S.** counts differently, looking at the total number of medals awarded.

But how good an achievement is third for the UK, a rich country with a population of a little over 60 million? The UK is certainly smaller than the U.S. and **China**, but other competitors are far poorer, and far smaller too.

How would their performance look if we were all competing on a level playing field?

The *Guardian* data team, with a little help from the Royal Statistical Society, gave it a try building a mathematical model to find out. It keeps the total number of medals constant, then corrects for either population, GDP or age, and it changes the rankings dramatically.

The tiny nation of **Grenada** is the big winner: its sole gold medal, coupled with its low GDP and population of 110,000, propel it to first in the rankings in both corrected tables: the single gold medal is equivalent to 112 when corrected for population, and 124 accounting for GDP.

China and the U.S. are the big losers, though. As both are large countries and (relatively) rich, their table-topping performances no longer look so great. By comparison, the UK does okay, ranking 10th when accounting for population, and 27th adjusting for GDP.

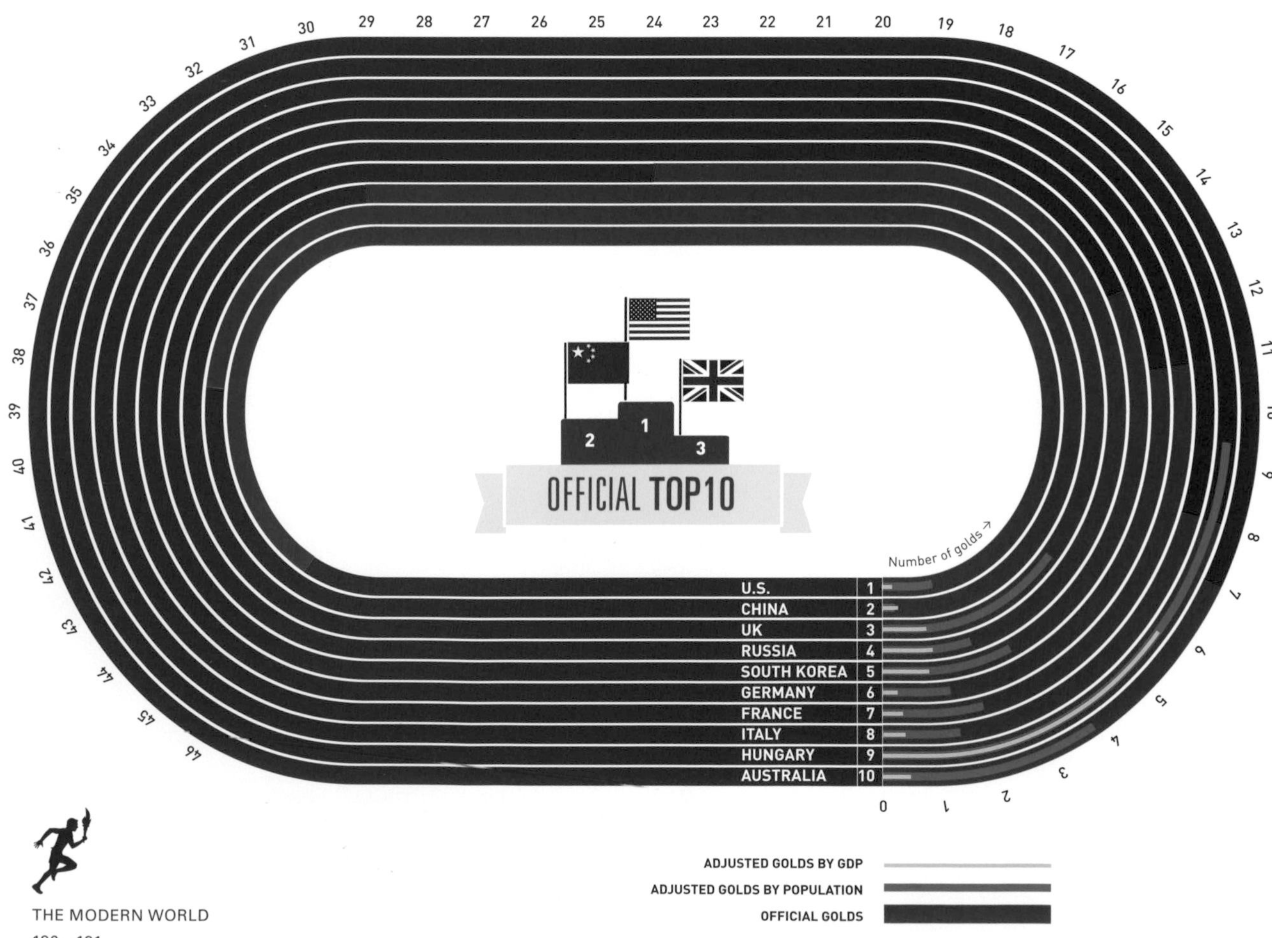

ADJUSTED TOP10

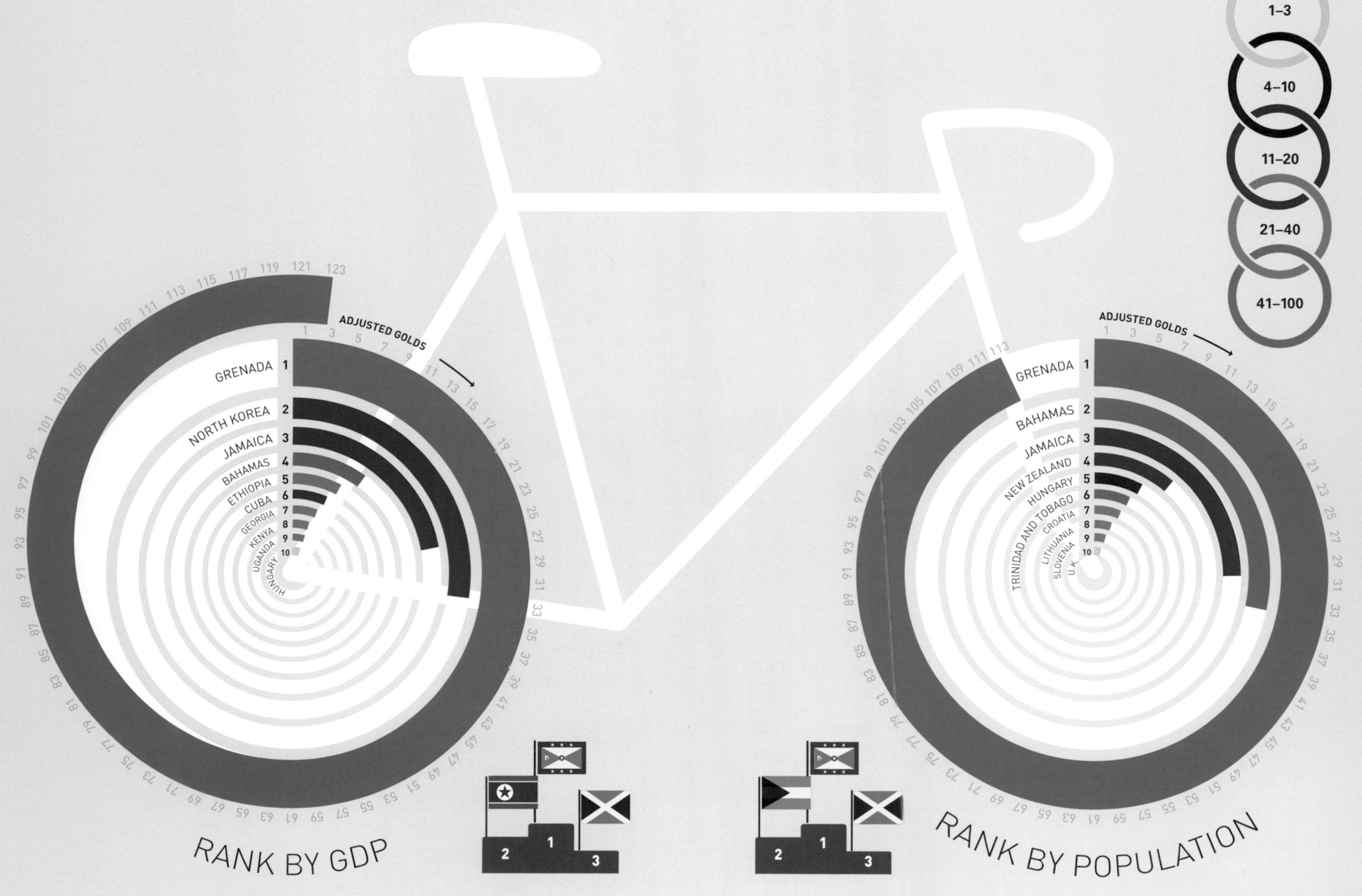

Harder, better, faster, stronger

Athletic events, whether they're watched by millions like the Olympic Games, or in front of a few dozen at a local arena, are as much a battle to better ourselves as to beat the competition.

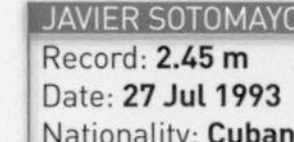

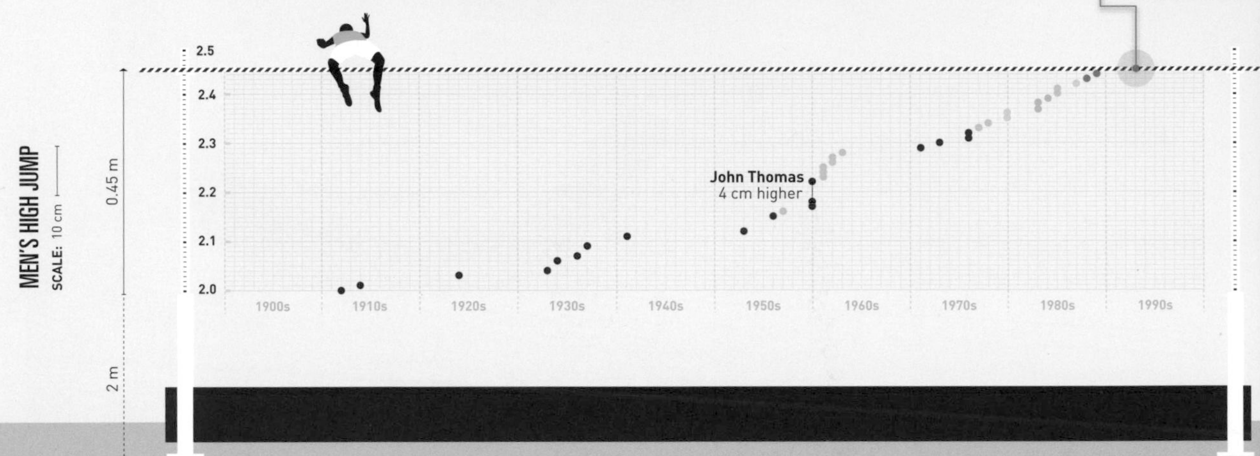

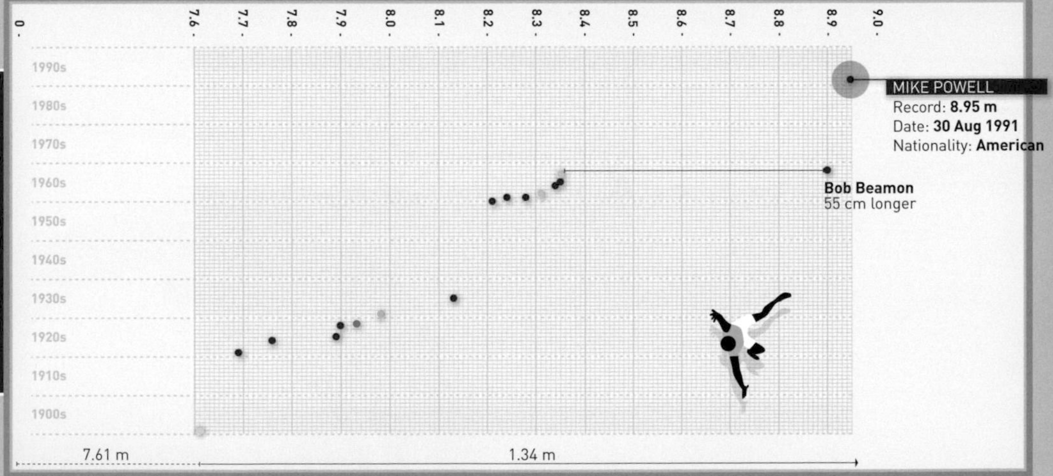

SCALE: 10 cm

Nowhere is that felt more than at the very top of the game, where the world's best athletes fight not so much to win a given event as to be noted in the history books as the world-record holder in their event.

But is that a challenge that's getting ever harder to accomplish? As our understanding of science and the human body increases, eking out extra performance gains without breaking sport's strict rules gets increasingly difficult. This might be particularly true in cycling, where the records that remain unchallenged from the dope-ridden 1990s and 2000s seem unlikely to ever be beaten, but a similar story is found in most sports.

Records from four events – from which we've excluded any shown to involve cheating, and ignored various timing and weather discrepancies – show how hard it's getting to get better.

In the **men's long jump**, for example, the world record has only been beaten 18 times since

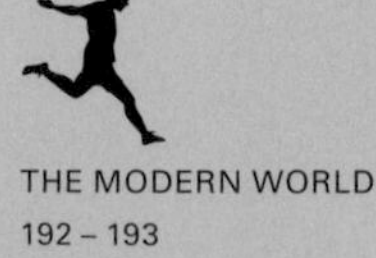

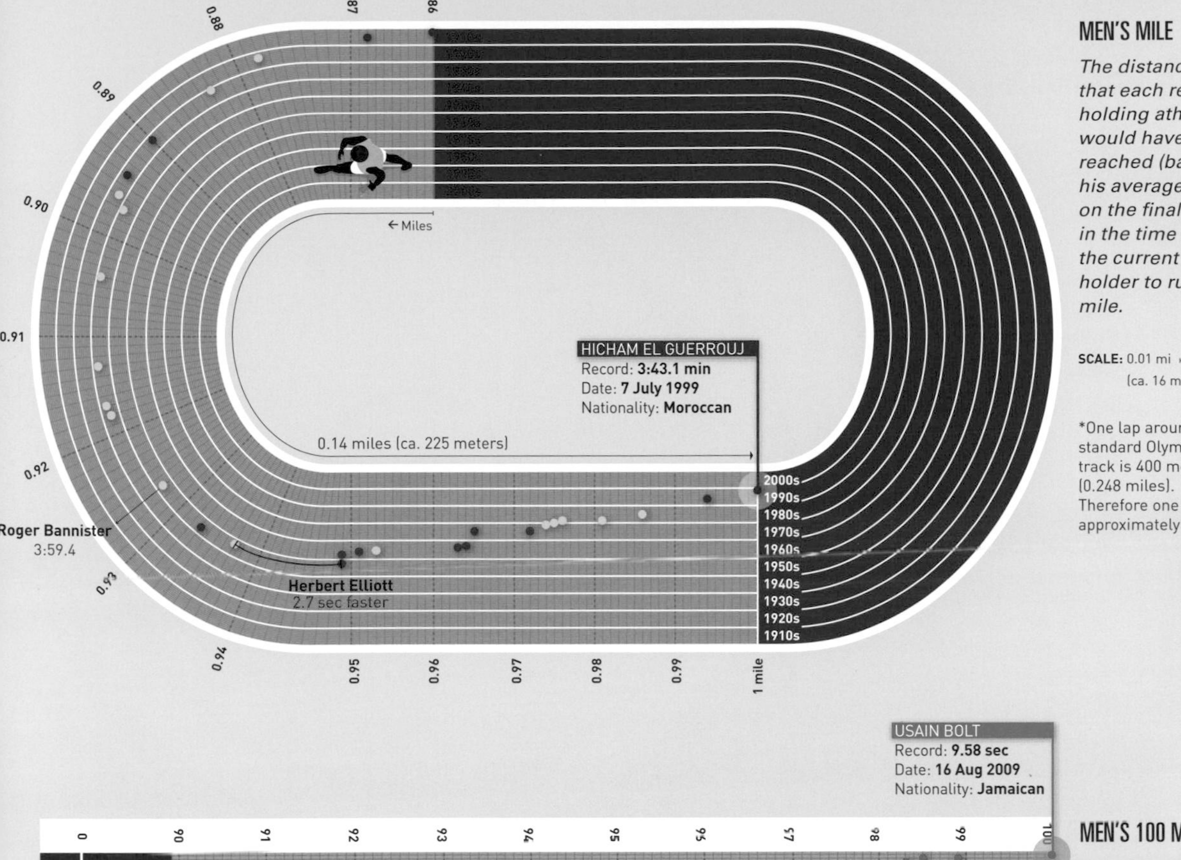

MEN'S MILE

The distance that each record-holding athlete would have reached (based on his average speed on the final lap) in the time it took the current record holder to run one mile.*

SCALE: 0.01 mi (ca. 16 m)

*One lap around a standard Olympic oval track is 400 meters (0.248 miles). Therefore one mile is approximately four laps.

USAIN BOLT
Record: **9.58 sec**
Date: **16 Aug 2009**
Nationality: **Jamaican**

0 · 90 · 91 · 92 · 93 · 94 · 95 · 96 · 97 · 98 · 99 · 100

2000s · 1990s · 1980s · 1970s · 1960s · 1950s · 1940s · 1930s · 1920s · 1910s

Charlie Paddock
0.2 sec faster

89.35 m · 10.65 m

MEN'S 100 METERS

A final 10-meter view of where each record-holding athlete would have reached (based on his average speed) at the time when the current record holder crossed the finish line.

SCALE: 1 m

1901. No one has managed any improvement whatsoever since 1991, and the **men's high jump** record has stood unbroken since 1993.

As for **running a mile** – a record central to the psyche after Roger Bannister famously became the first man to run a sub-four-minute mile in 1954 (he only held that world record for around six weeks, incidentally) – that record has been set 32 times since 1913, but no one's beaten it since 1999.

The record for the **men's 100 m**, arguably the most famous athletics event of them all, is a bit different. It's only been beaten 16 times since 1913 – but it's been beaten three times since 2008. What's the reason? New technology? New rules? New counting systems? The answer's much simpler, and only two words long.

The answer is this: Usain Bolt. He not only broke the record, he then broke his own record twice more in the space of 15 months. As ever, the latest record will take some beating.

ATHLETES' NATIONALITY BY GEOGRAPHICAL AREA

- AFRICA
- NORTH AMERICA
- SOUTH AMERICA & CARIBBEAN
- ASIA
- EUROPE
- OCEANIA
- RUSSIA

DRUG CONSUMPTION BY REGION

	TOTAL USERS	% OF POPULATION
	Number of people in each region that use X	Percentage of the population in each region that use X

	TOTAL USERS	% OF POPULATION
AFRICA		
AMERICAS		
ASIA		
EUROPE		
OCEANIA		

Each group of rings represents one type of drug. The size of the rings represents the total number of drug users. The size of the dots (below the rings) shows the number of drug users as a percentage of the population of each region.

ABSOLUTE NUMBER OF **CANNABIS** USERS BY REGION

PERCENTAGE OF THE POPULATION THAT USES **CANNABIS** BY REGION

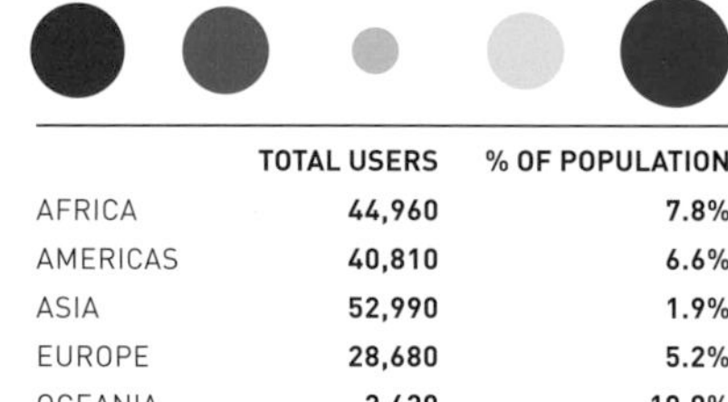

	TOTAL USERS	% OF POPULATION
AFRICA	44,960	7.8%
AMERICAS	40,810	6.6%
ASIA	52,990	1.9%
EUROPE	28,680	5.2%
OCEANIA	2,630	10.9%

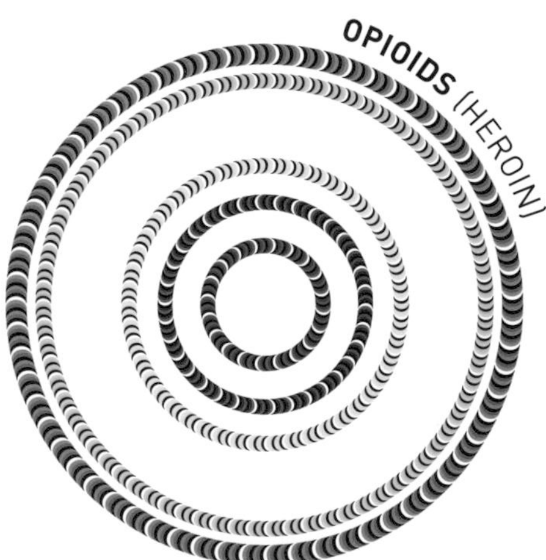

	TOTAL USERS	% OF POPULATION
AFRICA	2,200	0.4%
AMERICAS	13,230	2.1%
ASIA	10,560	0.4%
EUROPE	4,060	0.7%
OCEANIA	730	3.0%

	TOTAL USERS	% OF POPULATION
AFRICA	2,780	0.5%
AMERICAS	7,150	1.2%
ASIA	1,270	0.1%
EUROPE	4,650	0.8%
OCEANIA	370	1.5%

High times

The "War on Drugs" was declared by President Nixon in 1971. More than 40 years later, it's still being fought on every continent, and it's far from clear that law enforcement is winning.

The official UN figures for five of the top drug types alone (**cannabis**, **cocaine**, **amphetamines**, **ecstasy** and **heroin**) suggest there are more than 270 million regular drug users around the world.

For two of the most serious drugs – heroin and cocaine – the **Americas {■}** are over-represented: 42% of heroin and 44% of cocaine users are located there. But oddly, it's the "antipodeans" who really seem to hit the hard stuff.

The effect isn't small. If you were to run into an **Australian or New Zealender {■}**, picked at random, and a **European { }**, the Aussie would be four times more likely to be a heroin or ecstasy user, and twice as likely to use cocaine or cannabis.

Given there's a war on, it's perhaps no surprise that the CIA is keen to track where some of these drugs come from. Tracking cannabis is all but impossible (the stuff is grown everywhere), but more concerted efforts are made to track heroin and cocaine. And the story for both drugs is oddly similar.

Poppy cultivation is concentrated in three countries and the overwhelming majority of heroin is produced in Afghanistan (topped up by Burma, with more made in Mexico, almost all of which is sold in the U.S. as "black tar" heroin). From Afghanistan, it slips into Europe through one of two routes – through Iran to the Balkans and onward, or up and through Eastern Europe. Otherwise, it can head westward through Asia, or down (and through) South Africa and beyond.

Cocaine mirrors this pattern – Colombia makes the most (Peru and Bolivia come next), and from these three countries the drugs move: up through Mexico, around to Asia, or across the ocean to Africa, and up to Europe through Spain and Portugal, or round through Eastern Europe.

The problem for the U.S. and Western Europe? We're not only the drug cartels' sworn nemesis – we're their biggest customers. Hard to win a war when you're funding both sides.

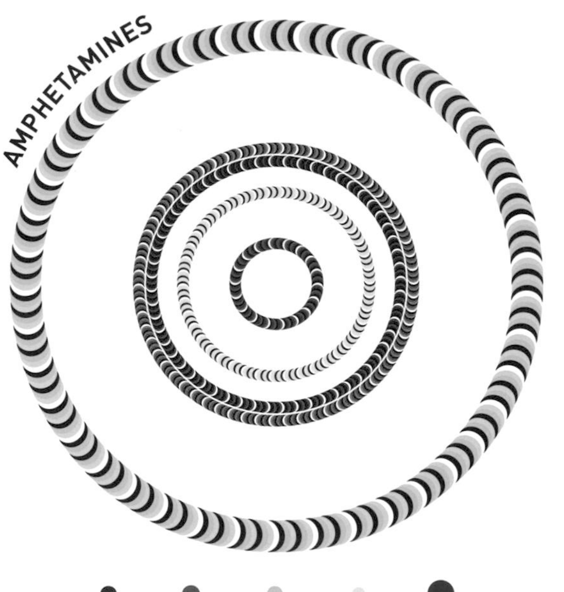

	TOTAL USERS	% OF POPULATION
AFRICA	4,730	0.8%
AMERICAS	5,790	0.9%
ASIA	19,570	0.7%
EUROPE	2,640	0.5%
OCEANIA	510	2.1%

ECSTASY

	TOTAL USERS	% OF POPULATION
AFRICA	1,160	0.5%
AMERICAS	3,230	0.4%
ASIA	10,380	0.2%
EUROPE	3,740	0.7%
OCEANIA	710	2.9%

WHICH COUNTRIES LIKE TO DRINK AND SMOKE?

Cigarettes and alcohol

"I was looking for action," complained Liam Gallagher in the mid-90s hit, "but all I found was cigarettes and alcohol."

Looking at the data, many of us could say the same – figures collected by the OECD show consumption of both remains a pretty common pastime, despite being potentially disastrous for us.

Let's get the health issues out of the way. Smoking kills. The estimates vary, but regular smoking reduces your life expectancy by somewhere between 10 and 18 years. On top of the many carcinogens contained therein, cigarette smoke is also radioactive (really) – it contains polonium, the radioactive material used to kill the Russian defector Alexander Litvinenko in London in 2006.

The evidence on alcohol is far more mixed – low levels of consumption may be beneficial to health – but alcoholism is deadly, knocking around a decade or so off life expectancy.

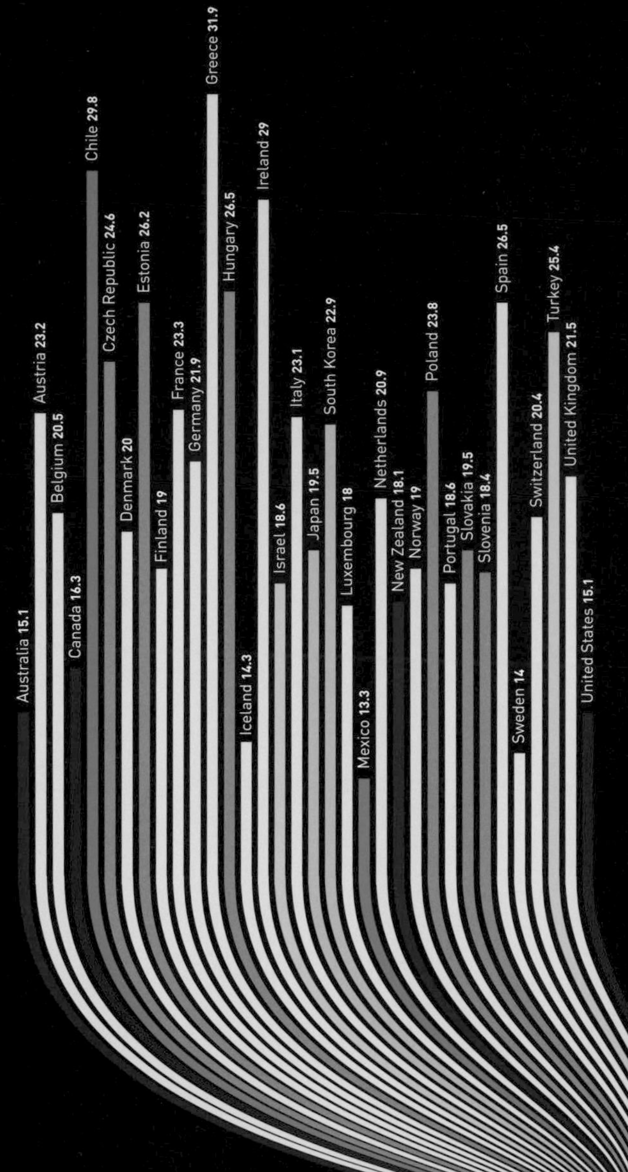

35
30
25
20
15
10
5
0

% DAILY SMOKERS →

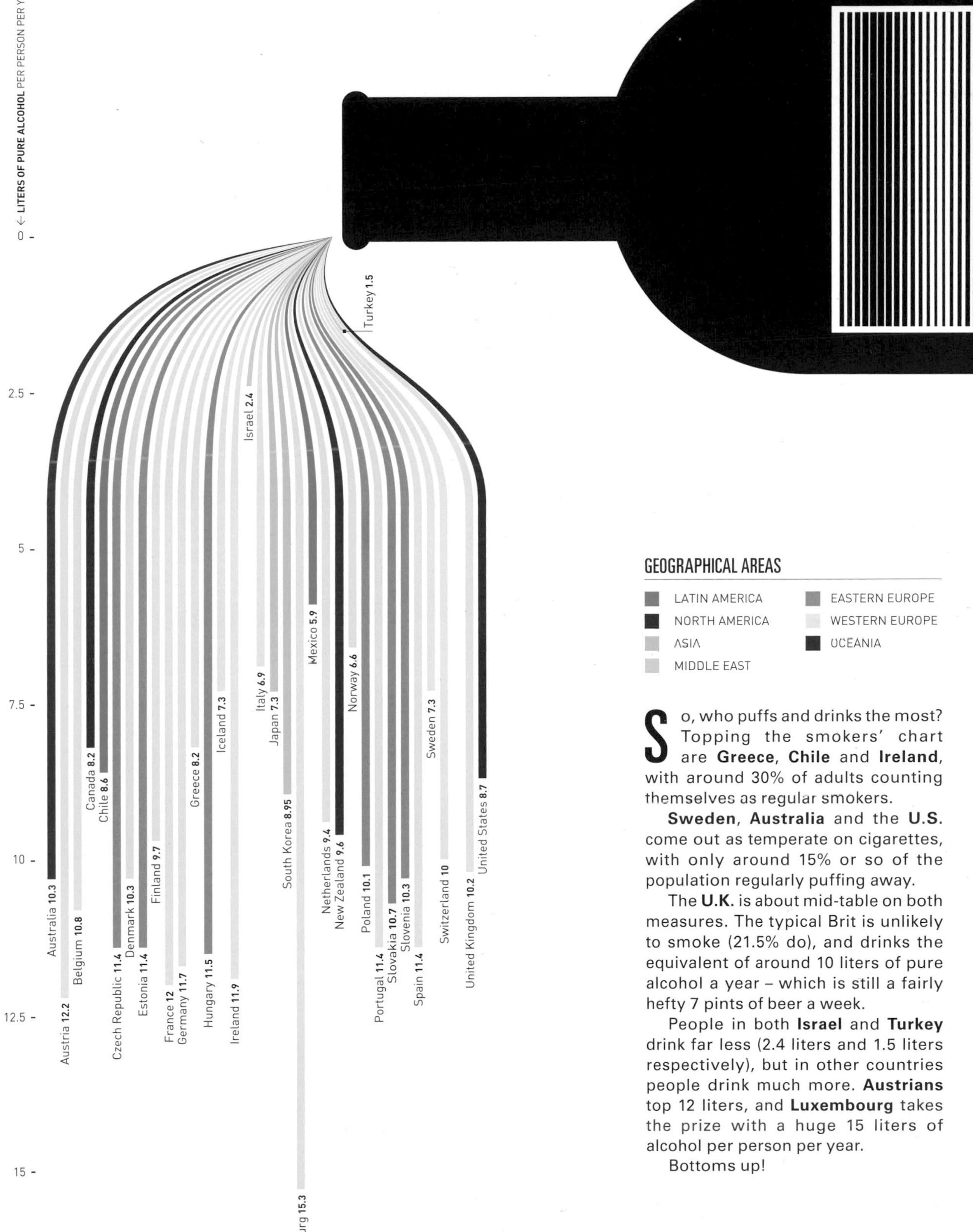

So, who puffs and drinks the most? Topping the smokers' chart are **Greece**, **Chile** and **Ireland**, with around 30% of adults counting themselves as regular smokers.

Sweden, **Australia** and the **U.S.** come out as temperate on cigarettes, with only around 15% or so of the population regularly puffing away.

The **U.K.** is about mid-table on both measures. The typical Brit is unlikely to smoke (21.5% do), and drinks the equivalent of around 10 liters of pure alcohol a year – which is still a fairly hefty 7 pints of beer a week.

People in both **Israel** and **Turkey** drink far less (2.4 liters and 1.5 liters respectively), but in other countries people drink much more. **Austrians** top 12 liters, and **Luxembourg** takes the prize with a huge 15 liters of alcohol per person per year.

Bottoms up!

History of the 'net

In our view, history isn't quick or willing enough to salute the nerds. From Charles Babbage (creator of the first computer) to wartime codebreaker Alan Turing, nerds have generally had to wait until long after their death for their accomplishments to be recognized.

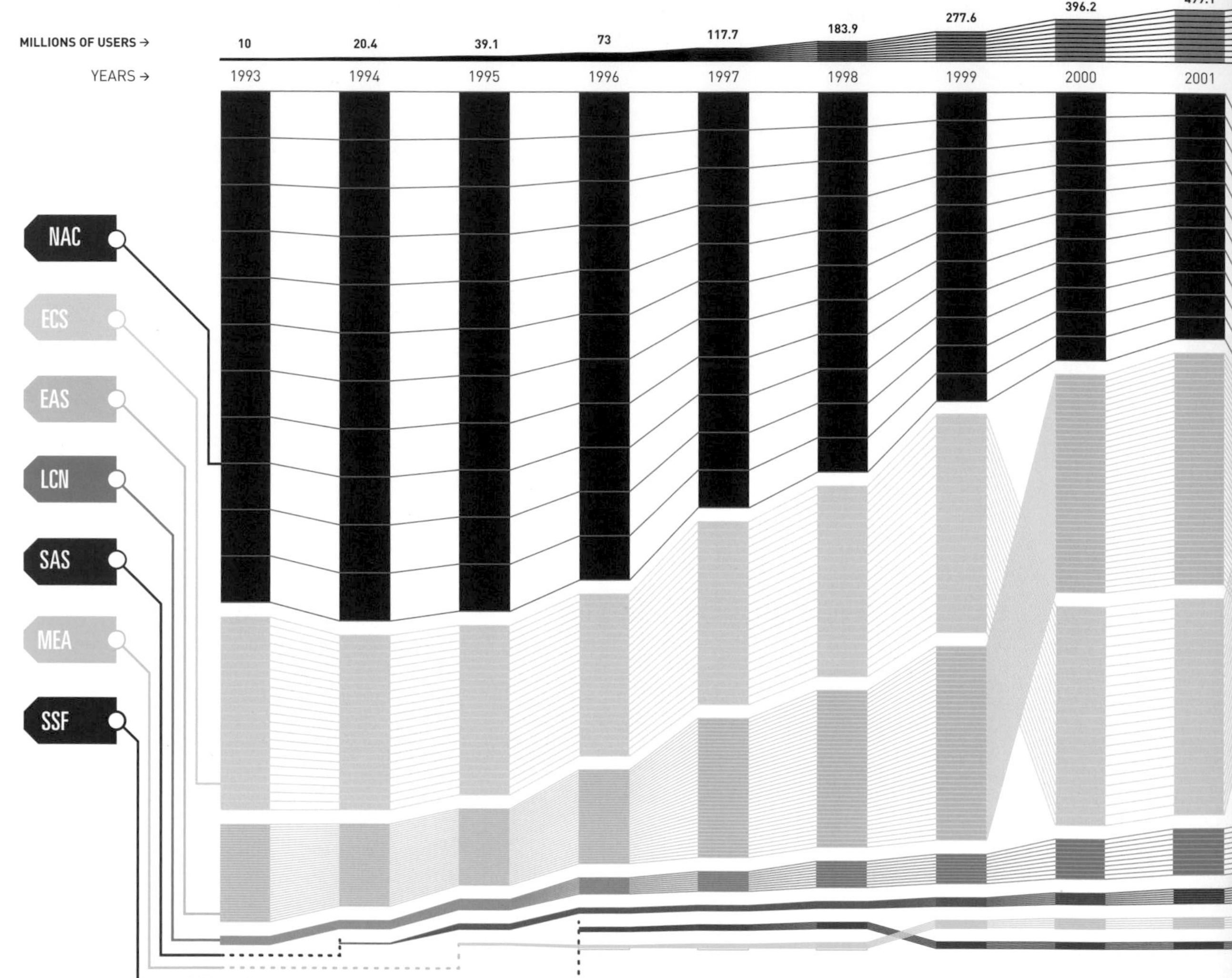

So it is, arguably, for some of the inventors of the internet, a network that's older than most of us realize. Its earliest precursor, the military network ARPANET, was first set up in 1969 and was a connection between four computers at four U.S. universities – rather smaller than the network we use today.

The very first piece of data sent across the network was "LOG" – the first three letters of the word "LOGIN." Shortly after the "G" was sent, the system crashed. Some things never change.

The growth of the early internet might not be described as astronomical. Data chronicling the early life of the 'net, set out in Hobbes' Internet Timeline, bear this out: by 1977 – eight years later – there were 111 computers hooked up to the network, spread across the U.S.. It took another seven years for the number of devices to top 1,000.

Come the '90s, though, things changed as home users and businesses started to log on. By 1992, one million computers spanned the

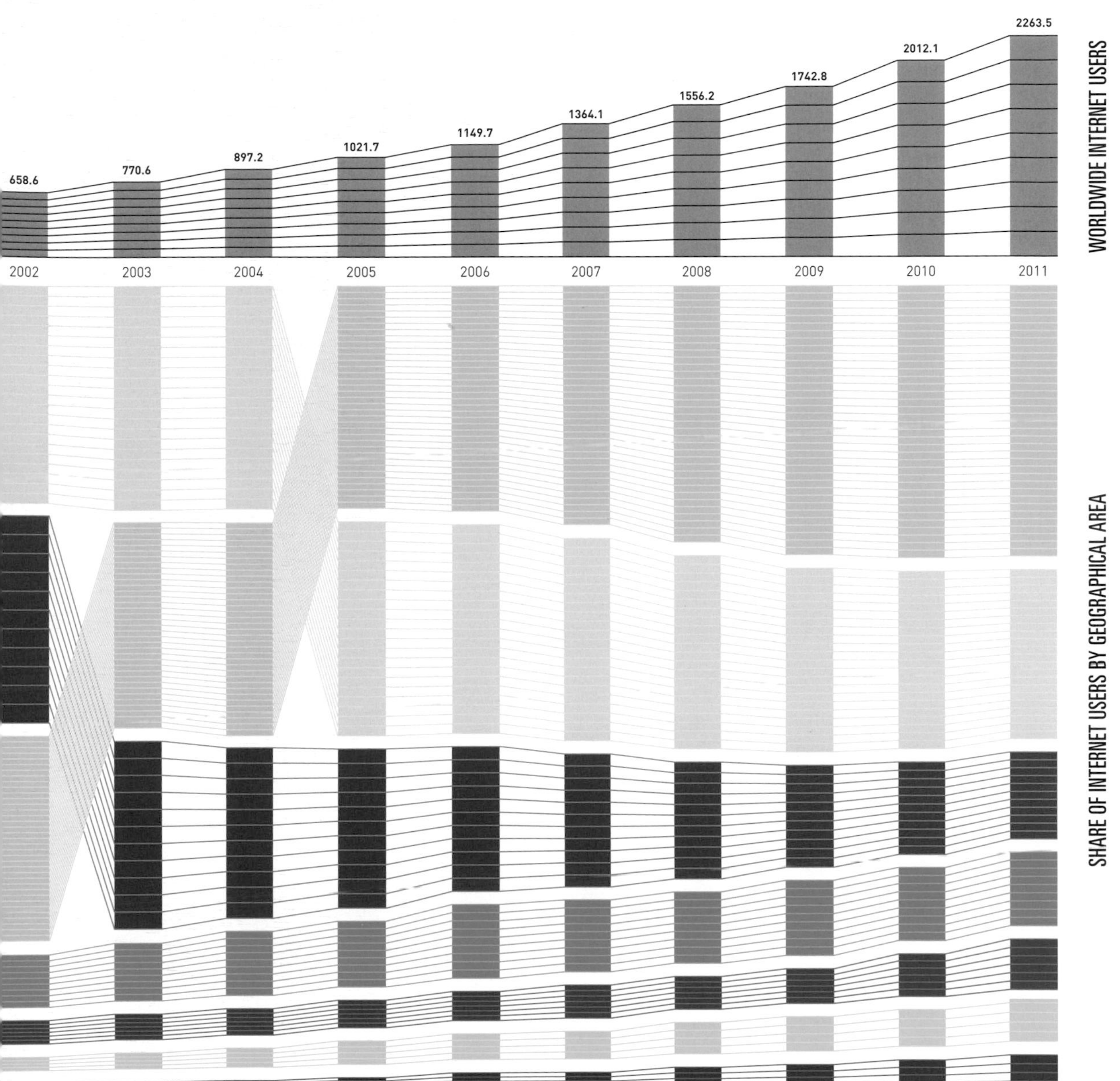

internet. By 1997, it was almost 20 million. And then things really got going. In 2000, around 400 million people across the planet had access to the internet. Today, it's more than 2.2 billion, and the technology has revolutionized our lives, our economy and our communications.

Almost everyone can name the inventor of the lightbulb. Who can name any of the ARPANET scientists from back in 1969? Anyone? It sucks to be a nerd. At least today's have their billion-dollar dotcoms as a consolation prize.

GEOGRAPHICAL AREA (COUNTRY CODE)

- **NAC** NORTH AMERICA
- **ECS** EUROPE & CENTRAL ASIA (all income levels)
- **EAS** EAST ASIA & PACIFIC (all income levels)
- **LCN** LATIN AMERICA & CARIBBEAN (all income levels)
- **SAS** SOUTH ASIA
- **MEA** MIDDLE EAST & NORTH AFRICA (all income levels)
- **SSF** SUB-SAHARAN AFRICA (all income levels)

The map of the 'net

More than two billion people around the world have access to the internet, more than five times as many as were online just a decade ago. An audience of this scale means far more than just a ready stream of people to upload videos of cats or baby pictures to Facebook. It's enough to make online giants rank among the biggest companies on the planet.

There's no shortage of places for that huge population to visit: when **Google {■ 1}** got going in 1998, it indexed around 26 million links. Two years later, with great fanfare, it reached one billion links indexed. Today that total stands at more than a trillion – that's one thousand million. Now lots of these point to the same pages, but even conservative estimates put the number of pages on the internet at somewhere between 8.5 and 40 billion unique pages.

Here's one troubling thought: even the most cautious estimates guess about 4% of those websites display what we could politely describe as smut (and searches for the stuff make up 13% of the total). That's at least 340 million pages of the stuff. Even at 30 seconds a page, that would take 647 years of browsing 24 hours a day. As to whether that's a good or a bad thing, we'd probably better leave that for others to judge.

Despite the unbelievable number of pages out there, the biggest sites on the net attract astronomical swathes of the audience: Google, the top dog, is visited by 48% of all internet users each month. Almost half of internet users (44.5%) visit **Facebook {■ 2}** each month too. The top twenty sites on the internet – and the audiences they reach – are set out here.

One final hint of the future is contained therein: 11 of the top 20 sites are in English, the lingua franca of the 'net. The remainder are in Chinese, Indian, Japanese and Russian.

TOP 20 WEBSITES BY TRAFFIC

1	GOOGLE.COM	11	LIVE.COM
2	YOUTUBE.COM	12	TAOBAO.COM
3	FACEBOOK.COM	13	MSN.COM
4	BAIDU.COM	14	SINA.COM.CN
5	YAHOO.COM	15	YAHOO.CO.JP
6	AMAZON.COM	16	GOOGLE.CO.JP
7	WIKIPEDIA.ORG	17	LINKEDIN.COM
8	QQ.COM	18	WEIBO.COM
9	GOOGLE.CO.IN	19	BING.COM
10	TWITTER.COM	20	YANDEX.RU

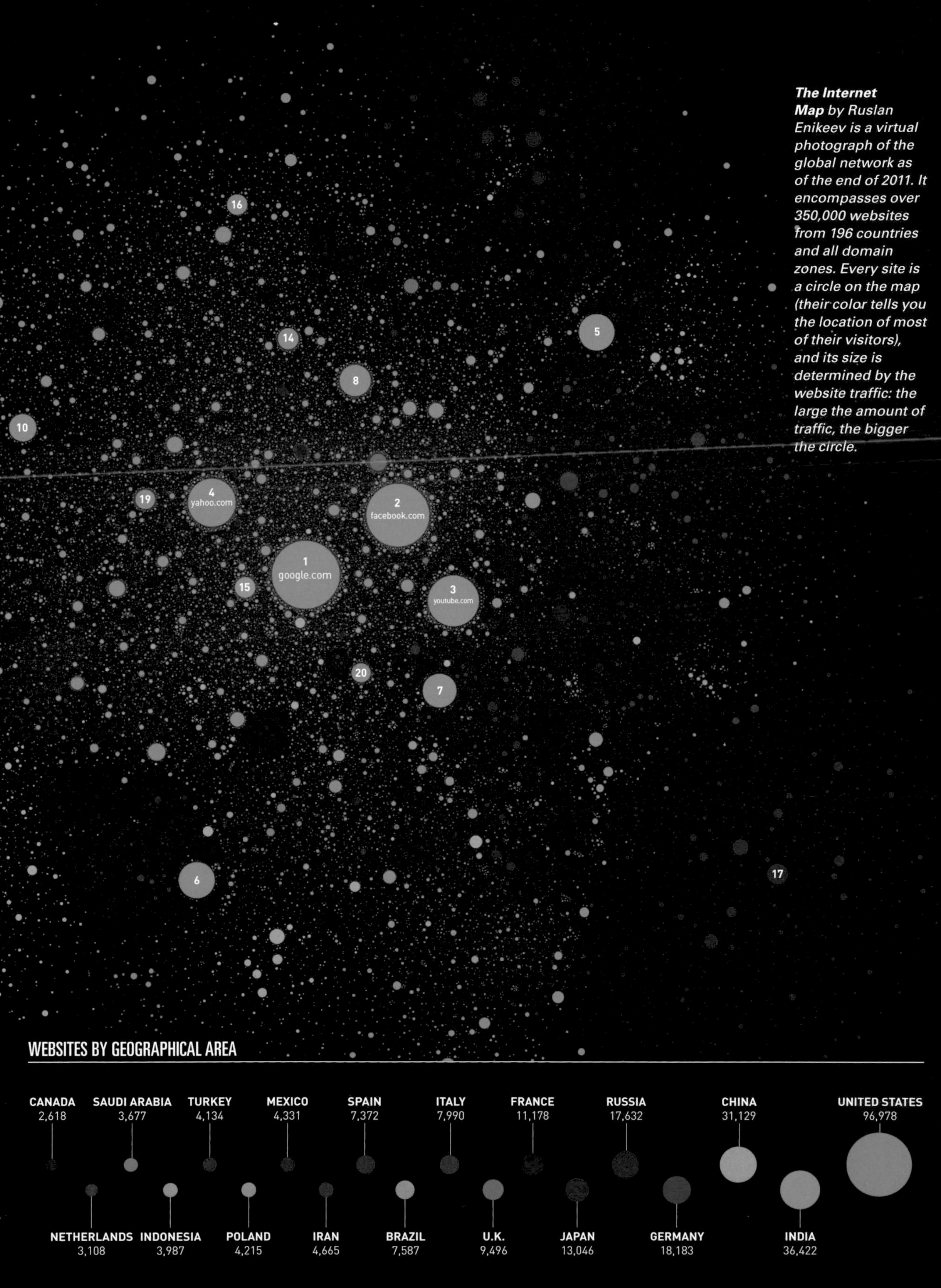

The Internet Map *by Ruslan Enikeev is a virtual photograph of the global network as of the end of 2011. It encompasses over 350,000 websites from 196 countries and all domain zones. Every site is a circle on the map (their color tells you the location of most of their visitors), and its size is determined by the website traffic: the large the amount of traffic, the bigger the circle.*

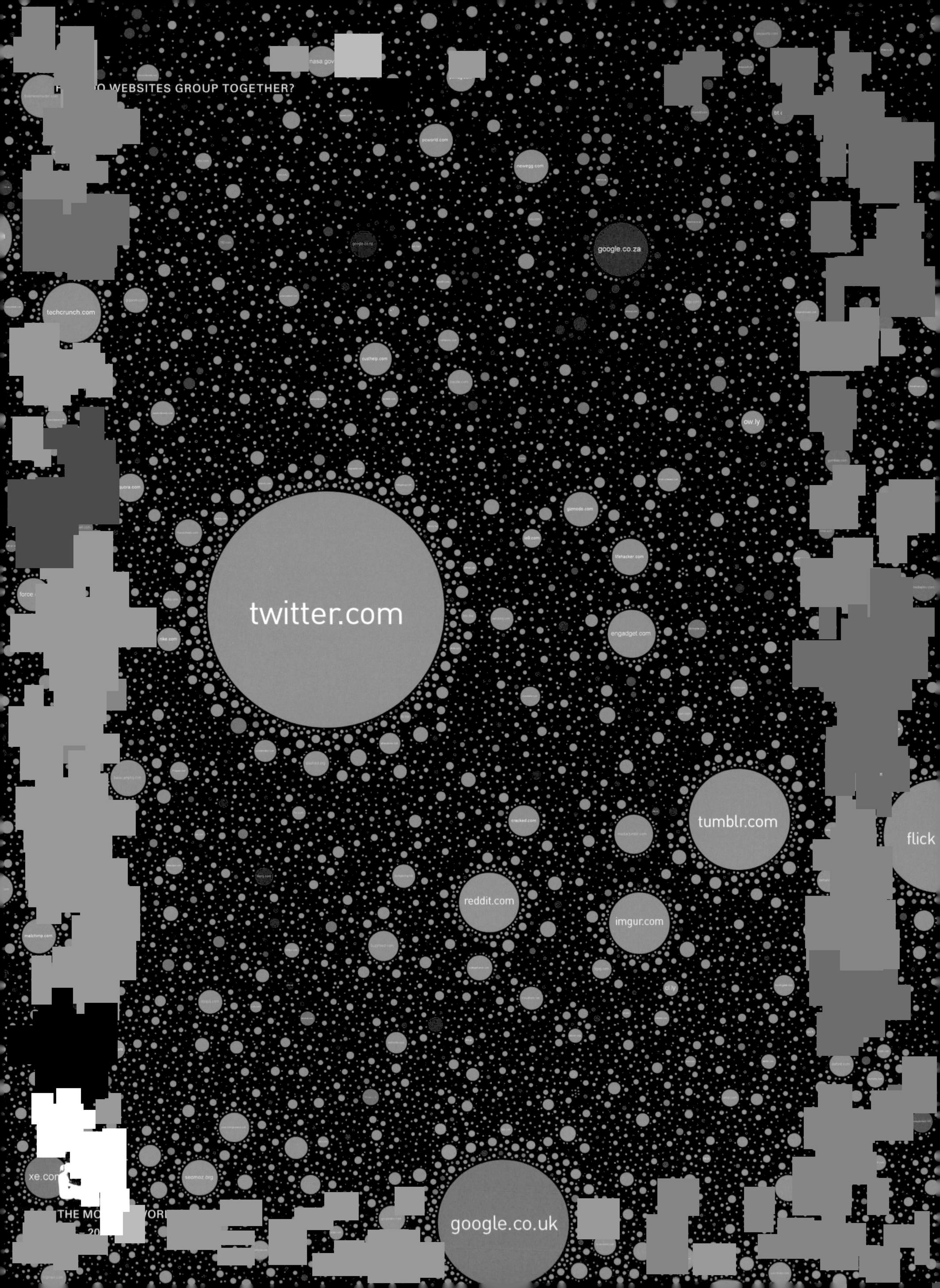

F... O WEBSITES GROUP TOGETHER?

nasa.gov
pcworld.com
newegg.com
google.co.za
techcrunch.com
custhelp.com
ow.ly
quora.com
gizmodo.com
lifehacker.com
twitter.com
engadget.com
nike.com
force...
tumblr.com
flick...
cracked.com
reddit.com
imgur.com
mailchimp.com
seomoz.org
xe.com
google.co.uk

THE MO... WORL...
20...

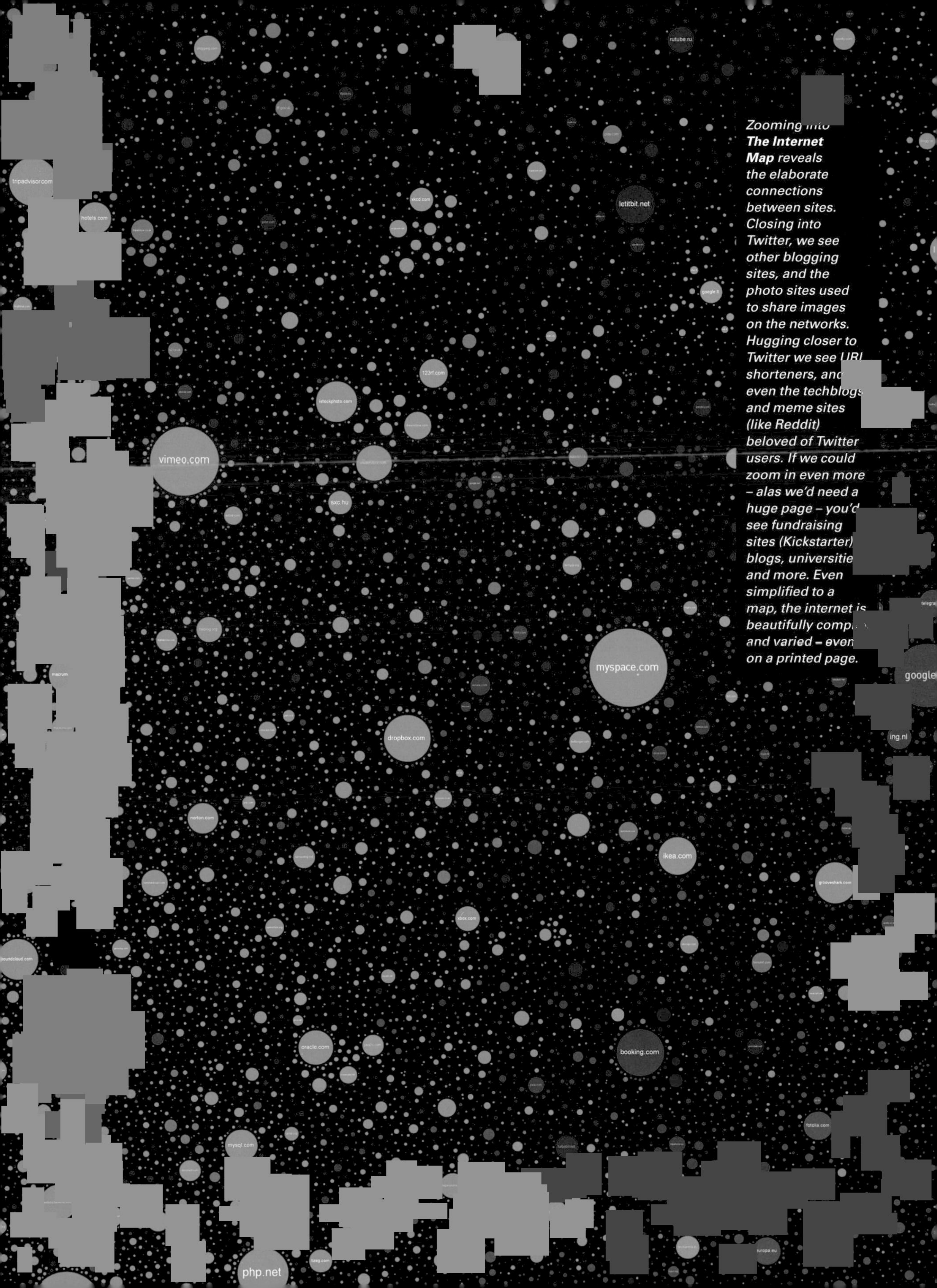

Zooming into ***The Internet Map*** *reveals the elaborate connections between sites. Closing into Twitter, we see other blogging sites, and the photo sites used to share images on the networks. Hugging closer to Twitter we see URL shorteners, and even the techblogs and meme sites (like Reddit) beloved of Twitter users. If we could zoom in even more – alas we'd need a huge page – you'd see fundraising sites (Kickstarter), blogs, universities and more. Even simplified to a map, the internet is beautifully complex and varied – even on a printed page.*

My army's bigger than yours...

Comparing our offensive capabilities is something that begins in the playground – "my dad's bigger than your dad" – and ends in the UN Security Council – "my air force is bigger than yours."

It's only natural, but when it comes to modern militaries, it's harder to do than you'd think. Our theoretical parade ground brings together the 30 countries with the most soldiers for a comparison of military might. **China** easily takes an unsurprising first place with 2.2 million active troops versus just under 1.5 million **U.S.** soldiers. But are **India** (1.3 million soldiers) and **North Korea** (1.1 million troops) really the 3rd and 4th greatest military powers on the planet?

Maybe not – because gear is a big factor, too: the U.S. has 8,700 tanks, 6,400 attack helicopters and 11 aircraft carriers. While impressive on their own, India's 5,900 tanks, 140 helicopters and sole aircraft carrier don't really stack up – just one example of the vast capability gaps between all those generals.

But money also talks – especially in America. The U.S. spends more than $700 billion a year on its military, which is not only more than any other nation, but more than the next 14 biggest spenders combined.

Perhaps it's not just the results, though, but also the commitment that counts. One way to measure this is to consider how much of a nation's GDP (its annual economic output) is spent on the military. In America this is a pretty hefty figure (around 4.7%). But that's nothing compared with North Korea, which spends more than 20% of its GDP on its armed forces.

Of course, in reality it's not conventional forces that would be likely to settle any full-on modern contest. We live in the nuclear era, after all, and between them the nations we're looking at have estimated stockpiles of more than 22,500 warheads. Maybe it's worth giving peace a chance for just a little bit longer, eh?

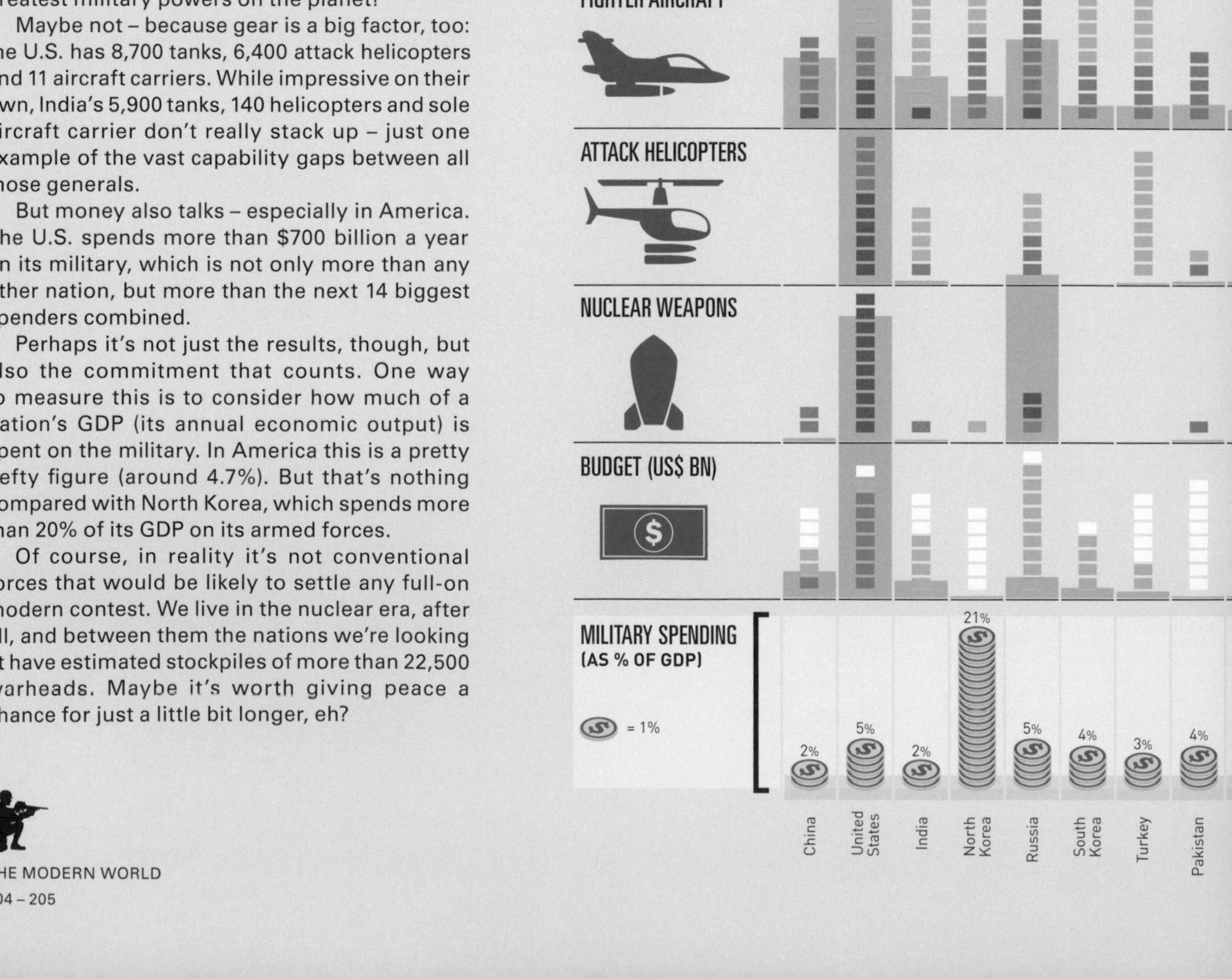

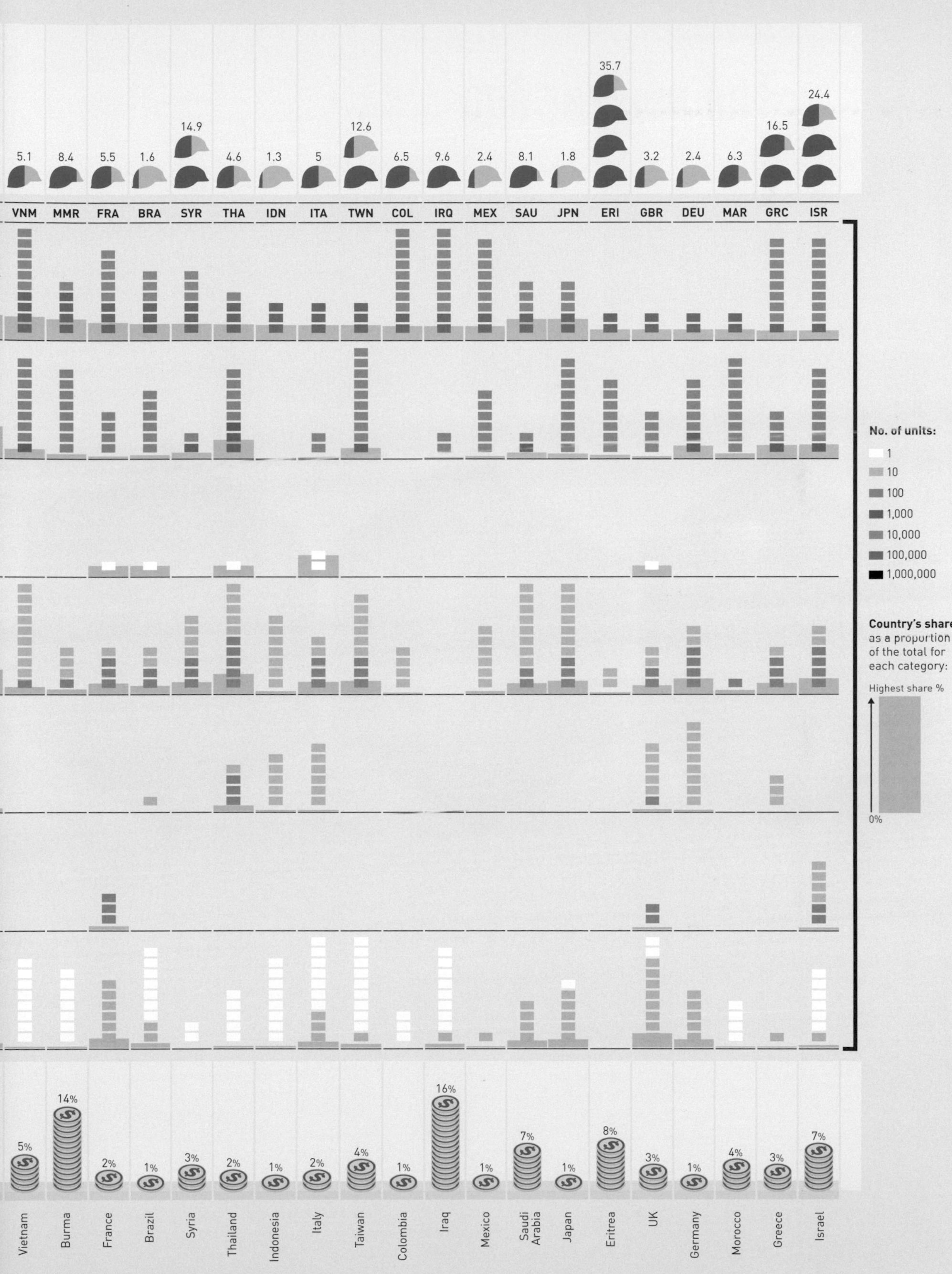

5.1
8.4
5.5
1.6
14.9
4.6
1.3
5
12.6
6.5
9.6
2.4
8.1
1.8
35.7
3.2
2.4
6.3
16.5
24.4
VNM
MMR
FRA
BRA
SYR
THA
IDN
ITA
TWN
COL
IRQ
MEX
SAU
JPN
ERI
GBR
DEU
MAR
GRC
ISR
No. of units:
1
10
100
1,000
10,000
100,000
1,000,000
Country's share
as a proportion of the total for each category:
Highest share %
0%
5%
14%
2%
1%
3%
2%
1%
2%
4%
1%
16%
1%
7%
1%
8%
3%
1%
4%
3%
7%
Vietnam
Burma
France
Brazil
Syria
Thailand
Indonesia
Italy
Taiwan
Colombia
Iraq
Mexico
Saudi Arabia
Japan
Eritrea
UK
Germany
Morocco
Greece
Israel

The nuclear age

If you're of a nervous disposition, you might want to skip this page. On 16 July 1945, U.S. scientists learned for the first time that the nuclear bomb they had developed worked. It took only 21 days for the new weapon to be used in the field when it was dropped on the Japanese city of Hiroshima.

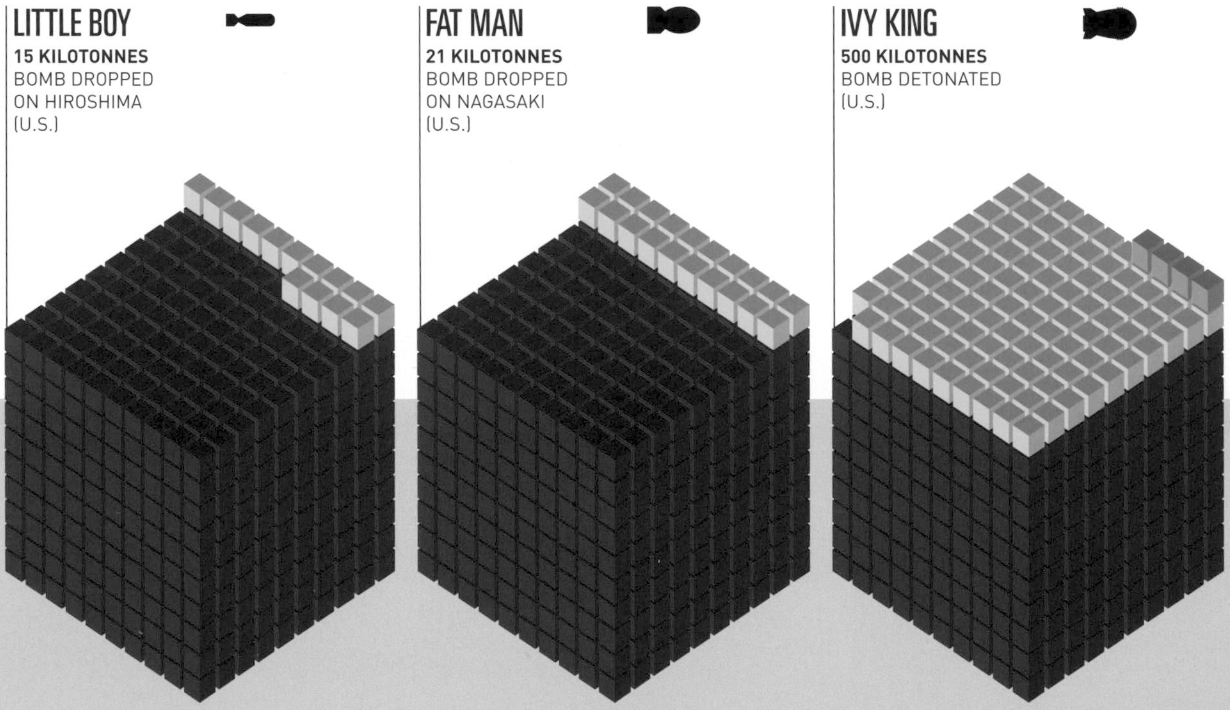

LITTLE BOY
15 KILOTONNES
BOMB DROPPED
ON HIROSHIMA
(U.S.)

FAT MAN
21 KILOTONNES
BOMB DROPPED
ON NAGASAKI
(U.S.)

IVY KING
500 KILOTONNES
BOMB DETONATED
(U.S.)

That attack killed around 70,000 in the initial explosion. What no one then knew was how terrible the after-effects – radiation sickness – would prove, killing a further 20,000 to 100,000 people (estimates vary hugely). That bomb, "**Little Boy**," was the equivalent of 15 kilotonnes of TNT. This graphic – an adaptation of work by the excellent Maximilian Bode – shows how the nuclear bomb dropped on Hiroshima compares with those detonated subsequently.

Each red cube represents one tonne of TNT. Each yellow cube represents 1,000 red cubes. But not even these yellow cubes are enough to let us fit the power of modern nuclear weapons on the page: we need blue cubes too – each representing 100 yellow cubes.

What does this mean? Put simply, the largest bomb on this page is equivalent to more than 3,300 **Hiroshima** bombs – destructive power virtually beyond imagination.

Still, surely we've managed to keep a lid on that kind of power? If only...

Today, the U.S. has around 7,700 nuclear warheads in total. Russia has more than 8,000. The U.K., France, China, Israel, India, Pakistan, and – quite probably – North Korea have nukes of their own.

Cheerful thought, that, isn't it? If you weren't nervous before, we'd wager you might just be by now.

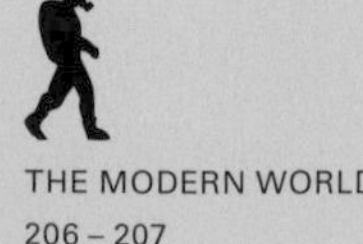

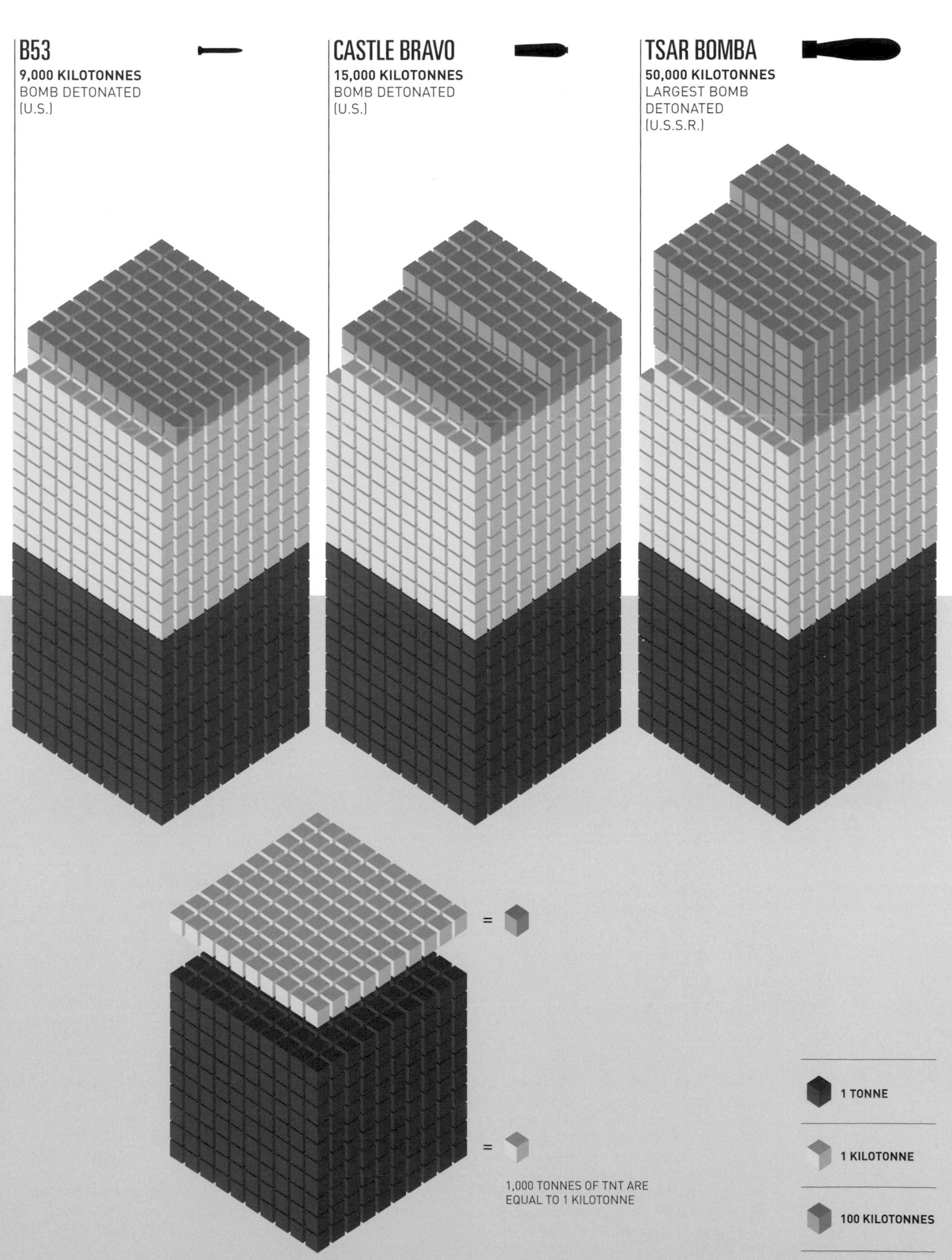

B53
9,000 KILOTONNES
BOMB DETONATED
(U.S.)
CASTLE BRAVO
15,000 KILOTONNES
BOMB DETONATED
(U.S.)
TSAR BOMBA
50,000 KILOTONNES
LARGEST BOMB
DETONATED
(U.S.S.R.)
=
=
1,000 TONNES OF TNT ARE
EQUAL TO 1 KILOTONNE
1 TONNE
1 KILOTONNE
100 KILOTONNES

Changing nation

Who's in the U.K.? How quickly is this changing? What's the U.K.'s national identity?

We live in a world where we can talk to someone 4,000 miles away almost as easily as to someone three desks over, and our access to transportation, communications and technology is beyond the imagination of people from even just one generation ago. But some of the most far-reaching changes are to attitudes – and all of these factors add up to a changing society.

It's interesting, then, to take stock of what these kinds of changes mean – and one rare opportunity to see what's really happened is that granted by a census. In the U.K., the census – a survey of the country's entire population – happens once a decade. The results for England and Wales from 2011 were published late in 2012 and show a nation changing at an astonishing pace.

But these country-wide figures, in millions and percentages, are hard to grasp. So we've reimagined the country as a village, which in 2001 had 1,000 people. How's it changed?

U.K. POPULATION
PAST AND PRESENT

U.K. population in 2001 and 2011 summarized according to ***ethnic group, religion*** *and* ***marital status*** *(based on a representative population of 1,000 individuals in 2001).*

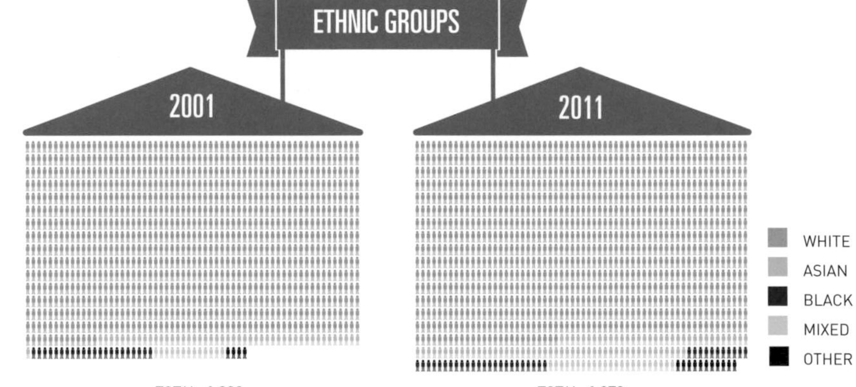

U.K. POPULATION
GROWTH AND CHANGE

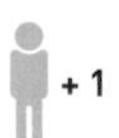

Each silhouette represents 1 person (ca. 5,200 inhabitants in real terms). An outlined silhouette upside-down indicates the deduction of 1 person in 2011 compared with 2001.

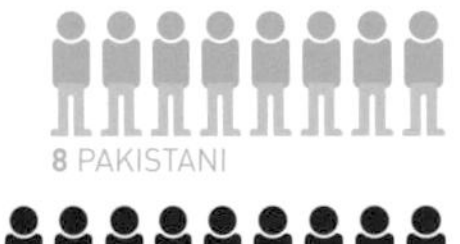

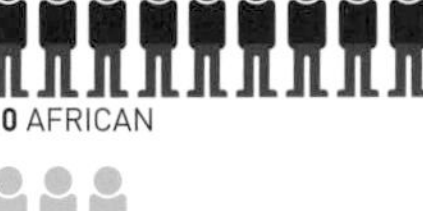

1 WHITE AND BLACK AFRICAN

3 OTHER MIXED

7 ANY OTHER ETHNIC GROUP

For one, the U.K.'s "village" is bigger now: there are 78 more people than there were before. It's more ethnically diverse, too: in 2001, 87 villagers were ***non-white*** *– now, it's 152; 19 villagers are (ethnically)* ***African*** *{■}, up from 9 ten years before, and 24 – up from 14 – are* ***mixed-race*** *{■}.*

Religion is also changing: despite the village growing, the number of ***Christians*** *{■} has fallen – from 716 to 639. The two fast-growing groups are* ***Muslims*** *{■} (numbering 52 out of every 1,000, versus 30 a decade ago) and* ***non-believers****, who've really rocketed: 148 professed no faith in 2001, versus 271 ten years later.*

Perhaps that has had an effect on the (relative) drop in the number of people who are ***married*** *{■}. Among the adults of the village, the number of* ***singletons*** *{■} has jumped from 240 to 302, and* ***divorcees*** *{■} have risen from 66 to 79. But love's not entirely dead. Of our 874 people of marriageable age, two have a* ***civil partnership*** *{■}. A decade ago, they didn't even have the option.*

RELIGIONS

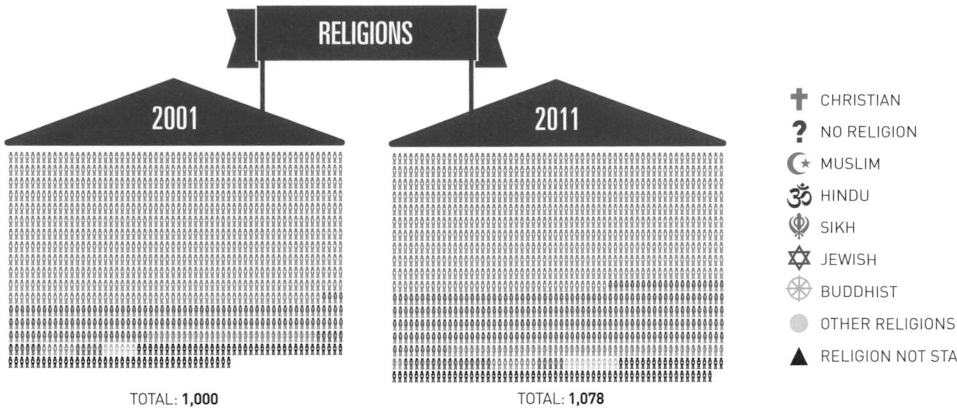

TOTAL: **1,000**

TOTAL: **1,078**

- CHRISTIAN
- NO RELIGION
- MUSLIM
- HINDU
- SIKH
- JEWISH
- BUDDHIST
- OTHER RELIGIONS
- RELIGION NOT STATED

-78 CHRISTIANS

123 NON-RELIGIOUS

22 MUSLIMS

5 HINDUS

2 SIKHS

2 BUDDHISTS

2 OTHER RELIGIONS

MARITAL STATUS

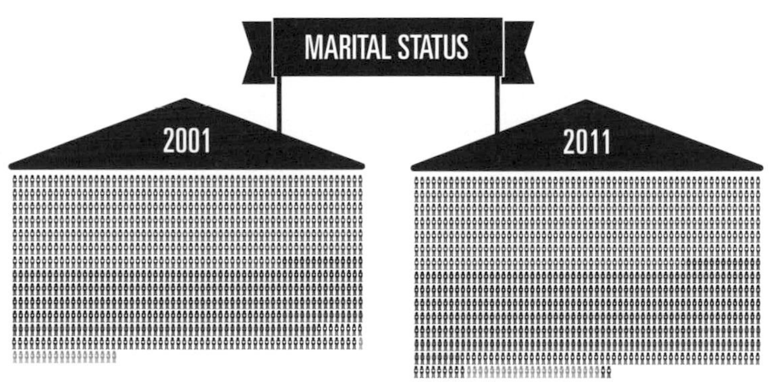

TOTAL: **798**

TOTAL: **874**

- MARRIED
- SINGLE (never married or never registered a same-sex civil partnership)
- DIVORCED (or formerly in a same-sex civil partnership that is now legally dissolved)
- WIDOWED (or surviving partner from a same-sex civil partnership)
- SEPARATED (but still legally married or still legally in a same-sex civil partnership)
- IN A REGISTERED SAME-SEX CIVIL PARTNERSHIP

1 MARRIED

62 SINGLE

13 DIVORCED

-6 WIDOWED

4 SEPARATED

2 SAME-SEX CIVIL PARTNERSHIP

I'll fly away

The first commercial flight – with a lone passenger – took place just 11 years after the Wright brothers achieved what's often called the first powered flight in 1903 (though some support other contenders. Nothing's simple.)

AIRPORTS
6,977

FLIGHT ROUTES
59,036

The 1914 flight took place between two cities in Florida, 23 miles apart, and took around 51 minutes. Terrifyingly, by modern standards, the flight never went higher than 50 feet, surging across a lake at treetop heights. Not surprisingly, flight didn't immediately take off.

Flight was sporadic between this point and the late 1920s, when a few semi-regular flight routes started to emerge. Regular cross-Atlantic flights took a while longer, beginning under American Overseas Airlines in October 1945. The flight took 17 hours 40 minutes. Today, that's down to between seven and eight hours, depending on wind conditions – but for a time, it was even shorter: while it was running, Concorde could do it in less than three.

As of January 2012, the OpenFlights Airports Database showed that there were more than **59,000 commercial flight routes {■}** across the planet, between more than **6,900 different airports {■}**.

The busiest ten of those routes might come as a surprise: no European or North American airport features on the list, which is dominated by Asian countries – and at least nine out of the ten are internal flights between two cities in the same nation.

The tenth, between Hong Kong and Taiwan, all depends on your interpretation – China refers to Taiwan as part of its nation, while the government of Taiwan disagrees. That's an argument your authors want no part of, lacking the substantial military budget of either party.

On a cheerier note, the first transatlantic route – between New York and London – the first one ever – is still one of the busiest in the world, with around 3 million passengers each year.

Bon voyage!

TOP SEVEN AIRLINES

This beautiful visualization, by James Cheshire at UCL, shows the routes flown by the world's seven largest airlines (as measured by the distance flown by their passengers, excluding domestic flights). The white points on the base map show areas of population density. Generally speaking, there is a clear correlation between where people live and where the big carriers fly to. The exceptions are India and China, which, relatively speaking, are served by fewer routes. For now.

Boldly going (and going, and going)

In some ways, space travel has become almost mundane. Commercial, unmanned flights to put GPS satellites, TV satellites and communications devices into near-Earth orbit are a reasonably regular occurrence – to the point where the amount of junk floating around our planet at high speed is a genuine concern.

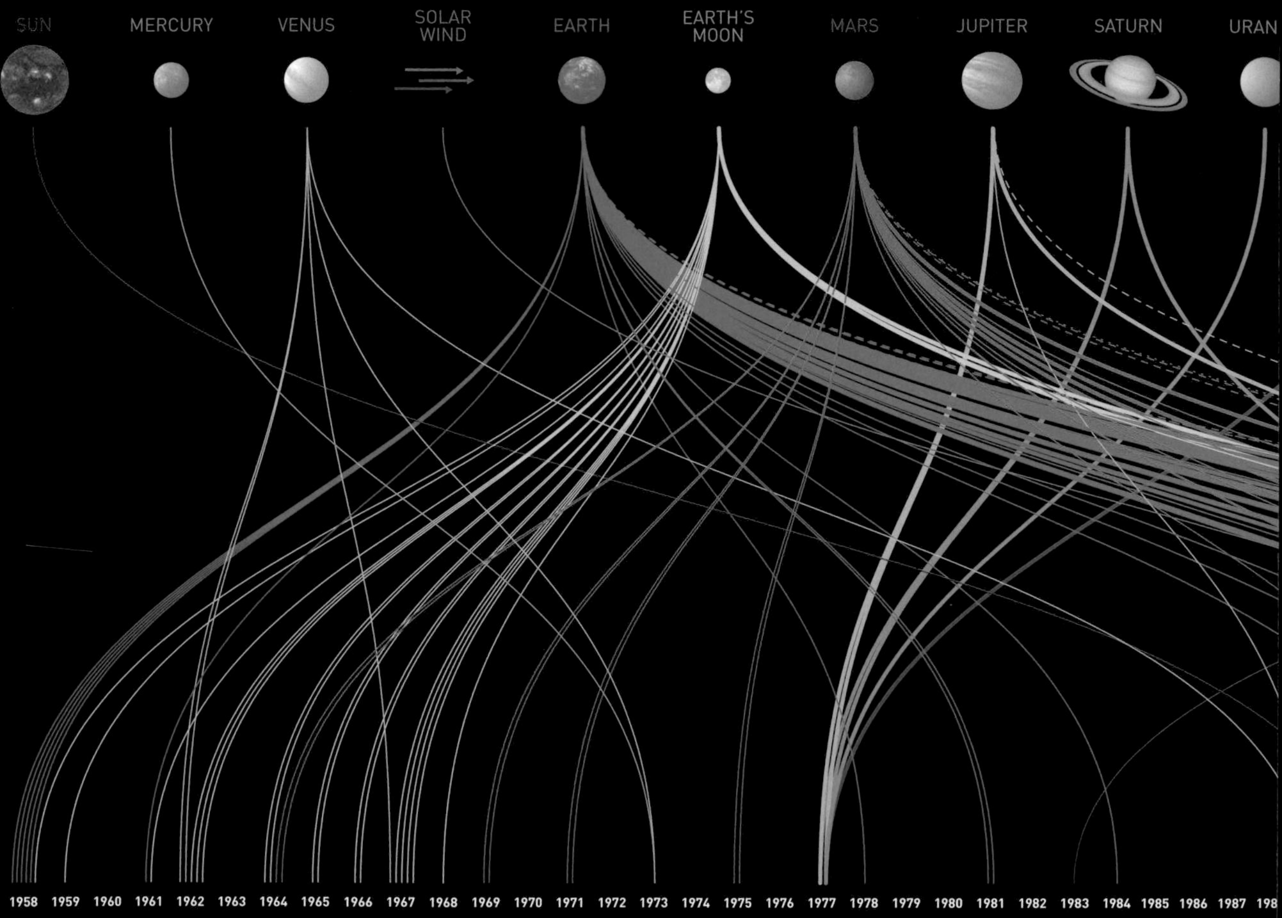

SUN MERCURY VENUS SOLAR WIND EARTH EARTH'S MOON MARS JUPITER SATURN URAN

1958 1959 1960 1961 1962 1963 1964 1965 1966 1967 1968 1969 1970 1971 1972 1973 1974 1975 1976 1977 1978 1979 1980 1981 1982 1983 1984 1985 1986 1987 198

But the number of crewed space missions – often runs for repairs, or for research – is higher than you might think, at more than 320. And with the regularity of modern space travel, it's easy to forget just what an incredible feat it is.

Easy, but totally unromantic – because the minority of flights that set out into the unknown are still truly remarkable. We've sent dozens of probes to explore, investigate, and then finally land a person on the Moon – but we know all about that.

What is less well known is that we've managed to land probes on Venus and Mars, send crafts to investigate the Sun, and even launch two vessels out of our solar system entirely. We're still in touch with one of them: Voyager 2. We're communicating with something further away than we'll probably ever go.

That said, the speed is nothing to write

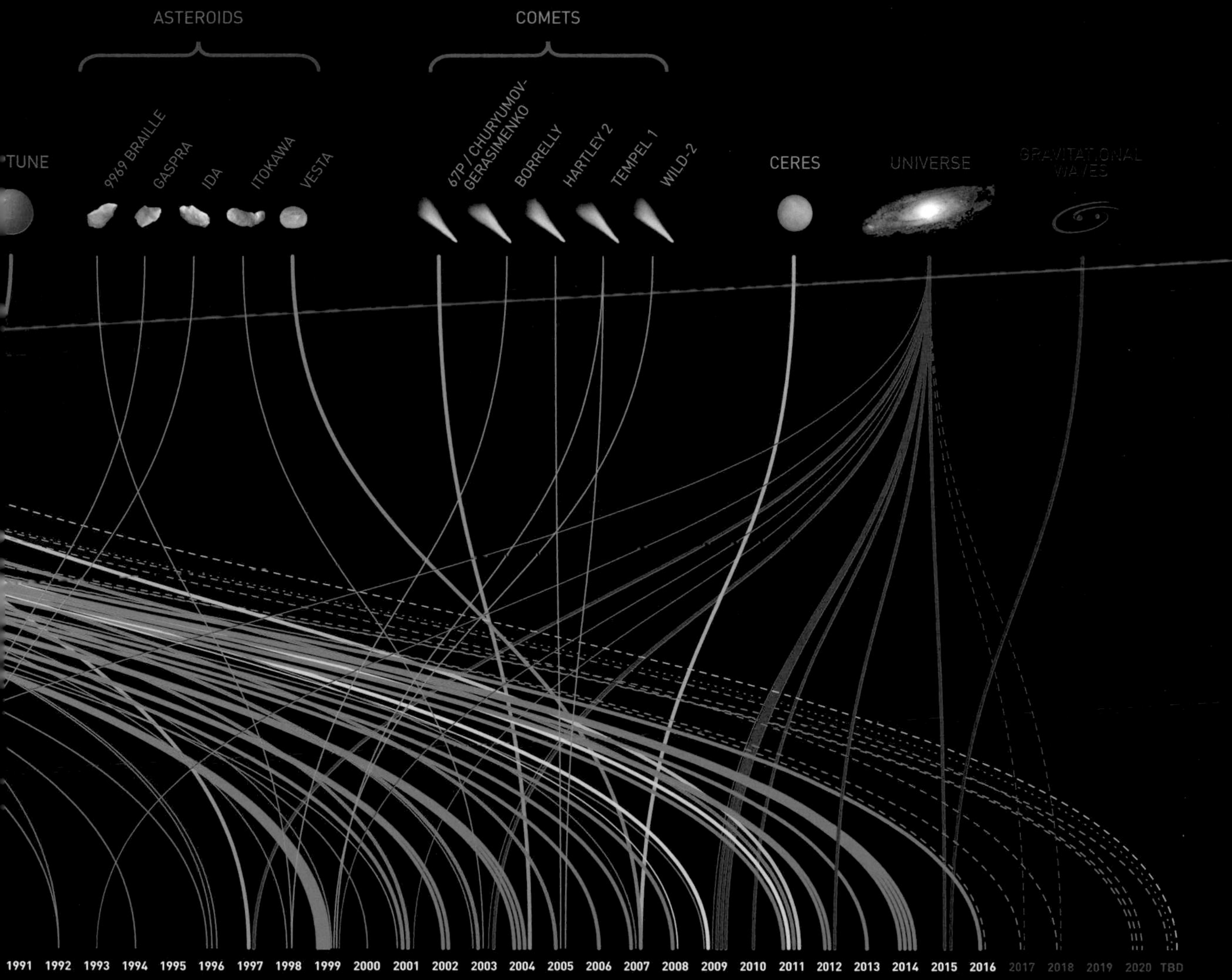

home about – less than one ten-thoundsandth of a typical home internet connection. But the principle is pretty cool. And other craft are headed its way even as we speak.

Here, NASA's Jet Propulsion Laboratory have chronicled what happened to the craft sent on space-exploration missions between 1958 and today. Hard to read it without a tiny tingle of awe, right?

JPL MISSION HISTORY

PAST
CURRENT
FUTURE
PROPOSED

What happens next?

So, that's the world from the birth of the universe up to the present day. What happens next?

Inevitably, at the end of any story lies death – though typically savvy authors throughout the ages have chosen to tie things up before then, or bring their yarns to an end with the ever-popular "happily ever after."

Thanks to the statistics in *How We Die*, though, we know that most of us reading this book in a developed country will most likely shuffle off this mortal coil at an advanced age, of natural causes (hurrah!). But what of our species as a whole?

There are a number of events that can trigger extinction: meteorites, earthquakes, super-volcanoes, radiation from space, and more. But these are all (in any given year) astronomically unlikely.

The odds of humans doing something stupid enough to wipe ourselves out, however, could well be higher – whether through something like climate change, or a nuclear holocaust.

During the Cuban Missile Crisis, President Kennedy estimated that the odds of the situation escalating to nuclear war were "somewhere between 1-in-3 and even." Estimating the chances of a natural disaster wiping out humanity at 1 in 5,000,000, we can consider a range of **optimistic** and **pessimistic** scenarios.

If we take the **ultra-pessimistic** view (but still maybe cheerier than Kennedy's) that in any given year we have a 1-in-100 chance of wiping ourselves out, our odds of surviving a century are less than 37% – and of surviving a millennium only around 0.01%.

A slightly **less pessimistic** 1-in-1,000 chance of self-inflicted wipeout gives us a 37% chance of seeing out a millennium, while a 1-in-10,000 chance gives us more than a 90% chance of being here in another 1,000 years.

AN IMPENDING ARMAGEDDON?

One in seven (14%) global citizens agree that "the world will come to an end during my lifetime," according to a new poll by global research company Ipsos on behalf of Reuters News.

How long will humanity last? These gauges give the odds if we assume different chances of self-inflicted wipeout and estimates of natural extinction.

OFF

HUMANITY'S CHANCES OF SURVIVING ANOTHER...

1-IN-10,000
99.0%

1-IN-1,000
90.4%

1-IN-100
36.6%

1-IN-1,000,000
99.9%

1-IN-100,000
99.9%

000100
YEARS

...CENTURY

1-IN-10,000
90.5%

1-IN-1,000
36.8%

1-IN-100
0.01 – 0%

1-IN-1,000,000
99.9%

1-IN-100,000
99.0%

001000
YEARS

...MILLENNIUM

1-IN-10,000
0.01% – 0%

1-IN-1,000
0.01% – 0%

1-IN-100
0.01% – 0%

1-IN-1,000,000
88.7%

1-IN-100,000
36.1%

100000
YEARS

...100,000 YEARS

BETWEEN 8 AND 20 BILLION TONNES OF FUEL

are required to send every human to another planet

14 billion tonnes of **FUEL (produced in 195 years)**

72 million tonnes of **FUEL**
(produced in 1 year)

Eventually, though, we'd have bigger problems. If we're still inhabiting the Earth in five billion years' time, and haven't been obliterated by natural disaster or nuclear winter, we're in trouble: the Sun will be beginning its red giant phase, and the surface temperature of Earth will rise to a point where the oceans evaporate.

To say the least, this would be bad news. Earth would be uninhabitable, and we'd need somewhere else to live – a problem that seems solvable in theory, but comes with one big headache. Even assuming we'd have somewhere to go, the travel arrangements would be somewhat tricky.

Randall Munroe of the popular *xkcd* webcomic worked out how much energy it would take to get all of the seven billion humans on the planet into space. Counting solely the weight of humans (**humanity** weighs about 400 million tonnes – we should start counting the pounds!), we'd need between 8 and 20 billion tonnes of fuel to get us there.

If we used **kerosene** (an oil-based fuel used in early-stage rockets), we'd require between 111 and 277 years of production of the stuff – assuming there's that much left in the ground. And that's before we count the weight of equipment, ships, food, the fuel itself and – most important of all, surely – pets.

It's possible that future technology – like a "space elevator" suspended on an unbelievably strong rope (look it up, it's a cool idea) – might save the day.

Leaving the planet gives our species much better prospects, if it were doable, but we still wouldn't be around forever, due to a problem known as increasing entropy.

The idea's simple: it's easy to scramble an egg, but almost impossible to reverse the process. It's easy to put a frog in a blender, but ... actually, let's leave that there.

Eventually – although we've got a good trillion years to wait – the universe's descent from order to chaos will lead to the stars running out of fuel, the end of viable life in the universe, and all matter spreading ever thinner, and thinner, to, essentially, nothing.

Which would frankly be a bit of a downer, if it weren't for one thing:

in the beginning, there was nothing, which exploded.

It's a tricky task condensing 13.8 billion years into 224 pages: it works out at around 61 million years per page. Naturally, that means we've had to leave a little bit out. Like so many history books before, there have been times when we've chosen to simplify things slightly or overlook a detail in order to highlight the most satisfying and interesting nuggets, but being data geeks we're keen to highlight the full complexity of the data where we can – and that's here, in the data appendix. For those interested in where our data came from and how we analyzed it, the spread-by-spread details are below. One general note: we have occasionally used Wikipedia as a source, particularly in the book's first two sections. Almost universally, we could check Wikipedia facts against their original source, but there are one or two occasions where we couldn't. Despite its notoriety as a source, the few (small) studies done to date compare it quite favorably with traditional references (you can look them up on Wikipedia, if you like). We could just refer to the original sources on these spreads, but to ignore that we got there via Wikipedia just to look good seems churlish. So we haven't.

022 **In the beginning**
The main challenge on these three spreads is conveying visually (and descriptively) numbers so large that they are difficult to think about meaningfully. Note that the viral comparison is based around a scale as if you had shrunk while everything else hadn't, and uses relative *length* or *distance*, not *area* or *volume*. We've used 80 years as a typical human lifespan, and have used 100 trillion years as an estimate for when star formation ends, though some estimates are as low as one trillion. There's no agreed "edge" to our solar system. We've been generous and taken a broader measure than some.

028 **Bang goes the neighborhood**
The information used for the specifications of the planet was taken from a (much more detailed) Wikipedia table, though several universities (and NASA) offer very similar lists.

030 **Producing a planet**
Details of the Earth's composition come from EnvironmentalChemistry.com, Georgia State University and Wikipedia. Note our parts-per-million figures include the atmosphere as well as the crust (because we're not geologists, we care about more than just the rock!).

032 **Evolution revolution**
Exact numbers are of course difficult to come by for this topic – working out our evolutionary trail is the ultimate detective mystery for some of the world's best scientists. This is an amalgamation of (we think) sensible picks from the correct approximate geological periods. Note that species are examples rather than the "definitive" first one with a given feature.

036 **Critical mass**
We've had to do a little fudging of the numbers here, given different estimates come from different sources, and some cited "dry" and others "wet" biomass. We used the average multiple of "wet" versus "dry" to make estimates (loosely) comparable.

038 **The impact zone**
This delightful dataset comes from NASA, as of the latter end of 2012. We think the overall picture is low-risk, but who knows if NASA has actually got it right?

040 **Distinctly extinct**
The primary source for the details of the "five great extinctions" here come from *Science*, *Nature* and Wikipedia. It's really important to remember our evidence comes from the fossil record, which might differ substantially from the species that were actually around during those periods. Our tree of life diagram uses data from Appendix A of Hillis et al: *Principles of Life*.

—

046 **All in the family**
This one's quite fun, no? We hope we avoided any of the finds later proved to be hoaxes, and we're still miffed we didn't find a mass estimate for *Homo ergaster*.

048 **What makes a man?**
Nothing too controversial here (estimates are gathered from public domain sources), but it's worth noting that composition is done by the mass, not the number of atoms, of each element.

050 **Our little friends**
These figures – which show species *diversity*, not number of microbes – come from the National Institute of Health Human Microbiome Project. Icky, aren't they?

052 **How we spread**
Early population estimates are (inevitably) almost all patchy and contradictory, so in essence we took one and ran with it, in our case McEvedy & Jones (1978). The 5,500 population figure for 70000 BCE is based on 2,750 couples. The actual figure from the data could be anywhere between 2,000 and 22,000.

054 **The taming of...**
All the livestock population estimates here come from the UN's Food and Agriculture Office, except for dogs (which is a FAO-endorsed estimate). The cats figure is the outlier – there's really no authoritative number. Which seems oddly apt. The hieroglyphs we use here are genuine, but each is multiplied by a thousand.

056 **City livin'**
Not much to say here, other than to stress that this is a selection of early cities, not a definitive measure of the earliest or largest – and also to note population estimates are necessarily rough.

058 **Dressin' it up**
The first instance of a common caveat here: invention dates are hard. Something resembling a bra dates back more than 500 years, but the garment's had its modern guise (and popularity) for far less long. Similarly, what we now think of as a kilt is less old than the original garment and was, as it happens, invented by an Englishman. What to count from when isn't hard and fast here, in other words.

060 **Makin' sweet music**
Multiple sourcing here, with some caveats again on exact dates. We've also decided to put piano and harpsichord with strings rather than percussion, largely arbitrarily.

062 **Painting by numbers**
Ancient art can be difficult to categorise. Take "stylized humans in art:" stick figures date back a very long time, but more detailed humans only appear in cave paintings less than 6,000 years old.

064 **Learnin' the lexicon**
The *Science* study on Google Scholar on the development of language is phenomenal, and should report more in time (we hope). Details on the various dictionaries come from Wikipedia and other corroborating sources.

066 **The language tree**
As with evolution, language development shouldn't be taken too strictly: this is indicative, not definitive. The information is taken from diagrams made by Daniel M. Short, and by Curzan and Adams' *How English Works.*

068 **Getting to the Iron Age**
Where the Iron Age ends and the Middle Ages start is largely arbitrary, as is (in some ways) the whole three-ages theory of history. There are several inconsistencies in dates between different sources here. We've tried to stick with the original on each, given everything comes from fossil records rather than documentation.

—

074 **I used to rule the world**
Lots of dates have been stripped out and simplified (trying to deal with Alexander the Great's effect on the ancient world is surprisingly tricky), but it provides a good general picture.

076 **What did they ever do for us?**
Who to credit for bricks? The first civilization to make any use of them, or the first to make widespread use? What do we actually count as the first woven "textile?" Neither is clear cut. Through tight calls (and negotiation), we've made particular decisions – but recognize that others might choose differently.

078 **Age of empires**
The core of this graphic's data comes from Wikipedia and FindTheData, with lots of embellishments and checks from elsewhere. Worth recalling that empires don't rise and fall smoothly – the real course of each won't be a smooth curve.

082 **Anatomy of a legion**
The modern figures for the British army were taken from the Guardian Datablog and verified against official figures. On the Roman side, sizes and structure of the army changed in different periods – we've taken midpoints and a small number of arbitrary calls.

086 **The medieval day**
The theory on the "segmented sleep" of peasants belongs to Roger Ekirch. The modern-day comparisons come from opinion polling (and therefore deserve a pinch of salt) gathered by the Mirror newspaper. The diagram assumes breaks are an hour long, but in reality they were likely to be shorter.

088 **Going crusading**
Different people number the crusades differently. We have stayed with the numbering system favored in Wikipedia, though diverge somewhat from there in other places. The complements for the 5th and 6th, and 8th and 9th crusades have been treated as the same, as each was essentially a continuation of another, or an attempt aborted due to widespread disease.

090 **The age of exploration**
We've been unfair to some explorers here (like Magellan) by focusing on landmass "discoveries" rather than those who first navigated straits and the like. It's also a little Western-Europe-centric – natives of the "new" lands already knew they were there, of course. The compass graphic shows the main explorations order by the relative location of the lands concerned, *not* the direction of travel of the explorer.

092 **Rule Britannia**
This is a guest graphic from James Cheshire, generated from an amazing dataset of ship logbooks from 1750–1800, gathered to help monitor long-term warming of the Earth's oceans.

094 **Long to reign o'er us**
Want a long rule? Be a monarch. This data excludes some unverified claims of long periods of rule, and some interrupted rules.

096 **All about the money**
Estimating GDP *this* year is tricky, so generating estimates for historical periods is clearly going to be approximate. Nevertheless, Angus Maddison's data is impressive and well worth a look.

100 **A rough guide to conflict**
This data was gathered from The Polynational War Memorial website. Note it generally attempts to include direct deaths and not others (particularly with say Israel/Palestine) caused as a result of conflicts or settlements.

102 **To end all wars**
This data was generated by Stephen Pinker, as part of his excellent book *The End of Violence.*

104 **An artistic streak**
This is a guest spread adapted from a graphic made by Giorgia Lupi.

106 **Read all about it**
These slightly demoralizing figures (for a newspaper journalist, at least) come from the March 2012 report of the Newspaper Association of America.

108 **Working men of the world, unite!**
A few caveats – was England's Glorious Revolution a revolution or a foreign invasion? Tricky. The casualty count of Iran's revolution is also disputed: a figure of 60,000 is included in the country's constitution, but not supported by evidence. We used the lower estimate in this case. Other revolutions come after years of unrest (sometimes including famine) – deciding which dates to use, and which deaths to count, differs.

110 **Give me freedom**
We decided to use this spread to show that slavery is still a modern-day issue.

Data comes from the International Labour Organization.

114 **A different kind of revolution**
The Industrial Revolution data here is taken from *The Fontana Economic History of Europe Vol. 4, Part 2.*

116 **A bunch of bankers**
Data here is sourced from UKPublicSpending.co.uk. Note that the GDP measure is corrected for inflation.

118 **Cash and the crisis**
This data, which adjusts GDP for inflation (for better comparison), is sourced from MeasuringWorth.com

120 **A question of faith**
This data comes from the Gordon-Conwell Theological Seminary, and the recent values were cross-checked against other sources. Some of the historical figures are perhaps questionable (are the atheist counts low?), but the data is thorough and seems scrupulous. The seminary also tries to project forecasts (but we haven't used these). If you're wondering why the totals don't add up to 100% (you observant thing, you), it's because we've excluded minor religions.

122 **I get around**
A short and simple note for pedants here: the "round the world" assumptions assume maximum speed, unlimited fuel, and (in the case of land transport traveling over water) magic.

126 **Who's in charge here?**
As you might guess, this is very much simplified: some dynasties/royal families have been merged or skipped over, for reasons of space and comprehensibility.

—

132 **Population pyramids**
This data, all sourced from the UN, highlights how different questions require different visualization. The top chart on the first spread shows the distribution of age groups across the world – the bottom makes age groups on each continent clearer. There's no single "right" way to look at it.

136 **How we die**
It's interesting to note in this data (from the *New England Journal of Medicine*) that the top two causes of death, though different, kill similar numbers of people each year in 1900 and 2010: it's only from the third cause and below that longer life expectancy manifests itself.

138 **Gendercide**
The data sources and fantastic *Economist* article are all noted in the copy – but it's worth noting China's disproportionate effect on the total is due to both its scale and ratio, while India has less of a ratio issue than Azerbaijan or Armenia, but a much bigger total of missing girls due to its sheer size.

140 **This woman's work**
Who thought of Italy as a great place for high-earning women before now? This data compared the median woman in one country to the median in another, and does the same for the 20th percentile and 80th percentile (low and high earners, respectively). The data is from the *OECD Employment Outlook 2011.*

142 **The patent race**
This data comes direct from the U.S. Patent Office. Important to stress quantity is not everything: most patents are junk. Bonus fact: Abraham Lincoln is the only U.S. President who ever held a patent (for a naval flotation device).

144 **Invention comprehension**
This is another topic that can turn into an interesting debate. Is something invented when it's patented, first demonstrated or first sold? We've generally gone with brought to market here, as that's what consumers see. With multiple inventors (working unaware of each other) and more than one date to choose from, some of these may be contentious. But we welcome debate!

146 **Written in a book that I've read**
The industry-wide figures relate to the U.S. and come from the U.S. Census Bureau, while the data on specific titles sold in the U.K. comes from Nielsen Bookscan, via the Guardian Datablog. A question: one million more people in the U.K. bought the fifth book in the Harry Potter series than bought the fourth. What's with that?

148 **Makin' music**
This data, highlighting the physical/digital shift, was assembled from public annual reports from the Recording Industry Association of America, and refers to U.S. sales. Individual record sales data for bestselling artists is taken from Wikipedia and uses only confirmed and verifiable sales (you often see far higher figures cited, without much basis).

152 **Who are the 1%?**
The data here is taken from the Credit Suisse *Global Wealth Report 2011.* Apologies for using such a leftist, hippie source.

154 **Global gluttony**
This data comes from the UN's Food and Agriculture Organization. We were a little mystified by Egypt's obesity given its relatively low consumption of fat and calories. Anyone know more?

156 **Hey, state spender**
This data was all produced by the Heritage Foundation. Interesting to see the difference between absolute government spending (even the U.S. scores highly on this) versus relative spending (% of the whole economy).

158 **Carbon sinks**
We gathered this data from a series assembled by the Guardian's environment desk. We think it's more useful to compare like with like (modes of transport, etc.) than just totals. Do note that the scale changes quite drastically between the top two entries and the others. Data on cell phone usage includes distribution and base-station energy use.

160 **The world in carbon**
This data is from the U.S. Energy Information Administration, and reflects the stalemate on carbon emission targets: China focuses on emissions per person, the U.S. on total emissions. It's important to note that this refers to carbon dioxide equivalent – there are other greenhouse gases. There was no 1992 data for Czech Republic.

164 **The end of cash?**
This breakdown of the ways we spend our money focuses on the U.K., and uses data from reports generated by the British Payments Council.

166 **The drugs don't work, do they?**
This fascinating dataset comes from the annual MixMag/Guardian drugs survey, which has respondents in the tens of thousands. Remember they're

not representative of the population as a whole, though.

168 **Ditched in the downturn**
Several caveats on this graphic, which was generated using International Labour Organization data. Firstly, it takes unemployment from its low point in each country (lowest quarter of 2007–8) and compares it with the highest quarter in 2009–2011. It excludes a couple of countries, notably Germany, where unemployment didn't rise. It also focuses on absolute numbers, rather than percentage of the workforce of each gender. There are dozens of ways to count unemployment – we show just one.

170 **Seeking refuge**
This data was published by the United Nations High Commissioner for Refugees in the annual report 'Global Trends of Forced Displacement' in 2015.

172 **Gotta get yourself connected**
This data all comes from the International Telecommunications Union. A bonus fact (and a pretty amazing shift that we didn't highlight in the text): in 2005, landlines outnumbered mobiles. By 2011, there were more than five times as many mobiles as landlines.

174 **Love and marriage**
This data is sourced from the OECD. Note on the right-hand diagram we've used 100 as a cap for the marriages-per-divorce ratio. Some, where divorce was to all intents and purposes impossible in 1970, would've been far higher still.

176 **State of mind**
These figures are somewhat approximate (don't take it as a top ten) as they exclude conditions such as autism, where figures are not as readily available (most are estimates). The prevalence stats refer to the US figures produced by the National Institute of Mental Health.

178 **Give me land**
It's worth noting that these figures can vary as some sources use total land, while others use 'inhabitable' land. This data is from the CIA's *The World Factbook*.

182 **Synthetic disaster**
The data used in the graphic here comes from the 2005 report *Global estimates of occupational accidents*, and will be significantly affected by substantial under-reporting in many developing countries.

184 **Shake it out**
This spread is a contribution by John Nelson of IDV Solutions.

186 **Lock 'n' load**
These graphics are based on recalculated figures produced from data on the Guardian Datablog. Note on the right-hand graphic on the second spread that the larger gun signifies far more guns per death, and therefore (arguably) *less* of a gun problem than the smaller ones.

190 **The Olympic spirit**
This data, especially the alternative medals tables, in taken from the Guardian Datablog, which drafted in several experts to help rebase the official medal tallies.

192 **Harder, better, faster, stronger**
These figures strip out records which 'tied' previous ones back when accuracy was lower. They also disregard any confirmed drugs cheats.

194 **High times**
This graphic is based on UN data. There are two ways to look at each of these – what proportion of the world's users of a particular drug come from each continent, or what proportion of people on a continent use drug X? We've tried to show both.

196 **Cigarettes and alcohol**
This data is gathered by the OECD and provides a fascinating top-line view. The real question for the future of both industries, of course, lies in smoking/drinking take-up and quitting rates, though.

198 **History of the 'net**
The data on the geographical split of internet users comes from the World Bank. The supporting narrative in the copy relied in part on Hobbes' Internet Timeline.

200 **The map of the 'net**
This is a mere extract of a fantastic interactive graphic by Ruslan Enikeev. The original is well worth a look – the level of detail available to zoom in on is impressive (http://internet-map.net).

204 **My army's bigger than yours**
The GDP and army size estimates were generated from multiple sources, as (particularly for countries like North Korea) they vary sizeably. Note the army stats at the top of the spread are showing rates, not total army sizes. The breakdown of kit comes from a terrifyingly thorough Wikipedia page. That site has some buffs, clearly.

206 **The nuclear age**
This is a contributor spread, adapted for the book from an online graphic created by Maximilian Bode.

208 **Changing nation**
All of this data comes from the latest UK census. Our village analogy tries to take into account both changing composition and a growing nation. More formally, you would typically look at either absolute figures or rates. Some of the values in the spread were altered due to issues about rounding up/down.

210 **I'll fly away**
This is an adaptation of a compelling graphic by James Cheshire. It excludes flights classed as domestic. Data source: OpenFlights.org.

212 **Boldly going**
If you're going to talk about space exploration, you might as well cut out the middleman and talk to NASA. Which is what we did for this contributor spread – this is from their Jet Propulsion Laboratory.

214 **What happens next?**
Our odds of survival use some formal sources for risk of natural disaster, then run different scenarios of our chances of ending ourselves – the rest is simply compound probability. The graphic uses a 1-in-10,000 chance of a man-made calamity, while the copy considers several different probabilities. The left-hand graphic comes from an Ipsos MORI poll, while the data on the second spread is adapted from a blog post by the excellent Randall Munroe of *xkcd*. In reality, kerosene (the 'fuel' referred to in the graphic) is only used for the first stage of rocket launches – our projection is therefore a little iffy, which, when it comes to projections, is generally the case.

IMAGE CREDITS

020 Inspiration: Gastrulation theory by Ernst Haeckel, 1877.

026–027, 036–037, 069 ©2013 by the University of South Florida, Clipart courtesy FCIT.

048–049 Inspiration: *Vitruvian Man* by Leonardo da Vinci, Venice, 1485–90.

065 Johnsons Samuel, *The Dictionary of the English Language,* 1755.
High res scan provided by Brandi Besalke (www.johnsonsdictionaryonline.com).

088–089, 118–119 ©2013 Type National Currency, Decade Typefoundry. *http://www.myfonts.com*

104–105 Courtesy Accurat (www.accurat.it): Giorgia Lupi, Gabriele Rossi, Simone Quadri, Davide Ciuffi, Federica Fragapane. Originally published on La Lettura, Corriere della Sera, 2012.

082 Warrior silhouettes, courtesy *http://all-silhouettes.com/*

092–093, 211 © 2012 James Cheshire.

155 Some food pictograms, courtesy *http://all-free-download.com*

184–185 © 2012 IDV Solutions, LLC. Visualisation of Earthquakes since 1898 by IDV Solutions, LLC and John Nelson. Reprinted by kind permission of John Dougherty, VP of Operations, IDV Solutions, LLC.

200–203 © 2012 Ruslan Enikeev.

206–207 © 2013 Maximilian Bode.

210 Courtesy OpenFlights Airports Database. http://openflights.org/

212–213 Courtesy NASA/JPL-Caltech Graphic created by Moore/Boeck.

RECOMMENDED READING AND INSPIRATIONS

Data visualization

Harmon, Katherine. *You are here: Personal Geographies and other Maps of the Imagination*. New York: Princeton Architectural Press, 2004.

Klanten, Robert, Nicolas Bourquin, Thibaud Tissot and Sven Ehmann. *Data Flow: Visualising Information in Graphic Design*. Berlin: Die Gestalten Verlag GmbH, 2008.

McCandless, David. *Information is Beautiful*. London: Collins, 2009.

Mogel, Lize and Alexis Bhagat (editors). *An Atlas of Radical Cartography*. Los Angeles, CA: Journal of Aesthetics & Protest Press, 2008.

Neurath, Otto. *From Hieroglyphics to Isotype: a visual autobiography*. London: Hyphen Press, 2010.

Pietsch, Theodore W. *Trees of Life: A Visual History of Evolution*. Baltimore, Maryland: The John Hopkins University Press, 2012.

Rendgen, Sandra, Julius Wiedemann (editor) and Paolo Ciuccarelli. *Information Graphics*. Cologne: T GmbH, 2012.

Rogondino, Michael and Pat Rogondino. *Process Colour Manual: 24,000 CMYK combinations for design, prepress and printing*. San Francisco, CA: Chronicle Books, 2000.

Tufte, Edward R. *Envisioning Information*. Cheshire, Connecticut: Graphics Press LLC, 1990.

Turchi, Peter. *Maps of the Imagination: the Writer as Cartographer*. San Antonio, Texas: Trinity University Press, 2004.

von Debschitz, Uta and Thilo von Debschitz. (editors). *Fritz Khan: Man Machine*. Vienna: Springer-Verlag, 2009.

—

History and factual information

Barach, Arnold and Rudolf Modley. *The New Europe and Its Economic Future*. New York: The Macmillan Company, 1964.

Dorling Kindersley Publishing Staff. *History Year by Year*. London: Dorling Kindersley Limited, 2011.

Gombrich, Ernst. *A Little History of the World*. Yale University Press, 2008 (this edition).

Haven, Kendall F. *100 Greatest Science Inventions of all Time*. Westport, CT: Libraries Unlimited, 2006.

Heck, J.G (editor). *Heck's Pictorial Archive of Nature and Science*. New York: Dover Publications Inc, 1994.

Palmer, Douglas and Peter Barrett. *Evolution the Story of Life*. London: Mitchell Beazley, 2009.

—

Typography and design

Baines, Phil and Andrew Haslam. *Type & Typography*. London: Laurence King Publishing, 2005.

Haslam, Andrew. *Book design*. London: Laurence King Publishing, 2006.

Lupton, Ellen, and Jennifer Cole Phillips. *Graphic Design the New Basics*. New York: Princeton Architectural Press, 2008.

Mitchell, Michael and Susan Wightman. *Book Typography: A Designer's Manual*. Marlborough, Wiltshire: Libanus Press Limited, 2005.

De Jong, Cees W (editor), Alston W Purvis and Jan Tholenaar. *Type: A Visual History of Typefaces and Graphic Styles Volume I 1628 – 1900.* Cologne: Taschen GmbH, 2009.

—

Web resources

The Guardian Datablog
http://www.guardian.co.uk/news/datablog

The United Nations Statistics Division
http://data.un.org

International Labour Organization
http://laborsta.ilo.org/

International Monetary Found Statistics
http://www.imf.org/external/data.htm

OECD StatExtracts
http://stats.oecd.org

ACKNOWLEDGMENTS

Nine months ago, I left a meeting at HarperCollins as a happy member of a new team – but more importantly, in love with the potential of what *The Infographic History of the World* might become.

Well, 1,674 emails, 100 infographics and 224 pages later, here we are, at the end of what has been an incredible journey.

My first big thanks goes to everyone at HarperCollins who made this book possible – and my fellow adventurers, James and Craig. Thanks for sharing the joy (and the pain) that came with this project.

Specifically, I want to thank James for the steady diet of amusing content and clever copy. And a special thanks to Craig for providing more than just feedback, research and ideas, but also a comprehensive lesson on how inspiring a hardworking editor can be. Thank you guys!

Huge thanks to Timothy Sondreal, who not only put up with it all, but also participated daily – offering constructive feedback to both shape the book and maintain my sanity.

A heartfelt thanks goes to Charlotte Hoyes for her design assistance and endless support in finishing the book.

Thanks to all our contributors who generously agreed to participate.

And I would like to extend my gratitude to all friends and colleagues who supported me – whether providing specific input or simply a friendly ear – thank you!

And to those who went beyond empathy – Chris Lloyd, Marie Laurent, Nicola Di Costanzo, Piero Zagami – thanks for your hands-on support. Finally, thanks to Miyuki Yamanaka, I wish everybody had a friend like you!

Last, but certainly not least, thanks to Maria Rita Testore – my most consistent source of stability and inspiration. Grazie mamma!

Valentina D'Efilippo

Producing a book – any book – is virtually like raising a child, though in this case on a time-schedule even more punishing. And much like parenting, getting this book to completion has taken a veritable village.

The first person to acknowledge can only be this book's absolutely phenomenal designer, Valentina, whose ability to turn a few hundred words and a little bit of data into something magical has consistently amazed, even after months. This book's moments of magic (in my view) virtually all belong to her (responsibility for any duff moments, alas, stays with me).

Second credit must go to a man who must be one of publishing's most tenacious editors, Craig Adams, who has in turn been editor, researcher, writer, diplomat and a dozen things besides, and this is as much his as anyone else's. (He's stuck with it now).

Further thanks must go to John Burn-Murdoch for his research assistance, and to all the phenomenal guest designers who contributed their work to the book.

Credit also to all of those whose data and research was used in the course of research, particularly my colleagues on the Guardian Datablog.

Apologies are due to those friends and relatives I've bored over the months, particularly those with whom I've shared a roof – Kevin Sullivan and Mary Jordan (plus Tom and Kate), Damian Clements and Simon Ward.

Finally, in case they skimmed over the dedication (entirely possible), thanks – for everything – are due to my Mum, and my Dad.

James Ball